Routledge Revivals

Building in the British Economy Between The Wars

When it was originally published in 1968, this was the first comprehensive study of the building industry in the inter-war years. The main theme of the book is an analysis of the influence of building in the British economy in terms of fluctuations and growth. The authors survey many aspects of the industry, including structure, labour and materials supplies, investment, technical change and efficiency and the demand and policy factors affecting the industry. The book produces interesting findings regarding the relationship between building, fluctuations and economic growth but it also relates and compares these with trends before 1914. Emphasis is placed on the role of non-monetary factors in the housing boom of the 1930s and the authors also suggest that the 1920s experienced a housing book. Following a quantitative and analytical approach to economic history, this book will be of value to professional economists and historians and students in economic history and industrial economics.

Building in the British Economy Between the Wars

Harry W. Richardson and Derek H. Aldcroft

Routledge Revivals
Routledge
Taylor & Francis Group

First published in 1968 by George Allen & Unwin Ltd.

This edition first published in 2025 by Routledge
4 Park Square, Milton Park, Abingdon, Oxon, OX14 4RN
and by Routledge
605 Third Avenue, New York, NY 10158.

Routledge is an imprint of the Taylor & Francis Group, an informa business

ISBN 13: 978-1-041-06578-4 (hbk)
ISBN 13: 978-1-003-63612-0 (ebk)
ISBN 13: 978-1-041-06580-7 (pbk)
Book DOI 10.4324/9781003636120

BUILDING IN THE BRITISH ECONOMY BETWEEN THE WARS

BY

HARRY W. RICHARDSON

Senior Lecturer in Economics
University of Aberdeen

AND

DEREK H. ALDCROFT

Lecturer in Economic History
University of Glasgow

London

GEORGE ALLEN & UNWIN LTD

RUSKIN HOUSE · MUSEUM STREET

FIRST PUBLISHED IN 1968

SBN 04 330120 7

PRINTED IN GREAT BRITAIN
in 10 *on* 11 *pt. Times Roman type*
BY SIMSON SHAND LTD.
LONDON, HERTFORD AND HARLOW

To Margaret
Wife and Friend

PREFACE

The publication of this book has been made possible by generous financial guarantees from the Carnegie Trust and the University of Glasgow.

We wish to express our sincere thanks to Professor Donald J. Robertson for his editorial duties and for expeditiously dealing with our drafts despite the pressure of his other work. We are also indebted to Professors Robertson, Maxwell Gaskin and Sidney G. Checkland for their many helpful comments on structure, content and style. While we are sure that they will recognize many improvements due to their influence, we must exempt them from responsibility for any remaining errors. We ourselves are, of course, jointly responsible for the whole book. There was, however, some specialization on the first draft, Richardson preparing the first draft of Chapters 1–4 and 10–12 and Aldcroft writing the first draft of Chapters 5–9, 13 and 14.

We are grateful to Dr. C. H. Feinstein for providing us with some of his unpublished statistics on pre-1914 capital formation and to Mr J. L. Marshall for letting us make use of his unpublished analyses of interwar housing statistics. We also acknowledge the help of Mr Donald I. Mackay on various points.

Last, but not least, we wish to thank all the typists who have coped with our many drafts and gross illegibilities with patience and good humour: Misses M. M. Hay, A. M. Fraser and Mrs A. J. King at the University of Aberdeen, and Misses M. Marlowe, S. Beaton, J. Moir, and S. Ross at the University of Glasgow.

DEREK H. ALDCROFT
HARRY W. RICHARDSON

CONTENTS

TABLES

Statistical Appendix to Chapter 2

FIGURES

INTRODUCTION

We have written this book in an attempt to fill a gap in the literature of the development of building and in the study of its interrelationships with the economy. Economic historians have analysed in some detail building fluctuations in the nineteenth century and their effects. There has also been a considerable resurgence of interest by economists in the contemporary situation, particularly in the problem of low productivity in the building industry and in the economics of housing generally. But the historians have stopped short in 1914, while the economists have been too busy with current problems and their implications to explore their historical origins.[1]

The chief aim of this book is to analyse the influence of building in the UK economy between the wars both in terms of fluctuations and of growth. This theme is developed in Chapters 10–14. As an essential part of this inquiry, however, we have to consider in some detail the building industry itself and the forces acting upon it. This involved an examination of the structure of the industry, the supply of men, materials and capital, productivity and technical change, the demand and policy influences operating in building. It also required a broad outline in quantitative terms of the industry's development in the inter-war period. Apart from being a corollary to the development of the analysis in the second half of the book, these chapters should be useful in adding some historical perspective to present-day research into building.

This book has no obvious precursors. There have been no major studies of the inter-war period since Marian Bowley's *Housing and the State, 1919–44* (1945) and H. W. Robinson's *The Economics of Building* (1939). These books, especially the former, concentrated on narrow questions. Indeed, although there is a reasonable amount of scattered work on British building between the wars it is very partial in scope. It tends to be limited to two main topics, housing policy and analysis of the housing boom of the 1930s. Although important work has been done in these fields, such as that of Stolper and Nevin on the latter,[2] there has been no general assessment of the role of

[1] Parry Lewis is a possible exception, but he deals briefly with the inter-war period, and the model he applies was developed to explain pre-1914 fluctuations (J. Parry Lewis, *Building Cycles and Britain's Growth* (1965), Chapter 9).

[2] W. Stolper, 'British Monetary Policy and the Housing Boom', *Quarterly Journal of Economics*, 55 (1941), and E. Nevin, *The Mechanism of Cheap Money* (1955), Chapter 8.

building over the inter-war period as a whole. Consequently, the overall impression of building's role has been somewhat distorted. For instance, very little work has been done on the relative roles of the private and public sectors in housebuilding or on the interaction between them. The emphasis on the housing boom and recovery in the 1930s has diverted attention from the subsidized housing boom of 1926–7, and led to an exaggerated importance of the role of cheap money in the housing boom and of the housing boom in Britain's general upswing after 1932. Finally, inter-war non-residential building has been seriously neglected.

Some subjects discussed, pre-eminently inter-war building fluctuations and the assessment of building's contribution to the growth of the economy during this period, have not been examined before in depth. In other parts of the book covering less untrodden ground we have made revisions to accepted views. For instance, in the survey of housing policy we believe that contemporaries, including the Government, exaggerated the alleviation of the housing shortage in the period, primarily as a result of relying on estimates of the net increase in families which were too low. Again, in accounting for the rise in private unsubsidized housebuilding from 1928 to 1934 too little emphasis has been given to the effects of falling building costs. The book also draws together much scattered and not easily accessible material on inter-war building.

This book could not have been written in its present form ten or fifteen years ago. It relies on the statistical estimates prepared by other researchers in the intervening period, of which the Cambridge series on national income and expenditure (Feinstein, Stone and Rowe, Chapman and Knight), Maywald's work on building costs and Lomax's on production indices are some of the main examples. The limitations of much of these data are serious, but whatever their deficiencies writing a book on inter-war building with their aid is a much easier task than it would have been in 1950 before these statistics had been compiled. Some of the more important of the indices are presented and discussed in the Appendix to Chapter 2, but they are used repeatedly in the main analysis of the book.

The outline of the book is as follows. In Chapter 1 the scope of building within this book is defined, the pre-1914 picture is outlined and the structure of the building industry is analysed. In Chapter 2 the development of building in the inter-war period is briefly summarized in terms of the data in the appendix. In Chapters 3 and 4 an attempt is made to assess the relative importance of some of the main influences on the demand for housing, and demand factors acting on non-residential building are also briefly considered. We analyse in Chapters 5–7 the industry's supply problems (in regard to men, materials, and to a lesser extent capital) and consider whether there were any supply inelasticities in the inter-war period and if so to what degree. In addition, the relationship between supply and costs is explored and the movement of aggregate costs is used as an aid to assess the overall productivity changes in building over this period. The extent of technical change, both in materials and their uses and in organization, is also discussed. Chapter 8 discusses the impact of government policy on building, particularly housing policy, not only the general subsidies of the 1920s and the slum clearance and overcrowding provisions of the 1930s but also the wider issue of the effects of rent restriction. The influence of monetary policy on housing is analysed in Chapter 9. These nine chapters together provide the necessary knowledge of the development of building and the influences acting upon housing which is a prerequisite for the analysis of the interrelationships between building and the economy in the second half of the book.

Chapters 10–12 are concerned with the cyclical aspects of inter-war building and the general character of the relationship between building and business fluctuations. These problems require some discussion of the special character of building fluctuations, the response of building activity to business cycle variables, inverse cycles in public and private housebuilding, and the connection between fluctuations in housebuilding and in non-residential building. The question of whether or not there is a causal relationship between fluctuations in building and business cycles is examined in Chapter 12. Chapters 13 and 14 move from a consideration of short run interconnections between building and the economy to an analysis of long-term forces, the interaction between building and growth. They deal with such questions as: Was the long-term weighting of building as a sector in the economy declining? Was the absorption of resources by building between the wars a handicap or a stimulus to growth? What was the nature of the relationship between building and growth? Is there any evidence to support the thesis of a transport-building cycle for Britain? Did new forms of transport supply the connecting link between the development of building and suburban growth between the wars? Were the difficulties encountered in the spread of suburban development solved satisfactorily, or were they aggravated by inadequate planning?

CHAPTER 1

HISTORICAL BACKGROUND AND STRUCTURE

I. *Scope*

The main emphasis in this book is placed on housebuilding, partly because of its quantitative predominance in total building but primarily because it tends to follow a path of its own with the capacity to offset or influence trends and fluctuations in the economy as a whole. On the other hand, we have not drawn the line as narrowly as this since most types of non-residential building are built mainly with the same materials, the same labour and by some of the same firms as housebuilding. Of course, there are obvious differences between residential and non-residential buildings. They cater for completely different markets: the main purchasers of houses are private individuals (owner-occupiers and housing investors), development companies or local authorities (who very often built the houses themselves); the customers of non-residential buildings vary according to the type of building, but are usually either industrial and commercial companies or public authorities.

The technologies involved are dissimilar too. The production methods used in building houses are largely traditional, and have changed little over time. The techniques of production used in large non-residential buildings (and in the construction of large blocks of flats) are not so stable; new materials and construction systems are intermittently introduced. This branch of building lends itself more to mechanization, while housebuilding until recently remained largely unmechanized. The result is that non-residential building is much more specialized than housebuilding, and is often carried out with the aid of specialized sub-contractors. The effects of changing techniques and improvements in site organization show themselves particularly in increased construction speed; it was estimated that the time engaged in building large projects between the wars was reduced by 30–40 per cent, though the speed of bricklaying operations had scarcely changed at all. Nevertheless, the similarities between the two kinds of building are closer than their differences. Therefore, most non-residential buildings such as factories, shops, offices and other commercial properties, schools, hospitals, libraries and other public buildings are included in the definition of building applied here. However, civil engineering works are excluded since these spill over into other supplying industries such as steel which have rather different problems from the building materials industries.

The omission of civil engineering works is more justifiable than it would be today since the use of steel in traditional non-residential buildings between the wars was not increasing at a fast rate. Although commercial experiments were being made and steel-framed buildings had been built in Britain since the first decade of the century, technical difficulties held up progress. Thus, the division between non-residential buildings and civil engineering works was more clear-cut than it is now. Also excluded are all forms of public works contracting—roads, bridges, sewers, gas mains, waterworks, railway works, harbours, docks, tramway lines, canals and telegraphic lines.[1] It is impossible to maintain this division between building and contracting in all cases especially in regard to labour, so that some of the statistics used refer to building and contracting as a whole rather than to building alone as considered above. But the analysis in the book is limited to building, including non-residential building, and ignores civil engineering and public works contracting.

II. *General Characteristics*

The building industry has its own characteristics. Its products are large in size and very durable. They are not transportable, and consequently the industry must be geographically dispersed. Its raw materials are bulky, thus the building materials industry is dispersed as well. The capital requirements of the industry are relatively small and overhead costs are low. Building products have a high labour content, and this leads to some rigidity in building costs. Because of variations between areas in regard to availability of types of building materials and because of significant regional differences in earnings, construction and cost conditions vary considerably between localities. An obvious feature is that the industry is a home market industry except for certain raw materials. The immobility of its products shelter it from foreign competition, though conversely of course it is unable to boost output via exports. Its rate of growth therefore depends on domestic forces, not on growth stimuli from

[1] Of course, where public works contracting is a component part of a pure building project, for instance the internal roads and footpaths of a housing estate built by the developer himself or the sewage systems from the house to a main sewer, it is included in building.

abroad. Because the bulk of its operations is carried on outdoors, the industry is dependent on weather conditions, and is therefore to some extent seasonal. For this reason, but also because of longer-term fluctuations in the level of building activity, there are great variations in the size of the labour force and the building industry retains only a very small permanent staff.[1]

A further characteristic of the industry is that non-residential buildings are often tailor-made while the majority of residential buildings is produced for speculative sale (or in this period to some extent for rent).[2] Buildings are also sold to a very large extent on credit; this is particularly true of houses which are primarily financed by the building societies, but is also sometimes the case with factory and commercial buildings financed by bank overdrafts. The degree of competition in building varies from sector to sector. For instance, it tends to be keener in housebuilding than in non-residential building. On the other hand, the building materials industries are mainly oligopolistic. Finally, perhaps the most characteristic feature of the industry is the diversity of firm sizes and the co-existence of a very large number of very small firms with a few large contractors. There is a high turnover of these small firms, many of which are primarily engaged on repairs and maintenance. The predominance of small firms is accentuated by the considerable degree of sub-contracting in the industry.

A. HISTORICAL BACKGROUND: BUILDING BEFORE 1914

Before embarking on a study of the building industry in the inter-war period and an analysis of the impact of building activity on the economy, it is desirable to survey briefly developments in the late nineteenth century up to 1914. The function of such a survey is to provide a broad historical setting for the detailed analysis of the inter-war years that follows.

I. *Structure and Organization before the First World War*

Hard facts about the structure of the building industry before 1914 are difficult to obtain. The Census of Production of 1907 gave no details about the size of firms. The Census results were tabulated from

[1] This generalization applies especially to small firms and was more relevant in the inter-war period than now.

[2] Excluding, of course, local authority houses.

about 45,000 returns. Apart from building work specifically excluded,[1] the compilers of the Census thought that only some of the very smallest firms had escaped their net. But since the Census returns referred to a total employment of only 514,000, less than one-half of the total labour force in building indicated by the Census of Population statistics of 1901 and 1911, we have considerable doubts about this assertion.[2] If we assume that few of the larger firms failed to make a return, the Census statistics indicate, since they show an average labour force of less than twelve men, a structure characterized by a great many very small firms. The pre-1914 and the inter-war structures were very similar, except that the average size of firm was probably smaller before the First World War and the proportion of large firms rather lower. But not all firms in the pre-1914 building industry were small. Firms of medium size (say about 200 men) had been quite common, at least in London, since the 1820s. By 1914 there were a few large firms operating over many parts of the country, and in one or two cases, overseas.[3] But the typical building firm remained very small (under ten men) often established by an ex-workman and primarily engaged on repairs or small new projects. With credit facilities available from building merchants and few technological scale economies, most building work could be carried out by small units. Company organization was rare in building because even the largest contractors could finance their work in progress by advance payments from their customers.

Although the structure of the building industry immediately before 1914 differed little from that found in the inter-war period, it would be wrong to think that the structure and organization of building had not changed over the sixty years before the First World War. Building employment had easily more than doubled in the second half of the nineteenth century. The direct contracts between the customer and the master craftsman familiar in earlier periods had broken down in favour of a system where the general builder, often an estate developer, co-ordinated the activities of several trades in schemes usually involving both direct work and subcontracting. This greater flexibility permitted a firm to operate in more than one area,

[1] For example, building work done by employees of public utility companies and manufacturing firms and jobbing work.

[2] *Census of Production, 1907*, PP v. 101 (1911) and occupational returns of the Population Census, as given by P. Deane and W. A. Cole, *British Economic Growth, 1688–1959* (1962), p. 143.

[3] For instance, the London firm of Holland, Hannen & Cubitts was engaged on large contracts in Liverpool before 1900, and in 1913 established a subsidiary in South Africa.

and also gave rise to the development of specialized firms such as in glazing and structural engineering. These specialist firms often developed to exploit new techniques of production and to use new materials. There were new technical developments in building in the late nineteenth and early twentieth centuries, though these were mainly applicable to the large non-residential buildings. Of these, the innovations of the fully load-bearing steel frame and reinforced concrete were probably the most revolutionary. It is significant that Britain's adoption of the first lagged twenty years behind the innovation in the US,[1] while the use of reinforced concrete, though not opposed as strongly since unlike the steel frame it did not divert work from builders to civil engineers, followed years after its exploitation on the Continent. Bowley shows that neither local authority by-laws nor the builders could be blamed for this lack of progress. The responsibility lay with the scepticism and opposition of the architects and other members of the designing professions.[2]

Although most non-residential buildings and the highest class residential dwellings were, as in the later period, custom-built, a feature of the half century before the First World War was the emergence of estate development for most houses. Houses were built in anticipation of the market, and the estate developers provided the necessary organization and capital. Profits were made not only from sales of houses but from rising land values, especially with suburban building. New methods of finance and new agencies catered for the expansion by replacing the earlier method by which small men built houses with their own capital. The expansion in building societies and development of the joint stock banks made mortgages and bank deposits, supported by merchants' credit, the normal instruments of finance. Co-operative Societies advanced funds to their members and occasionally undertook development directly, charitable trusts (predominantly in London) built working-class houses to let, and even local authorities obtained very limited powers to act as developers. In the financial and organization spheres, however, the inter-war years were to bring even more striking developments. Pre-eminent among these were the large-scale intervention of local authorities in housebuilding associated with financial provision by the State, and the expansion in building society business at an unprecedented rate.

[1] The first large steel-framed building was the Home Insurance Co. building designed by W. G. B. Jenney and erected in Chicago in 1883–5, while the first British example was the Ritz Hotel, London, erected in 1904.

[2] M. Bowley, *The British Building Industry: Four Studies in Response and Resistance to Change* (1966), pp. 3–35.

II. *Building in the Economy*

Some aspects of the growth in building activity before the First World War are illustrated by the statistics in Table 1. These are largely self-explanatory, and detailed comment is unnecessary. We shall confine ourselves to a few general comments. It will be seen later[1] that building was a much more important sector in the economy between the wars than before 1914, and this is true whatever indicators are examined (building's share in total investment or in gross national product, houses built, etc.). This change in building's importance occurred suddenly around the time of the First World War, and was not therefore a continuation of a trend established in the late nineteenth century. There was, in fact, no marked upward trend in building activity before 1914, and building's share in total investment remained much below the level of the 1870s. However, building activity was very unsteady, and was marked by quite severe fluctuations. The impact of these is that if we consider decade averages, as in Table 1, and start from 1880 we get an impression of a firm upward trend in the following three decades. This trend is, in part, an illusion. It reflects the building slump of the 1880s and the strong upward swing of the late 1890s with high levels of activity maintained in the early years of this century. The rate of increase in the housing stock and the rate of growth in employment were particularly high in the 1890s. Indeed, the labour force attained at the end of that decade compares well with the size of building's labour force between the wars up to the intense housing boom of the 1930s.

It is superficial, however, to interpret the swing from low building levels in the 1880s to high levels in the late 1890s and early 1900s as evidence of an upward trend. The annual output of houses in the four or five years before the war was lower than at any time in the period since 1870, and the number of houses built in 1876 was surpassed in only seven years up to 1914 (1898–1904). Finally, the stability of housing's share in total building is an indirect pointer to the absence of a firm upward trend in housing activity. If we accept that the main determinant of the trend in non-residential building is the rate of growth in the economy as a whole, and given the fact the overall rate of growth was probably falling and certainly did not rise in the 1870–1914 period, then a strong growth trend in building activity would have required a secular increase in the share of residential construction in total building.

[1] Especially in the next chapter and in Chapter 13 which deals with the relationship between building and economic growth.

Table 1: THE GROWTH OF BUILDING BEFORE 1914[1]

	(1) *Houses built, GB* ('000; *annual average*)	(2) *Investment in dwellings* (£m. 1900 *prices*)	(3) *Residential as per cent of total building*	(4) *Building as per cent of GDCF*		(5) *Housing Stock, GB (million)*	(6) *Per cent unoccupied houses*	(7) *Building employment (England and Wales)* ('000)
1870–9	101·0	20·2	56·6	38·0	1871		6·1	567
1880–9	79·8	17·2	60·4	30·8	1881	6·02	8·0	690
1890–9	107·7	26·0	59·6	33·0	1891	6·69	6·8	706
1900–9	130·6	35·2	59·0	32·0	1901	7·68	7·2	953
1910–14	61·9	19·2	48·8	27·3	1911	8·65	5·7	887
1905–14	88·8	25·5	56·0	29·5				

[1] SOURCES: Column 1, B. Weber, 'A New Index of Residential Construction, 1838–1950', *Scottish Journal of Political Economy* 2 (1955); columns 2, 3 and 4, C. H. Feinstein, see Chapter 13, Tables 27 and 28; columns 5 and 6, Census statistics; column 7, estimates by G. T. Jones, *Increasing Return* (1933).

III. *Pre-1914 Building Fluctuations*

The bulk of research into building activity in the nineteenth and early twentieth centuries has been concentrated on an analysis of fluctuations, particularly long swings, in housebuilding.[1] The outlines of these fluctuations and the major factors behind them are well known. However, it is clear that the relative importance of the different, sometimes conflicting but often complementary, explanations is not yet understood, and that the position still needs a final assessment. It would be beyond our scope to do more than summarize the present state of the argument.

Building activity tended to move in line with business cycles during the first half of the nineteenth century and beyond. From around the 1860s, however, fluctuations in building were detached from the cycle in the economy as a whole and followed their own course. Although most forms of non-residential building, except those directly linked with housebuilding, fluctuated in line with investment generally, and therefore moved pro-cyclically, housebuilding itself became subject to separate influences. The result was housebuilding cycles marked by a much longer periodicity than business fluctuations generally, and characterized by wider variations in amplitude. Building booms tended to overlap upswings in the economy as a whole, with building activity rising not only in the upswing itself but continuing to expand after the cyclical downturn. When the building booms broke, the reaction was strong and building slumps persisted for many years. The housebuilding cycle of the 1870–1914 period appeared to be about twenty years in length. Although different series show slight differences in turning points, consensus dates for troughs would be 1871, 1890 and 1912 and for booms 1876 and 1898 (though in the latter case housebuilding remained almost at peak levels up to, and including, 1903).

Given a housebuilding cycle of about 20 years, the problem is how to explain it? Researchers in the 1950s found their key clue in the American economy. It was found that housebuilding cycles in the US

[1] For example, B. Thomas, *Migration and Economic Growth* (1954); A. K. Cairncross, *Home and Foreign Investment, 1870–1913* (1953); J. Parry Lewis, *Building Cycles and Britain's Growth* (1965); E. W. Cooney, 'Capital Exports and Investment in Building in Britain and the USA', *Economica*, NS 16 (1949) and 'Long Waves in Building in the British Economy of the Nineteenth Century', *Economic History Review*, 13 (1960); S. B. Saul, 'Housebuilding in England, 1890–1914', *Economic History Review*, 15 (1962); H. J. Habakkuk, 'Fluctuations in Housebuilding in Britain and The United States in the Nineteenth Century', *Journal of Economic History*, 22 (1962).

tended to have a similar periodicity and furthermore that their timing was approximately opposite to British housebuilding fluctuations.[1] This phenomenon of inverse cycles in Britain and the US was beyond dispute. Of course, the inverse correspondence was not exact, and it was possible to argue that the inverse character of the fluctuations was partly, perhaps even primarily, fortuitous. On the other hand, the appeal to search for a causal connection was strong. The long swing in building could be observed in American data as far back as the 1830s, and there were grounds for believing that the development of the Atlantic economy from the 1860s, particularly the flows of capital and men which accompanied it, was responsible for these swings being transmitted, though inversely, to Britain. The hypothesis was plausible. Economic conditions in the US dictated when immigration (and capital inflows) from Europe would be high. When emigration from Britain was high, houses stood empty and building activity was low. But when emigrants were few, the domestic economy in general, and building in particular, boomed. Thus, immigration was the activating link between the inverse cyclical patterns on both sides of the Atlantic, and the building cycle was, in essence, 'a migration cycle in disguise'. Moreover, the hypothesis seemed to fit the facts. Brinley Thomas showed that 'spurts in building in the US were preceded by waves of incoming population, and that in Great Britain upward and downward movements in emigration tended to be accompanied after a short lag respectively by downward and upward movements in building'.[2]

The forces behind the inverse relationship were more complex than a simple migration model might suggest. Before 1914 migration and foreign investment were like Siamese twins. Booming conditions in the US induced an outflow of both capital and labour from Britain, and this foreign investment and emigration had several effects on building activity. Increases in foreign investment reduced the supply of capital available for building. Furthermore, to the extent that foreign investment was associated with expanding exports, then building costs would tend to be high during periods of foreign investment as a result of having to compete for productive factors with the export trades. Emigration reduced the supply of labour available for building, with adverse consequences on building costs, and also reduced the demand for houses, a factor tending to reduce rents. In

[1] Long suggested dates for United States building cycles in 1878 and 1900 with peaks in 1871, 1892 and 1912, C. D. Long, *Building Cycles and the Theory of Investment* (1940), p. 136.

[2] Thomas, op. cit., p. 175.

this manner, emigration squeezed builders' and investors' profit margins by narrowing the gap between building costs and rents. This would be reinforced by the fact that periods of high capital export would generally be associated with higher domestic interest rates than when foreign investment was low. Conversely, when foreign investment and emigration slumped, urban demand for houses, and therefore rents, was high and more labour and finance were available to enable the building industry to satisfy this increased demand. This type of explanation is consistent with the change in the character of building fluctuations from being similar to economy-wide fluctuations earlier in the century to longer twenty-year cycles, inverse to those found in the US, from about 1870, for there is no doubt that foreign investment and emigration were between 1870 and 1914 much more powerful determinants of activity in the British economy than previously.

Yet the Atlantic economy explanation of the building cycle is by no means watertight. The argument was often conducted in terms of *a priori* reasoning, and was given insufficient empirical verification. Facts could easily be found to support the hypothesis, while other evidence, less easily accommodated, was ignored. For example, many of the above arguments (particularly those relating to capital and labour shortages) fall to the ground in situations below full employment, and the lack of unemployment data before 1914 makes it very difficult indeed to test some of the arguments directly. Moreover, the inverse character of British and American building fluctuations may reflect accidental factors as much as the causal relationship described above. Two examples are sufficient to suggest that such an interpretation is at least possible. Firstly, the alternation of American and British housing peaks in the 1880s and 1890s partly reflects the difference in the rate and timing of the application of electricity (especially to traction) in the two economies. Secondly, the decline in building in London (obviously an important component of a national housebuilding index) after 1903 was clearly not associated with a revival in foreign investment and emigration. Instead, it was primarily due to local influences—the slow growth in consumer goods industries that figured prominently in the industrial structure of the metropolis, rising site values in the centre inhibiting an inflow of new industry, and delays in providing adequate suburban transport facilities.[1]

The relationship between emigration and British building cycles is not strengthened by the fact that fluctuations in the numbers of

[1] Habakkuk, loc. cit., pp. 226–30.

emigrants were in themselves too small to account for the variations in housing demand of sufficient magnitude to induce severe cycles. The rate of increase in total households was not much lower in periods of heavy emigration than at other times. The thesis can be salvaged only by linking fluctuations in emigration directly with fluctuations in urban growth. The argument requires low internal mobility in years of heavy emigration, and rapid growth in British towns when emigration is slight. It needs to be established that there was an inverse correlation, that the alternation, if it existed, was causally connected, and finally the mechanism of how changes in internal migration influence the building cycle has to be outlined. The first point is a matter for empirical observation, the second probably needs the assumption that the US competed with British cities and towns for migrants from the rural areas, and the third requires showing how high internal migration may result in an *increase* in the overall demand for housing. A case can be made on each of these three issues, especially in the 1880s, but the upshot is that the link between foreign investment, emigration and inverse building cycles is not as clear-cut as appears on first sight.

Because of these qualifications and others, there has been a reaction from the Atlantic economy thesis in recent years. The researches of Habakkuk, Saul and Parry Lewis have tended to highlight forces of domestic origin which could explain the long building cycle of the 1870–1914 period. Thus, it has been shown that the transformation from the short pro-cyclical building fluctuations of the first half of the nineteenth century to the long cycles of later decades is explicable by internal forces without resort to the growth in foreign investment and emigration. Early in the century internal migration was closely associated with periods of trade expansion, but after 1880 a much higher proportion of migrants was of middle-class origin whose movements were not subject to constraints imposed by the business cycle. In the second half of the century, increased financial stability and, particularly, the absence of financial panics at the upper turning point after 1866 combined with new sources of building finance to make it possible for building activity to be financed in general downswings. Also, income levels were maintained in years of depression at higher levels than previously. These influences enabled building booms to continue after general upswings had worked themselves out.

Perhaps of even greater importance was the tendency in the late nineteenth century for an increased share of housebuilding to be suburban building. Bursts of suburban building tended to persist for quite long periods of time, because once the minimum transport facilities and public utilities had been built, an area gave opportunities for extensive building. In other words, suburban housebuilding development tended to lengthen periods of building expansion. Another significant discovery is the diversity of regional housebuilding experience in the late nineteenth century. If the fortunes of different areas and towns varied considerably, this demands modification of the Atlantic economy thesis which is usually presented in aggregate terms. Moreover, regional variations in themselves provide an explanation of long building cycles. If regional building fluctuations vary in periodicity and amplitude, their aggregation may lengthen the national cycle even if the local building cycles are only of standard business cycle length.

Internal population changes and domestic credit conditions will also affect building activity, and even in the period of intense internationalization between 1870 and 1914 variations in these factors cannot be fully, or even primarily, explained by reference to external flows of labour and capital. For instance, the rise in the number of marriages from 2,047,000 in the 1880s to 2,393,000 in the 1890s was too high merely to reflect the reduced emigration rate. A similar point is that although higher exports, both visible and invisible, were important additions to income before 1914, the sources of income expansion were very often domestic. Fluctuations in the rate of growth of real incomes were a potentially important element in housing demand, and yet this factor has virtually no place in the traditional inverse building cycle thesis.

Finally, Saul has strongly criticized the Atlantic economy thesis on the ground that it assumes remarkably rapid responses to changes in market indicators (rents, building costs, interest rates, etc.). He stresses the speculative character of the industry at this time; for example, speculative builders would usually be halted only by shortage of cash, not by fine calculations of changes in costs and profitability. The housing market was very important, capital came from many quarters not merely from frustrated foreign investors, and housebuilding activity responded far more to changes in internal demand than to minor variations in rents and building costs induced by the rate of emigration. The Atlantic economy thesis assumes virtually no reaction lags with almost instantaneous responses to changes in market indicators. For example, it is well known that builders often used the level of unoccupied houses as a guide to the state of the market in an area. But, in practice, the lag between a high vacancy rate and a reduction in building activity was very great. The 'emigration – foreign investment – inverse building cycle' hypothesis is, in other words, rather too neat, considering the character of the building industry and its methods of operation in the late nineteenth century.

The last words have not yet been written on this controversy. A balanced appraisal of the character of pre-1914 fluctuations would probably call for considerable emphasis on both internal and external factors. The arguments of Habakkuk and Saul have shown up deficiencies in the Atlantic economy thesis. But they have not enthroned the domestic origins explanation in its place. Fortunately, this 'foreign *v.* domestic causation' need not harass us in our analysis of the inter-war period. Between the wars external forces could have had only a marginal influence on building fluctuations. The introduction of strict immigration controls in the US meant that the great era of international migration was over. Also, foreign investment was at a lower level, and the introduction of State financial assistance to housebuilding and the replacement of the direct investor in building by the owner-occupier financed by building society mortgages were fundamental changes in conditions. The diversion of capital abroad argument could only be maintained if overseas issues and building society shares and deposits competed for the same funds. In fact, the share capital of building societies increased as fast in the 1920s as in the 1930s when foreign investment activity was strictly controlled. Furthermore, in a period of persistent under-employment of resources many of the arguments ancillary to the Atlantic economy thesis ceased to be relevant. Finally, the First World War left such a severe shortage that the severe fluctuations in demand (whether related to internal or external factors) that dominated the nineteenth-century building cycles disappeared. A central feature of inter-war experience was a persistently high level of potential demand for houses kept in constraint only by economic and financial considerations.

B. STRUCTURE OF THE INDUSTRY BETWEEN THE WARS

An important characteristic of the structure of the building industry was the very wide range in firm sizes. At one end of the scale was a small group of very large contractors which combined civil engineering work with building. These operated over a wide area and included some very large firms, one employing more than 20,000 men. At the other end, there was a very large number of jobbing builders exclusively engaged on repairs and sub-contracting work. Such firms were usually run by working craftsmen and employed in 1939 an average of four men only. In between these extremes lay three other groups: medium-sized firms engaged in both building and civil engineering but operating locally rather than nationally; a large number of building firms primarily engaged in residential building work and developing estates to their own designs; a much larger group of general-purpose builders mainly employed on alterations and repairs but occasionally erecting a single house or a few houses. The largest national builders undertook all forms of building, while the regionally based large firms and the private estate developers did most forms of building, including local authority contracts, but usually concentrated on housebuilding. Many sub-contractors were specialized firms, again varying considerably in size, engaged in such activities as excavating, plastering, plumbing, etc.

In terms of numbers, the medium and large firms were swamped by the small ones. This is shown in Table 2.[1] Almost 84 per cent of the

Table 2: DISTRIBUTION OF BUILDING AND CONTRACTING FIRMS BY SIZE, 1930

Size by employment	*Number of firms*	*Percentage of total number of firms*
		per cent
0– 10	43,620	83·8
11– 24	3,749	7·2
25– 49	2,480	4·8
50– 99	1,339	2·6
100–199	549	1·0
200–499	263	0·5
500 and over	54	0·1
	52,054	100·0

total number of firms in the industry employed ten men or less while only about 1·6 per cent of the firms employed more than 100. The number of firms in the industry was probably increasing throughout the inter-war period but especially in the 1930s. The Census total of 49,900 in 1924 increased to about 52,100 in 1930 followed by a rapid expansion to 72,690 in 1935. By January 1942 there was an estimated 86,970 firms in building and civil engineering of which 1,280 were purely civil engineering contractors and another 1,705 undertook

[1] Based on the 1930 Census of Production reproduced in H. W. Robinson, *The Economics of Building* (1939), p. 12.

civil engineering as well as building work. These firms which were partly or wholly engaged in civil engineering were naturally the larger firms: the purely civil engineering contractors accounted for about 11 per cent of total employment in building and civil engineering (average employment eighty-six men) and the large mixed firms absorbed 39 per cent of total employment (average employment 240 men). Of the remaining 83,984 firms, 44,940 could be regarded as general building firms while 39,044 were involved in those trades allied to building (joiners, plumbers, painters and miscellaneous). If anything, the small firms had become more important since 1930, for 92 per cent of the firms (80,240) employed less than twelve men and only 1·4 per cent of the total (1,257) employed more than 100. On the other hand, the large building and civil engineering contractors created more employment (39 per cent of the total) than the 45,000 general builders (only 37 per cent of the total).[1]

The increasing importance of small firms in the industry was noted by Bowen in 1938, who argued that an increasing share of the building boom of the 1930s was taken by small firms whose commitments to *new* building almost certainly consisted of houses rather than non-residential buildings. The Census of Production data revealed an increase in the proportion of total employment to be found in firms of not more than ten employees; in broad terms, the proportion rose from one-fifth in 1924 to one-quarter in 1930 and one-third in 1935. The coverage of the Census was not comprehensive, possibly only 80 per cent, but the trend is beyond dispute. The available evidence suggests that the rise in the importance of small firms was explicable not in terms of an increase in their average size but by the growth in the number of firms. This is in line with general expectations that building booms will be accompanied by entry of new small firms into the industry and building depressions associated with many small firms leaving it.[2]

[1] 'Labour in the Building Industry', *Planning*, September 1943, Vol. X, No. 212.

[2] The supplementary indirect evidence assembled by Bowen is far from conclusive. For instance, between 1924 and 1938 new company registrations amounted to fifty-four public companies and 8,783 private companies, more than two-thirds of which were registered in the latter half of the period. But the increase in new companies was insufficient to match the increase indicated in the Census of Production. Many small building firms were, of course, too small to be registered as companies and the figures of company registrations merely show an upward trend in individual financial units in building. Bowen's other evidence, based on counting the postal addresses in telephone and other directories, is even less convincing. The rise of builders in the London area shown by this procedure could quite easily reflect an increase in new telephone subscribers as much as

It is consequently impossible to quantify the growing importance of small firms. However, there is no reason to doubt that the increasing predominance in employment and output of small firms as shown by Census data was typical of those parts of the industry not covered by the Census. Working from the Census of Production data, Hart estimates that in 1924 firms employing no more than ten men were responsible for 16·5 per cent of value added in building and contracting. The proportion had risen to 23·7 per cent in 1930 and 30·8 per cent in 1935.[1] Whatever the limitations of this evidence, it supports the view that the expansion of building output in the inter-war period created considerable opportunities for new small firms entering the industry either by building a few houses or concentrating on the jobbing and maintenance work vacated by larger firms moving into speculative housebuilding. The smaller firms accounted for a disproportionate share of the expansion in output between the wars, whereas the larger firms increased relatively little either in size or in number. Since Census data showed a lower average net output per worker in smaller firms, the increasing predominance of small firms in the industry may have had some effect on the course of productivity.

The increasing contribution of small firms in the inter-war period was undoubtedly associated with the fact that the competitive advantages of large firms were not great enough to keep the growth of small firms in check. Scale economies were few for many reasons: expensive capital equipment was not required for most types of building; builders' merchants reduced the need for firms to carry stocks; detailed site supervision is necessary whatever the size of organization; no special techniques or know-how are needed except for very large projects.[2] On the other hand, the number of firms employing more than 1,000 men increased from sixteen in 1930 to thirty-one in 1935. It is, therefore, probably more precise to say that very large and very small concerns were expanding at the expense of the medium-sized firm.

The most notable feature of the distribution of building output by type of product was the predominance of housebuilding; in 1935

---

new entrants to the building industry. (I. Bowen, 'Investment in the Building Industry', *Review of Economic Studies*, 6 (1938–9), Pt. II, pp. 204–8.)

[1] P. E. Hart, *Studies in Profit, Business Saving and Investment in the United Kingdom, 1920–62*, Vol. I (1965), p. 95.

[2] M. Bowley, *The British Building Industry: Four Studies in Response and Resistance to Change* (1966), p. 387.

new housing accounted for 48 per cent of total output and housing absorbed a high proportion of the 24 per cent of output going on maintenance.[1] The remaining 28 per cent was allocated between factories and warehouses (5 per cent), shops, offices and hotels (6 per cent), other new building works (8 per cent) and civil engineering maintenance (7 per cent). Of the 8 per cent of output catered for by other new building works, more than half was taken up in public buildings and schools. Of course, these proportions applied only to 1935 and did not remain constant from year to year. By 1938, for instance, the share of housebuilding had declined relatively to non-residential building in general, and factories, offices and public buildings in particular.

As argued earlier, the nature of the building industry requires it to be geographically dispersed. It tends to have a location employment quotient of around unity.[2] In fact, between the wars building was heavily concentrated in London and the South-East and grossly under-concentrated in Northern England, Scotland and Wales; the location quotient for South-East England was almost double those of the latter three areas.[3] The predominance of the building industry in London and the South-East reflected many factors: the clustering of commercial office and hotel building in London; the size and population density of the metropolis intensifying the need for suburban development; higher average income levels making the increased demand for housing effective; the predominance of new factory building in Southern England in the inter-war years. Despite the operation of these forces, the predominance of the South in the building industry was being reduced. The insured labour force in building expanded faster in the under-represented regions, except South Wales, than in the South-East between 1923 and 1937.[4] Especially in the 1930s, residential building activity proceeded at a higher rate in the North, Scotland and Wales than in the South. The changing proportions in houses built reflected the concentration of local authority building in the older industrial areas over the period and, in the 1930s, the filtering down of housing demand to the lower average income levels prevailing in these regions. Thus, although the building industry was not as evenly distributed over Britain as a whole in 1930 as

[1] According to figures based on the Census of Production as given by the *Working Party Report on Building* (1950), p. 2.

[2] This quotient for building in a given region measures the proportion of national employment in building accounted for by that region divided by the proportional contribution of the region to total national employment.

[3] See Table 31, Chapter 13.

[4] See Table 32, Chapter 13.

might be expected on *a priori* grounds, secular influences were at work leading to a more uniform spread.

Although the question of building labour is discussed in more detail later, a few introductory comments may be made on the structure of the labour force. A Ministry of Labour enquiry in July 1939 estimated numbers involved in building as 1,007,640 plus 354,180 in civil engineering. Of the labour force in building, slightly less than half (500,270) consisted of unskilled labourers while the remainder were skilled. Ranked in order of importance the main trades were carpenters (146,510), painters (140,000), bricklayers (108,310), plumbers and glaziers (43,830), plasterers (38,050), masons (21,440), and slaters and tilers (9,240).

These totals masked considerable regional differences. For example, craftsmen accounted for 64·8 per cent of total building employees in Scotland but only 46·1 per cent in London. The distribution of craftsmen by trade also varied widely. The extremes for each trade are as follows: carpenters 34·9 per cent of all craftsmen in Wales but only 26·0 per cent in London; bricklayers 30·2 per cent in the Midlands but only 10·8 per cent in Scotland; masons 11·0 per cent in Scotland but 0·8 per cent in the South-East; slaters 7·2 per cent in Scotland but only 0·3 per cent in the South-East and in Wales; plasterers 4·7 per cent in the South-East but 11·1 per cent in Wales; painters 35·4 per cent in London but only 19·8 per cent in Scotland; and plumbers 12·7 per cent in Scotland and 3·9 per cent in Wales.[1] The causes of these differences are sometimes obvious: more buildings made of stone rather than brick meant more masons and fewer bricklayers; variations in tastes such as a higher proportion of bungalow-type dwellings in Scotland meant more slaters; differences in classification of trades between regions, again particularly acute in the allocation between bricklayers and masons; variations in production techniques between areas and, associated with this, changes in the share of non-residential buildings in total building giving rise to differences in the ratio of skilled workmen in the total labour force. Finally, the ratio of craftsmen to all building workers changed over time, the ratio being high in slump periods but lower in times of building boom when the industry had to resort to less skilled labour in order to satisfy demand. In the period 1924 to 1938 the ratio fluctuated between 48 per cent and 53 per cent.

The structure of the building industry is a matter of some signifi-

[1] I. Bowen, 'The Building Industry in Wartime', *Economic Journal* 49 (1939), p. 669.

cance. The predominance of small firms and the ease of entry, especially in the residential sector, meant that the industry could respond to variations in building demand with a high degree of flexibility. On the other hand, market indicators were very imperfect and channels of communication within the industry were weak, so that there were often considerable time lags before a change in the direction of demand resulted in a change in the level of building activity. Once the industry had recognized and acted on, say, an increase in demand, however, expansion could be achieved by an inflow of new firms and by flexibility in the ratio of unskilled labourers in the labour force. The growth in the number of small firms in the building boom of the 1930s is an illustration of this kind of response. Quite severe fluctuations in building activity could be met by changes in the structure of the industry, that is by inflows and outflows of marginal firms, without placing unbearable strains on the permanent, usually larger, building firms.

CHAPTER 2

DEVELOPMENT

In this chapter, we offer some general observations on the development of building between the wars in the light of the statistical data assembled in the Appendix.[1]

I. *Residential Building*

There was a strong upward trend in the number of houses built in the inter-war period though the rate of expansion was not uniform. Up to 1924 the level of housebuilding was unduly low reflecting the slowness of the industry, especially the private sector, in readjusting to peacetime conditions. After 1924 the rate of building expanded attaining boom levels in 1926 and 1927. In 1928 there was a sharp decline due to cuts in Government subsidies. Between 1929 and 1932 the volume of housebuilding remained relatively stable and did not surge forward until 1933. The rate of expansion in 1932–3 was tremendous with an increase of over 36 per cent, but could scarcely be maintained. The increase in houses built in 1934 was nevertheless substantial, but housebuilding remained stable in 1935. The expansion in 1935–6 was also slight, an increase in houses built of only 5·5 per cent, and in 1937 and 1938 the number of houses built actually fell.

These fluctuations were not the result of similar movements in each type of housebuilding. Local authority housebuilding fluctuated violently in the 1920s, and was particularly high in 1921 and 1922 and in 1926 and 1927. Over the years 1928–35, on the other hand, the number of local authority houses built remained remarkably stable, a period during which housebuilding by the private sector expanded year by year except in 1934–5. There was a considerable expansion in local authority building between 1935 and 1938, especially in the last year, suggesting that the slum clearance and overcrowding provisions of the legislation of 1930 and 1936 were beginning to bite. The housing legislation of the early 1920s authorized subsidies even for

[1] For discussion of sources and methods, as well as the data themselves, see the Appendix. The aim in placing these in an appendix is to preserve a connected account in the text. It does not imply that these matters are unimportant, for in fact the argument of the book relies heavily on the Appendix Tables.

certain kinds of private housebuilding. This gave rise to considerable numbers of subsidized houses being built by the private sector. This kind of housebuilding though not on an insignificant scale in the years 1920–2 was very heavy in the period 1924–9, equivalent to 90 per cent of the number of private unassisted houses built over this period. After 1929, as private unsubsidized building expanded, subsidized housebuilding by the private sector virtually disappeared, averaging little over 4,000 houses per annum over the next nine years.

Unsubsidized building was slow to recover from the cessation of building during the First World War, and did not reach sizeable proportions until 1923. Over the period 1923–8 private unsubsidized building averaged very little over 65,000 houses per year. In 1929 and again in 1930 there was a rapid expansion in this sector. Between 1930 and 1932 the increase was rather modest, but again private housebuilding surged forward in 1933 and in 1934. After 1934 private unsubsidized building declined almost year by year down to 1938, the fall in output being especially rapid in 1937–8. Looking at the annual contribution of subsidized (both local authority and private) housebuilding and unassisted building, the striking feature is the contrast between the 1920s and the 1930s. In every year of the 1920s the total number of unassisted houses built was less than the level of subsidized building with the exception of 1923 when subsidized housebuilding was at a very low ebb between the running down of the 1919 Act and the passage of the new legislation of 1923 and 1924. In the 1930s, on the other hand, subsidized building was swamped by private unsubsidized building. In most years, the private sector was at least twice as important as the contribution of the local authorities and in 1934 and 1935 almost four times as important. Thus, the high level of housebuilding in the later 1920s was based on subsidized building just as the housing boom of the 1930s was based on the private unassisted sector.

The impression of the share of local authority building in total residential building given by the statistics of capital formation is rather different from that based on houses built. This is partly because the estimates of private expenditure are buttressed by the inclusion of private subsidized dwellings and partly because local authority houses were cheaper. Consequently only in the period 1920–2 was local authority spending on housing higher than private spending. Even in 1927 when local authority building was at its peak, local authority housing expenditure stood at little more than 60 per cent of the level of private spending. Its share was within the range of 35–40 per cent over the period 1929–32 but after 1932 declined markedly. In 1934 the local authority share was only 17·5 per cent of private housing expenditure, and even in 1938 when local authority housebuilding had revived strongly and private housebuilding declined the share was 46 per cent. In terms of houses built, on the other hand, local authority houses accounted for 30·7 per cent of all houses built between April 1, 1920, and March 31, 1939, and over the same period new local authority houses equalled almost 53 per cent of the private unsubsidized houses built.

The course of total expenditure on housebuilding moved upwards over the inter-war period up to 1934, apart from slight recessions in 1922 and 1923 and some drop from the peak of 1927 in the following year or two. After 1934 capital formation in residential buildings declined modestly over the rest of the inter-war period. The expansion up to 1934 was by no means even. Instead the growth was clustered in three relatively short periods: 1920–1, when local authority building expanded sharply under the stimulus of the 1919 Housing Act; 1923–7, the longest upward phase of the inter-war period, again accounted for by a revival in local authority building from the depression year of 1923 and growth in subsidized building; finally, the sharp upswing of 1932–4 based entirely on private building.

The total UK housing stock not surprisingly expanded year by year in the inter-war period.[1] Apart from periods when the stock is run down by the effects of war damage, the housing stock will only decline at times when the population is declining rapidly or in periods of complete shutdown in the building industry since an essential prerequisite for a fall in the stock is that the level of new housebuilding should be exceeded by housing demolitions. The upward trend in housebuilding coupled with a low demolition rate resulted in an acceleration in the rate of growth of the housing stock through the inter-war period. Since after the middle 1920s the housing shortage was progressively alleviated it follows that the rate of building did not vary directly with the size of the housing shortage. On the other hand, there was over the period as a whole a similar absolute increase in the number of families as in the stock of houses. This correspondence and its significance is explored in Chapter 3.

Factors influencing the demolition of houses and replacement are discussed in Chapter 4. It is clear that the absence of demolitions in the years 1920 and 1921 reflected the intolerable post-war housing shortage. The basis of the estimates of 1922–31 is so approximate that no firm comments can be made about them. After 1934 the year by year rise in the number of demolitions reflected the increased

[1] See Appendix, Table 2.

intensity of the slum clearance programme subsidized by the State. Moreover, now that the chronic housing shortage had been relieved to some extent there was less pressure to maintain property which ought to have been pulled down.

On the other hand, taking the inter-war period as a whole the most notable feature about housing demolitions was their abnormally low rate, varying between one-tenth and less than one-half of a theoretical annual 1 per cent depreciation rate.[1] Since a substantial proportion of the housing stock consisted of old dwellings overdue for renewal, only the severity of the housing shortage explains the low level of replacement building between the wars. People preferred to patch and repair old houses rather than pull them down and replace them, while the pressure for slum clearance and relief of overcrowding was all the weaker because 'additional' demand for residential accommodation was high.

The number of unoccupied houses shows a firm upward trend after 1926. The relative stability up to that time is explained, of course, by the acute housing shortage. The rise in houses left unoccupied after 1926 up to 1935 reflects to some extent the alleviation of the housing problem. But the main factor as suggested by the concentration of the increase in the period 1932–35 was the results of inter-regional migration which left many houses in the depressed regions of the UK, temporarily at least, unoccupied. A further not unconnected factor was the close correspondence between the rise in unoccupied houses and the expansion in private housebuilding. The sharp increase of 1932–5 may consequently have been due in part to a temporary rise in vacancies associated with the movement of families into new houses. What is clear, however, is that the cause of the upward trend in unoccupied houses was certainly not the emergence of a housing surplus. Even at the end of the inter-war period the number of families was still in excess of the size of the housing stock, and this says nothing about the fact that many houses in the current stock were in urgent need of replacement.

II. *Non-residential Building*

The course of non-residential building moved rather differently from that of housebuilding.[2] Using £60 million at 1930 prices as indicating the boundary between low and high non-residential building activity, years of high investment were 1920 and 1921, 1928–30 and 1934–8.

[1] See Appendix, Table 1, columns 8 and 9.
[2] As shown in Appendix, Table 3.

These differed markedly from the peaks of residential building in 1926–7 and 1933–4. Moreover, the strong upward trend in residential building was not pronounced in other forms of building. The post-war boom level of £80 million in 1920 was surpassed only in 1930 and 1936–8. Instead, the cyclical nature of non-residential building was more in evidence, and non-residential building moved closely in line with the index of business activity especially in the 1930s.

The three main sub-sectors in non-residential building investment were manufacturing, retail distribution and social and public services. Leaving aside any over-estimation due to the inclusion of civil engineering works expenditure in the manufacturing series, the three components between them covered a high proportion of total non-residential building investment—between 70 per cent and 90 per cent and averaging about 80 per cent. However, the course followed by each sector was different, suggesting that the close correlation between non-residential capital formation and business activity could partly be accidental. The trend of investment in building and works in manufacturing, for example, was clearly downwards to 1932. After the boom year of 1920 investment in this sector slumped in every year up to 1932–3, apart from 1923–5 and 1928–9, and in the first of these three years the expansion was only slight. From 1932, however, investment in buildings in manufacturing moved pro-cyclically, expanding slowly up to 1935 then sharply up to 1937, finally suffering a severe relapse in 1938. Capital formation in social and public services buildings contrasted sharply with manufacturing, since this sector experienced a sharp upward trend, the average level of 1935–8 being five times as great as the average level of 1920–3. Only in 1931–3 when public expenditure at both the central and local levels was pruned back in response to the economy campaign did investment in this sector decline. The course of investment in shop-building was different again: no sharp upward trend, and severe depressions in 1921–2 and to a lesser extent in 1931–2. The upswings were steep only in 1922–4, 1927–9 and 1932–4, and after 1934 such investment remained stable while investment in factories and public buildings boomed. However, as is noted in the Appendix, the estimates of investment in shops were not independently determined especially for the 1930s, but were assumed to move in proportion to the changes in investment in residential building. For this reason the series is almost useless for assessing the character of fluctuations in shop-building in the 1930s and instead shows a very close correspondence with residential building fluctuations from which the series is derived. The fluctuations in the amount of shopbuilding actually carried out may be very different from the cycle shown in column 3 of Appendix, Table 3. In fact, the estimates for the 1920s suggest that shopbuilding investment lagged one or two years behind housebuilding. Since this accords with normal expectations about the relationship of suburban building to the development of utilities and ancillary services, the actual course of shopbuilding investment in the 1930s probably exhibited the same lag, a lag obscured by the method used in constructing the estimates for this period.

The deficiencies in the Weber-Parry Lewis industrial building plans approved series are so great that detailed comment would not be valuable.[1] It is practicable, however, to use the series to check the year by year direction of change in the building and works in manufacturing investment estimates discussed above. If a one-year lag is assumed to allow for the transition from plans to completions in industrial building then the fluctuations in both series show a very close correspondence. The direction of change is the same for every year throughout the period apart from 1925–6 when total manufacturing investment fell while the partial series shows a modest expansion, and 1929–30 when the overall series shows stagnation and a slight decline whereas industrial building plans approved shows a marked increase. In both these instances the plans approved series may be misleading. The apparent rise in expenditure in 1926 refers on the assumption made above to plans approved in 1925; in the year of the General Strike a higher than normal proportion of plans approved may have failed to result in actual building. Similarly, in 1930, a higher proportion of the peak industrial building plans approved in 1929 may have been shelved with the onset of the depression. The two series, constructed by entirely different methods, consequently provide some kind of check to each other.

III. *Building as a Whole*

Building investment as a whole followed a strong upward course between the wars, and its level by the end of the period was twice as great in real terms as at the beginning. Falls in activity occurred only in 1921–2, 1927–8, 1930–2 and 1937–8.[2] In the first and last years of decline both housebuilding and non-residential building fell, but the decline of 1927–8 was explained by the collapse of housebuilding alone, while in the period 1930–2 it was non-residential rather than residential building which slumped.

[1] Appendix, Table 3, column 5. [2] See Appendix, Table 4.

Housebuilding accounted for a high proportion of total building activity, apart from the early 1920s. Normally, housebuilding accounted for between three-fifths and three-quarters of total building activity. The share of housebuilding tended to move against the business cycle, being high in the mid-1920s and in 1932–4 but low in the late 1920s and the later 1930s. This was primarily to be explained by the strong pro-cyclical movement in industrial and commercial building while housebuilding followed its own path which failed to correspond either directly or inversely with general business activity.[1]

Building's share in total gross capital formation fell within the range of 37 per cent to 58 per cent over the period as a whole. These percentages underestimate the share of construction as a whole because civil engineering activities are expressly excluded from the scope of the book. On the other hand, building accounted for over one-half of aggregate capital formation only in 1926 and in the period 1933–5, all of which were years of high residential building activity. The share of building in total investment varied, often considerably, from year to year but pursued no particularly regular or cyclical pattern. The most notable feature was the fact that on average building accounted for a much higher proportion of total investment in the 1930s than in the previous decade. This belies the generalization based on US experience that the twentieth century has witnessed a fall in the relative importance of building in advanced industrial economies. Investment in residential dwellings accounted for a substantial proportion of total investment. The role of housebuilding was at its peak in two periods, 1926–7 and 1932–5. In these years housebuilding accounted for between 35 per cent and 44 per cent of total investment activity.

The Lomax index of building and contracting (given in Appendix, Table 4, column 4) was not constructed independently of sources used elsewhere in this chapter and in most writings on inter-war building. Its value depends on Lomax's weights allocated to the individual indicators used in interpolating Census data in construction of the index, and probably underestimates the importance of non-residential building. Leaving aside the question of the accuracy of the year to year magnitudes of change, it is nevertheless worth pointing out that the index shows a close correspondence with the gross capital formation in building series at least as far as the direction of change is concerned. The only exceptions to this generalization are 1922–3 and 1929–30 when the capital formation series

[1] See Chapters 10–12.

remained virtually stable while the Lomax index declined quite noticeably in both instances. The discrepancies are probably accounted for by the latter's overemphasis of housebuilding, since the number of houses built fell more than negligibly both in 1922–3 and in 1929–30.

The available estimates of repairs and maintenance expenditures on buildings are probably not very accurate. However, they point to marked stability up to the middle 1920s and a firm upward trend thereafter. It is not, of course, surprising to find evidence of such a trend partly because the size of the building stock was growing markedly at this time, and partly because an upward movement in maintenance expenditures on houses could be expected in conditions of extreme housing shortage. The remarkable feature of the upward trend was the climacteric in 1930–1 when the estimates of maintenance expenditures show a proportionately greater expansion than over the rest of the decade taken together. No satisfactory explanation of this fact is known. It could be due to an unknown change in the basis of the statistics, though one element is likely to be a rise in maintenance expenditures on industrial and commercial building to offset the sharp fall during the first year of depression of new investment in non-residential buildings. A minor influence could also be the stimulus to higher expenditures on repairs of rented dwellings given by the gradual steps towards rent decontrol. In addition, resources were released for repair work on an abnormal scale in 1930–1.

The estimates of profits in construction are not very reliable. Moreover, they refer to profits in construction firms whose activities in some cases spilled over outside the scope of strictly building activities into civil engineering and related fields. Another drawback is that lack of data about capital employed makes it impossible to estimate changes in the profitability of the industry in the sense of annual return on capital employed. Nevertheless, the series quoted in Appendix, Table 4, give a rough guide to fluctuations in profits earned in the industry. It is not surprising to find that the peak years of the 1920s were 1926 and 1927 when housebuilding boomed, while in the 1930s profits were high and rising over the period 1934–8 probably in this case because of expanding opportunities in industrial and commercial building which were more profitable. Since housebuilding stagnated after 1934, it was unlikely to be the source of higher profits. Between 1930 and 1932 profits fell considerably, despite the fact that building activity was well maintained. The relatively high levels of building activity in the depression were only made possible by the acceptance of lower profit margins by firms in the building industry.

The Lomax index of building materials production is based on several very different sources with the overall figures for building plans providing a guiding light for movements in building materials taken as a whole. The index is referred to here because certain questions relating to building materials, particularly on changes in costs, are discussed in Chapter 6. Not surprisingly, the fluctuations in the index are broadly in the same direction and of similar magnitude to fluctuations in building activity. This is partly but not wholly accounted for by Lomax's reliance on the building plans approved series in constructing his index. There are close similarities between the movements in total capital formation and the building materials index. The series consequently provide some kind of check on the reliability of each other.

IV. *Employment, Unemployment and Strikes*

Employment in building expanded far more quickly in the 1930s than in the 1920s.[1] The difference was only partially explained by the higher level of building activity in the 1930s than in the previous decade, and is probably explicable in terms of supply constraints in regard to skilled building craftsmen in the 1920s. It is significant that between 1924 and 1929 total building employment expanded by 19·3 per cent against a rise of only 7·4 per cent in employment among craftsmen.[2] That the industry may have been handicapped even up to the later 1920s by this problem is indicated by the relatively low level of employment in the peak year of 1927, and by the continued expansion in building employment up to 1930 despite the stagnation in building activity as a whole and the sharp fall in house building. In the 1930s there was some fall in employment in the depression from the 1930 peak matched by a fall in building capital formation between 1930 and 1932, but the 1930 level was surpassed by 1934 and building employment expanded by over 35 per cent between 1932 and 1937. The estimates of local authority building employees show that local authorities accounted for between one-fifth and one-sixth of total building employment. This proportion was lower than the normal contribution of local authorities to building

[1] See Appendix, Table 5.

[2] There is little evidence to suggest that this differential could be due to changes in the relative demands for skilled and unskilled workers accounted for by technological advances and/or productivity increases.

and contracting output, but discrepancies are to be explained by the fact that considerable local authority building work was subcontracted out to private firms. The rate of expansion in local authority building employment was much lower than that in total building employment. After a steady rise from 1922–30 a peak was reached and the number of local authority building employees never re-attained the 1930 peak in the 1930s. This reflects the predominance of the private sector in the building boom of the 1930s. On the other hand, after 1932 building workers employed by local authorities increased in numbers back towards the peak of 1930, an expansion explained by the gradual resurgence of local authority housebuilding and the upward trend of building in the public and social services.

Building and contracting accounted for a steadily increasing proportion of total employment rising from 4·7 per cent in 1920 to 6·2 per cent by 1938. The only exceptions were 1921 when the economy suffered in the post-war slump far more than building, and 1932 and 1933 due to a rapid expansion in employment in non-manufacturing industries and in some services.

Unemployment in building stood at a relatively high level throughout the inter-war period, the percentage out of work in building being higher than the average unemployment percentage for the economy as a whole, especially in the 1930s. At first sight this does not seem consistent with the rate of expansion in building output between the wars. The explanation is to be found in the casual character of the building labour market so that in times of general unemployment unskilled workers formerly attracted to other industries were prone to seek work in building. Not unnaturally the unemployment rate in building varied cyclically. Nevertheless, the rise in unemployment in the depression was much higher than the relative stability in building activity would suggest. One of the factors in the increase in unemployment was that the high rate of public expenditure on housing in 1926 and 1927 attracted an excess of labour into the industry. This labour was only partly absorbed by private building when the public building programme was cut back. Moreover, the unemployment rate was only gradually whittled down after 1932 because the building boom's increased demand for labour was met more by the attraction of new labour from outside than by the absorption of the reservoir of unemployed in building. Although the unemployment rate amongst building craftsmen was not surprisingly always lower than in building as a whole, the gap narrowed in 1931 and 1932. But after 1932 the gap widened in comparison with the experience of the 1920s, and this tends to confirm the above point that the building boom of the 1930s failed to mop up the reserves of unskilled labour that had drifted into the building industry in the depression.[1] On the other hand, the cyclical swings in the number of craftsmen unemployed were very wide, from 15,000 in 1925 to 108,300 in 1932, falling to 28,900 in 1936 (July of each year). Craft labour suffered from the instability of building activity equally as much as unskilled labour.

The estimates of numbers employed in brick, cement and non-metalliferous mining manufacturers in the inter-war period follow a path very similar to that of building activity, with a pronounced peak in 1927 in the first post-war decade and a continuous rise in employment in these trades between 1932 and 1938. But employment in this, the largest, sector of the building materials trades increased considerably faster than employment in building and contracting generally; in fact, numbers employed more than doubled. This differential increase was not to be explained by differences in productivity rates between building and contracting on the one hand, and building materials production on the other. Rather it was due to a switch in emphasis from contracting to building, resulting in an increased demand for bricks, cement and other basic materials. Thus, the output of the main product of the group, bricks, more than doubled in the inter-war period in line with the increase in numbers employed in the group. The unemployment rate in the building materials trades moved in line with building activity apart from the year of the General Strike when unemployment stood at a high level due to the shortage of coal. The unemployment rate was considerably lower than in building and, indeed, than in the economy as a whole. The building materials trades were not, of course, as non-specialized as the unskilled sections of building itself, so they never attracted unemployed workers to the same extent.

The final column of Appendix, Table 5, indicates the effects of strikes in building on employment in the industry. As in many other industries, the early 1920s were a period of many labour disputes and a relatively large number of working days was lost. A major cause of the disputes was pressure for wage increases in the post-war boom, when prices were rising quickly, and resistance to wage cuts in the ensuing slump. From the middle 1920s, however, the industry was relatively free from disputes with an annual loss of over 100,000 working days in only four years—1927, 1931, 1934 and 1938. In other years, working days lost through disputes were very low falling to only 9,000 days in 1933. In fact, over the inter-war period there was only one year when building activity was noticeably affected by dis-

[1] See Appendix, Table 5, columns 6 and 7.

putes. In 1924 some 3,145,000 working days were lost, more than in all the other years of the period 1920–38 put together. This was a special case to be explained by a seven-week stoppage (July 5th–August 25th) in the summer caused by the reluctance of Liverpool building workers to accept national wage rates and negotiating machinery.[1]

V. *Building Societies*

The building societies expanded rapidly between the wars and were a vital permissive factor in the growth of the owner-occupied sector of the housing stock. Both shares and deposits increased about ninefold over the period, the annual amount advanced on mortgage rose by five to six times, and there was a tenfold rise in the balance due on mortgage.[2] The growth in the business of the societies obviously had two main aspects: the inflow of funds and the great increase in the demand for mortgages. There were many reasons for the accumulation of funds by building societies. Although building society assets did not increase very much during the war because of the diversion of savings to the Government, the societies were left with considerable excess funds at the end of the war because advances had been so low. During the inter-war period large shareholdings became increasingly important. Higher income tax rates had made building societies with their favoured tax position a more attractive outlet for those liable to tax. The decline in the supply of new rented houses was accompanied by former housing investors placing their money in building societies. From 1932 cheap money and low equity returns made building societies more attractive relatively to Consols and other forms of investment. At the same time, building societies assisted the spread of the investment habit to lower income groups, partly because of the inducement of fixed capital values and high liquidity. The inflow of funds into building societies was not, however, a passive phenomenon resulting from factors outside the societies' control. The building societies did more than a little to induce the inflow by increased expenditure on advertising, by offering different kinds of investments to cater for individual needs, and by the emergence of national as opposed to regional societies.

The structure of building society liabilities changed within the

[1] For further details see *Ministry of Labour Gazette*, 32 (1924), pp. 237–8, 278, 318.

[2] See Appendix, Table 6.

inter-war period. At the outset deposits were equal to rather more than one-quarter of shares, but from the middle 1920s the preponderance of shares increased still further. From 1932, however, deposits reverted to their share of the early 1920s, partly because building societies placed restrictions on the expansion of new share investment. Thus, in the period 1927–32 share capital rose by £208·1 million while deposits increased by only £28·2 million; between 1932 and 1935, on the other hand, deposits increased by £57·4 million while share capital went up by £66·3 million.

The increased demand for mortgages in the inter-war period was inextricably involved with the influences changing the character of the housing stock, such as an increased desire for owner-occupation and the rise in incomes which enabled this desire to be satisfied, an unfavourable environment for investment in rented housing and the failure of local authorities to fill the gap left behind by the withdrawal of the housing investor. Apart from a dip in 1921 and 1922, building society advances expanded year by year up to 1936 by which time the private housing boom of 1930s had passed its peak. Despite the fact that building societies were almost the only available source of mortgages in the period 1919–22, there was little expansion in mortgages, partly because of the low levels of housebuilding, partly because of the expected fall in building costs and house prices which militated against granting large advances in case the value of a property might fall below the outstanding mortgage debt. Between 1922 and 1928 there was a steady but unspectacular rise in advances, but after 1928 the annual amount advanced on mortgage accelerated in line with the expansion in private unsubsidized housebuilding. There was stagnation in the unsettled years of 1931 and 1932, but between 1932 and 1934 advances rose by more than 50 per cent. Mortgage rates had begun to fall and real incomes were rising. Since the number of borrowers rose by only 23 per cent in the same period, this suggests that a higher proportion of borrowers required mortgages for new, therefore more costly, houses. In fact, despite considerable year to year fluctuations in advances in the 1930s the number of borrowers rose more or less steadily, and in fact increased two and three-quarter times between 1928 and 1939.[1]

An indication of the changing liquidity of building societies is given by comparing the net yearly addition to building society shares and deposits with annual mortgage advances minus repayments. The building societies' overall liquidity situation may be assessed by placing total share capital and deposits alongside the

[1] See Appendix, Table 6, columns 3 and 6.

outstanding balance due on mortgage.[1] This shows considerable variation over the inter-war period. At the beginning of the period shares and deposits exceeded outstanding mortgages by more than 20 per cent, but this deteriorated especially in 1926 and 1927. In the late 1920s and early 1930s the position was reversed, but from the middle 1930s the building societies' liquidity position declined once again. A continued high level of demand for new mortgages was accompanied by a much slower rise in shares and deposits than had been experienced earlier in the decade. The liquidity position of building societies is the net result of influences on the effective demand for owner-occupied houses on the one hand, and factors governing the rate of accumulation of building society funds on the other. Of course, essential elements in these two sets of forces include building society policy regarding advances and the rates of interest they pay on shares and deposits. Consequently, the change in liquidity in the later 1930s reflected increasing liberalization of terms and conditions relating to advances alongside a declining ability to compete with other investment outlets.[2]

VI. *Some Determinants of Building Activity*

To conclude this chapter, it may be useful to comment on some major determinants of the level of building activity which are referred to repeatedly in later chapters. Changes in the level of building activity are sometimes explicable in terms of such variables as rents, building costs, interest rates and incomes.[3]

After a hump in 1921 and 1922 connected with the severe housing shortage and as a delayed reaction to the high prices of the post-war boom which preceded these years, rents settled down in 1923 and 1924. From that time, rents displayed a virtually steady rise throughout the inter-war period. This upward trend in rents continued even in the 1930s despite the increased supply of houses. The point was that demand had not remained constant, but increased rapidly because of a high rate of net household formation. Moreover, the rent index included controlled as well as decontrolled houses so that gradual decontrol in the 1930s obviously assisted the upward move-

[1] In other words, by comparing columns 1 and 2 of Appendix, Table 6, with column 5.

[2] In addition to the data in the Appendix, this section relied on E. J. Cleary, *The Building Society Movement* (1965), Chapters 10–12 and A. A. Nevitt, *Housing Taxation and Subsidies* (1966), Chapter 3.

[3] For the course of these in the inter-war period, see Appendix, Table 7.

ment in the rent index. Moreover, available rent indices include rates which were also moving upwards for the greater part of the inter-war period. Yet the overall increase in rents was not very high showing a rise of only 8–9 per cent between 1924 and 1938.

The rise in rents was matched by a growth in the share of rents and rates in total consumers' expenditure. Again, however, the main spurt occurred in 1920–2 reflecting in addition to the factors mentioned above a 40 per cent increase in controlled rents in 1920. The share then stagnated until 1925. From 1925 there was a steady rise year by year up to 1933, but after 1933 there was a slight decline in the percentage share of rents and rates in consumers' expenditure. This stagnation was due to a certain upward inflexibility of rents as well as to faster rates of expansion in other categories of consumers' expenditure such as durable goods.

The trend of building costs was clearly downwards between the wars, the downward trend being interrupted only in the years 1923–5 when productive factors were in short supply, especially labour, and after 1933 (particularly after 1935) when booming overall building activity induced rising costs. Costs were exceptionally high in 1920 and 1921 because of high wages and severely restricted supplies of building materials in the post-war boom, but fell dramatically in the ensuing general slump. After the temporary recovery in 1923–5, building costs started to fall again, a decline which on this occasion continued until 1933. The fall in costs was rather uneven but was most rapid in the depression years 1930–2, a decline of more than 8 per cent overall which was, however, much more marked in materials than in wages. From 1933 building costs started to recover and surpassed the 1930 level by 1937. The increase in costs was concentrated in the period 1935–7; this was especially due to soaring raw materials prices in the boom of 1936–7 since the annual rate of increase in building wages was more or less uniform between 1924 and 1938.

Interest rates, as illustrated by the yield on Consols, remained remarkably stable in the 1920s after the exceptionally high rates of 1920 and 1921. The yield on Consols dropped sharply in 1932 and continued to fall, if less dramatically, down to 1935–6. There was some hardening of interest rates from 1936, but the yield on Consols only reverted to the 1933 level in 1938. The sharp change in interest rates after 1931 had, as will be shown later, a marked impact on building. The fall in gilt-edged yields drove investors into the building market for the favourable returns from investing in property and for the higher yield on capital offered by the building societies. In the

1920s the yield on Consols had been about equal to the interest on building society shares. But between 1931 and 1936 investors were able to obtain with equal security a higher return from investing in building societies, since their shares offered a margin of 0·8 per cent higher than the yield on Consols in 1932, and margins which varied between 0·3 per cent and 0·7 per cent in the period 1933–6.[1] In 1937 and 1938, on the other hand, the margin closed, for the yield on Consols had begun to recover while the interest offered on building society shares continued falling, if slightly.

The only noticeable similarity between the movements in annual average real earnings and net national income is that both series exhibited an upward trend in the inter-war period, though the trend in aggregate income was much more marked than in real wages. A better comparison would be between real wages and incomes per head; because population was increasing the difference in trend would be less marked if the aggregate income series were deflated by population changes. Of course, there is no inherent reason for real wages and aggregate income to move together, since a rapid growth in income could easily be associated with a shift in expenditure towards investment (both private and public) or a faster growth in non-wage than in wage income. In fact, the year to year variations in the two series are very marked. The major determinant of changes in real wages is the differential movements in money wages and the cost of living, and real wages are likely to alter considerably in periods characterized by rapid changes in the overall price level regardless of the rate of economic progress. Conversely, the course of national income will be more sensitive to variations in the economy's production potential; for instance, the national income series shows a marked decline in 1926 due to the effects of the General Strike. As for the course of real wages, annual average real earnings stood at a low level in the post-war boom because of the impossibility of wage demands being met promptly enough to keep pace with rising prices. From 1923–9 real wages increased rather unsteadily up to 1929, but in the depression after 1929 the rate of increase accelerated, partly because prices as a whole were falling too fast for wages to be pared down in proportion, partly because import (especially food) prices were falling faster than export prices. From 1933, however, the rise in real earnings levelled out and in 1935–7 the index actually shows a decline primarily because of a rapid rise in prices and particularly in the cost of living. The aggregate real income index, on the other

[1] Tax advantages made the building society margin even more favourable than these figures suggest.

hand, moved as expected in line with business activity, expanding between 1922 and 1930, apart from the interruption in 1926, falling between 1930 and 1932 due to the effects of the slump but rising again quite rapidly in the recovery of the 1930s though at an uneven rate.

The widely divergent movements in average annual earnings and aggregate income are not surprising. This is not a source of difficulty because the two series are not, or intended to be, substitutes for each other as influences upon building. In fact, in the analysis developed later in this book the two indices are put to different uses. The index of annual average earnings is used to indicate changes in the ability to pay rents and to account for the spread of house ownership to lower income groups, in other words as a factor in the demand for houses. The aggregate income index, on the other hand, is mainly employed in relation to fluctuations in building activity since a comparison of building activity with movements in aggregate income gives some guide to the responsiveness and sensitivity of building to changes in general business conditions.

VII. *Summary*

It is not easy to summarize a general introductory chapter of this kind which takes a broad sweep on the one hand but confines itself to description on the other. Consequently, only the briefest précis will be attempted. There was a strong upward trend in building activity between the wars, though not a smooth rise since there were marked fluctuations from year to year. Housebuilding followed a different course from non-residential building: for instance, its trend was steeper. Movements in determinants of the level of housebuilding, such as rents, building costs and real income, were on balance a strong net stimulus. The entry of local authorities and the rapid expansion in building societies reflected changes in the character of residential building. The trend of building output was not matched by a parallel change in employment for the labour force expanded relatively slowly and heavy unemployment persisted.

STATISTICAL APPENDIX

This Appendix brings together some of the more important statistics relating to building in the inter-war period, and comments on the sources and reliability of the data. The statistics are assembled in a number of main tables, each relating to one aspect of building:

Table 1: RESIDENTIAL BUILDING IN THE UK, 1920–38

Year	Houses built (calendar years)	1920=*Year ending March* 31, 1921 Houses built by LAs	Private subsidized houses	Private unsubsidized houses	LA expenditure on dwellings	Private expenditure on dwellings	GDCF in dwellings	Assumed depreciation	Estimated replacement investment
			('000)		(£ million; 1930 prices)			(£ million; current prices)	
	(1)	(2)	(3)	(4)	(5)	(6)=7–5	(7)	(8)	(9)
1920	48	17	13	— } 60	19	17	36	56	..
1921	121	87	22	— } 60	49	25	74	47	5
1922	109	67	11	— } 60	37	29	66	39	18
1923	94	20	5	69	13	47	60	37	14
1924	146	24	49	71	18	67	85	39	4
1925	185	50	67	68	32	75	107	40	5
1926	237	84	84	66	49	85	134	41	10
1927	258	120	78	62	56	91	147	41	16
1928	197	70	52	66	41	74	115	41	20
1929	228	73	54	93	35	95	130	42	11
1930	208	61	6	131	33	89	122	43	11
1931	219	77	5	133	35	92	127	42	5
1932	223	67	6	149	31	97	128	41	5
1933	304	70	11	212	29	139	168	42	6
1934	345	75	1	292	28	160	188	44	10
1935	348	70	—	280	31	148	179	46	16
1936	366	87	1	282	38	140	178	49	20
1937	364	92	3	265	46	121	167	53	25
1938	359	122	4	233	52	113	165	56	n.a.

.. =negligible

residential building, the housing stock and its utilization, non-residential building, building as a whole, employment and labour, building societies and determinants of building activity.

TABLE 1: RESIDENTIAL BUILDING IN THE UK, 1920–38

1. The estimates of houses built each calendar year for the United Kingdom are based on the official statistics as given in returns to the Ministry of Health reprinted in the annual *Statistical Abstract for the UK.* The original estimates refer to years ending March 31st, and these have been readjusted to a calendar year basis. However, the readjustments have been made only for houses built in England and Wales; the houses built in Scotland and Northern Ireland have been added simply by making the year ending March 31, 1921, for instance, the figure for 1920. Because the houses built in Scotland and Northern Ireland are such a small proportion of the total, this is not a major drawback though it introduces another element of approximation into these estimates.

2, 3 and 4. These columns classify the volume of housebuilding according to whether houses were built by local authorities or by the private sector. Privately built houses are in turn subdivided into those built without State assistance and those which were built with the aid of State subsidies, a number which were quantitatively significant in the years 1924–9. These estimates refer to years ending March 31st, and therefore aggregates of the three columns do not match exactly the calendar year estimates of column 1. The numbers of private unsubsidized houses are not available annually up to March 1923, but approximately 60,000 houses of this type were built in the three years 1920–2. The totals for each column are obtained by aggregating six monthly totals (ending in September and March) as given in the *Statistical Abstract.*

5. The estimates of total authority expenditure on dwellings are based on figures given in *Local Government Financial Statistics* compiled by R. F. Bretherton *et al., Public Investment and the Trade Cycle* (1941). Adjustments were made to these by C. H. Feinstein, *Domestic Capital Formation in the United Kingdom, 1920–38* (1965), p. 216, on three counts. Firstly he made adjustments for the purchase of land and legal costs, an amount on average equal to 6·2 per cent of expenditure. He also excluded sums repaid to lenders or transferred to sinking funds, approximately a further 2 per cent of total local authority expenditures. Finally, reductions were made to the estimates for the years 1920–3 to exclude sums not spent on houses.

The resulting estimates were in current £ millions, and these were reduced to a common base of 1930 prices by deflating them with the Maywald index of building costs.

These estimates show considerable divergences from the alternative estimates prepared by G. P. Braae, 'Investment in Housing in the United Kingdom, 1924–38', *Manchester School*, 32 (1964), p. 22. Braae's estimates were constructed by multiplying the number of local authority houses built annually, obtained from the Ministry of Health returns, by the average tender price of contracts for the standard 'three-bedroom non-parlour type house'.

6. The annual amounts of private expenditure on dwellings are a residual obtained by deducting local authority housing expenditures from total gross capital formation on dwellings as estimated in column 7.

7. The annual estimates of gross capital formation are obtained by taking the estimated total number of houses built each calendar year, as given in column 1 above, and multiplying these by the estimated average cost per dwelling. The figures for average cost per dwelling are based on collected monthly data from 146 local authorities, and are obtained by dividing the total cost of dwelling plans by the number of housing units involved. These average cost figures are subject to limitations. The 146 local authorities covered are not necessarily a representative sample because they include only urban authorities and they also exclude the area controlled by London County Council. Other weaknesses are doubts about the basis of costs, for example whether the cost of land is excluded or not, and the fact that it is not clear whether the costs are those ruling at the time the plans are approved or those expected at the time of construction. On the other hand, the advantages of the series are that it covers a very large sample of urban houses, is continuous and allows for changes in size and type. Following Feinstein, the series has been reduced by 5 per cent because it very likely exaggerates costs—it is intended to include all professional fees and legal charges but to exclude costs of site development. The final figures of capital formation obtained from this multiplication are of course in current prices, and these were reduced to 1930 prices.

8. The estimates of depreciation investment in residential dwellings at current prices are from Feinstein, op. cit., p. 219. These estimates are calculated on a straight line depreciation method based on an assumed life of 100 years. Thus, Feinstein takes the first cost value of the housing stock at the end of each year and represents 1 per cent of this figure as depreciation. The estimates would be reasonably accurate only if the housing stock was homogeneous, if each house lasted one hundred years and if the rate of housebuilding had been constant over time. If these conditions were satisfied, then actual replacement investment might approximate to these estimates of depreciation. (It should be noted that Feinstein's estimates refer only to replacements since estimates of depreciation in the sense of repairs and maintenance of the existing stock are made elsewhere in his book.) But in the inter-war period scrapping of dwellings equalled little more than a sixth of the assumed depreciation rate. This fact illustrates how misleading depreciation estimates calculated on these theoretical assumptions can be. Feinstein's estimates of net capital formation in residential dwellings are consequently so wide off the mark as not to be used in this book. Incidentally, the predominance of housing in total investment makes Feinstein's estimates of net capital formation for the whole economy subject to very great margins of error as a result of his serious underestimation of net investment in housing.

9. It is believed that the estimates of replacement investment in this column, though by no means free from error, give a far better guide to replacements than Feinstein's depreciation estimates and provide a sounder basis for estimating net housing investment from the gross capital formation estimates. These were obtained by taking the estimates of housing demolitions discussed below (see notes to Appendix, Table 2, column 3) and multiplying these by the average local authority three-bedroom non-parlour house contract price (excluding land and site development) for each year. There are a number of drawbacks to this procedure. As pointed out below, the estimates of houses demolished for individual years are very approximate for the 1920s. Moreover, they refer to the year April 1st–March 31st, not calendar years (the year ending March 1930, for instance, is counted as 1929), and this introduces another error. Using local authority tender prices implicitly assumes that local authorities built the replacements for demolished dwellings, an assumption which though obviously not true of all cases is probably not far off the mark. There may also have been some differences between the tender prices and the actual prices of local authority houses built under contract. The source of houses demolished figures is given below, while the local authority contract prices are taken from M. Bowley, *Housing and the State, 1919-44* (1945), especially pp. 276–8. Contract prices were not available for 1922 and 1923, and estimates had to be made in the light of movements in the average cost of all dwellings.

There are clearly very wide differences between Feinstein's estimates of depreciation and these estimates of replacement investment. The latter obviously have considerable deficiencies particularly for the 1920s, but they are more logically based than Feinstein's estimates, and if subtracted from gross housing investment would provide a firmer guide to the levels of net housing investment. In particular, they make some attempt to be related to actual replacements rather than to an assumed theoretical depreciation rate and thereby avoid the danger of seriously understating net housing investment in the inter war period.

TABLE 2: THE HOUSING STOCK, 1920–38

Year ending March 31st	*Stock of houses, UK (million)* (1)	*Unoccupied houses* ('000) (2)	*Houses demolished* ('000) (3)
1920	9·262	123	—
1921	9·29	93	—
1922	9·361	123	8
1923	9·448	121	38
1924	9·516	131	30
1925	9·615	139	9
1926	9·771	144	11
1927	9·968	160	22
1928	10·189	173	38
1929	10·37	177	55
1930	10·532	195	32
1931	10·71	200	33
1932	10·895	213	14
1933	11·1	257	15
1934	11·341	326	22
1935	11·64	370	35
1936	11·952	357	52
1937	12·258	356	64
1938	12·56	363	70

1. The UK housing stock estimates are taken from J. R. Stone and D. A. Rowe, *Measurement of Consumers' Expenditure in the United Kingdom, 1920–38*, Vol. 1 (1954), p. 221. The stock estimate for 1929 refers to the year ending March 31, 1929, and likewise in preceding and successive years. The basic estimates are taken from the Census of Population returns in 1921 and 1931, and for intermediate years additions to stock due to building are taken from the *Statistical Abstract*, i.e. this source gives the number of houses built each year and when the number of houses demolished is subtracted from the annual totals the net addition to the housing stock remains. The basis of the annual estimates of houses demolished is shown in the notes to column 3 below. Adjustments were made to account for houses in Northern Ireland; the number of houses in Northern Ireland amounted to 2·8 per cent of the number in Great Britain in 1926 and 2·48 per cent in 1937. This figure was linearly interpreted and extrapolated to find the UK stock of houses.

2. The annual estimates of unoccupied houses are also compiled by Stone and Rowe. The 1921 and 1931 totals are again given in the Census returns. Estimates were found for other years by interpolation and extrapolation on the basis of data for several large cities—London, Birmingham, Leeds, Newcastle, Edinburgh and Glasgow. Because no account is taken of differences in rates of migration from large cities, other urban areas and rural districts, the estimates are bound to be approximate. But the large cities account for a high proportion of the housing stock, so the resulting errors are probably not large.

3. These estimates are also taken from Stone and Rowe, p. 221. The total houses demolished in the period 1921–31 were obtained by taking the 1921 Census estimate of the stock adding all the houses built in the inter-census period and subtracting the housing stock of 1931 according to the Census from this total. This total estimate of houses demolished between 1921 and 1931 was distributed between individual years by assuming that houses demolished each year were in proportion to local authority housebuilding in the previous year relative to other years over the period.

The estimates of houses demolished after 1931 are much more accurate being based on returns of houses demolished under the slum clearance sections of the Housing Acts of 1930 and 1936.

TABLE 3: NON-RESIDENTIAL BUILDING IN THE UK, 1920–38

The total estimates for building investment, excepting dwellings (column 1), and for individual sectors (columns 2–4) are those of Feinstein. The final column shows the estimated cost of new factories and workshops for which plans were approved for 146 local authorities at 1930 costs; these were compiled by B. Weber and J. Parry Lewis, 'New Industrial Building in Great Britain, 1923–38', *Scottish Journal of Political Economy*, 8 (1961). Some comment is necessary on how these estimates are constructed.

1. The total estimates of capital formation in buildings other than dwellings exclude civil engineering works. These are constructed mainly on the 'ownership side' as opposed to the 'supply side', i.e.

Table 3: NON-RESIDENTIAL BUILDING IN THE UNITED KINGDOM, 1920–38

Year	*GDCF in other buildings*	*Building and works in manufacturing*	*Buildings in retail distribution*	*Buildings in social and public services*	*Estimated cost of new factories and workshops (£ million; 1930 prices)*
		(£ million; 1930 prices)			
	(1)	(2)	(3)	(4)	(5)
1920	80	41	10	5	—
1921	61	29	8	6	—
1922	42	22	4	5	—
1923	49	18	12	5	3·22
1924	57	20	16	6	3·46
1925	60	28	14	8	4·09
1926	56	23	12	9	3·52
1927	54	20	11	11	4·74
1928	61	19	13	11	5·27
1929	72	26	15	13	6·24
1930	81	25	12	18	4·58
1931	56	14	10	20	2·77
1932	49	13	9	17	3·26
1933	53	15	12	14	4·08
1934	68	17	15	15	6·70
1935	77	19	16	18	7·91
1936	82	27	16	23	10·01
1937	105	38	16	27	8·68
1938	98	31	17	32	6·99

by measuring the amount spent on building by various categories of future owners rather than by trying to extract items from the total output of the building industry which form part of the flow of fixed assets. The final figures are the aggregate totals for seven separate sectors: agriculture, forestry and fishing; mining and quarrying; electricity, gas and water; manufacturing; transport and communication; distribution and other services; and the social and public services. The sectoral estimates were constructed by aid of a variety of methods, and were subject to different degrees of accuracy. The overall estimates in the table are deflated in terms of 1930 building costs and are taken from Feinstein, op. cit., p. 38. His guess of the margin of error involved is between 7 and 15 per cent. If this is the case, and if the margin of error varied significantly from year to year which is certainly a possibility, it means that the later analysis of non-residential building fluctuations is subject to the limitations of the data. On the other hand, when Feinstein's *total* gross capital formation estimates are compared with the independent figures of Jefferys and Walters the average discrepancy between the two series is only 4 per cent (ibid., p. 250).

In some of the sectors and sub-sectors, such as manufacturing, electricity supply and wholesale distribution, it was impossible to separate buildings from works and the solution to this, scarcely satisfactory, was to assign an estimate covering both in full to whichever was the predominant component. In the national figures any errors on this account would tend to cancel out, but the net effect was likely an understatement of capital formation in buildings. Other sources of error included the fact that factories and warehouses owned by financial institutions, property owning companies and firms in retail distribution were omitted, while shops owned by firms in the manufacturing, wholesale distribution and public utilities sectors were duplicated because capital formation in shops was estimated primarily from the supply side. In fact, though most of the estimates were obtained from owners' accounts and similar sources, shops, hotels, theatres, halls and cinemas and farm buildings were all estimated on the supply side. As the example above illustrates, this lack of uniformity in methods of estimation resulted in some errors.

2. The estimates of gross capital formation in building and works in manufacturing in this column are taken from Feinstein, Table 8.00, p. 102. Because it was not possible to separate out buildings from civil engineering works, the value of investment in buildings alone is overstated. Works in this instance meant such items as site development and private sidings and ports. The estimates for all but one of twenty-two manufacturing groups (i.e. cotton) are based on samples of company accounts, and on Inland Revenue wear and tear allowances and rates of depreciation. The company accounts yield direct estimates of net fixed capital formation. Gross capital formation figures were then obtained by adding back *assumed depreciation* sums by the reducing balance method. Firms may have actually written off for depreciation sums quite different from the assumed figures. This was particularly likely in years of poor profits when little was actually allocated by companies to depreciation. In industries where depreciation added is large compared with net capital formation the possible errors may be large. For the cotton industry, the extensive reorganization of the inter-war period rules out use of company accounts. Instead estimates for plant had to be worked out in physical terms, and estimates for buildings obtained by data relating the stock of buildings to the stock of plant. The resulting estimates were very approximate. The estimates of investment in buildings in individual industries were in many cases rough, because of the coverage of the sample. For two industrial groups, tobacco and cement, the sample covered more than 80 per cent of the group; for many more (wool and worsted, other textiles, wood and cork, glass and pottery, and miscellaneous manufacturers) the coverage was less than 20 per cent. However, the small samples referred mainly to small unimportant industries, and Feinstein argues that the estimates for manufacturing taken as a whole are fair.

3. A different method was used for estimating the amount of investment in buildings in retail distribution. Gross capital formation in shops was obtained as a proportion of the estimated total new work in buildings, The latter series based on *Census of Production* reports is to be found in Feinstein, p. 60. The proportions required for 1920–9 were derived from the gross annual value of building assessed to Income Tax, Schedule A, for the first time, using the ratio of shop to all buildings covered by Schedule A. The required data were not collected after 1929, and a less reliable procedure had to be adopted. The assumption was that shops and residential building moved together each year and the share of shops was assumed to be a fixed proportion of the share of residential dwellings in each year from 1930 to 1938. The fixed proportion employed was the average ratio of first assessments for shops to those of houses under Schedule A in the period 1920–9. It is clear, therefore, that these figures have to be used with caution, though Feinstein still believes that they have a fair reliability. The estimates are reduced to a base of 1930 prices, and are taken from Feinstein, p. 188. Here they are rounded off to the nearest £ million.

4. The estimates of gross capital formation in buildings in social and public services are made from four separate sub-sectors—schools and libraries, hospitals, local authority non-trading services and specified civil and revenue departments of the central governments. Of these the last was quantitatively insignificant accounting for an annual average of less than £1 million over the inter-war period. The data used were obtained from *Local Government Financial Statistics* and for hospitals from *The Hospitals Year Book*.

In regard to schools and libraries, local authority accounts gave no division of capital spending into types of asset. On the basis of data given in *Memorandum on the Board of Education Estimates*, Cmd. 4824 (1935), it was assumed that 70 per cent of the purchases comprised buildings. Major omissions were capital formation by private schools and by universities: the 1935 Census of Production gave a figure of £1·5 million for new construction of private schools, while annual average expenditure on buildings and equipment by the universities stood at about £750,000 in the 1930s. For hospitals, a sample of specifications for new buildings and extensions recorded in *The Hospitals Year Book* in the 1930s suggested that 83 per cent of total purchases were composed of buildings. For local authority non-trading services, the amounts taken were total loan expenditure for specified services which could be roughly classified into the 'buildings' category of assets. The list of services comprised police stations, courts, poor-relief buildings, baths and other public health services. For expenditure by the central Government the information was obtained from the *Appropriation Accounts* of the Treasury. Buildings were taken as 90 per cent of the capital expenditure on new works (the remaining 10 per cent assumed to be for land). The total capital formation in buildings was aggregated from these four sub-sectors and deflated to 1930 prices. The annual estimates are to be found in Feinstein, p. 202. The reliability of the estimates for education is for the reasons stated above the lowest of the four sub-sectors. The aggregate estimates, however, are on balance probably as reliable as those in columns 2 and 3.

5. The estimates of the cost of new factories and workshops given in Weber and Parry Lewis are based on the value of building plans passed for 146 local authorities, deflated in terms of 1930 building costs. The data were collected by the Board of Trade, and were given in the *Ministry of Labour Gazette* with adjustments in the *Abstract of Labour Statistics*. As comparison with column 2 shows, they are far from comprehensive and are probably useful only as a check to the course of fluctuations as given in column 2. The authors' own verdict on the series is that it is 'a somewhat hazardous estimate of costs of intended new building in a non-representative sample of towns'.

The value of the series is depreciated by several factors. The measure is of plans approved, not work done: only a varying proportion of the plans approved would actually be carried out, the classification by type of building was imprecise, and the lag between the approval of plans and their completion varied often markedly over time. Moreover, the value of plans approved was based on estimates, not actual costs. Even more serious is the fact that the sample of plans was grossly unrepresentative. The London County Council area was excluded, and the sample covered only about one-third of all industrial building done. For these reasons the series should only be used to check the year to year direction of change in other series, and even for this purpose the question of varying length of lags provides a major difficulty.

TABLE 4: BUILDING IN THE UK, 1920–38

1. The estimates of gross capital formation in total building exclude civil engineering works and are simply the aggregates of column 7, Appendix, Table 1, and column 1, Appendix, Table 3. The notes to the above tables should be referred to for comments on the methods used in constructing the estimates for the individual components.

2. Similarly this column expresses the estimates of column 7, Table 1, as a proportion of column 1 above. In view of the possible errors in both series the percentages are most unlikely to be as accurate as the decimal place in the column suggests.

3. Column 1 as a percentage of gross domestic capital formation as given by Feinstein, op. cit., p. 38. The overall capital formation estimates are built up sector by sector. For a brief summary of the methods used for calculating capital formation in individual sectors see ibid., pp. 18–21, and for more details Chapters 5–12.

4. The index for building and contracting in this column is taken from K. S. Lomax, 'Production and Productivity Movements in the UK since 1900', *Journal of Royal Statistical Society*, 122A (1959), pp. 122–3. The original index was based on 1924; in Table 4 it has been reworked to a base year of 1930 to bring it into line with other series used in this book.

The index relies heavily on Census of Production statistics for Census years. For interpolation between Census points, Lomax used the following sources: estimates of building plans passed as given in the *Ministry of Labour Gazette* and obtained from a private source; the numbers of new buildings assessed for income tax as given in the

Table 4: BUILDING IN THE UK, 1920–38

Year	*GDCF in total building* (*£ million*) 1930 *prices* (1)	*Residential as per cent of total building* (*per cent*) (2)	*Share of building investment in total GDCF* (*per cent*) (3)	*Index of building and contracting* (1930=100) (4)	*Maintenance and repairs* (*£ million*) 1930 *prices* (5)	*Gross profit in construction* (*£ million*) (6)	*Index of building materials production* (1930=100) (7)
1920	116	31·0	43·4	50·4	62	11	71·4
1921	135	54·8	44·1	69·9	61	8	69·1
1922	108	61·1	38·3	57·8	61	6	60·0
1923	109	55·0	37·7	48·1	62	5	68·6
1924	142	59·9	42·1	76·2	61	6	81·9
1925	167	64·1	43·4	97·3	62	11	93·1
1926	190	74·4	50·9	113·1	67	15	95·1
1927	201	73·1	48·4	124·4	68	17	105·4
1928	176	65·3	42·8	100·2	73	6	97·4
1929	202	64·4	46·7	108·3	74	13	104·8
1930	203	60·1	46·7	100·0	77	9	100·0
1931	183	69·4	42·9	94·5	92	8	94·1
1932	177	72·3	47·6	89·1	98	9	90·7
1933	221	76·0	57·6	103·6	101	13	103·4
1934	256	73·4	54·8	116·8	102	15	120·1
1935	256	69·9	52·7	119·6	103	15	129·2
1936	260	68·4	49·1	130·9	103	19	140·6
1937	272	61·4	49·6	136·5	104	19	147·2
1938	263	62·7	47·3	130·8	106	20	138·0

Statistical Abstract; returns of houses built as given by the Ministry of Health; and for construction expenditure by local authorities interpolation was made on the basis of local authority loan expenditure.

Although the Lomax index is widely used, it is probably less reliable than others used in this book, for instance column 1 of Table 4. None of the sources used are independent of those used in the construction of other estimates. The index probably understates the role of non-residential building. In particular it is considered a serious under-estimate for the years 1920–3, because some of the series used in the compilation of the index did not begin until 1923.

5. The estimates of maintenance and repairs expenditure on building were again taken from Feinstein, op. cit., Table 4.22, p. 60, given in current prices and deflated to 1930 prices for inclusion here.

The series is based on Census of Production data for 1924 and 1935. According to the Census of 1924 the value of repair and maintenance work on buildings in current prices was £60 million plus a further £8 million for non-reporting firms; in 1935 the Census estimate was £95 million. The 1930 Census estimate could not be used because it excluded small firms which were responsible for a high proportion of total maintenance work. For other years the Inland Revenue series of annual maintenance allowances (given under the heading 'Repairs, etc., to Houses and Buildings') under Schedule A of Income Tax were used as an index to extrapolate the Census figures. Further adjustments were made to the series for the years 1920–3 because the sharp fall in building costs over this period was not adequately reflected in the Schedule A allowances for these years. The series is probably not very accurate, especially in view of its heavy dependence on the reliability of the two Census estimates. It is suspicious that in no year between 1924 and 1938 does the series show a reversal in the upward trend in repairs and maintenance expenditures.

6. The estimates of gross profit in construction are taken from P. E. Hart, *Studies in Profit, Business Saving and Investment in the United Kingdom, 1920–62*, Vol. I (1965), p. 93. The estimates refer to private firms only, and the building and contracting activities of local and central government authorities are excluded. The basic source was a sample of firms in the industry used by the Oxford Institute of Statistics in making estimates of profit in benchmark years 1927, 1932 and 1936–8. Estimates for years between the benchmark years were obtained with the aid of the index of gross profit for construction obtained from the estimates of the gross margin in building and contracting according to Census of Production data for 1924, 1930 and 1935 (ibid., p. 96). It must be stressed that the reliability of the estimates is low, and the degree of error involved may well be over 10 per cent. Nevertheless, the series is worth mentioning because it gives some idea of fluctuations in building profits (though not, unfortunately, in profitability) in the inter-war period.

7. The index of building materials production given in this column was constructed by Lomax, loc. cit. pp. 192–3. Like the index in column 4, it has been reduced from the original 1924 to a new base year 1930. It relies heavily on Census of Production data, but information used to interpolate the Census points was obtained from many sources. Data on brick and fireclay production were obtained from a sample of private firms, on china and earthenware from estimates of home consumption of ball and china clay, on cement from information supplied by the Cement Makers' Federation, and on glass from private firms. A defect in the index is that it ignores many lesser materials and in particular takes insufficient account of newer materials. The statistics of building plans passed provided some guide to the course of building materials production taken as a whole.

TABLE 5: EMPLOYMENT IN BUILDING AND BUILDING MATERIALS, 1920–38

1. The estimates of numbers employed in building and contracting are those of A. Chapman and R. Knight, *Wages and Salaries in the United Kingdom, 1920-38* (1953), p. 18. Numbers employed in 1(a) include salary earners and employers while 1(b) refers to wage earners only. Both columns include those working for the local and central governments as well as those in private firms. The estimates are not based on Census of Production data which show a far lower total employment, because the coverage of the Census of Production was far too narrow and excluded government employees.

The procedure adopted for key years by Chapman and Knight in making their estimates of total numbers employed can best be explained by example. For 1931, for instance, they started from a figure of numbers employed according to the Population Census of 987,400, an estimate including operatives in building and contracting and in electrical wiring and contracting and also including 139,500 in building occupations listed in the Census under local government. This provided the basic estimate which was then made more accurate by certain refinements. Firstly, there were two major additions: 35,000 were added as an estimate for employers, directors and managers, and since the Census returns referred only to England and

Table 5: EMPLOYMENT IN BUILDING AND BUILDING MATERIALS, 1920–38

Year	Numbers employed in building ('000) (1) (a) Total	(1) (b) Wage earners	LA building employees ('000) (2)	Building employment as per cent of total employment (3)	Insured craftsmen ('000) (4)	Unemployed craftsmen ('000) (5)	Per cent craftsmen unemployed (6)	Average per cent unemployed in building (7)	Numbers employed in building materials ('000) (8)	Average per cent unemployed in building materials (9)	Number of working days lost through strikes in building ('000) (10)
1920	840·4	763·9	157·9	4·7	419·2	4·8	1·2		84·0		789
1921	805·9	732·7	153·5	5·3	436·6	41·1	9·4		77·7		557
1922	734·5	667·9	141·8	4·8	393·3	38·0	9·7		8[illegible]·1		179
1923	754·7	686·4	147·6	4·8	396·7	27·9	7·0	12·2	95·7	7·6	394
1924	775·2	705·1	153·6	4·9	369·9	19·1	5·2	12·5	10[illegible]·1	7·9	3,145
1925	841·9	765·9	169·0	5·2	363·4	15·5	4·3	10·5	12[illegible]·4	6·8	85
1926	856·0	777·4	173·8	5·5	394·1	24·4	6·2	12·1	12[illegible]·4	15·2	38
1927	920·5	837·7	189·4	5·5	392·2	18·6	4·8	11·1	134·5	6·9	129
1928	922·8	839·9	192·2	5·5	392·4	29·6	7·6	13·9	13[illegible]·8	12·4	84
1929	925·2	842·2	195·1	5·5	397·2	20·4	5·1	14·3	13[illegible]·2	11·5	28
1930	946·4	861·5	202·0	5·7	389·5	44·2	11·3	16·2	13[illegible]·6	13·0	46
1931	922·0	837·6	190·9	5·7	411·0	69·3	16·9	22·7	12[illegible]·5	18·0	145
1932	851·6	772·0	170·8	5·3	424·2	108·3	25·5	30·2	12[illegible]·6	21·5	36
1933	901·5	815·4	174·8	5·4	440·1	69·7	15·8	29·0	13[illegible]·9	20·2	9
1934	987·3	891·1	184·8	5·7	448·4	48·5	10·8	21·3	14[illegible]·9	13·3	172
1935	1,044·7	940·9	188·5	6·0	462·0	39·3	8·5	19·7	15[illegible]·9	11·9	37
1936	1,110·5	997·9	192·8	6·1	481·8	28·9	6·0	19·8	16[illegible]·7	11·7	44
1937	1,157·3	1,037·7	192·8	6·1	497·2	33·3	6·7	14·6	17[illegible]·0	8·2	39
1938	1,158·8	1,036·7	184·9	6·2	522·8	46·0	8·8	16·7	17[illegible]·3	9·1	115

Wales and Scotland 13,500 were added as an estimate of building employment in Northern Ireland. The subtractions were rather more extensive: 30,500 were taken away as representing the deficiency in the Population Census 'out of work' category as compared with the numbers of insured employees listed by the Ministry of Labour, the estimate was reduced by 59,900 to adjust from April 1931 to the average 1931 level of employment and by a further 23,500 to account for differences in classification, rounding, etc. The resulting estimate is 922,000 as given in the Table. For interpolation between Census years Ministry of Labour data on building employment and changes in unemployment were used.

2. The estimates of local authority building employees are also taken from Chapman and Knight, pp. 111–12. The estimates relate to all work of construction including alterations and repairs (except public utilities, canals, docks, harbours and road transport) carried out by employees of local authorities as recorded by the Census of Production. Since, according to the Census, 97 per cent of output reported under local authorities consisted of construction work it was assumed that 97 per cent of local authority employees engaged in production were employed in building and construction.

3. Building employment as given in column 1 as a proportion of total employment in all fields—manufacturing, non-manufacturing industries, services, professions and Government employment. The estimates of total employment used in this series are also those of Chapman and Knight aggregated from estimates for individual sectors. Chapman and Knight should be referred to for details of how the individual estimates are constructed.

4, 5 and 6. Columns 4 and 5 provide estimates of insured building craftsmen and numbers unemployed, while column 6 gives the unemployment rate for this group by dividing (5) by (4). The data was extracted from the *Ministry of Labour Gazette*. The main tradesmen included consisted of carpenters, bricklayers, masons, slaters, plasterers, plumbers and painters, and the unemployment estimates refer to July of each year. The statistics are more accurate after 1924 than before. The 1923 estimate refers to May rather than July. Also for 1923 and earlier years slaters were excluded along with a few minor skilled trades for which separate data were not available. Since only about five thousand workers of these categories were involved, their omission makes a difference of only slightly more than 1 per cent to the estimates. The series therefore provide a reasonable guide to the growth of the insured skilled labour force in the building industry between the wars, and to the variations in unemployment.

7. The average unemployment rates in building quoted in this column are based on published data in the *Ministry of Labour Gazette* and quoted in the *Statistical Abstracts*. The rate quoted is the average of the January and July rates of each year (apart from the 1923 figure which refers to July alone). Workers under 16 are excluded, while after 1928 people over 65 were not counted. Also the basis changes for the 1938 figure, since the method of counting unemployed changed in September 1937.

8. The estimates of the numbers employed in building materials are not comprehensive since they only refer to the largest Census of Production industrial classification in the building materials field, that is to 'brick, cement and other non-metalliferous mining manufactures'. These estimates are based on Census of Production data, and the mean of numbers employed in 1924, 1930 and 1935 is used as the base for interpolation. In the use of the Census data one qualification is that 2,275 employees working in quarries owned by cement companies were assigned to mines and quarries in 1930 but in 1924 had been classified as being in the cement industry. This was compensated for by the fact that 2,000 people assigned to building and contracting in 1924 were transferred to building materials in 1930, and consequently no adjustment was made for these changes.

9. The estimates of the average unemployment rates in the building materials trades are taken from the *Ministry of Labour Gazette* and are constructed in the same way and subject to the same qualifications as the unemployment percentages for building in column 7. It should be noted, however, that the building materials trades classification used by the Ministry of Labour is a very wide one embracing workers in industries such as glass and pottery, not all of whom were working on the production of building materials.

10. This column shows estimates of working days lost through strikes in the building industry. Working days lost are probably a much more effective indicator of strike activity than, say, the number of disputes each year, and in fact shows far different results. For instance, the number of strikes starting in 1924 was small by the standards of the early 1920s yet more working days were lost through strikes in that year than in the rest of the period 1920–38 put together (excluding the effects of the General Strike). The estimates in the column are taken from the *Abstract of Labour Statistics* up to 1936, and from *Annual Abstract of Statistics, Vol.* 84 (*1935–46*), for 1937 and 1938. The estimates of working days recorded as lost include days lost by workers at establishments where disputes occurred even though they were not directly involved in the dispute.

On the other hand, they do not include days lost at other establishments. The 1926 figure does not include working days lost because of the General Strike, since such losses were not the result of a dispute in building itself.

TABLE 6: BUILDING SOCIETIES OF GREAT BRITAIN, 1920–39

All the data in the table with the exception of column 5 are taken from the *Statistical Abstracts of the United Kingdom* and the *Annual Abstract of Statistics*, Vol. 84 (1935–46). The statistics were supplied for inclusion in these Abstracts by the Chief Registrar of Friendly Societies. The headings are self-explanatory. It should be noted that they refer not to calendar years but to years ending January 31st, i.e. 1930 means February 1, 1930, to January 31, 1931. The numbers of borrowers were not available before 1928.

5. This column, which lists the average mortgage rate charged by most societies for each year 1920 to 1939, is taken from A. A. Nevitt, *Housing, Taxation and Subsidies* (1966), p. 35. It refers to the rate charged on new mortgages and differs somewhat from the overall mortgage rate obtained by expressing total annual interest payments to building societies as a percentage of the outstanding balance due on mortgage. The new mortgage rate seems the more appropriate rate as far as the analysis in this book is concerned, since our main preoccupation is with the acquisition of new, rather than existing, houses.

TABLE 7: RENTS, COSTS AND INCOMES, 1920–38

1. This column gives the annual average index of rents (that is, average of twelve monthly values) as used in the construction of the Ministry of Labour monthly cost-of-living index. The figures are extracted from the *Ministry of Labour Gazette*. The index is based on the July 1914 value of 100, and estimates of changes in the value of the index were obtained by a sampling method based mainly on large towns and cities. The index is heavily biased in favour of working-class dwellings. It consequently refers to controlled as well as uncontrolled rents, and for this reason fails to give an accurate impression of the market movement of rent. The index, moreover, refers not merely to rents but to rates and water charges as well.

2. The index of average value of rents, rates and water charges in this column is taken from Stone and Rowe, op. cit., p. 221. It is not

Table 6: BUILDING SOCIETIES OF GREAT BRITAIN, 1920–39

Year	Share capital	Due to depositors and other creditors	Amount advanced on mortgage during year	Balance due on mortgage	New mortgage rates (per cent)	Number of borrowers ('000)
	(£ million)					
	(1)	(2)	(3)	(4)	(5)	(6)
1920	63·9	18·3	25·1	68·8	6½	
1921	70·9	19·1	19·7	75·5	6	
1922	80·4	21·0	22·7	83·7	6	
1923	93·5	24·4	32·0	98·8	6	
1924	109·0	28·1	40·6	119·7	6	
1925	127·8	32·4	49·8	145·9	6	
1926	147·7	35·7	52·2	171·2	6	
1927	172·8	38·6	55·9	197·8	6	
1928	213·2	41·4	58·7	227·5	6	554
1929	250·2	46·8	74·7	268·1	6	629
1930	302·8	50·8	88·8	316·3	6	720
1931	341·8	57·3	90·3	360·2	6	803
1932	380·9	66·8	82·1	388·4	6	869
1933	395·5	81·5	103·2	423·5	5½	949
1934	424·3	104·1	124·6	476·2	5	1,067
1935	447·2	124·2	131·0	529·7	5	1,180
1936	480·7	141·3	140·3	586·6	4½	1,295
1937	517·5	154·8	136·9	636·4	4½	1,392
1938	548·3	169·0	137·0	686·8	4½	1,479
1939	559·1	152·0	94·3	706·1	4½	1,527

Table 7: RENTS, COSTS, AND INCOMES, 1920–38

Year	Index of rents (Ministry of Labour) (1914=100)	Index of average value of rents, rates and water charges (private houses) (1929=100)	Rents, rates, etc, on private dwellings as per cent of consumers' expenditure	Index of building costs (1930=100)			Yield on Consols (per cent)	Annual average real earnings (1930=100)	Real net national income £m. 1930 prices	(1930=100)
	(1)	(2)	(3)	(4) (a) wages	(b) materials	(c) total	(5)	(6)	(7) (a)	(b)
1920	142·0	83·6	5·4	146·8	196·8	171·8	5·3	84·1	—	—
1921	155·0	97·2	7·2	127·6	153·3	140·5	5·2	88·5	3,259	78·5
1922	150·0	100·1	8·4	103·4	123·7	113·6	4·4	91·5	3,252	78·4
1923	147·0	97·2	8·5	98·8	114·9	106·9	4·3	90·4	3,308	79·7
1924	147·0	96·2	8·4	104·3	117·4	110·9	4·4	90·7	3,392	81·8
1925	147·3	96·2	8·2	104·7	117·4	111·1	4·4	90·8	3,572	86·1
1926	149·2	97·5	8·6	105·2	110·4	107·8	4·6	91·9	3,458	83·3
1927	151·0	98·9	8·8	105·4	106·3	105·9	4·6	95·1	3,755	90·5
1928	150·8	99·1	8·9	102·8	100·6	101·7	4·5	95·1	3,813	91·9
1929	152·5	100·0	9·0	102·6	101·8	102·2	4·6	96·5	3,995	96·3
1930	152·8	100·5	9·4	100·0	100·0	100·0	4·5	100·0	4,149	100·0
1931	154·0	100·9	9·9	97·7	94·7	96·2	4·4	105·6	4,031	97·2
1932	154·2	100·9	10·3	95·0	88·7	91·8	3·7	106·5	3,965	95·6
1933	155·8	101·5	10·5	92·4	87·5	90·0	3·4	108·8	4,180	100·7
1934	156·0	101·6	10·4	92·5	87·8	90·2	3·1	109·2	4,468	107·7
1935	157·3	102·5	10·4	95·0	89·9	92·0	2·9	109·2	4,581	110·4
1936	158·7	103·3	10·4	97·9	93·3	95·6	2·9	108·3	4,681	112·8
1937	159·0	103·5	10·0	100·2	100·6	100·4	3·3	105·2	4,718	113·7
1938	159·8	104·1	10·2	103·3	101·3	102·3	3·4	107·1	4,867	117·3

entirely independent of the rent index of column 1 since it is also based on the Ministry of Labour figures but refined in the light of Stone and Rowe's own estimates of consumers' expenditure on rents, rates and water charges referring to private dwelling houses but also to hotels and institutions. To obtain their index the average of monthly Ministry of Labour indices of rent was multiplied by the square root of the ratio of the value index to the quantity-price index of consumers' expenditure on rents, etc. This gave an average value series which moved in line with the actual total value series. As Stone and Rowe point out, their estimates are more reliable for later years of the inter-war period than for the early 1920s.

3. This column is also based on Stone and Rowe. It refers to estimated personal expenditure on rents, rates and water charges for private dwellings (that is, for residences and specifically excluding hotels and other institutions), taken from Stone and Rowe, p. 221, as a percentage of total consumers' expenditure, again as estimated by Stone and Rowe and quoted in LCES, *Key Statistics of the British Economy, 1900–62* (1963), Table E. The ratios of personal expenditure on rents and rates to Schedule A gross values and total rates collected were calculated for 1936–7 from the rateable value of all hereditaments in England and Wales. Modifications were made to take account of the rest of the UK and the ratios were interpolated with ratios from the Inhabited House Duty returns. Separate estimates were made for expenditure on water per head. Allowance was also made in estimating expenditure on rent for the number of houses unoccupied. Total expenditure on rents, rates and water charges as obtained in this way was then divided into a domestic and an institutional sector. For this division a constant proportion was taken based on the gross values in the two groups in the returns under the Inhabited House Duty for 1913–14. A list of probable errors involved in calculating the estimates and a brief discussion of their reliability are to be found in Stone and Rowe, pp. 219–20.

4. The index of building costs given in this column is from K. Maywald, 'An Index of Building Costs in the United Kingdom, 1845–1938', *Economic History Review*, 7 (1954–5), p. 152. Maywald constructed two indices, one referring to buildings with roofs and the other without roofs. The index used here is the former which most clearly relates to the ground covered in this book. It includes weights given to materials used in roofing, installation and painting. The index is combined from an index of wages and one of building materials, and equal weight is given in the combined index to labour costs and costs of materials. As is suggested from the evidence given in Chapter 5, this probably exaggerates the contribution of labour costs. The sources used by Maywald were as follows: for wages he took the average recognized wage rates per hour for adult workers in thirty-nine large towns taken from the *Statistical Abstracts* and covering bricklayers, masons, carpenters and joiners, plasterers, painters and labourers; for materials he obtained information mainly from *The Builder* complemented by the *Annual Statements of Trade of the United Kingdom* and by *The Economist*. The materials index was based on bricks, stone, cement, wood, two kinds of iron, tiles, lead paint and glass. The combined index has other deficiencies apart from the strong possibility of incorrect weighting for labour and materials. The use of wage rates can only give a rough approximation to labour costs because of the differential movements in rates and earnings and the effects of overtime. Since the trend of prices of different building materials varied markedly between different materials, the question of the accuracy of the weights in the materials index can be of critical importance. The weights assigned by Maywald were probably too imprecise. On the other hand, some of the errors undoubtedly offset each other and there is no reason not to accept the Maywald index as giving a useful approximation to the course of building costs.

5. The yield on Consols is taken from the *Statistical Abstract of the United Kingdom*. This series is given as presenting an approximate guide to the course of interest rates, for which the yield on Consols is often regarded as being the best single indicator. It is not of course a rate of interest directly used in building, where the mortgage rates of building societies and bank overdraft rates to builders are the most relevant series. But rates varied between building societies and other institutions offered mortgage finance, while the terms of credit facilities to builders varied considerably according to size and nature of firm and other factors. Moreover, the yield on Consols is relevant in the sense that it formed a predominant influence on the rate of influx of investment funds into building, both directly via investment in rented houses and indirectly into the building societies. In view of these factors, the yield in Consols conveys some idea of the course of fluctuation in interest rates, suggesting how the influence of the interest element on building varied over time.

6. The estimates of annual average real earnings are taken from Chapman and Knight, op. cit., p. 30. They are based on their detailed estimates of average annual money earnings for all industries deflated with the Ministry of Labour cost-of-living index. The limitations of this index are well known, that it is weighted according to the expenditure of working class families only and that the weights used are based on pre-1914 budget studies, but it is the only continuous series available (since the Bowley index ends in 1936, and even this index was regarded only as an approximation by its originator). The estimates are probably reasonably reliable, and as the column shows the index is based on 1930=100.

7. The first part of this column presents estimates of net national income in 1930 prices, while part (*b*) converts these estimates into an index with 1930 as the base year. The estimates are based on the most recent published estimates of national income in current prices by C. H. Feinstein given in his article 'National Income and Expenditure, 1870–1963', *London and Cambridge Economic Bulletin*, No. 50 (1964), p. xi. The series used is that of gross national product as estimated by the expenditure method minus estimates of capital consumption. These result in estimates of net national income in current prices which were then deflated to reduce them to 1930 prices in order to obtain a guide to the course of real income.

CHAPTER 3

DEMAND I: POPULATION, INCOME AND TASTES

The main objective of this chapter and the first half of Chapter 4 is to analyse the formative influences on housing demand and to attempt to relate this demand to changes in housebuilding output or, to be more precise, to changes in the total housing stock. Supply relationships will be ignored since they are treated elsewhere.[1] Consequently, the two chapters present a one-sided view of the problem and by isolating demand factors for consideration neglect important determinants of building activity.

The main influences on the demand for residential dwellings can be classified into certain broad categories: (1) changes in the size and structure of population; (2) variations in the rate of growth and distribution of income; and (3) changes in tastes.[2] The forces operating on (4) investment demand and (5) replacement demand are also relevant, but these are considered in the next chapter.

I. *Demographic Forces*

a. Population Growth and Family Formation

While it is obvious that rapid population growth must result in a rise in the demand for houses, it would be most surprising to find that the relationship between population and housing demand is constant. The key demographic variable is not so much the size of the population as the number of families. Within this number should be included not only the groups of people occupying separate premises but all the persons desiring to occupy a separate dwelling, a proportion of the total population which may vary markedly as the institutional environment and economic circumstances change. For instance, an increasing tendency for family and household fragmentation has been one consequence of rising incomes, better education and a more elastic building supply. Population growth may show itself in a rise in the number of families, but an expanding population is not a necessary condition. Even with a constant population, the

[1] See Chapters 5–7.

[2] Changes in credit conditions may also influence demand. However, these are considered separately in Chapter 9 below.

number of families may increase if the age structure and composition of the population is changing in the appropriate direction, and in this case it follows that there will be a fall in average household size. Finally, even with both constant population and family size families may exert a strategic influence on the demand for dwellings if the geographical distribution of the population is changing markedly. Because people are mobile while houses are not, a net migration of families from one part of the country to another (or even from cities to suburbs) will increase the total demand for dwellings.[1]

It should be stressed that the number of families determines only the *potential* demand for houses. Whether this can be made effective or not depends upon income levels and upon the willingness of public authorities to provide houses for low income households at subsidized rents. With given tastes and without State intervention, concentration on the number of families will over-estimate effective housing demand. The number of families when considered beside the stock of houses is probably much more useful for estimating housing needs than housing demand.

In discussing the role of demographic factors in housing demand, it is not possible to establish a relationship between annual population changes and the number of houses built each year. This is because, firstly, annual fluctuations in housebuilding are very wide whereas annual changes in the size of the population do not vary a great deal from year to year—though some writers such as A. Losch have argued that there exist population cycles which provide the basic cause of fluctuations in general economic activity.[2] Consequently, even if there is a long-term association between population growth and houses built population changes cannot explain short run fluctuations in building. Secondly, the number of houses built each year includes a proportion which are merely replacements for houses demolished or otherwise rendered uninhabitable. It is not easy to identify from annual statistics houses which cater for additions to households and those houses which replace obsolete dwellings. The problem can be obviated, however, by relating changes in population to changes in the overall stock of houses. Given a reasonable estimate of the initial stock of houses in a base year, annual data for houses built and estimates of annual (or periodic) demolitions and houses left derelict, the construction of a time series

[1] NBER—Universities Conference, *Demographic and Economic Change in Developed Countries* (1960), p. 359.

[2] A. Losch, 'Population Cycles as a Cause of Business Cycles', *Quarterly Journal of Economics*, 51 (1936–7), pp. 649–62.

of changes in the total stock of housing is a straightforward operation.[1]

It is easily demonstrable that changes in the size of the UK population *per se* were not a major element in the growth of the housing stock in the inter-war period. If the average size of households remains constant, and if population influences are the vital factor in changes in the housing stock, then the stock of housing will tend to grow nearly in proportion to population. In fact, between 1921 and 1938 an expansion of 7·8 per cent in the population was matched by an increase of 37·5 per cent in the stock of housing. More strikingly, the absolute increase in the stock of houses over the same period (3,487,000) was slightly greater than the increase in total population (3,467,000). Emphasis, therefore, should be placed on changes in the number of families rather than on total population.

The total number of families including all those desiring to occupy a separate dwelling, plus a 'normal' vacancy rate to cover the fact that at any one time a certain proportion of houses will lie empty due to movements between and within areas, gives an approximate guide to the normal need for shelter.[2] This may bear little relation to the effective demand for housing, but is a rough pointer to potential housing demand as given by demographic influences. It is not easy, however, to estimate the number of families in the country or annual changes in this number. The Census definition of 'family' was defective because it classified as a family those people living in a separate unit of accommodation which made the stock of occupied houses and the number of families identical. Thus, the Ministry of Health Report for 1932–3 argued that the Census estimate for the number of families in England and Wales was deficient to the extent of 400,000.[3] Definitions of a household have to be modified from time to time, since changing social attitudes could lead to a disintegration of housing groups formerly classified as families resulting in an increased demand for separate housing units. Similarly, there are several problems involved in estimating the net increase in the number of families each year. The annual number of marriages plus allowances for single people requiring separate accommodation gives the gross increase, but account has to be taken of dissolution of families through death. Stolper made estimates of these for England and Wales and his method has been used to take account of Scotland and

[1] See Chapter 2, Appendix, Table 2 and the explanatory notes relating to it.

[2] J. B. D. Derksen, 'Long Cycles in Residential Building: An Explanation', *Econometrica*, 8 (1940), p. 99.

[3] Ministry of Health, *14th Annual Report*, 1932–3, p. 95.

Northern Ireland.[1] The estimates are given in Table 3. The procedure is to some extent crude and arbitrary, but is more accurate than estimates which assume a constant replacement factor for families in inter-census years.

The number of families increased by about 3,515,000 between 1921 and 1938, that is, rather more than the increase in the population as a whole! It follows that the average size of households fell markedly. Indeed, Britain was experiencing a secular decline in the number of persons in each house, a trend which was particularly marked in the inter-war years. Estimates comparing the pre-1914 period with the end of the inter-war years point to a fall in the size of the average family from 4·35 in 1911 to 3·59 in 1939. Over the same period the number of families of one to three persons rose from 3,625,000 to 6,760,000 while the number of families of six or more persons fell from 2,455,000 to 1,660,000.[2] If the average size of household falls this is consistent with a rate of growth in the housing stock far higher than the rate of population growth. The question as to what determines the rate of household formation and changes in average household size is therefore important. National income is an obvious factor since a rising trend in incomes will reduce 'doubling up'; this

Table 3: ESTIMATED INCREASE IN NUMBER OF FAMILIES IN THE UNITED KINGDOM, 1920–38

('000)

1920	240*	1930	199
1921	214*	1931	189
1922	188	1932	186
1923	191	1933	184
1924	184	1934	217
1925	182	1935	222
1926	171	1936	218
1927	186	1937	217
1928	167	1938	225
1929	175		

* Very approximate.

[1] W. Stolper, 'British Monetary Policy and the Housing Boom', *Quarterly Journal of Economics*, 56 (1941), pp. 83–9. His method involved adding to the number of marriages the numbers of unmarried and widowed people who would prefer to maintain their own home and subtracting from this total estimates of the number of families dissolved because of death or some other reason. Although errors were admitted in constructing the estimates they tended to cancel each other out. For more details reference may be made to Stolper.

[2] M. Abrams, *The Condition of the British People, 1914–45* (1945), p. 41.

influence may have had some effect between the wars because the overall rise in real incomes was substantial. On the other hand, its impact was limited by the fact that 'doubling up' is much more prevalent among the lower income groups who suffered heavily from unemployment, while the middle income groups benefited disproportionately from rising national income. Movements in national income may also affect family formation via their influence on the marriage rate. The number of UK marriages in the period of relative boom 1935–8 averaged 403,300 per annum compared with an average of 351,700 in the years of depression 1930–2; and was it merely coincidence that the number of marriages in the year of the General Strike was considerably lower than in any other year between the wars?[1] Changes in social customs such as the age of marriage and the extent of family ties may also be important; nothing will be said here on this account beyond noting that the trend to earlier marriages had not yet become firm and that family ties were probably already loosening compared with the nineteenth century.

The age distribution of the population plays an important role in any change in average family size. The most obvious change under this head was the decline in the average number of children in each family. Taking England and Wales as an illustration, the birth rate between the mid-1920s and 1938 averaged less than half the level of the 1880s, while the proportion of the population aged under 20 was only about 35 per cent in 1931 and 28 per cent in 1951 compared with 45 per cent in 1851 and 42 per cent in 1901.[2] The total expansion in families was further boosted by a longer average life expectancy of couples after their children had married. Finally, the number and size of families may alter because of the demographic effects of random shocks. The First World War was a major shock of this kind, for it gave rise to a temporary bulge in the marriage rate in 1919–21 and in the birth rate in 1920 and 1921. 'Echo' effects of the war on population and housing replacements are discussed in a little more detail in Chapter 10.

There is a strong prima facie case that demographic influences on housing demand were the major factor in the growth of the housing stock between 1921 and 1938 because, given the degree of error in the estimates, the correspondence between the 3·487 million additions to the housing stock and the 3·515 million increase in the number of families was very close. An easy inference to draw would be that the

[1] Registrar-General's statistics given in B. R. Mitchell, *Abstract of British Historical Statistics* (1962), p. 46.

[2] Ibid., p. 12.

net expansion in the number of houses was very close to the increase in the potential demand for houses, and therefore that the potential demand was more or less realized. Such a conclusion would be misleading for several reasons, though it would be going too far to break the link between family formation and additions to the housing stock altogether. The first objection is that the argument assumes an initial equilibrium in 1921 between the housing stock and families, but the interruption to housing during the war and its slow revival thereafter had disturbed any equilibrating tendency. Consequently, by 1921 there was a severe housing shortage and a substantial proportion of the inter-war housebuilding is best considered as an attempt to make up the shortage rather than catering for the needs of expansion in the number of families. In addition, a substantial proportion of the existing stock was obsolete. Finally, the argument refers to the national economy neglecting regional considerations. The aggregate demand for additions to the stock of houses in the country as a whole depends not on the national increase in families but, because of the immobility of houses, on the sum of positive increases in the number of families in each area of the country.[1]

It is sometimes argued that demographic influences are the long-run determinants of residential building activity, and other (primarily economic) factors the short-run influences. Certainly, any correlation between houses built (exclusive of replacements) and net family formation found from looking at the inter-war figures considered as a whole disappears entirely in year by year comparisons. This is apparent even from a decennial point of view. In the 1920s the expansion in families was far greater than the increase in the housing stock partly because of the low level of housebuilding in the early 1920s. The 1931 Census indicated a marked increase in 'doubling up' since 1921, an increase in multi-family dwellings from 803,000 to 867,000 and a rise of more than 216,000 in the number of families sharing accommodation. In the 1930s, on the other hand, additions to the housing stock far exceeded the growth in the number of families. The correlation disappears even more convincingly in the annual statistics. This can be shown by using a concept, *the marginal housing*

[1] For example, the argument neglects the fact that provision for a vacancy percentage is an essential component of housing need, and an allowance for this widens the gap between potential demand and additions to stock. This criticism is strengthened in a period of marked inter-regional shifts of population when the vacancy rate rises. It is estimated that the number of unoccupied houses rose from 93,000 in 1921 to 200,000 in 1931 to 363,000 in 1938, an increase which reflected the southward movement of population not an elimination of the housing shortage.

coefficient, first elaborated by R. A. Gordon.[1] His coefficient measures the *net* increase in the housing stock in real value terms per additional household each year. However, Feinstein's estimates of net capital formation in dwellings are too unreliable for this purpose, so instead the coefficient has been expressed in physical terms. The coefficient thus expresses the relationship between the annual *net* increase in the number of houses and the annual net increase in the number of families. Thus, changes in the average quality and size of houses built are neglected, but the distortions on this account are less than those resulting from Feinstein's 1 per cent straight line depreciation assumption in calculating his net residential capital formation estimates. The results for 1920–38 are plotted in Fig. 1 (p. 325). If annual increases in the stock of houses were to be accounted for entirely by expansion in families, the coefficient would tend to be stable and in the region of unity. As Fig. 1 shows, apart from an upward trend in the coefficient there were sizeable year to year fluctuations, trough and peak values being 0·2 in 1920, 1·32 in 1926, 0·88 in 1930, 1·57 in 1933 and 1·28 in 1938. Thus, short-run movements in additions to the housing stock bore no relationship to short-run increases in families. The conclusion is that, despite first appearances, the aggregate increase in the number of families was not a sufficient explanation of the growth in the housing stock between the wars, though there are stronger grounds for maintaining a long-run rather than a short-run association.

b. Regional Migration

The last major demographic factor in housing demand was the effects of regional migration. A high rate of regional migration, if primarily in a given direction, will boost housing demand far more than in a situation where the geographical location of the population remains stable. Although an increase of population in one area may be cancelled out by a decline in another, an expansion of families in one region due to migration means a net increase in housing demand and cannot be cancelled out by a surplus of houses in another area due to a fall in the number of families there. Of course, interregional migration is not the only relevant spatial movement in population. International migration has to be considered. Net emigration from the UK totalled 667,000 in the inter-census period 1921–31, and between 1931 and 1939 there was a net immigration of

[1] R. A. Gordon, 'Population Growth, Housing and the Capital Coefficient', *American Economic Review*, 46 (1956), pp. 307–22.

514,000. Thus, relatively high emigration in the 1920s reduced the demand for housing (the extent depending on how many of the migrants consisted of families rather than, say, young unmarried sons, though most of these would presumably have soon married had they remained in Britain), while demand was intensified in the 1930s by the return of emigrants from abroad where economic conditions generally remained depressed. Secondly, the demand for housing will also be affected by migration from town to country or vice versa within a small area due to changing customs and changes in incomes and prices. In this case the areas will usually be close enough together for the housing markets not to be entirely independent. If population moves into the suburbs or to the outskirts of towns and cities, the houses left in the cities are not rendered unoccupied or useless but merely less desirable. The result will not be a higher vacancy rate but a fall in property values, and suburban movement of population influences housing demand primarily by hastening the rate of obsolescence of houses in old city and town areas. Partly because city and suburban house markets are interdependent, partly because the movement of population into the suburbs is more the consequence of changes in tastes than an autonomous factor, the relationship between the development of suburban housing and housing demand is considered under changes in tastes rather than under demographic factors.

Spatial movements of population may be a stronger demographic influence on housebuilding activity than natural increase because spatial movements may occur suddenly and are more intense. Interregional migration between the wars meant a substantial increase in *potential* housing demand. We stress potential demand, because if it is argued, as Marian Bowley does, that the demand of the middle classes for new houses was the dominant factor in the housing boom then the effects of regional population shifts are easily exaggerated; she suggested that the net gain to the South-East in middle-class families by migration was much less than 50,000 families.[1] But it is undoubtedly possible that the associated shifts in the location of industry and population to the South of England could have meant a major demographic influence on housing demand, despite the small change in overall population. Generally speaking, the number of families desiring to live in any particular area will depend primarily on economic opportunities there relative to elsewhere. Between the wars there were striking differences in prosperity between the South

[1] M. Bowley, 'Some Regional Aspects of the Building Boom, 1924–36', *Review of Economic Studies*, V (1937–8), p. 182.

and Midlands and Northern England, Scotland and Wales, and these disparities resulted in a southward movement of population (see Table 4).[1] Apart from the changes noted in the table, Scotland lost 392,000 between 1921 and 1931 and a further 25,000 between 1931 and 1939 while Northern Ireland lost 103,500 and 5,000 respectively, though in the 1920s many of these went overseas rather than to

Table 4: MIGRATION IN ENGLAND AND WALES, 1921–36
('000; *+means net immigration, —net emigration*)

South-East and Midlands	+1,147
of which:	
South-East, excluding London	+ 689
Northern England	− 610
of which:	
Northumberland and Durham	− 295
Wales	− 371
of which:	
South Wales	− 343

England. The North–South migration did not result in a dearth of housebuilding activity in the North and in Wales between the wars for two main reasons. Firstly, the average age of the housing stock was much older in these areas so that replacement demand was higher. This fact, considered with lower average income levels, resulted in a much higher degree of subsidized building by local authorities than in the South. Secondly, high levels of net migration from the relatively depressed regions did not necessarily result in declining populations there, since migration was offset by higher rates of natural increase. An extension of this point is that North-East England and South Wales had larger households than elsewhere (3·92 in the 1930s compared with 3·68 for Great Britain as a whole)[2] which influenced the character of housing demand in these areas. Nevertheless, there were net falls in population in some areas, 161,000 in Glamorgan and Monmouthshire and 31,000 in North-East England between 1921 and 1937 compared with a rise of 1,803,000 in London and the Home Counties alone.[3] Housebuilding activity was heavily concentrated in the South of England especially in the 1920s,

[1] R. M. Titmuss, *Poverty and Population* (1938), pp. 279–80.
[2] Ibid., p. 238.
[3] *RC on Distribution of Industrial Population* (*Barlow Report*), Cmd. 6153 (1940), pp. 22–3.

but as this concentration remains even after accounting for population changes there were obviously other explanations beyond regional migration. It is very difficult to isolate the effects of regional migration on housing demand, so matters can be left with the generalization that when the rate of inter-regional migration is high as between the wars the level of housing demand will be much higher than with an immobile population. At the same time, unless the effects of outward migration are swamped by a very high rate of natural increase, the number of unoccupied houses will be heavily concentrated in regions from which population is moving.

II. *Income Effects*

Changes in income are normally the most important factor in whether the potential demand determined under (I) is translated into effective demand.[1] Long-run rises in income (or expectations of such) will boost housing demand, though to what extent is indeterminate since it is not settled whether the income elasticity of demand for houses is high or low. An overall rise in income may stimulate demand in different ways: by encouraging a move to larger or superior houses, by making existing houses obsolete or by reducing 'doubling up'. Short-run cyclical movements in income are less likely to influence housing demand, since *total* housing consumption is more a function of permanent than transitory income. But, as with other consumer durables, the rate of additions to the housing stock may be quite sensitive to cyclical changes in income because the decision to move into a new home is easily postponed. Changes in the distribution as well as the level of incomes will also affect housing demand. For instance, in periods when the private housing sector predominantly caters for houses for sale, shifts in the distribution of income in favour of the middle groups will stimulate housing demand because in this group potential house-purchasers are heavily concentrated. Finally, a fall in the price of necessities relative to other goods will free spending power for other goods including housing and in this way be equivalent to a rise in income. On the other hand, if house prices rise faster than the prices of other goods potential housing demand may be choked off (though the rising house prices may be the *result* of a rising level of housing demand). This type of effect

[1] This neglects multicollinearity between demographic and income changes. For instance, the numbers of new families and the size of existing ones are to some extent subjectively determined by changes in the level of incomes. This point is discussed below.

may show itself more strongly in a reduction in quality (as measured by number of rooms or extent of fittings) rather than in terms of quantity (number of dwellings demanded).

Of course, the effects of higher incomes are not necessarily independent of demographic factors. The income structure of the population may be a potent factor in housing demand if families in different income groups tend to be, on average, of dissimilar size. Income changes may result in demographic movements; for example, a rise in average incomes may increase the marriage rate or result in increased urbanization or affect emigration from, and immigration into, the country. Conversely, demographic forces may also have income effects. A trend toward smaller families alters the pattern of consumption expenditure, freeing disposable income from spending on necessities (food and clothing) for spending on improved housing or consumer durables, while at the same time altering the character of demand for housing by shifting demand in favour of smaller dwellings.

The consequence of changes in income for housing demand are not easily established *a priori*. Some adhere to the view, originating with Engel, that housing accounts for a constant proportion of income. Others support the Schwabe law of rent—the higher the level of income the lower the proportion spent on housing. Yet others, in the light of recent empirical finding, believe that housing-income ratios rise noticeably with average incomes. There is no simple formula; the income elasticity of demand for housing will vary over time and in different institutional environments partly of course because housing expenditures are subject to forces other than income changes which vary in intensity through time.[1] Thus, it was compatible in the 1930s for the income elasticity of demand to be low in the US[2] due to the long-lasting depression and to the fact that housing demand had been blunted by the tremendous housing boom of the 1920s, but relatively high in the UK during the housing boom. In Britain over the interwar period as a whole, an approximate increase of 50 per cent in real net national income and an increase in average annual real earnings of 25–30 per cent were associated with a 38 per cent net increase in the number of houses and a rise of almost 85 per cent in the real

[1] For a full discussion of the above points see M. G. Reid, *Housing and Income* (1962).

[2] An estimate by I. Bowen suggested an income elasticity of demand for housing in the United States of +0·33 for the period 1929–42, 'The Future Output of the Constructional Industries in the United States', *Economic Journal*, 56 (1946), p. 222.

value of the net housing stock.[1] These figures are too approximate to lend themselves to firm conclusions. However, a reasonable assumption might be that the increase in the volume of the stock reflected expansion in the number of families (and the effects of higher income on 'doubling up', a factor which could only have been operative in the 1930s). This leaves a close association between the trend of national income and real earnings and a rise in housing standards denoted by the appreciation in the real value of additions to the housing stock. Although rising housing standards are explicable by factors other than income growth, for instance shifting consumer preferences, they are difficult to reconcile with the general hypothesis of a low income elasticity of demand for housing.

The growth in incomes between the wars was a secular expansion. Real net national income went up year by year with the exception of a slight fall in 1921–2, a decline in the year of the General Strike, 1926, and a temporary fall in the depression, 1930–2. On the other hand, the rate of increase varied considerably and was particularly rapid in the early years of the recovery in the 1930s, 1932–4.[2] Annual average real earnings followed a similar pattern with falls only in 1922–3 and 1935–7, though the upward curve was rather shallower.[3] It is more justifiable to relate housing demand to the trend of incomes rather than to their cyclical movement because few houses are bought with cash but are financed through credit, so that ability to finance house purchase over a long period of time is an important condition.[4] This ability will depend far more on long-run expected, or permanent, income than on short-run fluctuations in income. Unless cyclical changes in income are severe or prolonged they will have little impact on long-run expected income. Even sharp cyclical falls in income will not induce a contraction of the housing stock because of its extreme durability, though it may have an impact on new housebuilding by temporarily holding up decisions to move to new or better houses. Normally, short-run changes in income will be too mild to influence housing expenditures and long-run expected income will be geared more to past long-run changes in income than to current levels. To the extent that short-run income changes affect spending on housing, they will be more effective when the change is

[1] Based on Stone and Rowe's housing stock estimates, Chapman and Knight's average annual earnings series and Feinstein's estimates of national income and housing stock values.

[2] See Fig. 1, p. 325.

[3] See Fig. 2, p. 326.

[4] Income changes are, of course, more influential in the owner-occupied than in the rented sector.

positive rather than negative. Thus, the acceleration in real income growth in the early 1930s may have been a vital factor raising demand in the housing boom of that period. But this question is closely interrelated with changes in income distribution since the real incomes of the middle income groups were rising at the expense of profit-earners and the unemployed. The conclusion is that it is the *trend* of real incomes which should provide the best guide to the effect of income on housing demand. A rise in income *per capita* should tend to increase the size of the housing coefficient. But as Fig. 1 shows, the marginal housing coefficient fell sharply between 1927 and 1930 and again between 1933 and 1938 in periods when the expansion in real incomes continued unabated. Thus, short-run fluctuations in housebuilding cannot be explained by income (or even demand) factors alone.

A permanent rise in income will increase the overall demand for house room (for instance, by inducing people to move into larger houses) and *ceteris paribus* will raise the level of house prices and rents. Stone and Rowe's estimates show a 12 per cent rise in rents in the years 1920–2,[1] a slight fall over the next two years then a gradual rise through the inter-war period. Total expenditure on rents, rates and water charges for private dwelling houses almost doubled between 1920 and 1938, and in the 1930s averaged 10 per cent of total personal expenditure. The Ministry of Labour index of rent follows a similar course, a temporary hump in the early 1920s due to high prices and the critical post-war housing shortage then a gradual rise through the inter-war period.[2] Rents, therefore, traced a similar path to income except that they did not fall off in the early 1930s, due to their notorious 'stickiness'; in fact, the share of rent in total consumers' expenditure rose year by year from 1925 to 1933, and fell slightly thereafter. H. W. Robinson argued that the influence of changes in real national income on housebuilding was fully accounted for by their impact on rents,[3] but in fact in the housing boom of the 1930s there was little connection between building expansion and rents. Rents continued their gradual rise with an acceleration after 1934–5, whereas the *a priori* sequence should have been a high level of rents stimulating building with the subsequent relief to the housing shortage showing itself in falling rents or at least in a deceleration in their upward path.

[1] The main factor in increased expenditure on rents in the early 1920s was a 40 per cent statutory increase in controlled rents in 1920.

[2] See Chapter 2, Appendix, Table 7.

[3] H. W. Robinson, *The Economics of Building* (1939), p. 155.

The link between movements in income and rents was further weakened by the operation of forces other than those of the free market. A sizeable proportion of the housing stock was subject to rent control and many new additions to the housing stock were built to let at subsidized rents. These two factors tended to hold down rents particularly in the 1920s,[1] whereas gradual decontrol was one factor in the rise of rents in the 1930s. Moreover, the influence of rising incomes on housing demand did not show itself fully in movements in rent at a time when there was an extensive shift from rented dwellings to owner occupation. A vital element in housing demand was the percolation of opportunities for house purchase down the relative income scale. The overall rising trend in incomes helps to explain the appearance of lower-income house-buyers in the 1930s, but salaried and skilled manual workers also benefited from favourable shifts in income distribution due to improved terms of trade and the wage-price lag in the late 1920s and early 1930s. Institutional changes also worked in the same direction. The provision of unemployment pay reduced income fluctuations so that the fear of unemployment was not an impossible obstacle to house purchase. Relaxation of lending terms by building societies brought house-buying within the range of larger numbers by requiring smaller deposits and monthly repayments. In one sense, the liberalization of building societies' terms and conditions increased the influence of cyclical income movements. For many households the main obstacle to house purchase was an insufficient down-payment. Temporary rises in income sometimes provided the means through which a deposit could be saved.[2]

Just as the change in total income was an aggregation of varying rates of change for different income groups, it was also the resultant of different rates of change between regions. Average incomes were lower in the old industrial regions where the relatively depressed basic industries clustered and these regions had a lower middle class content. Defining middle class in terms of income and taking as an approximation an income of more than £4 per week in the 1930s as the definition, the 26·6 per cent middle-class ratio for Britain was

[1] On the other hand, their influence was partly offset by a sharper rise in rents in the free market sector associated with the limited supply of houses. How important this was is difficult to estimate because the large block of controlled and subsidized dwellings held demand for other houses lower than it otherwise would have been.

[2] This argument should not be overstressed for the timing was not quite right. Whereas real income rose fastest in the early 1930s the major steps in building society liberalization were not taken until the middle of the decade.

compounded from a range of 31·8 per cent for London and the South-East to 21·2 per cent for North-East England and 20·1 per cent for South Wales.[1] The distribution of wealth, which may also be a factor in housing demand, was much more concentrated than the distribution of income. Regional variations were important since the demand for owner-occupied houses in the 1930s remained, despite the downward percolation, predominantly a middle-class demand. The higher proportion of middle-class incomes and the higher overall level of income in southern England could perhaps be expected to have resulted in a higher rate of housebuilding there than in the less wealthy regions. To some extent it did, but with qualifications: the gap in private housebuilding in the North and in Wales was partially filled by local authority building; even more important lower incomes in the poor regions were compensated by low rents and house prices. The Ministry of Labour Family Budget Enquiry of 1937–8 revealed a range of average weekly rents from 9·1 and 9·2 shillings in Wales and the North to 11·2 and 15·7 shillings in the South-East and in London.

Other income effects may be mentioned briefly. A long-term rise in incomes will reduce 'doubling up', by reducing the numbers of young couples living with parents and by expanding the number of single people wanting separate homes. As pointed out above, this influence did not operate in the 1920s when multi-family occupation increased. In the 1930s, on the other hand, houses built exceeded the increase in families by an amount far in excess of the rise in unoccupied houses. This is a *prima facie* case that rising incomes reduced 'doubling up', though in the absence of a census in 1941 there is no conclusive evidence. The expansion in unoccupied houses does not affect this argument, partly because of their disproportionate concentration in certain regions partly because the fact that unoccupied houses did not have to bear rates gave no incentive to their owners to bring them on to the housing market. A rise in incomes may also affect housing demand via changes in tastes, for example, by strengthening preferences for new houses. But influences of this kind are best considered under (III) below since they operated in the same way as an increasing propensity to spend on housing out of a given income.

One income effect remains to be discussed, the influence of falling prices, If prices other than house prices fall this is equivalent to a rise in real incomes. Indeed, the method used to measure changes in individual real income is to deflate money wages by a cost-of-living index which is nothing more than a weighted index of prices in the

[1] R. M. Titmuss, op. cit., pp. 236–7.

basket of goods making up a typical family budget. Nevertheless, it is sometimes necessary to distinguish a rise in real incomes due to an increase in the economy's productive capacity (and output) from a rise due to a fall in the cost of living, which may occur with a static productive capacity as a result of improving terms of trade or of a wage-price lag. In the first case, money wages may rise but prices remain stable so that relative prices between goods remain unaffected. In the second case, money wages remain stable but the price of certain types of goods, say imported foodstuffs, falls. Thus, relative prices change. If the demand for the now cheaper goods is elastic the lower prices will stimulate increased purchases. If completely inelastic, the same amount of the good will be bought as before and because the price has fallen this commodity will now account for a smaller proportion of total income than if the rise in real income had been due to rising money wages. Although this is a limiting case, it illustrates the point that an increase in real incomes through a fall in the cost of living (i.e. selective price reductions) may, if demand for cheaper goods is inelastic, free a larger margin of income for spending on other goods or for saving than if the increase in real incomes was caused by other factors.

Moreover, because expenditure on necessities is closely geared to family size, the declining birth rate of the inter-war period meant falling rather than stable physical levels of basic necessities per household. The combination of falling cost of living and declining birth rate freed disposable income for spending on other goods, probably consumer durables, or for saving. This did not necessarily mean increased housing expenditures, since such expenditures would be affected by relative price movements between housing and other consumer durables. In fact, these relative price movements were unfavourable to housing. Although both building costs and house prices fell secularly, the extent of the fall was not so steep as for motor cars (where prices more than halved) or for electrical appliances. Cars were becoming an increasingly important item of consumer capital and may have tied up income which could have been used to purchase houses. On the other hand, this may have been outweighed by the fact that houses stood higher on consumers' scale of preferences. Finally, it must be stressed that while a long-run fall in the cost of living should stimulate housing demand short-run changes may not because moving house is a costly and inconvenient business. The cost of living (other than rent) fell almost steadily and substantially between the wars up to 1933–4. Then it started to rise again at quite a sharp rate. Perhaps it was not mere coincidence that the rise in the cost of living (other than rent) from 1934 was associated with a sharp fall in residential capital formation in the private sector.

To sum up, the faster rise in the real value of the net housing stock than in the number of houses suggests one impact of rising incomes on housing demand was an improvement in the standard of new houses. One aspect of this was a major shift away from rented to owner-occupied houses. The long-term fall in the cost of living combined with a declining birth rate freed disposable income which was probably used more and more to spend on housing. The stratum of potential house-buyers was widening, not only because of higher incomes but due to relaxations in building society lending terms and conditions. Although the demand for housing may have shifted suddenly in the early 1930s under the stimulus of rising real incomes in the depression in combination with other favourable factors, the association between rising incomes and expanding housing demand is normally long run. Changes in income cannot adequately explain short-run fluctuations in housebuilding activity, as is shown by the fact that periods of rapidly expanding real income were sometimes characterized by falls in the marginal housing coefficient. This last objection is not as strong if changes in *real wages* are compared to fluctuations in the marginal housing coefficient since average annual real earnings expanded only very slowly between 1927 and 1929 and declined after 1934, both periods witnessing falls in the housing coefficient.

III. *Changes in Tastes*

With a given level of income and a constant number of households, a shift in consumer preferences in favour of housing will shift the demand curve to the right. Changing tastes may also affect the *structure* of housing demand, for example by moving in favour of smaller modern houses and/or suburban houses. Such changes in tastes may be induced by technological change, such as the invention of labour-saving devices which can more easily be fitted into a modern new house or by transport developments, mainly those concerned with the motor car, which stimulate the demand for suburban housing. Alternatively, the changing tastes may be precipitated by social forces in society at large. For instance, the increased demand for smaller houses was partly to be explained by the consequence of reduced attractiveness of domestic service in face of competing employment opportunities elsewhere.[1]

[1] ILO, *Housing and Employment* (1948), pp. 79–80.

Changes in tastes may be more than a marginal influence on housing demand. The NBER investigation into residential capital formation in the US between 1890 and the 1950s found that the real *per capita* value of the housing stock had stagnated,[1] a surprising finding in view of the rise in incomes over the period and not fully explained by the slowing down of population growth. It was concluded that a revision in consumer preferences away from housing in favour of other goods was the only satisfactory explanation. A number of arguments, some ingenious, were used in support: that consumers spent part of their increased incomes not on housing itself but on consumer durables related to the house, that motor cars competed successfully with houses for consumer income, that higher maintenance and running costs affected the amount of capital outlay on house, that people were buying smaller cheaper houses because of housekeeping problems and the shift of leisure activities away from the home, and that a reduced quantity of inputs (for example, much lower ceilings) lowers the real value of additions to the housing stock by reducing costs yet at the same time raises consumer satisfaction.[2] This is no place to argue the virtues of the individual arguments, but it must be stressed that the change in tastes was regarded as *the* major cause of retardation in residential capital formation. Some observers have explained the British housing boom of the 1930s in similar terms, except of course that consumer preferences were revised in the opposite direction. Thus, Bellmann interpreted the boom as being caused by 'revolutionary' changes in the community's concept of acceptable housing standards, while Bowley argued that 'the single most important factor was the development of the demand by the middle classes for the new commodity, a modern house on the outskirts of the bigger towns'.[3]

Changes in tastes may favourably influence housing demand in several ways. The main instance is where demand switches in favour of new houses. This stimulates new housebuilding directly, but also results in a more rapid obsolescence of the existing housing stock by attracting attention to the outdatedness of old houses. Moreover, the demand for new houses will be exercised predominantly by existing families moving from old to new houses rather than by new families.

[1] L. Grebler, D. M. Blank and L. Winnick, *Capital Formation in Residential Real Estate* (NBER, 1956).

[2] L. Winnick, 'Housing: Has there been a downward shift in Consumers' Preferences?', *Quarterly Journal of Economics*, 69 (1955), pp. 85–98.

[3] H. Bellmann, 'The Building Trades', p. 432 in British Association *Britain in Recovery* (1938) and Bowley, loc. cit., p. 184.

In consequence, the effective demand for new houses influences the replacement of the existing stock though in most cases the abandoned old houses will find new occupants. But if old houses are scrapped more quickly this will stimulate the building of new houses in the future.

A preference for new houses may arise for many reasons. Growing scarcity and cost of domestic service may boost the demand for new labour saving kitchens. New houses may be stimulated by improvements in architects' designs or by product innovations not only in building but in, say, electricity supply. This has repercussions on the demand for electric lighting, heating and household equipment which may be more effectively satisfied in new than in old houses. New houses may be demanded because of a reduced desire to live in cities, and is therefore associated with the development of suburban housing—stimulated between the wars by the growing use of motor transport and by suburban extensions of public transport systems. Small families may lead to a demand for smaller houses, more easily satisfied by building new houses though it may also induce conversions of existing houses into two or three flats. An increased demand for new modern suburban houses may arise as result of complex changes in social attitudes originating in a source which is unidentifiable, at least to the economist. Moreover, a collective change in tastes may be more influential since it can be enforced by legislative action, for example, by placing condemnation orders on old properties.

Influences of this kind have been regarded as playing some role in raising housing demand in Britain in the inter-war period. It may be admitted that this role was far from negligible. The higher real values of additions to the housing stock are reasonable evidence of an improvement in housing standards. There can be little doubt of the acceleration in the rate of suburban building in the 1930s. Consumer preferences were shifting in favour of houses, and in favour of a particular kind of house. But were these shifts due to changes in tastes alone independent from other demand factors? It is most unlikely that they were. The rise in housing standards was closely associated with the rise in real incomes and may not have occurred had the average income level remained constant. The demand for smaller, new suburban houses may easily have been due to demographic influences (i.e. the trend to smaller families) rather than to a pure change in tastes. On the other hand, changes in the social attitudes of the middle income groups who were buying the new houses of the 1930s should not be underestimated. From time to time, shifts in tastes may have a significant influence on the demand for houses, and even if these shifts are inextricably interrelated with other demand factors such as income or demographic change this fact does not detract from their importance.

CHAPTER 4

DEMAND II

In this chapter we are concerned with two quite different topics. In the first half of the chapter we complete the discussion of the determinants of housing demand by considering factors influencing investment demand and replacement demand. Although both these demand forces were less important than formerly, the first because the private housing investor was constrained by the demand for owner occupation and local authority rented houses, the second because the severe housing shortage resulted in a low scrapping rate for obsolete dwellings, they were nevertheless of some significance. In the second half of the chapter we analyse briefly some of the major elements in the demand for non-residential buildings, with particular emphasis on the demand for industrial building between the wars.

A. THE DEMAND FOR HOUSES (CONTINUED)

I. *Investment Demand for Houses*

Apart from the demand of owner-occupiers for houses, investors may buy a house to obtain a return from it by letting and/or by resale for a capital gain. The relevance of the second objective depends largely on investors' expectations about future movements in house prices. Investing in a house for the purposes of an annual income depends on the returns from letting houses compared with the returns from other forms of investment. The yield from investing in a house will primarily be determined by the ratio of the annual rent (net, after repair and maintenance charges) to the cost of buying the house, which is mainly influenced by the rate of interest and building costs—even the market value of old houses will bear some relation to current building costs. This will give a yield as a percentage return which may be compared with the yield as from other relatively safe investments such as fixed interest bearing securities.[1] However, the rent-cost ratio is only a guide to housing investment decisions, since the main ques-

[1] C. E. V. Leser, 'Building Activity and Housing Demand', *Yorkshire Bulletin of Economic and Social Research*, 3 (1951), pp. 145–8.

tion governing such decisions may be whether the investor can sell or let the house at a price or rent which covers his outlay yet gives a reasonable return, and this will depend more on expectations of future rents, house prices and interest rates than on actual changes. The relative profitability of investment in housing will tend to rise in periods of low interest rates, because interest is usually a cost in housebuilding, while low market rates are likely to be associated with low returns from other investment in general.[1] Slump conditions will have a certain favourable impact upon housing investment because the depression will be characterized by low yields from industrial investment, while the yield from housing investment may rise because of falling building costs (and interest rates) and the relative inflexibility of rents.

The investment aspect of housing demand was much less important between the wars than it had been before 1914. Of the 1914 housing stock, virtually no houses had been built by local authorities, only 10 per cent were owner-occupied and 90 per cent consisted of houses rented privately. A high proportion of inter-war housing, on the other hand, was absorbed either by building for owner-occupation or by subsidized building by local authorities (almost 31 per cent of the houses built between the wars). Whereas before 1914 only about 850,000 houses were owner-occupied, a return in 1938 based on a substantial proportion of the housing stock (in fact 8·25 million houses) revealed that 35 per cent (2·88 million) of the houses covered were owner-occupied.[2] Even if only a very small proportion of the 4·25 million houses not covered by the survey were owner-occupied, most of the 2,757,000 houses built by private enterprise in England, Wales and Scotland between 1920 and 1938 must have been built for owner-occupation.

The UK housing boom of the 1930s differed from all previous residential building booms in that it was a sales boom and was not based upon a large volume of rental housing production. This is true, and housebuilding for investment purposes was now demoted compared with its former importance. But it must be stressed that it was by no means negligible. Of the houses built of a rateable value below £13 in England and Wales, 29 per cent were privately built to let in 1934 rising to 45 per cent in 1938, a total of 190,224 houses between October 1, 1933, and March 31, 1939. Of the houses with rateable values between £13 and £26, one-sixth were built to let in 1934 rising to one-quarter in 1938, as many as 144,679 houses between October

[1] Moreover, the costs of borrowing will be lower for housing investors.

[2] Quoted by Stone and Rowe, op. cit., p. 204.

1933 and March 1939. Indeed, of the privately built houses of less than £26 rateable value, 28·3 per cent were built to let between October 1933 and March 1939.[1] In addition, of course, local authority houses, despite the lower levels of public housebuilding in the 1930s, accounted for 21 per cent of new houses built in 1934 rising to 34 per cent in 1938. The view of the 1930s housing boom as being based on houses built for sale must, therefore, be accepted more cautiously than has often been the case in the past.

Conditions for housing investment were considerably less attractive in the 1920s. The reasons for this are easy to understand. The demand for houses for investment purposes depends on the profitability of investment in housing relative to other forms of investment. The profitability of investment in housing depends on alterations in the expected net yield from new houses (i.e. the level of rents after making allowance for maintenance) and the cost of ownership (determined by building costs and interest rates). Over the inter-war period as a whole the trend of rents was upwards whereas building costs and interest rates (taking the yield on Consols as an indicator) were falling secularly.[2] If rents on new houses moved in sympathy with rents as a whole, these trends should have been favourable to investment in housing. But in the 1920s (apart from in 1925–7) rents were not moving upwards as fast as in the 1930s. Moreover, though building costs were falling steadily after 1925, interest rates remained high until 1932. High interest rates meant better returns from other forms of investment: gilt-edged yields averaged at least 4·5 per cent in the 1920s, industrial yields were much higher[3] and prospective returns on foreign investment were good. Another adverse factor in the 1920s was that investment in the housing market was characterized by considerable uncertainty. The policies of rent control were an investment hazard because of real fears that rent control might be extended to new houses which would widen the gap between net yields from housing and from other sectors, while the very fact of rent control undermined the market indicators with which the rental housing investor could estimate his prospective yield.[4] In addition, a large section of rent controlled properties meant that many house-

[1] Statistics supplied by J. L. Marshall.

[2] See Fig. 2, p. 326.

[3] An estimate based on the Moodies Services Index suggested an average dividend yield on ordinary shares of over 6 per cent in the late 1920s and an average earnings yield of over 10 per cent, LCES, *Key Statistics of the British Economy, 1900–62* (1963), Table A.

[4] L. Grebler, *Production of New Housing* (1950), p. 136.

holders were very reluctant to move into new rented dwellings at much higher rents.

In these circumstances, very few privately built houses to let should have been built in the 1920s. Had market prices been the only consideration very few such houses would have been built. But houses built to let by the private sector were eligible for subsidy (indeed, in the early years under the Housing Act of 1919 houses *for sale* could be subsidized!) in the 1920s. In the period 1924–9 privately built houses to let accounted for a substantial proportion of additions to the housing stock. Over these years an average of 64,000 privately built subsidized houses was constructed each year, that is, almost 31 per cent of the total houses built.[1] So, despite unfavourable market conditions private houses for renting were an important section of total housebuilding output in the late 1920s. However, most of these houses would not have been built without the stimulus of subsidies, and for this reason do not properly fall within the ambit of investment demand considerations.

In the 1930s the market environment became much more favourable for investment in housing. Rents continued to rise at least as rapidly as in the past and the depression had no effect upon this trend. Real incomes (for those in work) were rising, therefore the ability to pay rents was unimpaired, the housing shortage of the 1920s had scarcely been alleviated and gradual decontrol helped the rent index continue upwards. In addition, other factors such as long tenancies, the landlords' superior bargaining power and inconveniences involved in tenants changing their accommodation resulted in rigidity of rents. Building costs continued downwards at least up to 1933, and interest rates fell sharply indeed. Thus, the returns from investing in housing were far higher than in the 1920s. The development of an investment demand was accentuated by poor returns available from other investments. Cheap money meant low yields from gilt-edged and other fixed interest securities, depression had deleterious effects on returns from industrial investment, and economic uncertainty abroad, not to mention the foreign loan embargo, led to almost a complete drying up of another formerly important investment outlet.

In the early 1930s conditions were very favourable to investment in rental housing. From 1935 the relative profitability of housing investment declined. Building costs were now rising, primarily because of competition from industrial and commercial building, and interest rates showed signs of beginning to harden. Rents, though

[1] Chapter 2, Appendix, Table 1.

still rising, were not increasing fast enough to outweigh higher costs and interest rates. At the same time the strong industrial recovery meant a revival of profitability in investment in industry. Yet the proportion of privately built houses for letting continued to rise. This is not easily explained. One consideration was that the potentialities of housing as an investment outlet spread slowly, and therefore lagged extensively behind market conditions. Moreover, the demand for owner-occupation at current income and price levels was beginning to flatten out, while a great number of households not yet willing to enter commitments to buy a house could now after the long preceding expansion in incomes face more easily the prospect of paying an economic rent. Finally, a higher proportion of the dwellings built in the later 1930s consisted of flats, which at this time were more likely to be built to let than for sale. What is surprising considering the favourable market conditions was that investment demand was so low in the period 1932–5 relative to demand for owner-occupation. In the early 1930s consumer preferences for owner-occupied houses were very strong indeed.

II. *Replacement Demand*

Lack of data and too many imponderables make it difficult to pass firm comments on this aspect of demand. There are no accurate estimates of replacement investment in residential dwellings.[1] The difference between Feinstein's estimates of gross and net capital formation at first sight seems to provide an approximation, but the basis for this difference is simply the assumption of a straight line depreciation method based on a life of 100 years. He estimates the first cost value of housing stock at the end of each year and takes 1 per cent of this figure as representing depreciation. This cannot be equated with replacement. If the housing stock were homogeneous, if each unit had a finite life of exactly one hundred years and if additions to the stock had been distributed equally over time, these estimates would have yielded reasonable results. But in the inter-war period scrapping of dwellings was equal to only 17 per cent of the depreciation required (on the assumptions given above).[2] The life of

[1] We have attempted to make estimates of replacement investment based on housing demolitions and average tender prices. These were presented in Appendix, Table 1, Chapter 2. Although very approximate, these estimates are far more reliable than Feinstein's. However, we do not use them in this section since we confine our analysis to the *numbers* of houses demolished rather than considering their replacement value.

[2] Feinstein, op. cit., p. 50.

a house is not determined purely by physical considerations where the time of replacement is fixed by wear and tear. Identical houses built at the same time may have lives of different length according to the regularity and thoroughness of repairs and maintenance expenditures. The durability of a house gives plenty of leeway between the minimum and maximum potential life, and the timing of replacement will depend primarily on economic considerations. The current demand position relative to supply will be one influence; for example, in a time of severe housing shortage the rate of replacement will be low. An improvement in acceptable housing standards will *ceteris paribus* induce a higher replacement rate, while a change in tastes may have a similar effect particularly if it takes the form of an increased desire to live in new houses in new areas. The rate of replacement investment will not be independent of the level of building costs because high costs affect the margin between abandoning a house and incurring the expense of renovating it. For these and other reasons, there are few signs of replacement cycles removed by a fixed number of years from net investment cycles in the past. Finally, even to the extent that such echo effects exist they do not result in a constant volume of replacement building because the rate of housebuilding varies markedly over time. For instance, in the nineteen-year period 1920–38 the number of houses built exceeded by more than 50 per cent the number built in the previous thirty years, 1890–1919.[1] Thus, any discussion of replacement investment without empirical evidence is bound to flounder because influences on replacement investment cannot be determined *a priori*.

It would be defeatist to conclude that nothing may be said about replacement demand, since approximate numbers of demolitions may be obtained for the inter-war period which give a rough guide to the level of replacement demand. A difference between investment in houses and investment in plant, equipment and to some extent industrial buildings is that in the first case it is usually impossible to relate the replacement unit to the one scrapped. With a machine the same firm scraps and replaces, and usually on the same spot. But only in some cases are houses demolished and replaced by dwelling houses on the same site and often only after a considerable lapse of time. When a machine is scrapped the firm may decide to replace it or not to replace it; with a house there is usually no way of knowing whether it was abandoned or demolished for replacement (except where slum inhabitants are rehoused prior to demolition). If the latter, the replacement may be built by a person or institution differ-

[1] Feinstein, op. cit., p. 218.

ent from the one doing the scrapping. The consequence is that it is impossible to identify from aggregate housebuilding statistics the houses which are replacing those worn out. The solution to this problem is to equate replacement building with the number of houses demolished. The procedure is not too unsatisfactory. By the 1930s demolition and replacement building were largely in the hands of one body, the local authority, under the slum clearance legislation of 1930. More important, so long as the total number of households is growing then houses which are demolished will need to be replaced.

Stone and Rowe have prepared annual estimates of houses demolished in the UK between the wars, excluding Northern Ireland, which accounted for only a small proportion, about 2·5 per cent of the housing stock.[1] These estimates are reasonable for the 1930s since houses demolished were officially returned under the Housing Acts of 1930 and 1936. But the annual distribution of total demolitions in the period 1921–31 according to the extent of local authority building in the previous year is a very unrealistic procedure, primarily because the general subsidy schemes of the 1920s were in no way related to slum clearance but instead were aimed at alleviating the overall shortage by making *net* additions to the stock. For this reason, for the 1920s only the estimates for the decade as a whole will be referred to in the following comments.

In the period 1920–9 there were about 179,000 demolitions in England and Wales and 32,000 in Scotland. This was equal to an annual replacement rate of 0·23 and 0·29 per cent respectively. If the 100-year life is accepted as a reference norm and the housing stock assumed equally distributed over time, this was a very low replacement rate. Of course, the age distribution of the housing stock was biased in favour of houses built after 1890. Even so, of the housing stock built before 1914 and still in existence by 1938 over 3 million out of 7·5 million houses had been built prior to 1855.[2] A high proportion of the oldest units of the stock had been 'jerry-built' at a time when Northern and Midland towns and cities had been growing very rapidly under the impetus of industrialization, and these houses were not generally of a quality which could be expected to last a century. Moreover, the upward drift in acceptable housing standards over time and new techniques and housing amenities were accelerating the obsolescence of older houses. As a result, Britain faced in the inter-war period an entirely new problem of urban renewal, stemming from the fact that almost a century had elapsed since the new towns

[1] See Chapter 2, Appendix, Table 2.

[2] Feinstein, op. cit., p. 218.

and cities of the most rapid industrialization period had been built.

Why was the replacement rate so low? One factor was undoubtedly the overall housing shortage of the 1920s. Replacement is easily postponable, so at a time when families are in excess of houses and building resources are heavily employed making up the deficiency old properties will be kept in the stock by patching repairs rather than replaced by new houses. Another factor, a contrast with the 1930s, was the absence of specific provision for slum clearance, for in the 1920s if slums were to be cleared by local authorities it had to be done on their own initiative. Finally, rent control slowed down replacement. Rent controls were operative on old buildings, thereby widening the differential between rents on old and on new dwellings. This severely dampened any desire to move from old controlled to new decontrolled properties, and families had a financial incentive to stay in old houses as long as they were habitable.

In the 1930s the replacement rate accelerated, moderately in England and Wales (258,000 houses demolished between 1929 and 1938, an annual rate of 0·29 per cent), markedly in Scotland (79,000 houses over the period or a rate of 0·67 per cent). The annual figures (Table 5)[1] show relatively fewer demolitions in the years 1932–4 but then a marked acceleration culminating in 1937 and 1938. In the latter two years houses demolished accounted for 24·5 per cent of

Table 5: HOUSES DEMOLISHED IN THE UNITED KINGDOM, 1931–8
(Year ending March 31st)
('000)

	UK	of which *Scotland*		*UK*	of which *Scotland*
1931	33	7	1936	52	14
1932	14	4	1937	64	12
1933	15	6	1938	70	9
1934	22	8			
1935	35	11			

total inter-war demolitions. The main reason for the higher rate of the 1930s and the yearly variations was the operation of slum clearance schemes from 1930,[2] buttressed by financial assistance to local authorities and by some pressure from the Ministry of Health. The low demolitions of 1932–4 are explained by severe cutbacks in local authority spending in those years, while the higher rate of the late 1930s reflected the easier financial position of local authorities and the alleviation of the housing shortage by the housing boom thereby

[1] Taken from Stone and Rowe, op. cit., p. 221.

[2] See Chapter 8.

permitting attention to be diverted to the problems of replacement. Thus, in the 1930s there were much closer links between scrapping and rebuilding than in earlier periods. Replacement demand was increasing but more in response to policy decisions than to market forces. Whatever the motive force, the rise in local authority building for slum clearance in the latter 1930s at a time when private housebuilding had started to decline provides a clear example of replacement demand maintaining total building activity. Historical experience suggests that replacement building will normally be high when 'additional' housebuilding is high.

From the figures given above, it may be observed that replacement demand was higher between the wars in Scotland than in England and Wales, and that the differential widened greatly in the 1930s. The main reason for this was probably a higher proportion of slum or otherwise obsolete properties in Scotland, and the acceleration in replacement investment when official slum clearance schemes were introduced in the 1930s supports this view. In addition, the high rate of demolitions may have been partly due to the greater predominance of local authority housebuilding in Scotland than in the rest of Britain. Local authorities were more likely to be interested in redeveloping sites than private builders who would find it more profitable, taking into account demolition costs and the fact that building land was not yet scarce, to build on new undeveloped land. A supplementary minor explanation of the higher proportion of the housing stock scrapped in Scotland in the inter-war period is that some houses were abandoned as a result of rural depopulation of marginal land.

III. *The Demand for Houses: Conclusions*

The higher level of housebuilding activity in the inter-war period compared with before 1914 was closely associated with the shift to the right in the demand curve for housing. The potential demand for houses was related to a rapid increase in net family formation despite the deceleration in population growth. The effects of this were stronger because as a result of migration the new households were disproportionately concentrated in certain regions. The high level of inter-regional migration in the inter-war period necessitated a rising vacancy rate. Potential demand was also stimulated by changing tastes, at least among the middle income groups. These groups were demanding a newer type of house with modern fittings and situated in new residential suburbs. This factor boosted the demand for new houses, though its effects were partially offset by the filtering down of existing middle-class houses for occupation by lower income groups. The increase in potential demand was made effective by a secular rise in real incomes for most groups except the unemployed. Investment demand for houses was considerably reduced in the inter-war years because of the consequences of State intervention in the housing market and shifting tastes in favour of owner-occupation, but was far from negligible especially in the 1930s when low returns from gilt-edged rising rents and reduced fears of an extension of rent control led to considerable numbers of houses being built to let. The replacement demand for houses was much lower than the existing condition of the housing stock warranted, but reflected the fact that for the first half of the period family formation proceeded at a rate higher than new housebuilding and this meant a continuing housing shortage.

While demand factors are possibly the major explanation of why housebuilding activity ran continuously at a higher level between the wars than before 1914, they fail to provide a sufficient explanation of variations, especially in the short run, in the rate of housebuilding within the period. Demand factors are far more useful for explaining long-term shifts than short-run changes. For a total explanation reference must be made to the supply side, particularly to the effects of State intervention and housing subsidies and to the consequences of changes in the costs of housebuilding and house purchase.[1] The need to consider explanations of shifts in supply as well as in demand is confirmed by the downward trend in house prices between the wars. Had the supply curve remained fixed, increased demand would have showed itself in rising house prices. Supply conditions were changing independently and have to be examined before causes of variations in the rate of housebuilding can be understood.

B. THE DEMAND FOR NON-RESIDENTIAL BUILDINGS

Non-residential construction was such a large proportion of total building activity, accounting for between 24 and 45 per cent of the total in normal years of the inter-war period, that some consideration must be given to the demand influences acting upon it. It is clear that the primary demand forces on housebuilding are not very relevant to non-residential building. Because the major part of the non-residential sector consists of industrial and commercial buildings and is subject to commercial and profitability considerations, it is not surprising to

[1] See Chapters 5–9.

find that non-residential construction behaves much more like investment in general than housebuilding. Thus the demand for, say, industrial buildings is explicable in terms similar to industrial investment demand as a whole. The similarity is so great that it is difficult to distinguish characteristics about the demand for industrial buildings peculiar to this demand alone. Obviously, this book is not the place for a discussion of the theory of investment in general. Consequently, this section will be confined to a few bare generalizations about the demand for non-residential buildings.

I. *Some General Considerations*

Although the traditional approaches to the theory of investment can be applied to building investment, at least in principle, there are problems in its application. Take, for instance, the marginalist approach where the level of investment is dependent upon the expected profitability of investment and the cost and availability of required funds, and the prevailing level of investment is determined by the intersection of the marginal efficiency of investment and the marginal cost of funds schedules. The marginal efficiency of investment schedule is related to expected profitability, but a problem arises because indivisibilities make it far more difficult to estimate the profitability of a new building as opposed to that of a machine. Similarly, the cost elements which enter into profitability differ from those of investment in general since the relevant costs are building costs the course of which will differ from the cost of capital goods (such as machinery prices) generally. As for the cost of funds schedule, it is possible that different rates of interest may be charged for financing investment in buildings than in equipment—due, for instance, to longer pay-off periods. The relevancy of accelerator theories where the level of investment is dependent upon the rate of change of output (demand) to buildings is also open to dispute. Admittedly, most investment in buildings would normally be regarded as being *induced* by changes in past demand (or expectations of demand changes), whereas some investment in machinery could be looked upon as autonomous if it involved innovations. On the other hand, the demand for investment in buildings cannot always be explained in terms of response to changes in demand. A high proportion of such investment could be described as autonomous in the Hicksian sense of being 'only expected to pay for itself over a long period'. And certainly, investment in factories built to produce *new* goods is clearly autonomous, while the demands of the Government and other public authorities for non-residential buildings are strongly related to social needs and policy considerations, and for this reason are autonomous. Residual fund theories, where the level of investment is dependent upon the level of reserves and retained earnings remaining after 'normal' dividend payments have been made, thereby making investment a function of lagged profits, are probably less applicable to buildings than to equipment since the high capital costs involved in the former are more likely to require outside finance.

A simpler approach to the question of the demand for non-residential buildings is to consider the individual types of building within this sector. The high and relatively stable levels of investment in retail distribution, for instance, reflected the major changes in the structure and character of distribution between the wars. The growth of large-scale production methods in the consumer goods trades facilitated the use of large-scale distribution methods. A consequence of this was a marked increase in the number of department stores from a very approximate total of 200 in 1914 to about 500 in 1938 and a rapid increase in the number of multiple shops, especially in the 1920s.[1] These developments were probably induced more by intensified competition than by a rise in expected profitability, while the lack of expansion in the demand for new investment in shops in the 1930s rules out the influence of cheaper building costs and low interest rates.

The almost continuous rise in investment in public buildings between the wars suggests independence from movements in costs, interest rates and profitability considerations. Investment in this sector only declined between 1931 and 1933, and this was due far more to the economy campaign than to the cyclical forces of depression. The demand for schools, hospitals and similar buildings depends on population growth and changes in its structure and upon the Government's standards of what the social services should be. Although this type of building investment might tend to show a slight anti-cyclical tendency because of the influence of costs, this could be compensated for by the healthier state of Government revenue in times of prosperity. Even if current business conditions had an influence on this sector, the lag would be considerable because of long planning periods and completion schedules. Investment in public buildings may be strongly subject to policy influences where the Government employs such investment for stabilization purposes. In this case, the level of public building investment may remain high even in the depressions. But the relatively high level of investment in

[1] J. B. Jefferys, *Retail Trading in Britain, 1850–1950* (1954), pp. 59 and 61–5.

buildings in the social and public services in Britain between 1930 and 1932 was accidental rather than the result of deliberate policy.

The largest and most important sector of non-residential building investment is industrial and related buildings. There are two main divergent explanations of factory and commercial building activity. The first explains changes in building plans almost entirely by reference to the level of business activity and the desire for increased productive capacity. The second tends to stress the influence of building costs and interest rates and regards only exceptionally high or low levels of business activity as having much impact on decisions to build, and then very often after a lag.[1] The evidence seems to favour the former explanation rather than the latter. Gross investment in non-residential building as a whole moved very closely in line with the *Economist* index of business activity,[2] that is pro-cyclically, and consequently showed little obvious response to changes in interest rates and building costs which moved downwards until 1934. This suggests that interest rates were not generally important in the demand for non-residential buildings, though it is possible that many small new firms were able to finance new factory building with the increased availability of credit attendant upon cheap money. The lack of a relationship between non-residential construction and the course of building costs also leads to the view that cheaper building costs were not much of a stimulus compared with profit expectations (and the availability of reserves from past profits for financing investment).

If the demand for industrial buildings responds more to business activity than to changes in building costs and interest rates, it will tend to be directly related to the expansion of industry. An increase in business activity will lead to an increase in factory and commercial building and vice versa, though the size of the response will depend on the initial level of excess capacity and on the number of vacant factories in existence. Of course, the aggregate relation is rather misleading. Correspondence between factory building and national business activity neglects the migration of industry as a factor in demand, an influence of some significance in the inter-war period. Moreover, changes in business activity will show themselves in different degrees of change in individual industries. The demand for factory and commercial buildings is determined by the expansion and contraction of individual firms throughout the whole economy and by the rate of entry and exit of firms. Rapidly expanding firms

[1] H. W. Robinson, op. cit., p. 155.

[2] See Fig. 8A, p. 332.

and new entrants will obviously tend to cluster in industries faced with a rapid secular growth in demand, and in such industries many new factories will be opened.[1]

Since profitability gives the signal for such action, investment of this kind is primarily influenced by future expectations (which correlate closely with profits). Certainly as far as new entrants are concerned new factories and premises are usually an essential prerequisite of production, and in these cases cannot be explained as a response to past changes in demand.

II. *Industrial Building*

Thus, although the demand for non-residential building as a whole in the inter-war period was determined by the level of economic activity, falling in the slump following the post-war boom in 1920–2, rising between 1922 and 1930, apart from the interruptions of 1926 and 1927, falling again steeply between 1930 and 1932, then displaying a marked recovery up to a peak in 1937, the relationship was only approximate. Leaving aside public building, demand was dependent upon the entrepreneurial decisions to build of firms in *individual* industries and on the locational decisions which accompany them. Evidence available to support this view is very scanty, but reference may be made to Feinstein's estimates of gross capital formation in five major industrial groups (textiles; metals and metal-using industries; food, drink and tobacco; chemicals, leather clothing and paper; and wood, clay and miscellaneous manufactures) and to Board of Trade estimates of factories opened, closed and extended, listed by both industry and region.[2] The industrial groups for which estimates of building and works have been made by Feinstein are obviously too wide for detailed comment to be made. In textiles gross investment was negative over most of the 1930s reflecting primarily the extensive scrapping in cotton. In none of the groups was there an upward trend in building though there were marked fluctuations broadly in line with the business cycle. But there were marked differences: in the chemicals, clothing and related group building was at its peak in the late 1920s and the average level of 1924–9 was not regained in the 1930s; in the metals and metal-using trades (a category which included the newer industries) there were periods of peak industrial building in 1920–1 and in 1936–8 but

[1] Robinson, op. cit., pp. 59–61.

[2] Feinstein, op. cit., pp. 105–32, and Board of Trade, *Surveys of Industrial Development* (1932–8).

a relatively stable and low level in the intervening years; in food, drink and tobacco the peak of the early 1920s was not surpassed in the inter-war period. The Board of Trade data, on new factories opened, in Table 6 support the view that the demand for industrial buildings was high only in certain industries where opportunities for profit were good. The data merely list numbers of factories and say nothing about their size, and for this reason do not give any clear impression of the industrial distribution of building investment. However, it is perhaps significant that the ratio of new factories opened, to factories closed in the period 1933–8 was high in the building materials groups (bricks, pottery, glass [2·9], non-metalliferous mining trades [2·6]), in vehicles (1·9) and in food, drink and tobacco (1·8) but extremely low in depressed industries such as textiles (0·5) and clothing (1·1).

The demand for new industrial buildings was also distributed unequally by regions between the wars. This was accounted for, of course, by the shift in the location of industry to the South and Midlands which in turn was associated with the concentration of population increases in these regions: the Midlands and the South, whose share of UK population in 1921 amounted to 44 per cent, accounted for 88 per cent of the increase in population between 1921 and 1938. In any event, non-residential building was concentrated in the South of England due to the influence of London as the major administrative and commercial centre. This meant that the major demands for office and hotel building arose in London. Evidence for the higher level of demand for non-residential buildings in the Southern, more prosperous areas of the country is very scanty, but again the Board of Trade figures of factories opened and closed in the period 1932–8 inclusive stood at 2·6 in the South and South-West, 1·9 in Wales, 1·7 in the Eastern region and 1·5 in Greater London. At the lower end of the scale the Midlands ratio was 1·05, North-East England and Scotland both had ratios of just under unity, and in the North-West region the ratio was 0·9. The surprising point was the high ratio for Wales and the relatively low figure for the Midlands. The Welsh figure is explained by the small absolute numbers involved and the facts that the predominance of coal mining in Wales meant that there were fewer industrial factories in existence and therefore fewer closures, while the Special Area policy induced a number of factories into Wales in 1937 and 1938. The Midlands figure is partly explained by the co-existence of rapidly expanding and heavily depressed industries in the region, while the figure looks more flattering when the high rate of factory extensions in the Midlands is considered. Nevertheless, a clearer impression of the regional demand for industrial buildings is given from the excess number of factories opened over those closed by region: these were +506 for Greater London, +102 for the South and South-West, +48 for the Eastern region, +30 for Wales, +23 for the Midlands, compared with deficits of –4 for Scotland, –15 for North-East England and –101 for the North-West. To sum

Table 6: FACTORIES OPENED, CLOSED AND EXTENDED

A. *By Region*, 1932–8

Region	*Opened*	*Closed*	*Extended*
Southern and South-Western	167	65	73
Greater London	1,562	1,056	332
Wales	62	32	21
Midlands	508	485	243
Eastern	117	69	52
North-West	722	823	239
North-East	320	335	149
Scotland	146	150	43

B. *By Industry*, 1933–8

Industry	*Opened*	*Closed*	*Extended*
Non-metalliferous mining	76	29	14
Bricks, pottery, glass	118	41	36
Chemicals	95	73	27
Iron and steel	185	155	112
Engineering	347	238	168
Vehicles	159	85	91
Non-ferrous metals	54	46	25
Textiles	347	703	115
Leather	60	46	8
Clothing	654	581	151
Food, drink and tobacco	202	114	69
Timber	280	214	52
Paper, printing	186	141	63
Miscellaneous	179	129	56

up: apart from the public sector, the main element in the demand for non-residential buildings was the prevailing level of economic activity and the expected rates of profitability associated with that level. Consequently, in aggregate terms there was close correlation between investment in non-residential buildings and the index of general business activity. However, the national picture blurred quite marked differences at both the industry and regional levels. The demand for industrial buildings was dependent upon the expansion potential in individual industries and was distributed unequally between regions because of the clustering of new industrial development in the South of England. On the other hand, it would be untrue to explain the demand for industrial building at all times in purely economic terms divorced from external considerations. Other factors had some influence; for instance, the heavy investment in rearmament factories in the late 1930s was largely stimulated by Government defence policy.

III. *Conclusions*

Finally, a few concluding statements may be made about differences in the character of demand for non-residential buildings and the demand for houses on one hand and investment demand in general on the other. Most non-residential buildings are tailor-made on specific orders; the strong speculative element which influences the demand for houses is therefore lacking. Because buildings are more durable than machines and other types of investment, net investment is much more important than replacement investment in building and works relative to other types of investment. But it is misleading to consider the demand for non-residential buildings as being entirely an independently determined demand. As suggested earlier, it is difficult to disentangle the special characteristics of this demand from investment demand generally. In many cases, a rise in investment means an increased demand for both new machines and new buildings. Probably even more significant is the fact that a sizeable volume of non-residential building is directly generated by housing construction. This is especially true when suburbs are built since the development of housing estates induces a demand for shops, other commercial properties and public buildings including schools, libraries and hospitals. In some situations, therefore, the demands for houses and non-residential buildings are closely associated with each other. Despite this, it is generally true that the demand for non-residential buildings approximates closer to the demand for investment goods as a whole than to the demand for houses. The consequence is that the course of investment in non-residential building differs markedly from the course of housing investment. The divergences have considerable repercussions on the character of building fluctuations as a whole, and their influence is considered in some detail in Chapter 10.

CHAPTER 5

MANPOWER

I. *Introductory: Some General Aspects of Supply*

A study of the building industry would be incomplete without an examination of the main features of supply. Clearly the expansion in building output in the inter-war years could never have taken place without a comparable increase in the supply of inputs. This and the following chapter will, therefore, be devoted to a general discussion of the problems of supply, with particular reference to manpower and building materials. It will then be possible to proceed to an analysis of the changes in, and determinants of, aggregate costs in building in relation to changes in efficiency and technology. In order to facilitate the more detailed discussion on manpower and materials which follows a few introductory comments on the chief characteristics of supply will be helpful.

The main inputs required in the construction of buildings are labour and materials, which together account for the bulk of the costs incurred. Estimates vary as to their relative importance but as a rough guide it is usual to attribute about one-third of the total costs of construction to labour and the remaining two-thirds to building materials. According to the Laidlow Committee the proportionate cost of materials, labour and management was in the ratio 55:36:9.[1] These proportions will obviously vary somewhat, depending upon the type of construction in question. The proportion of labour and material costs to total costs in non-residential building, for example, was probably slightly lower because of the fact that more capital was used in this type of work.

Apart from these two items there are, in addition, two other imputs—land and capital. Neither of these forms a significant share of the total cost of construction; together they probably account for no more than 10 per cent of the final cost of building work. Of the two, the price of land is the most important, and it is generally assumed that it represents on average less than 10 per cent of the first cost value of the buildings and sites.[2] It is obviously somewhat unrealistic

[1] *Report of the Committee on Scottish Building Costs* (HMSO, 1948), p. 17.

[2] Feinstein suggests a ratio of 7 per cent. C. H. Feinstein, *Domestic Capital Formation in the United Kingdom, 1920–38* (1965), p. 15. Cf. K. Maywald, 'Fire

to assume that the land value of building work remained constant since the price of land varied over time and between regions. Moreover, the cost of land per unit of output will vary depending upon the type of building (e.g. flats, office blocks or houses) and the average density per acre. Thus, in practice, the value of land inputs is likely to vary considerably. It would, however, be impossible to take account of such variations and for this reason we have taken the average as the norm.[1] Capital is a less difficult problem. Fixed capital per unit of output is relatively low in the building trade and, apart from the case of large contractors, it is a very small item in total costs. Short-term finance or builders' credit is important since much construction work is financed on this basis, but again this factor only forms a very small proportion of the costs incurred by builders. Fluctuations in the rate of interest, and hence the price of credit, can have an important influence in determining the timing of building starts though, as we shall argue below, this factor was probably far less influential in the inter-war years than it had been in the nineteenth century.

On the whole, it would be true to say that there were no revolutionary changes in the way in which buildings were supplied in the inter-war period. The production of houses in particular depended, as in the nineteenth century, on the assembly at scattered sites of an enormous number of small units of different materials by craftsman and general labourers using very little capital equipment. A notable feature of the industry was the large number of small firms engaged in house construction, many of them producing only a few units a year.[2] Despite their size such firms were able to operate a single process or product on a large scale, largely by virtue of the fact that they could draw upon the services of many specialist firms or subcontractors. Thus the small firm usually employed only a few men directly, most of whom were either bricklayers or general labourers engaged upon producing the outside shell of the house. At the later stage much of the work on interior fittings, etc., was of a specialized nature and this was sub-contracted out to independent firms of

---

Insurance and the Capital Coefficient in Great Britain, 1866–1952', *Economic History Review*, 9 (1956), App. I, p. 101.

[1] It is fairly certain that because of the higher standards adopted in the inter-war years, especially for housebuilding, the input of land per unit of output was greater than before 1914.

[2] The importance of the small firm and speculative builder in housing construction tended to increase during this period, see Chapter 1, pp. 32–8.

craftsmen such as joiners, plumbers, carpenters and painters. The materials required for the building—sand, bricks, cement, timber, etc.—were either supplied directly to the builder by the manufacturers or through their distributing merchants, or, alternatively, they were provided by the sub-contracting agents.[1] The whole process was financed largely on the basis of an elaborate system of short-term credit supplied mainly by the banks and the material suppliers, though in some cases the builder received part payment on account before completion of the work.

At the other extreme there were some very large general builders, many of which combined both building and civil engineering. Their output was generally substantial, consisting not only of houses and flats but also general office blocks and large public buildings. Some of these firms employed directly a wide range of specialized personnel, including architects, engineers and building craftsmen, and were able, consequently, to dispense with the services of many specialist sub-contracting firms. But by no means all these firms were self-sufficient producing units. Many large building contractors were organized on the lines of an assembly factory in that their main function was to co-ordinate the work of a large number of specialist sub-contractors on the building site. This latter group probably increased in importance during the inter-war years since, with the increasing complexity of construction (especially of large non-residential buildings) and the introduction of new structural materials such as steel, reinforced concrete and mass produced factory fittings, the degree of specialization increased thus favouring the growth of the large general sub-contracting firm.

In general it was the large firm which was mainly responsible for the introduction of new technical processes into building operations. This of course is not surprising since these firms were the chief producers of non-residential buildings where the scope for the application of new structures using steel, concrete and glass was much greater than in the case of housebuilding. Similarly, the size of firm dictated the degree to which machinery was used on the site; because of the scale of operations the large firm could utilize capital equipment fairly effectively. It was these firms, therefore, which were mainly responsible for the extensive application of mechanical appliances such as cement mixers, steam shovels, woodworking machinery, hydraulic and pneumatic riveters and mechanical cranes. Such changes gained little ground in housebuilding, however, partly

[1] Similarly, in the initial stages of development the small builder was heavily dependent on qualified experts, for example, architects.

because of the dominance of the small firm in this sector and partly because the spread of new techniques was frustrated by the fact that consumer demand continued to favour the construction of houses of a traditional type.

Yet even housebuilding was not completely unaffected by new technical developments. Admittedly houses still continued to be built in much the same way with bricks, timber, cement and tiles as their basic ingredients but there was a number of new additions to the range of materials available. The most notable examples were the new common Fletton brick and the concrete tile, both of which were applied extensively during the period. Less notable, but still important, was the increasing use made (in the 1930s especially) of asbestos cement sheet, fibre and plaster board and mass produced joinery fittings. Occasionally experiments were made with steel, concrete and timber frames in housebuilding though none of these became commercially viable propositions. Few of these materials, however, resulted in any significant reduction in the cost of the assembly operation itself, though considerable reductions occurred in the cost of producing the basic building materials as a result of improvements in technical efficiency in these trades.

Thus although technical progress was by no means absent in the inter-war period there was no dramatic change in the general conduct of operations. New structures and improvements in the techniques of assembly were confined mainly to the large firms engaged in non-residential work. Housebuilding benefited from the introduction of new materials and cost reductions in the production of many materials but such developments did not alter appreciably the basic methods of construction. New methods of assembly associated with prefabricated and industrialized systems of building were still very much in the experimental stage in these years. By and large the building industry as a whole remained largely traditional in that the type of labour employed, the materials used and the techniques of assembly did not change radically from those prevailing before 1914. There was, for example, no significant shift in the proportions of skilled and unskilled labour employed in the industry, a situation reflecting in part the relatively slow rate of technical change and the limited use made of mechanical equipment. Throughout the period the production of buildings remained very much a labour intensive process. This is borne out by the fact that capital employed per worker in 1924 and 1935 amounted to only £71·7 and £63·2 respectively as against £235·8 and £201·5 for all manufacturing industry.

Technical changes and efficiency in the building industry will be considered in more detail when we deal with the pattern of overall costs in building. This brief commentary on the supply problem will serve, however, as a background to the following analysis of manpower and building materials.

II. *Structure of the Labour Force*

Employment in the building industry consists of two main types: the skilled worker or craftsman and general labourers.[1] The former are employed in one of seven trades as carpenters, bricklayers, painters, plasterers, plumbers, masons and slaters; of these categories the first three are by far the most important accounting for about three-quarters or more of the total craftsmen engaged in the industry. The ratio of craftsmen to all building workers remained relatively stable for most of the inter-war years within the range 48–53 per cent, though it is probable that the relative importance of the unskilled labour component had increased compared with before the war.[2] National averages, however, tend to conceal significant regional variations; in Scotland, for example, the proportion of craftsmen in the total labour force was nearly 65 per cent in 1938 whilst in the London area it was only 46 per cent. These are, of course, extremes and in most regions the ratio of skilled labour was around 50 per cent or slightly below.[3] There are similar regional differences in the proportions in which particular craftsmen were employed. Some of these variations were quite marked as Table 7 shows and they reflected either differences in types of materials used or maladjustments in rates of supply. Masons, for example, featured far more prominently in the South-West, Scotland and Wales than elsewhere, whilst the Midlands and London area had a higher propor-

[1] That is excluding salaried employees; this group accounted for around 10 per cent of the total numbers employed.

[2] A number of writers (e.g. H. W. Robinson, *The Economics of Building* (1939), p. 14) have remarked upon the growth in importance of unskilled labour between 1911–31. Such observations, however, are based upon census data which adopts a somewhat different system of classifying occupations compared with the Ministry of Labour's employment returns. Unfortunately the latter did not become fully comprehensive until 1924 and so it is not possible to check the assertion. However, if allowance is made for unemployment, there was a steady fall in the proportion of craftsmen actually employed in the 1920s (from 53·9 to 40 per cent, 1921 to 1930) but in the 'thirties the proportion rose again and reached 46 per cent in 1938, roughly the same as it had been in 1925.

[3] I. Bowen, 'The Building Industry in Wartime', *Economic Journal*, 49 (1939), pp. 666 and 669.

Table 7: PERCENTAGE OF CRAFTSMEN EMPLOYED IN VARIOUS REGIONS IN 1938

	London	*South-East*	*South-West*	*Midlands*	*All Northern*	*Scotland*	*Wales*	*UK*
Carpenters	26·0	32·6	32·0	29·6	30·3	30·3	34·9	30·1
Bricklayers	19·1	26·6	18·7	30·2	23·8	10·8	19·0	21·7
Masons	1·8	0·8	10·7	1·5	3·3	11·0	10·3	4·4
Slaters	1·0	0·3	0·4	1·0	1·7	7·2	0·3	1·7
Plasterers	8·5	4·7	6·1	6·1	7·8	8·3	11·1	7·3
Painters	35·4	28·0	25·7	23·5	23·0	19·8	20·5	26·1
Plumbers	8·2	7·0	6·4	8·0	10·1	12·7	3·9	8·7
	100	100	100	100	100	100	100	100
Total craftsmen employed as a percentage of all building employees	46·1	51·5	52·0	50·4	55·8	64·8	48·9	52·5

SOURCE: I. Bowen, 'The Building Industry in Wartime', *Economic Journal*, 49 (1939), p. 669.

tion of bricklayers and painters in relation to other crafts. Variations also occurred with the size of firm. The tendency was for the proportion of craftsmen employed to fall as the size of the unit increased, though in all but the largest firms craftsmen outnumbered the unskilled labourers. Thus in 1941 the proportion of craftsmen in firms employing 100 workers or more was only 38 per cent, whereas for very small firms (less than twenty employees) it was as high as 64 per cent.[1]

As one might expect there were considerable differences in the training, organization and methods of recruitment of the two groups. Craftsmen were trained under a rigorous apprenticeship system to which entry was restricted.[2] The length of apprenticeship was about five years during which time wages were low. The interests of the craftsmen were jealously protected by a number of small close-knit craft unions, though even by 1938 by no means all skilled workers belonged to a union. In contrast, the unskilled workers had no standards of training and apprenticeship and they were far less extensively organized than the craftsmen. No unions catered specifically for their needs though building workers could join the large general unions, such as the Transport and General Workers Union, which served many interests other than their own. Similar differences also existed in the way labour was recruited. Much of the unskilled labour was hired casually on a weekly or even daily basis, and often when building activity was at a peak such labour was drawn from a variety of occupations. Craftsmen, on the other hand, were engaged on a longer-term basis, and sometimes, particularly when labour was scarce, building contractors would retain skilled men on their books after the original project for which they were engaged had been completed. Nevertheless, the differences in this respect were less marked than in the case of training and organization of building workers. The labour market was highly imperfect and methods of recruitment remained haphazard throughout the period. Despite the existence of labour exchanges most building workers were taken on directly and even in the case of craftsmen many were recruited on a casual or semi-casual basis.[3] Often they moved from

[1] See 'Labour in the Building Industry', *Planning*, September 1943, p. 6.

[2] That is the number of apprentices allowed into the industry was regulated. In 1926 there were 4·4 journeymen to each apprentice in the building industry. The proportions varied a great deal, however, between trades and regions.

[3] For the London area the proportion of engagements made through Labour Exchanges was only around 30 per cent in 1936. See R. G. D. Allen and B. Thomas, 'The London Building Industry and its Labour Recruitment through Labour Exchanges', *Economic Journal*, 47 (1937).

other skilled occupations to the building industry and back again depending upon the state of employment. In general, employment in building was not the most attractive of occupations. Conditions in the industry were poor. The work was demanding physically, wages were low, there were few welfare amenities and little security. Though some improvements took place in the inter-war years conditions of employment still remained less favourable than those in many other industries.

III. *Skilled Shortages*

Craftsmen, therefore, were the aristocrats of the building industry and because of the length of training involved it was usually in this field that shortages of labour first occurred which tended to hold up the expansion of the industry. In this respect the early 1920s were no exception. Immediately after the war the shortage of labour was acute because of the run-down in building and the draft of workers into the armed forces during hostilities. The situation was aggravated, moreover, by the low level of productivity in the industry.[1] Unfortunately the statistical data on building workers is not complete, and the estimates we have are at best only approximate since the Ministry of Labour's returns were constantly being reclassified in this period. Pre-1914 comparisons are not, therefore, easy to make. Nevertheless, roughly comparable figures were obtained for the number of insured craftsmen and unskilled labourers for the years 1914–25 (Table 8), and from this data it is possible to make some comments about the available supply of building workers.

It can be seen from Table 8 that by 1918 and 1919 the building labour force had been badly depleted. Most crafts were undermanned and the skilled labour force as a whole was only 55 per cent of the pre-war level whilst the number of unskilled labourers was only about one-third less. This deficiency was not as bad as it seemed, however, since building activity was still fairly low in the first half of 1919. Within the next eighteen months the release of men from military service helped to swell the ranks of the building trade and by July 1920 the total labour force (skilled and unskilled) was not far short of the pre-war figure. There was still a serious shortage, however, of most types of craft labour apart from carpenters, and this deficiency was undoubtedly one of the chief obstacles to the rapid production of housing. In 1920 there were few building schemes in

[1] This is dealt with later.

Table 8: NUMBERS INSURED IN BUILDING TRADES

	July 1914	*July 1918*	*March 1919*	*July 1920*	*July 1921*	*July 1922*	*May 1923*	*July 1924*	*July 1925*
Carpenters	148,763	95,785	96,979	143,425	147,230	135,560	135,210	126,410	114,030
Bricklayers	78,417	41,643	42,275	64,632	62,410	63,060	60,960	58,170	65,120
Masons	46,676	20,626	20,076	29,058	27,240	24,240	23,870	22,520	23,840
Plasterers	24,038	10,461	10,431	16,848	18,230	17,530	17,150	15,970	17,880
Painters	149,672	70,117	71,513	121,938	134,570	116,580	116,210	107,080	108,590
Plumbers	41,680	26,338	26,768	43,321	46,880	36,289	37 301	34,520	28,610
Total:									
Craftsmen	489,246	264,970	268,042	419,222	436,560	393,259	390,711	364,670	358,070
Unskilled Labourers	301,092	191,910	204,206	349,581	406,040	378,400	372,598	350,530	390,740

NOTES: The figures for craftsmen exclude one or two minor skilled trades, e.g. slaters, for which separate data is not available. The data for unskilled labourers is only approximate since it is difficult to get accurate figures because of the Ministry of Labour's continual reclassification of occupations in this period.

SOURCE: *Ministry of Labour Gazette.*

progress on which an adequate supply of labour was employed.[1] The Government realized that unless some action was taken to relieve the situation its housing programme would be placed in jeopardy. Discussions were therefore held between the Ministers of Health and Labour and representatives of both sides of the building industry. Little materialized, however, from these negotiations apart from a scheme for training 50,000 ex-servicemen with a view to their admission to the skilled ranks after only two years' training. This scheme was carried out by the building industry itself on a voluntary basis and was put into operation in April 1921.

By the latter half of 1921 the labour supply situation had eased considerably. There had been a considerable increase in the numbers in skilled occupations during the preceding two years (see Table 8) and the collapse of the post-war boom brought a decline in the demand for industrial and commercial building. This, together with the cut-back in local authorities' housing programmes later in 1921, had a considerable moderating effect on the labour market. Unemployment amongst craftsmen rose sharply in 1921 and remained at a fairly high level for the next two years. Thus, although the supply of skilled labour was still below that of pre-war it could hardly be said that the lack of manpower acted as a serious brake on the industry in 1922 and 1923. There were of course still shortages in particular trades and regions. The painting trade remained badly undermanned and in Scotland plasterers and bricklayers were difficult to obtain. But by and large the supply of skilled labour was adequate.

In 1924, however, the labour market became tight again. This situation was caused by a number of adverse factors. The sharp contraction in building output after 1921, and the increasing activity in the economy generally a year or two later, encouraged a drift of labour from building into other occupations. Thus between July 1921 and July 1924 the skilled labour force had been depleted by almost 72,000. Hence the sharp increase in building output between 1923 and 1924 and the launching of the Government's new housing programme in the latter year came at the worst possible time. The industry's skilled labour force in 1924 was probably well below what it had been in the summers of 1920 and 1921, when building activity was lower, and in some trades, e.g. bricklaying, plastering and painting, the shortage was very acute indeed. According to a com-

[1] The position was worst in Scotland where it was estimated that at least double the number of employees was required. *Second Annual Report of the Scottish Board of Health*, 1920, Cmd. 1319 (1921), p. 131.

mittee set up in 1924 to examine the situation the labour shortage had been aggravated by the fact that employers had failed in previous years to take up their full quota of apprentices allowed by the union rules. In 1921, for example, only 21,000 apprentices were actively in training for the crafts of bricklaying, masonry, joinery, slating and plastering as against 56,400 who could have been trained on the basis of one apprentice to four journeymen.[1] Accordingly efforts were made to increase the flow of skilled labour. The Minister of Health appointed a committee composed of representatives of employers and trade unionists to assist him in carrying out the Government's housing programme. This led to a 'gentlemen's agreement' between the industry and the unions whereby the latter agreed to modify their rules governing apprenticeship so as to shorten the period of training and to throw open the trade to semi-skilled adult workers who had undergone a special course of training. At the same time local authorities were requested to ensure that a larger proportion of apprentices was employed on building works financed by them.

It is difficult to say how effective this agreement was in increasing the number of skilled workers in the industry. Between 1925 and 1927 the number of insured craftsmen rose by nearly 30,000 but it is unlikely that all of this increase was due to the relaxation of the apprenticeship regulations. Nevertheless, for a time certain trades, e.g. plumbing, plastering, still remained undermanned. After 1926, however, there is little evidence of a serious labour shortage despite the fairly high level of building output in 1927 and 1929 and the relatively low rates of unemployment among craftsmen compared with the early 1920s.[2] If the heavy unemployment is anything to go by the position was even better in the first half of the 1930s. Unemployment rates averaged well over 10 per cent in most skilled trades during the years 1930–4, and apart from one or two local shortages, which were only temporary, the industry had no difficulty in finding the labour it required. In 1935 the labour market began to tighten again and by the later 1930s the shortage of skilled labour became acute in some trades. The Scottish region was most affected by the shortage and many housing schemes were seriously delayed because of the lack of bricklayers and plasterers.[3]

[1] *Report on the Present Position of the Building Industry* . . ., Cmd. 2104 (1924).
[2] See Table 5, Appendix, Chapter 2.
[3] See *Report on Scottish Building Costs*, Cmd. 5977 (1939), p. 15, and 10th *Annual Report of the Department of Health for Scotland, 1938*, Cmd. 5969 (1939), p. 28.

In contrast the supply of unskilled labour appears to have been adequate throughout the period apart from the exception of the immediate post-war years. With heavy unemployment prevailing in most years it was relatively easy for the builders to attract untrained labour from other trades when necessary. On average unemployment was much higher among unskilled labourers than it was among craftsmen which suggests that builders had a reserve pool of labour on which they could draw. This was particularly useful at times when craft labour was in short supply, for it was possible in the short term, e.g. 1924–5, to dilute the craft labour force by employing more unskilled workers.

IV. *Employment and Output*

The preceding paragraphs have been concerned with the supply of labour rather than the relationship between employment and output. How did employment respond to changes in the output of the building industry? Unfortunately the data is not accurate enough to present comparisons with 1914 but an overall picture can be traced for the period 1920–38 by comparing the Feinstein capital investment data for all buildings with the course of actual employment, that is after making adjustments for unemployment. For this purpose we have used the Chapman and Knight figures for total man years in employment together with the Ministry of Labour's estimated numbers engaged in the skilled trades.[1] On the whole, the data tend to confirm the conclusion that the building industry's progress was never seriously held back by a shortage of labour except in the early 1920s. The trend in actual employment follows fairly closely the course of building output though as we have already noted skilled employment was slow to respond to the upswing in building after 1923, whereas in the 1930s it ran parallel with the building boom. In fact in the latter decade total employment responded fairly readily to changes in output and continued to rise sharply after 1934–5 when building activity began to flatten out. But a general picture of this type tends to be somewhat misleading. For one thing it obscures temporary shortages of labour which occurred in particular regions or crafts and which we have already commented upon. And secondly it gives the impression that the labour supply increased (or contracted as the case may be) at the same rate as the output of the building industry. Nothing could be further from the truth, however. As Table 9 shows employment increased much less than the

[1] These are produced in Table 5, Appendix, Chapter 2.

output of the industry in every period listed. This is especially true of the early 1920s (1920–5) when output rose by nearly 44 per cent yet the labour supply remained virtually unchanged. Over the period as a whole (1920–37) the growth in employment was very modest compared with the rise in output. Moreover, in the 1920s the total labour force expanded more rapidly than craft employment, whilst in the following decade the reverse was the case.

The discrepancies between the growth in output and employment are not easy to explain precisely. There are a number of possible solutions, but statistical verification is difficult owing to the paucity of data. It will be helpful to review briefly some of the possible explanations at this point.

Table 9: PERCENTAGE INCREASES IN OUTPUT OF BUILDING WORK AND EMPLOYMENT OVER SELECTED PERIODS

	Output of building work	*Total employment*	*Craft employment*
1920–37	134·5	35·8	11·9
1920–1	16·4	−4·1	−4·6
1929–32	−12·4	−8·3	−16·2
1932–7	53·7	34·4	46·8
1924–37	91·5	47·1	32·2

SOURCES: Based on *Ministry of Labour Gazette*; C. H. Feinstein, op. cit., and A. L. Chapman and R. Knight, *Wages and Salaries in the United Kingdom, 1920–38* (1954).

The relatively slow expansion of the craft labour force in the 1920s can be partly accounted for by the substitution of unskilled labour, since the percentage of craftsmen to total employment fell steadily during this period.[1]

But we are still left with the problem of explaining why the total labour force expanded so much more slowly than the output of the building industry. The most obvious explanation would seem to be a secular improvement in the productive efficiency of the building industry. However, recent estimates suggest that productivity growth in building was only very modest in the inter-war years,[2] and it is highly improbable that it could have accounted for the discrepancies in output and employment except perhaps in the early 1920s when productivity rose rapidly from the low level reached after the war.

On the other hand, the aggregate productivity data may not reflect short-term or temporary changes in productivity which were determined by the degree of capacity utilization rather than by

[1] From 53·9 in 1921 to 44·7 per cent in 1929.

[2] Around 1 per cent per annum. See Chapter 7.

technical improvements. The productivity of labour often fluctuated quite sharply from year to year or even from month to month depending on the level of output in relation to capacity, and it is probable that the industry was able to use its resources much more effectively when fully employed. The building industry is notorious for the under-utilization of its labour force, especially in times of slack or even moderate demand largely because of the inevitable discontinuities between projects. Thus when output increased rapidly additional labour requirements did not increase in the same ratio since labour previously under-utilized was put to better use. It is difficult to say precisely what importance to attach to this explanation since statistical proof is non-existent, but it may well have been an important factor in times of rapid expansion.

An alternative explanation is that relating to hours or work. Owing to the erratic nature of building work overtime is not uncommon, especially in summer. When output expanded rapidly to near full capacity it was often easier to extend the hours of work than employ more labour, especially as additional craft labour was difficult to obtain at short notice. Because of this, fluctuations in output may have been much greater than the employment figures would suggest. Evidence on overtime work is scanty but it does support the tenor of the argument. An inquiry made by the Ministry of Labour into earnings and hours of labour in October 1938 found that over 50 per cent of building and contracting workers were employed in excess of the normal working week. This high proportion of overtime might seem surprising at a time when unemployment was still heavy but apparently it was quite common in other occupations though not to the same extent as in building.[1]

Both of these factors occurred as a once-and-for-all bonus at times of peak output, the effect of which was to reduce, relatively speaking, the demand for additional workers. This built-in ability to draw upon under-utilized reserves of labour enabled the industry to increase its output quite sharply from one year to the next without too much pressure being put on the labour market. Unfortunately, little statistical proof can be given, but according to Bowen this is what happened in the early 1930s, and the same is probably true also of the early 1920s.[2]

[1] See R. B. Ainsworth, 'Earnings and Hours of Manual Wage-Earners in the United Kingdom in October 1938', *Journal of Royal Statistical Society*, 112 (1949), Pt. 1, Series A, pp. 38 and 52.

[2] I. Bowen, 'Investment in the Building Industry, 1930–5', *Review of Economic Studies*, 6 (1938–9), p. 201.

V. *Wages*

The course of wages in the building industry confirms the view that apart from the early 1920s there was never any severe pressure on the labour market. Despite the increasing, though fluctuating, demand for building labour in the inter-war years, wage costs remained fairly steady for most of the period. This is not true, of course, for the years prior to 1922. The war and post-war boom had pushed wage rates up sharply, as in most other industries, and by the middle of 1920 average rates in building were about 200 to 225 per cent higher than before the war. The real cost of labour was, however, even greater than this figure suggests. Unskilled labour's wages had risen more rapidly than those of craftsmen and if, as suggested earlier, there had been a shift in the proportion of unskilled to skilled labour used in building it follows that there was also a relatively greater increase in on-cost labour during the period. Over and above the increase in wage rates, it became customary in the early years after the war to attract labour by special allowances which were not operative before 1914. These included allowances for time taken in travelling to and from the work-sites, payments for broken time, e.g. because of bad weather, and increasing overtime payments. In 1920, when wage rates began to be negotiated nationally, there was a reduction in the average working week of about five hours without any loss of pay. Finally, real costs were enhanced by the fall in productivity of building operatives during these years. It is difficult to estimate the magnitude of the decline but by all accounts it was considerable.[1] The chief factors responsible for the low level of productivity were the wartime disruption of the building industry and the subsequent delays in completion of work due to serious shortages of skilled labour and materials.

After 1920 wage rates in building fell sharply with the collapse of the post-war boom and in 1922 they were slightly more than double the pre-war level.[2] Apart from one or two minor fluctuations (see Table 10) they remained at this level until 1930. Between that date and 1933 they dropped by about 8 per cent, after which they rose slowly until 1938. At the latter date they were exactly the same as in 1922. Thus, apart from the sudden drop in the early 1930s, wage

[1] One writer has estimated that the bricklayers' output averaged 300 bricks a day in 1920 compared with nearly 1,000 in 1914. M. J. Elsas, *Housing Before and After the War* (1945), p. 2.

[2] From 1920 wage rates in building were negotiated nationally on a sliding scale basis.

rates remained more or less constant throughout the period. Neither were there any marked fluctuations, apart from the sharp fall in the early 'twenties, in average earnings of employees in the building trades, though the slight rise in the 1930s tends to confirm the view that wage costs as a whole were tending to creep up again in this period (see Table 10). On the other hand, there were no marked divergencies between average earnings in building and those in

Table 10: WAGES AND EARNINGS IN THE BUILDING INDUSTRY

	Index of wage rates (1930=100) (1)	*Average annual earnings of all employees in building and contracting* (*in* £) (2)	*Average earnings in all industries* (£) (3)	*Ratio* (4) *col* 2÷*col* 3
1913	48·6	—	—	—
1919	112·8	—	—	—
1920	146·8	225·0	192·0	1·17
1921	127·6	208·7	183·5	1·14
1922	103·4	165·1	153·6	1·08
1923	98·8	151·3	144·2	1·05
1924	104·3	155·6	145·6	1·06
1925	104·7	158·6	146·5	1·08
1926	105·2	159·7	145·0	1·10
1927	105·4	159·0	146·1	1·08
1928	102·8	157·1	144·9	1·08
1929	102·6	157·3	145·2	1·08
1930	100·0	157·7	144·9	1·09
1931	97·7	153·9	142·8	1·08
1932	95·0	149·5	140·5	1·06
1933	92·4	147·6	139·7	1·06
1934	92·5	148·1	141·1	1·05
1935	95·0	151·1	143·1	1·06
1936	97·9	152·5	145·9	1·05
1937	100·2	155·4	148·6	1·05
1938	103·2	158·4	153·1	1·04

SOURCES: K. Maiwald, 'An Index of Building Costs in the United Kingdom, 1845–1938', *Economic History Review*, 7 (1954–5), p. 192, and A. L. Chapman and R. Knight, *Wages and Salaries in the United Kingdom, 1920–1938* (1954), p. 27.

industry as a whole, though there was a tendency in the 1930s for average earnings in building to lag behind the general average. If nothing else this tends to lend support to the theory that the building trade was not subject to any undue pressure from rising wage costs.

There were, no doubt, considerable local variations in wage earnings since it was common, especially in the later 1930s, for employers to pay craftsmen bonuses or extra payments to encourage greater output.[1] On balance, however, it is probable that, although after 1922 monetary wage costs did not vary very much, the real cost of labour was falling slightly owing to the steady rise in productivity. This point will be discussed more fully when we come to survey building costs as a whole.

VI. *Supply Elasticity*

Generally speaking, therefore, the building industry was not seriously hampered by a shortage of labour in the inter-war years. The supply was fairly elastic especially in the unskilled trades but it is noticeable that at times when building activity increased suddenly a shortage of craftsmen developed as in the immediate post-war years, in the middle 1920s and again in the later 1930s. The effect of these temporary scarcities was to cause delays and raise costs since it was difficult to increase the supply of skilled workers quickly. On the other hand, it would appear that the industry was able to achieve substantial increases in output with a less than proportionate increase in the labour force (this was especially true of the 1920s) which suggests a substantial improvement in the way in which resources were utilized. Certainly for most of the 1920s the industry was operating with a smaller labour force than pre-war[2] yet at the same time achieving a far greater output.

It may seem strange to talk about labour shortages at a time when unemployment levels were notoriously high. The fact is, however, that the labour market in the building industry was, and still is, highly imperfect and because of the nature of the work it was quite common to get serious maladjustments in the demand and supply of labour between various trades and regions. The separate trades were disproportionately manned in relation to each other over the whole country. In Scotland, for instance, the total number of painters was much greater in proportion to the work available than the number of bricklayers and plasterers. Similarly, it was quite common to find a surplus of one class of skilled labour in one district whilst a shortage of the same class existed not far away. These imbalances in labour

[1] Payment by output (or piece-rates) never became common in building since the unions insisted on time-rates being paid.

[2] This is certainly true of craftsmen and there is no reason to suppose that the same conclusion is not also true of the total labour force.

supply had the unfortunate effect of causing delays and pushing up costs at times when the pressure on the building industry was severe. Moreover, the lengthy apprenticeship training of building craftsmen precluded any sudden increase in supply even though there might be unemployed labour resources in the economy as a whole. Nevertheless, had there not been heavy unemployment in these years the industry would undoubtedly have found much greater difficulty in recruiting labour.

CHAPTER 6

BUILDING MATERIALS

I. *Introductory*

As we have already seen, materials accounted for a fairly high proportion of the total costs in building construction. The range of materials required by the industry is enormous; in 1948 the Simon report estimated that some 250 different categories of materials were produced by at least 2,500 firms.[1] Many of the individual items were of no great importance and only a few, such as bricks and timber, accounted for a significant share of the total cost of materials. Roughly two-thirds of the cost of materials used in building can be attributed to timber, bricks, slate goods, cement and concrete products, whilst the remaining third was accounted for by glass, roofing felts, paint, varnish and wallpaper, iron, brass, hardware and holloware, sheet metal and other metal products.[2] With the exception of timber, the bulk of which was imported, requirements of most of the materials were met largely by domestic production. Although there were a large number of firms engaged in the manufacture of materials and components the industry as a whole was by no means a freely competitive one. Conditions varied, of course, a great deal from one industry to another, but broadly speaking it would be correct to say that in many cases—and this is particularly true of the less important materials—the bulk of the output was produced by one or two large firms which operated on a national scale. In contrast the numerous small firms accounted for only a small proportion of total output. These firms tended to be scattered geographically; they served a local market and their position was sheltered by rela-

[1] *Report of the Committee of the Distribution of Building Materials* (HMSO 1948).

[2] A rough breakdown of the proportionate contribution of the main materials to total materials costs for an average house is as follows:

Aggregate	2·3	Drainpipes, gutters, etc.	3·6	Joinery	15·4
Bricks	18·6	Grates and ranges	2·6	Slates	12·8
Cement	3·1	Hardware goods	4·5	Timber	13·9
Concrete	2·5	Lead	3·1	Miscellaneous	17·6
				Total	100·0

These proportions will differ, of course, depending upon the type of construction. See Political and Economic Planning, *Housing England* (1934), p. 59.

tively high transport costs. Moreover, restrictive arrangements affecting the distribution and price of building materials were common, since most producers belonged either to national or to regional associations, of which there were nearly one hundred. In fact there were few materials used in building construction whose price was not regulated at one time or another by either a combine, ring or other selling arrangement. The method of distributing materials was highly complex and led to further restriction. The bulk of builders' materials and components passed through the hands of builders' merchants, though some of the heavy products such as bricks and cement were distributed direct from manufacturer to contractor.[1] Altogether there were around 2,500 to 3,000 merchants of this sort and agreements between the producer and merchant as regards terms of sale made it difficult for the individual contractor to gain any advantage by purchasing direct.

In view of the wide range and variety of materials used in building it will be impossible to discuss them all separately. Nor would any great benefit be gained by doing so. Initially our main concern is with the price and supply of building materials as a whole in relation to demand. In particular we need to know whether building expansion was limited by either a shortage of materials or high prices. A second point which is worth consideration is the extent to which the cost of materials was reduced either by improvements in methods of production or by the introduction of new materials. This will obviously necessitate a more detailed discussion of the separate industries though reasons of space and availability of data will limit our review to one or two of the more important materials such as bricks and cement. Finally, we shall examine briefly whether the restrictive arrangements relating to the sale and distribution of building materials affected their price and supply in a manner detrimental to the building industry.

II. *Output, Price and Supply*

From the point of view of the building industry the position seems to have been almost ideal. The supply of materials was extremely elastic and output followed closely that of the building industry.[2] For most of the period it would appear that the supply of materials was adequate and the general downward trend in prices after 1920

[1] In 1948, for example, 50 per cent of the bricks were delivered direct to the user whilst 49 per cent were ordered but not stored by the merchants.

[2] See Table 4, Appendix, Chapter 2.

supports this conclusion. Temporary or local shortages did occur, however, from time to time. Immediately after the war the supply of all building materials fell far short of demand since production was well below the pre-war level. The output of most materials was probably less than 50 per cent of the pre-war level (see Table 11). This was largely due to the fact that many firms had ceased production during the war,[1] or had been taken over by the Government and used for purposes other than producing materials. Plant and buildings were badly in need of renewal by the end of the war. Timber supplies were also very short at this time; stocks were less than one-third the normal and current supplies were only sufficient to meet half the pre-war demand.[2]

Table 11: ESTIMATED OUTPUTS OF CERTAIN BUILDING MATERIALS IN 1918 AND 1921 AS PERCENTAGE OF THREE YEARS PRIOR TO WORLD WAR I

	Average three years prior to World War I	*1918*	*1921*
Bricks	100	33	117
Cement	100	56	108
Roofing tiles	100	6	87
Light castings	100	32	112

SOURCE: *Report of the Departmental Committee on the High Cost of Building Working Class Dwellings*, Cmd. 1447 (1921), p. 38.

Recovery in the production of building materials was extremely rapid indeed and by late 1920 and 1921 output of most commodities was about the same or above the pre-war level. One or two materials, notably timber and roofing tiles, remained scarce, however. The production of roofing tiles recovered more slowly than in the case of other materials, and though timber imports rose quickly to pre-war levels, supplies of really good, well-seasoned timber were extremely scarce for a few years.[3] Despite the recovery in production prices of building materials rose rapidly in the first two years or so after the war, though the building materials producers were in no way to blame for this increase. To a large extent it was a result of badly timed Government policy. At the end of the war it was quite clear

[1] Roofing tile manufacturers were worst hit in this respect; during the war 90 per cent of the firms closed down their works entirely. *Final Report on the Stone, Brick and Clayware Trades*, Cmd. 1209 (1921), p. 7.

[2] *Report of the Committee on the Building Industry after the War*, Cmd. 9197 (1918), para. 17.

[3] See M. Bowley, *Innovations in Building Materials* (1960), pp. 127–8.

that building materials were scarce and even more important that they would remain in short supply in relation to anticipated demand from the building industry for about two or three years. Yet early in 1919 the Government released nearly all building materials from wartime control. Although the operation of the wartime system of price and allocation controls for materials was far from being perfect it would have been preferable to continue control for a year or two longer in view of the conditions prevailing at the time, for, given the shortage in supply, the free market simply allowed prices to rocket upwards. Within a matter of months the price of some materials had nearly doubled and in 1920 the average price of all building materials was about three times the pre-war level. The pressure on prices was aggravated by two other factors. Throughout 1919 and for a good part of 1920 the transport system was disorganized and congested and this caused innumerable delays in the movement of materials. It is impossible to say precisely what impact this had on prices though it was considerable. According to one estimate, for example, congestion added £10 a standard to the cost of timber in freights and charges.[1] In addition there were increases in railway rates, wage and fuel costs in 1919–20. The second factor was the launching of the Government's housing programme in 1919–20 which brought further pressure to bear on the industry's depleted resources. The impact of the housing programme on the level of materials prices and costs of building has probably been exaggerated,[2] however, since work on the programme did not really get under way until late in 1920 by which time a decline in prices had already set in. Nevertheless, there seems little doubt that the rise in costs was accentuated by the decision to speed up the rate of housebuilding combined with a policy of unlimited subsidy.

Until 1921, therefore, the shortage and high price of building materials set a limit to the rate at which the building industry could expand. Price was probably the major deterrent in 1920 since builders were reluctant, even had sufficient materials been available, to construct houses when costs were at their peak. But apart from this it is probable that output of materials was getting back to normal in 1920 since in the following year a substantial increase in building output took place without any increase in the production of materials. After 1921 the curtailment of the local authorities' housing programmes relieved the pressure on the market and for the next two or three years the supply of materials remained adequate though there were, of course, one or two local shortages. Prices fell sharply in these

[1] *Report on Timber*, Cmd. 985 (1920), p. 6.

[2] See J. Sykes, *A Study in English Local Authority Finance* (1939), pp. 7–8.

years though even in 1923–4 they were still more than double the pre-war level (see Table 7, Appendix, Chapter 2). Thus when building activity increased substantially in 1924 the material producers had sufficient spare capacity to meet most of the demand. During the course of the year, however, local shortages of materials began to develop. In Scotland, for example, a number of building projects were delayed owing to inadequate brick deliveries.[1] The committee set up to look into the position regarding the supply of labour and materials had warned the Government earlier in the year that there was no great reserve of materials and that there was already a shortage of bricks and slates.[2] Although manufacturers of materials assured the Government that arrangements would be made for a substantial increase in supply to meet the full requirements of the new housing programme this could not be accomplished immediately. The result was that a temporary shortage of materials occurred in 1925 and 1926 though it is unlikely that this was very severe since the prices of materials hardly changed at all in these years. One thing is certain, however; the sharp increase in the cost of houses between 1924 and 1926 was not caused by a shortage of materials.[3] In the latter half of the 1920s the supply of materials kept pace with demand and prices fell slowly.

One result of the temporary shortages and relatively high prices of materials and labour in the early 1920s was that it encouraged a search for new materials and new methods of construction. The Government took an active interest in these questions. Between 1918–21 at least two official committees were set up to investigate the possibilities and a number of committees dealing with housing in general devoted part of their reports to these questions. In 1924 a further committee was established to make a special examination of new methods of building construction for the guidance of local authorities. After producing a number of interim reports dealing with steel, timber and concrete houses and substitutes for traditional materials, this committee, like the earlier ones, disappeared from the scene.[4] The impact of these investigations was very slight indeed, however. In 1921 a Building Research Station was set up (as a branch of the Department of Scientific and Industrial Research) to carry out

[1] *Sixth Annual Report of the Scottish Board of Health*, Cmd. 2416 (1925), p. 31.

[2] *Report on the Present Position of the Building Industry*, Cmd. 2104 (1924), p. 20.

[3] See below for a more detailed discussion.

[4] There is an excellent summary of these investigations in R. B. White, *Prefabrication: A History of its Development in Great Britain* (1965), pp. 42–62 and 73. See also the International Labour Office, *Housing Policy in Europe* (1930), p. 90.

scientific research into building methods and materials. It produced a series of important but dull reports to which few people paid any attention. In addition, a number of experiments were made with new materials and new methods of construction. The Government carried on a fairly active propaganda campaign and granted larger subsidies for the erection of experimental houses in various parts of the country in which steel and substitutes for plaster took the place of the usual materials. Moreover, a clause was inserted in the Housing Act of 1924 to the effect that if local authorities refused without valid reason to adopt approved building methods, the subsidy contribution from the Treasury would be reduced. Despite these attempts to encourage new techniques it is doubtful if more than 50,000 'non-traditional' houses of all types were built in the 1920s.[1] There were certain technical and other difficulties to be overcome before substitute materials and new methods of construction became generally acceptable. But perhaps a more important factor which delayed progress in this direction was the fact that most of the new materials and methods could not compete in price with traditional materials, especially after the price of the latter began to fall in the second half of the 1920s.

Certainly in the later 1920s and for most of the 1930s the price and supply of most materials was such as to give little incentive to the adoption of substitutes or new building methods. The index of building material prices fell steadily after 1925, and by 1933 a reduction of 25 per cent had taken place. It is true that prices began to rise slowly in the later 1930s but even in 1937 they were no higher than in 1928 and substantially below the level of the early 1920s. The supply of materials responded remarkably closely to the increased demand from the housing market in the 1930s, and only in the last few years before the war were there any real signs of supplies becoming difficult. In fact, the shortages were local in character and largely confined to Scotland. Here the position became quite acute in 1937 when many houses projects were delayed because of a shortage of bricks and Scottish slates.[2] By 1938, however, the position had eased considerably owing to a substantial increase in capacity in the preceding year.

Apart then from the temporary dislocating effects of war the supply and price of materials remained favourable to the expansion of the

[1] White, op. cit., p. 88.

[2] See *Report of the Committee on the Scottish Building Costs*, Cmd. 5977 (1939), p. 19, and *Tenth Annual Report of the Department of Health for Scotland, 1938*, Cmd. 5969 (1939), p. 28.

building industry throughout most of the inter-war years. The output of most materials expanded fairly rapidly and prices fell steadily between 1925 and 1934, and, though they rose again in the later 1930s, they were still about 13 per cent below the 1925 level in 1938. But as can be seen from Table 12 the decline in the price of building materials was much less than that of industrial materials and manufactures taken as a whole. Moreover, the fall in prices was by no means uniform for all materials; timber and cement prices fell much more rapidly than those of clay tiles and sheet glass whilst changes in brick prices were quite modest (see Table 12). Whilst the general downward trend in the price level was not conducive to the introduc-

Table 12: PERCENTAGE PRICE CHANGES OF CERTAIN BUILDING MATERIALS

	1925–34 *per cent*	*1934–8* *per cent*	*1924–38* *per cent*
All building materials	−25·2	+15·4	−13·7
Timber (1924–33)*	−41·0	n.a.	n.a.
Bricks—common Flettons (1925–35)	− 9·4	− 4·2	−13·0
London stocks (facings)	− 1·8	+16·0	+13·6
Sheet glass†	−24·3	− 3·5	−28·0
Cement	−37·0	+11·0	−30·0
Clay tiles	−22·3	− 5·2	−23·0
Clinker blocks‡	−28·0	0·0	−28·0
Roofing slates	−24·4	+ 6·1	−19·0
All industrial materials and manufactures	−33·0	+15·4	−28·1

* Swedish and Finnish 7-inch unsorted, per standard.
† Sheet 21 oz. price per foot super.
‡ 2 in. clinker blocks, price per yard super.

SOURCES: Maywald, op cit.; Bowley, op. cit., pp. 151–5; PEP, *Housing England* (1934), p. 108.

tion of new or substitute materials, the expansion in the demand for traditional materials led to considerable improvements in methods of production and part of the fall in prices can be attributed to increased efficiency on the part of manufacturers of materials.[1] Some idea of the way in which expansion affected the production of materials can be gained by considering one or two of the more important materials in some detail.

[1] That the price of building materials did not fall as fast as non-building materials can be explained partly by the fact that demand for the former remained more buoyant in the inter-war years.

III. *The Chief Materials*

a. Bricks

It is doubtful whether improvements in productive efficiency were always passed on fully to the consumer in the form of lower prices. This is especially true in the case of bricks which remained the chief walling material in building in this period. The output of bricks more than doubled in these years, the rate of expansion being most rapid in the 1930s (see Table 13). The most notable innovation was the rapid extension in the use of the new Fletton brick, the output of which rose fourfold between 1912 and 1937, and by the latter date they accounted for one-third of the total brick production. Flettons became generally acceptable as a common brick after the war largely on account of their cheapness,[1] made possible by the physical properties of the

Table 13: OUTPUT OF BUILDING BRICKS IN THE UK
(million bricks)

	Fletton	*Others*	*Tota*
1912	450	3,271	3,721
1924	n.a.	n.a.	3,939
1930	n.a.	n.a.	4,723
1937	2,600	5,169	7,769

Oxford clay used and their adaptability to large-scale production. The average output of Fletton plants was nearly ten times greater than that of ordinary brick works, and by 1937 one firm, the London Brick Company, dominated the market, accounting for about 60 per cent of the Fletton production. For most of the period the use of Fletton bricks was restricted geographically to Southern England (particularly London),[2] since transport costs made them uncompetitive with local bricks further afield. But in the years before the war Fletton producers were developing a nation-wide system of marketing and were beginning to compete effectively with local producers in many parts of the country.[3]

[1] Actually the price superiority of Fletton bricks was largely confined to South-Eastern England, which was the chief market for Flettons. In the inter-war years, Flettons were the cheapest bricks available in the London area but this was largely because there was an absence of competing supplies of cheap local bricks. The price of most London bricks, both Flettons and non-Flettons, was above that in most other areas except Bristol and Hampshire, and it was not until later on in the period that Flettons became competitive with local bricks outside London and the South-East.

[2] This was the main centre of production.

[3] On technical and aesthetic grounds, Flettons were not good substitutes for traditional facing bricks.

Productivity in the brickmaking industry as a whole rose fairly rapidly especially in the 1930s. Rostas has estimated that between 1907 and 1935 output per man rose by 31 per cent and output per man-hour by 47 per cent. For the years 1924 and 1937 Salter suggests a rise in output per operative of the order of 27 per cent together with a fall of about 25 per cent in the unit costs of materials and wages.[1] It is significant that the greater part of the productivity increase occurred in the early 1930s when expansion was most rapid and the average output per establishment rose from around 5 million to 7·2 million bricks per annum. This suggests that there were considerable economies to be derived from increasing the scale of production.[2] No doubt much of the improvement which took place was attributable to the Fletton group of producers whose large-scale mechanized plants were much more productive than those of the traditional brick producers. In 1935, for example, the man-hours required to produce 1,000 bricks in Fletton works was 9·6 as against 20·8 for all other brick producers. But the general expansion in output also encouraged modernization in non-Fletton works. Although there were no fundamental changes in the methods of producing bricks in these years considerable improvements in the design of machinery and kilns and in the methods of controlling, drying and firing the bricks were carried out. The great extension of plant and opening of new works encouraged mechanization and the use of best-practice techniques. In both the mining and moving of clay, for example, mechanized techniques spread rapidly. Before 1914 'clay-getting' was an arduous process and hardly touched by mechanized means; yet by 1937 only the clay for 37·8 per cent of the brick capacity and from 57 per cent of the clay-pits was obtained entirely without mechanical aids. Even so there were still considerable scope for greater improvements in efficiency. By the later 1930s production methods in brickmaking were still largely traditional. Apart from the Fletton branch little real attempt had been made to secure economies by large-scale production, or by reorganization of plant layout. The average annual output in 1935 was around 7 million bricks, which was far too small to permit complete mechanization. The optimum output was about 20 million and most of the brickworks of this size were Fletton establishments. In general the majority of brickworks was small,

[1] L. Rostas, *Productivity, Prices and Distribution in Selected British Industries* (1948) and W. E. G. Salter, *Productivity and Technical Change* (1960), p. 178.

[2] Rostas found that output per head increased almost continuously with the size of establishment and that plants in the largest size group were nearly twice as productive as those in the smallest. Rostas, op. cit., p. 123

badly planned and they wasted a great deal of labour in unnecessary handling of materials due to the old-fashioned conception that production was a non-continuous process. It has been estimated that up to 15,000 men or about one-quarter of the 1938 labour force could have been dispensed with had brickworks been reorganized and mechanized on modern lines.[1]

The building industry seems to have derived little benefit from the improvements which occurred in brickmaking in this period. Few of the productivity and cost gains were passed on to the consumer until 1934–6 when severe competition between brick producers forced down prices. During the 1920s and early 1930s brick prices remained remarkably stable, and even the price of Flettons fell by only 13 per cent between 1923 and 1936, and most of this reduction occurred within the last two years.[2] Compared with a 35 per cent reduction in the price of Portland cement in the same period the achievements of the brick producers appears decidedly poor, and it seems safe to conclude that the Fletton producers in particular were not over-anxious to extend the market for their products. Furthermore, the competition of Fletton producers does not appear to have stimulated innovations or improvements in the efficiency of traditional brick producers sufficient to enable them to compete. If anything the competitive gap between Fletton and non-Fletton producers widened during this period.

In view of the relative stickiness of brick prices in the inter-war years it is perhaps surprising that the supremacy of the brick as a walling material was never seriously challenged. This can be explained quite easily, however. Although prices were fairly steady, Flettons were considerably cheaper than the ordinary common brick and the range of their competition was increasing geographically throughout this period. This in itself limited the incentive to try out substitutes for the brick especially as there was always a danger that Fletton prices might be reduced sharply if an alternative material appeared as a serious competitor. In a way the Fletton producer safeguarded traditional producers from outside attacks for if Flettons had never appeared on the market the supply of bricks might well have been much less elastic and prices high enough to make other materials attractive as substitutes. As it was there was no great pressure from the supply side to replace the brick and although experiments were made with concrete, clinker blocks and certain cladding materials

[1] *Labour Requirements in the Brick Industry: First Report of the Technical Committee of the National Brick Advisory Council* (HMSO, 1947), p. 16.

[2] In fact the price of facing bricks rose steadily in the 1930s.

none of these provided a satisfactory substitute for the brick either because they were too costly or because they were technically or aesthetically inferior.

b. Cement and Concrete

Cement manufacturers achieved a much more creditable record than the brick industry in this period. Between 1912 and 1938 output almost trebled[1] and in the inter-war years (1924–38) the price of cement fell by nearly one-third, a larger reduction than for any other domestically produced building material. In 1938 the price of cement was only 60 per cent higher than in 1914 whereas brick prices, which fell only slowly in this period, were anything from 100 per cent above the pre-war level. Price reduction in cement was essentially the product of two factors: improved efficiency and severe competition in the cement market.

In the thirty years or so before 1939 the cement industry changed radically from an empirical trade, that is one based on old-established techniques and rule-of-thumb methods, to one organized and directed scientifically by the chemist. Technical innovation was extremely rapid though many of the changes which occurred in the inter-war years represented the application of earlier inventions or techniques. The emphasis was on the massive application of labour-saving devices. The old fixed kiln, for example, was completely replaced by the much more productive rotary kiln between 1907 and 1925 and from thence onwards development turned towards the application of much larger kilns. In addition, there was a rapid extension of mechanized or labour-saving techniques, the main ones being hydraulic drying and mechanical conveyance of the raw materials and finished products. In effect nearly all the capital equipment in use early in the twentieth century had been scrapped and replaced and capital per worker increased substantially. These changes were reflected in an enormous increase in efficiency. Between 1907 and 1938 average output per operative more than trebled whilst wage costs, which amounted to one-quarter of the gross output in 1907, had fallen to 13·5 per cent in 1935. The decline in the unit cost of manufacturing, which occurred as a result of these innovations and a fall in material prices, was not all passed on to the consumer, however. Between 1924 and 1935, for example, output per man-hour rose by 110 per cent whilst material costs fell by 43 per cent, giving in all a 46 per cent

[1] 1912, 2,722,000 tons; 1924, 3,240,000 tons; 1930, 5,056,000 tons; 1938, 7,715,000 tons.

reduction in prime costs which resulted in a decline of only 31·5 per cent in the ex-factory price of cement.[1]

It is doubtful, however, whether cement prices would have fallen as much as they did had fierce competition not forced prices down. Price wars had been frequent in this industry in the late nineteenth century and the effect had been to concentrate production in the hands of a small number of firms. By 1914 Associated Portland Cement Manufacturers dominated the market controlling about four-fifths of the total output. This, however, did not put an end to competition since a number of new competitors (e.g. the Red Triangle Group) emerged after the war with the result that by the later 1920s there was considerable excess capacity. Fierce price cutting developed in the trade which became particularly intense in the early 1930s with the collapse of the export market.[2] As a consequence most producers of cement joined together to form the Cement Makers' Federation in 1934 which provided for price fixing and the regulation of output on a quota basis. Henceforward price competition was eliminated though the agreement did not seriously restrict the supply of cement to the home market. It is worth noting, however, that the most significant reduction in the price of cement took place mainly during the period of acute competition between 1928 and 1934, and at a time when wholesale prices in general were falling rapidly, whilst in the later 1930s prices tended to remain stable or rise slowly. On the other hand, it should be noted that most of the productivity gains occurred before 1934 and that between 1935–8 output per operative rose by only 10 per cent.

Despite the substantial fall in price in this period concrete never seriously challenged the brick as a walling material, though it had long been in use for floors, frames and other internal work. Although many experiments were made to use cement for this purpose, especially at times when bricks were in short supply, it never became established as a satisfactory external walling material apart from one or two special cases. It tended to be considerably more expensive than brick and aesthetically it was much inferior. As an external facing material cement is cold and depressing and time and weather tend to make it dirty and untidy. Moreover, it is subject to cracking, crazing and shrinkage and suffers from moisture movements common to all concrete products. On the other hand, where appearance did not matter, as in the case of partition walling, breeze and concrete clinker blocks became accepted as a technicaly efficient and cheap

[1] Rostas, op. cit., p. 81.
[2] Exports of cement were halved between 1930 and 1933.

substitute for the common brick though for load-bearing walls their use was restricted by building regulations. Apart from this, however, many new developments in the use of concrete—e.g. pre-cast concrete wall units and light-weight aggregates[1]—still remained in their experimental stage and were generally unacceptable either because of their high cost or technical deficiencies.

c. Tiles

In one respect, however, concrete scored a resounding success in a new field. This was in its use as a roofing material. The concrete tile had been introduced as early as 1893 but by the end of the war it had made little headway and clay tiles and slates still remained the chief external roofing materials. Within the next few years the concrete tile became a serious competitor on account of its cheapness and by 1935 it accounted for about one-third of the total output of tiles (see Table 14). Although the price of clay tiles and slates fell considerably after 1927 the concrete tile remained a much cheaper product, the price differential being as much as 20s per 1,000 for the London market in 1938. The success of the new tile can largely be attributed to the founder members of the Marley Tile Company, the

Table 14: OUTPUT OF ROOFING TILES AND SLATES IN THE UK

	1912	*1924*	*1935*
Clay roofing tiles			
'000 tons	—	376	834
million	217	408	736
Concrete roofing tiles			
'000 tons	—	—	408
million	—	—	320
Roofing slates			
'000 tons	335	251	249

Aisher family, who began producing them in a small way in Kent shortly after the war. They realized that though the concrete tile was technically adequate it would remain an inferior roofing substitute and that its greatest compensating advantage would be one of cost. Accordingly they exploited the cost-reducing aspects of the innovation by producing tiles on a large scale with mechanized techniques. By the middle of the 1930s, when the original family firm had been converted into a public company, Marley Tile accounted for nearly

[1] That is concrete composed of cinder, clinker or other light-weight materials in place of crushed stone, gravel and sand.

two-thirds of the output of concrete tiles. It is possible that the competition of concrete tiles was one factor causing the decline in the price of slates and clay tiles since as far as is known there were no remarkable improvements in productive efficiency in these two branches during the period.[1]

d. Glass

Important cost-reducing innovations also occurred in the glass industry in the inter-war years. The two main sectors of the industry—sheet and plate glass—both experienced major innovations in this period. Briefly the effects of the new processes were to transform glass making into a fully continuous mass production process. At the same time considerable improvements in the quality of glass produced were realized which made it possible, among other things, to produce glass sheets and plates of almost any size or shape. These changes resulted in a rapid rise in productivity and falling costs of production. Between 1924 and 1937 the output of the glass industry as a whole (including the container section) doubled, whilst labour productivity increased by about 52 per cent. During the same period the unit costs of wages and materials fell by 20 to 25 per cent.[2] It is debatable, however, whether the effects of these innovations were reflected fully in reductions in price to the consumer. For example, the price of rough plate glass hardly changed at all after 1924 and by 1938 it was actually higher than in the former year.[3] Sheet glass prices, on the other hand, fell by about 28 per cent between 1924 and 1936, but since the major part of this reduction occurred prior to 1930 before the new techniques had really become effective it suggests that it was foreign competition (mainly from Belgian producers) more than anything else which was responsible for the fall. During the 1930s glass prices remained remarkably steady yet it was in this period that productivity increased most rapidly.[4]

Despite the substantial reduction in prices in the sheet glass section and the ability of producers to manufacture their product in almost any size and shape, there was no revolution in the uses made of glass in construction work. It continued to be used largely for windows of

[1] See Bowley, op. cit.

[2] Salter, op. cit., p. 178.

[3] Bowley, op. cit., p. 285.

[4] Output per operative increased as follows:

1924=100
1930=111
1935=135
1936=152

the traditional size. New architectural ideas (mainly of French origin) on how to employ glass extensively for roofing and exterior walling gained ground very slowly in this country and only a few experiments—mainly office blocks and flats—were made which used glass lavishly. To a large extent this slow acceptance was simply one of resistance to new fashion though there were other factors involved which retarded its adoption. Aesthetically glass may well have been equal to brick, but it had a number of disadvantages, the most obvious one being that of durability. A further defect was that it had limited resistance to extremes of heat and cold. Large glass buildings were likely to be extremely uncomfortable unless properly insulated from the elements. The cost factor was not entirely irrelevant either. Even though glass became cheaper in these years framing costs remained high which meant that the cost advantages in favour of using more glass in place of brick were very fine indeed.[1]

e. Timber

Undoubtedly the most important material used in building (that is, in terms of costs) was, and still is, timber. Its importance varies, of course, depending on the type of building, but roughly 15 per cent of the cost of an average house can be accounted for by timber including joinery. Changes in the conditions of supply and price of timber are likely, therefore, to have an important impact on the total cost of construction. In the inter-war years the bulk of the timber used in building was imported and hence the supply in this country depended very much on the state of things in the world market. Unfortunately statistical data relating to timber supplies is very incomplete and unsatisfactory but the information available on prices makes it possible to say something about general trends. In the immediate post-war years there is no doubt that timber was very scarce. During the war imports had been cut drastically and by 1918 they were barely 20 per cent of the 1913 level. Stocks of timber in Britain were the lowest on record, whilst timber supplies coming on to the world market were only about half the pre-war level. The price of timber even under official Government control was about three to four times greater than pre-war.

The decision to remove control from timber in 1919 inevitably led to a further rapid increase in prices—for some varieties of timber prices almost doubled between 1919 and 1920. High prices did, however, encourage a rapid increase in imports, even though the world supply situation was far from normal. One of the chief causes

[1] Bowley, op. cit., p. 290.

of the scarcity was the absence of Russian supplies which had been responsible for about one-third of Britain's timber imports before the war. It was not until after 1920 that the position really began to ease as alternative sources of supply, mainly Swedish and Finnish, became available. Then prices fell dramatically; by 1922–3 timber prices were less than half the 1918 level and probably not much more than double the pre-war price. Supplies continued to increase in the 1920s[1] and the reappearance of Russia as an important timber exporting country later in the decade brought a further sharp fall in prices in the early 1930s. By this time some classes of timber were almost as cheap as pre-war,[2] and on average the price of timber fell by about 40 per cent in the decade 1922–32. This reduction was substantially greater than for most other materials, and in view of the relative importance of timber as a cost item in building it was obviously an important factor in reducing the overall costs of construction in this period. For most of the 1930s the supply and price of timber remained favourable to the building industry. According to one authority imports of timber specifically for building doubled between 1931 and 1936 (£20·5 to £47·0 million).[3] In the later 1930s (1936–8), timber prices rose sharply due to speculation and a rise in freight rates. However, there is no evidence to suggest that building contractors found any real difficulty in obtaining adequate supplies of timber except perhaps in Scotland.[4]

IV. *Distribution and Credit*

Insufficient data precludes an examination of the other less important materials used by the building industry. There is, however, little evidence to suggest that the trends in the price and output of these materials were markedly dissimilar from those of the major material inputs. But a few general remarks must be made about the distribution of building materials since contemporary writings often ques-

[1] Imports of softwood (the chief type used in building) rose by 50 per cent between 1922 and 1927, from 3·9 to 6·0 million loads.

[2] E.g. carcassing timber £14 10s a standard in July 1931 as against £14 in April 1914.

[3] R. F. Bretherton, F. A. Burchardt and R. S. G. Rutherford, *Public Investment and the Trade Cycle in Great Britain* (1941), p. 297.

[4] The Scottish position is rather curious. For some reason timber prices there rose very rapidly in the later 1930s. Possibly the explanation lies in the fact that much Scottish wood was drawn from Baltic sources and it was here that speculation in the trade and freight increases were most prominent. See *Report of the Committee on Scottish Building Costs*, Cmd. 5977 (1939), p. 21.

tioned whether the delivery of building materials through builders' merchants was as cheap and efficient as it might have been.

As far as the large building contractor was concerned the system of distribution was far from ideal. Many of the merchants' yards were small, old-fashioned, badly equipped and run by people without any special knowledge of the business. Their dealings tended to be in small lots since margins were greater on such transactions. Moreover, the existence of a large number of distributive channels prevented the standardization of materials and components, and in effect offset the economies of large scale production which would normally have followed from the placing of large continuous orders. The unsatisfactory nature of the system was evidenced by the fact that some large contractors began to buy certain materials in bulk direct from the manufacturer, though the benefits to be derived from this approach were often more apparent than real on account of the agreements between manufacturers and merchants to maintain uniform conditions of sale for materials. It seems probable, therefore, that the large-scale contractor was forced to pay more for his materials than would have been the case had more efficient and less restrictive arrangements for the distribution of materials been available.

On the other hand, the merchant system was possibly of some considerable benefit to the small contractor and was one of the factors which made entry into the building industry relatively easy. The Simon Committee which investigated the system in 1948 were satisfied that the services provided by merchants were essential for the efficient functioning of the industry, and that a steady improvement in the range of facilities offered had taken place during the inter-war years. The merchant fulfilled two main functions: he carried adequate stocks of a variety of building materials which could be delivered to the contractor at frequent intervals and he provided the builder with credit facilities, technical advice and information. Whether the merchants performed their services as well as the Simon Committee would have us believe is another matter. Many of the concerns were too small and badly organized to perform the services properly and efficiently and in effect all that they were doing was acting as selling agents for the manufacturers.[1] Probably their most useful function was in the provision of credit facilities. Unlike the large-scale contractor, whose operations were financed mainly by issues of share capital, the small firm or specu-

[1] A fact which did not escape the Committee's notice entirely. See *Report on the Distribution of Building Materials and Components* (HMSO, 1948), p. 48.

lative builder with little capital equipment relied mainly on short-term finance. The builders' merchant and the banks were the two main sources of credit the charges for which varied with the rate of interest.[1] Although credit was not a very significant item in the total costs of building construction it is probable that easier credit terms in the 1930s encouraged a greater amount of speculative building than in the previous decade when interest rates were high.[2] But fluctuations in the supply and price of credit were certainly not an important factor in determining changes in the volume of building work as they had been in the nineteenth century.[3]

Builders carrying out contract work were, however, less dependent on these sources for financing their operations. In most building contracts provision was made for payments to be made on account. Thus the builder was paid at regular intervals whilst the work was in progress though usually 10 per cent or so of the valuation payment was withheld for up to a year after the contract had been completed in order to ensure that he made good any defects in the work which might later arise. By this process it was possible for the builder to proceed with only a limited call on the services of credit agents.

V. *Conclusions*

In general the supply of traditional building materials was fairly elastic in response to rising demand throughout the inter-war years. Temporary or local shortages did occur, especially immediately after the war and in Scotland, but they were never of sufficient duration to act as a serious check to the volume of building, or encourage an intensive search for substitutes. Furthermore, the nature of the market for building materials was not such as to encourage the rapid development of alternative materials. Generally speaking, apart from experiments in industrial building, there were no fundamental changes in the design or construction of buildings which were likely

[1] There is scarcely any reliable statistical information regarding the respective importance of the two sources of credit. The Macmillan Committee on Finance and Industry (*Report*, Cmd. 3897 (1931), p. 298) suggested that the London Clearing Banks had £47·8 million worth of advances outstanding to the building trade at the end of 1929. In relation to the total volume of building work at this date the amount is quite high and one might therefore reasonably conclude that bank credit was the more important of the two.

[2] It has been argued that in the later 1930s speculative building was encouraged by easier credit terms. See *Report on the Distribution of Building Materials and Components* (HMSO, 1948), p. 37.

[3] See J. Parry Lewis, *Building Cycles and Britain's Growth* (1965).

to provide a market for new materials. This is particularly true of residential accommodation which simply required a greater quantity of materials of the traditional type. These conditions provided, of course, opportunities for innovations and improvements in the manufacturer of building materials and as we have seen in some cases (e.g. sheet glass and cement) the improvements led to substantial reductions in price.

On the other hand, it would be wrong to assume that there were no new developments in the field of building materials. The rapid expansion in the use of the Fletton brick and concrete tile would certainly not support such a conclusion. In addition, many experiments were being made with less important materials some of which became firmly established by the 1930s. The most notable examples were the use of asbestos cement sheet as a cladding and roofing material and the development of fibreboard and plasterboard as substitutes for lining and partitioning work. Furthermore, in non-residential building work reinforced concrete and steel structures were gaining ground albeit slowly.[1] But few of these developments could be said to have been brought about by changes in design or pressure from the supply side of traditional materials. To a large extent they were simply the product of the growth of the market which no doubt favoured the development of cost-reducing innovations many of which were adopted by private builders catering for the mass market. Otherwise conditions in general were not conducive to the rapid development and adoption of new materials or alternative uses for old ones in the inter-war years. Apart from the reasons we have already mentioned, it was often the case that they were technically and aesthetically inferior substitutes, and it took time before they were accepted by the general public.

Prices of most materials tended to be in a downward direction for most of the period, though the magnitude of the reductions which took place varied considerably. Timber prices fell more rapidly than other materials, whilst brick prices did not decline very much in spite of a considerable improvement in manufacturing methods. It is almost certain, however, that prices of most materials were not as low as they could have been. In the first place not all the improvements in manufacturing were passed on to the consumer; the most notable case in this respect is that of bricks though the same is also true to some extent of the cement and glass industries. Secondly, there was clearly scope for further considerable improvements in the

[1] M. Bowley, *The British Building Industry; Four Studies in Response and Resistance to Change* (1965), Chapter VII.

efficiency of production methods especially in the brick industry, which would have reduced costs and hence prices. Thirdly, it is possible that the prices of some materials were higher than necessary on account of restrictive agreements among producers and the relatively ineffidient methods of distribution. The price of nearly all materials used in building was controlled either by trade associations or one or two producers.[1] It is difficult to say how effectively prices were regulated as a result of these agreements. Generally control tended to be intermittent since it often broke down when competition became acute. It is unlikely, therefore, that the trade associations ever managed to maintain prices at unduly high levels, though the conclusion of agreements often led to price increases. The first effects of the cement makers' agreement of 1934, for example, was that prices were raised by about 20 per cent.

[1] E.g. 98 per cent of the wallpaper was produced by three firms.

CHAPTER 7

TECHNICAL CHANGE, EFFICIENCY AND AGGREGATE COSTS

A reduction in the costs of building can be obtained in one of two ways: either by a fall in the costs of inputs, that is labour and materials, or through an improvement in the industry's efficiency. We have already seen that the trend in labour and material prices was downward for a good part of the inter-war period and it now remains to be shown whether there was any improvement in technical efficiency which would have facilitated the cost-reducing process further. It will then be possible to examine the course of aggregate costs of the building industry.

I. *Changes in Efficiency*

Unfortunately the task is by no means an easy one owing to the difficulty of constructing reliable estimates of productivity for an industry whose product is so differentiated. Moreover, there are considerable problems of definition and classification, whilst the absence of a reliable and continuous series of labour statistics makes comparisons with pre-war extremely hazardous. The first attempt to estimate productivity was made by a Working Party Report inquiry into the man-hours required to produce local authority houses.[1] It came to the conclusion that output per man-year in 1937 was between one-third and one-half greater than in 1924. But since it was reckoned that a sharp fall in productivity had occurred between 1914 and 1924 the authors concluded that output per man could not have exceeded the pre-war level by a very large margin. Apart from the fact that this inquiry was limited to one sector of building it seems likely that the estimate for the years 1924–37 was inflated unduly largely because it was based on the assumption that building productivity was low in 1924. It is unlikely, however, that recovery after the war was so slow and, given the fairly rapid expansion in output between 1920 and 1924–5 without any significant increase in the labour force, it would be reasonable to conclude that productivity increased considerably in these years. Recent estimates suggest a

[1] Ministry of Works, *Working Party Report on Building* (HMSO, 1950), p. 80.

fairly steady improvement in output per operative hour in building and contracting between 1907 and 1935 although the performance between 1924 and 1935 was well below that of industry as a whole (see Table 15).

Table 15: ANNUAL RATE OF PRODUCTIVITY INCREASE IN THE UK (per operative hour, per cent per annum)*

	1907–24	*1924–35*
Total all industries	1·6	2·2
Building and contracting	1·7	1·2

* Cf. Feinstein who gives an annual compound rate of 1·0 per cent (output per man-year) for the construction industry between 1924 and 1938. Feinstein, op. cit., p. 53.

SOURCE: K. S. Lomax, 'Production and Productivity Movements in the United Kingdom since 1900', *Journal of Royal Statistical Society*, 122 (1959).

Though the productivity gains made in these years were by no means spectacular it is almost certain that by the late 1920s the industry was more efficient than it had been in 1913. Moreover, compared with the nineteenth century the 1 per cent or more annual growth in productivity in the inter-war years was quite creditable. According to G. T. Jones physical output per man year in the London building trade rose by only 17 per cent in the period 1850 to 1910.[1]

II. *The Role of Technical Progress*

Even for the inter-war period the productivity estimates are still very tentative and it could well be that the improvement in efficiency was greater than the data suggest. But on the basis of what we know about changes in techniques in building during this period it seems highly improbable that productivity growth could have been much higher. Technical progress was by no means absent, of course, but there is little evidence of a massive application of new techniques or radical change in the organization of the building trade which could have resulted in a rapid rise in the industry's efficiency.[2] A brief

[1] G. T. Jones, *Increasing Return* (1933).

[2] See *Working Party Report on Building*, op. cit., p. 80. This conclusion seems to be borne out by American experience as well. According to one notable authority the application of large-scale cost reducing techniques has been almost as limited as in Britain with the result that productivity advances in building construction in the twentieth century have been very slight indeed. See L. Grebler, D. M. Blank and L. Winnick, *Capital Formation in Residential Real Estate* (1956), App. C, pp. 354–7.

summary of the main technical changes and their impact will make this point clear.

At least three types of technical improvements can be discerned in building in this period. First of all a number of new building materials were introduced some of which were applied fairly extensively. The most notable examples were the common Fletton brick and the concrete tile both of which were discussed in some detail in the previous chapter. Other new materials coming into use included asbestos cement sheet, fibre and plasterboard, steel and reinforced concrete, though rarely were they used on a wide scale. In most cases new materials were simply substitutes for, or variations of, older traditional materials. Moreover, their introduction did not lead to improvements in the efficiency of the assembly process, though in so far as they were cheaper than the older products they did help to reduce the overall cost of building construction.

The second major technical advance was the development of new structures in place of the traditional brick and stone. Several experiments were made with standardized, prefabricated structures using steel, cast iron, reinforced concrete and timber. Such experiments were generally carried out on large-scale projects such as blocks of flats or office accommodation where standardized steel frames were increasingly used to speed the process of construction. It has been estimated that the time required for the erection of large projects was reduced by up to 40 per cent when prefabricated steel structures were used for the shell of the building.[1] Even in housebuilding new structures were introduced, though rarely did they get past the experimental stage in this period. In addition, there was an increasing tendency for large building firms to use prefabricated fittings such as metal doors, windows and cupboards which were produced in factories and then fixed into the buildings by semi-skilled workers.

Finally, as regards the actual assembly process on the building site, there was some progress towards the introduction of labour-saving equipment. In fact new mechanical appliances became quite common on the larger building sites, though most of them were used in the early stages of construction. They included such things as cranes, hydraulic and pneumatic riveters, rock drills, steam shovels, hoisting engines, concrete-mixers, woodworking machinery, cement-guns and paint-sprays. Furthermore, seasonal stoppages in building work were reduced by the use of braziers and artificial light and by the erection of the roof at an earlier stage of the proceedings. On the other hand, many of the traditional crafts of bricklaying, plastering and painting

[1] H. W. Robinson, *The Economics of Building* (1939), p. 16.

remained largely untouched by mechanization and as a result the efficiency of these workers improved very little throughout the period.[1]

In sum, therefore, the technical improvements hardly constituted a revolution, and it is not difficult to see why productivity gains in building were only modest. Of the technical developments which occurred only those relating to new structures and mechanical equipment were likely to have had any real direct impact upon the efficiency of the building industry. But their application was far from extensive. It has been estimated that the technical changes as a whole (including new materials) related at the most to about one-quarter of the value of the output of the building industry.[2] For the most part it was the large contractors who adopted new methods of construction and mechanical equipment and even then their use was generally confined to large industrial and commercial buildings, office blocks and flats. The most important sector of the industry, residential building, remained virtually unaffected by the new methods. By and large the process of housebuilding remained much the same as it had been in the nineteenth century, a labour intensive, traditional craft occupation in which mechanized techniques were rarely applied. That mechanization did not proceed very far in the building industry is borne out by the very low, and virtually unchanged, level of capital equipment per worker employed in the industry.[3]

Certainly compared with the nineteenth century there were some notable changes in the inter-war years but there still remained considerable scope for further improvements in technical efficiency. The planning and management of building operations both before and during the course of construction were particularly defective and much time was often lost through a failure to co-ordinate properly the various components of the assembly process. Most contemporary authorities were of the opinion that the organization and methods of the building industry were grossly inefficient and that considerable cost reductions could have been achieved by the widespread adoption of best-practice techniques.[4] The reasons for this failure to do so are not difficult to find. In the first place the existence of so many

[1] H. W. Robinson, *The Economics of Building* (1939), p. 16.

[2] H. Barham, *The Building Industry* (1945), p. 5.

[3] See Chapter 5, p. 119.

[4] E.g. Political and Economic Planning, *Housing England* (1934), pp. 10–12; H. W. Robinson, *The Economics of Building* (1939), p. 16; International Labour Office, *Housing Policy* (1945), pp. 9–10.

small units in the building industry acted as a barrier to progress since it was often uneconomic to adopt new techniques unless operations were carried out on a large scale. Many firms, for example, would have found it difficult to provide the necessary sequence of operations to justify a heavy initial outlay on capital equipment. Moreover, the small firm was unable to secure economic advantages by purchasing raw materials and standardized fittings in large quantities.[1] Secondly, apart from the immediate post-war years the supply and price of materials and labour was such as to give little encouragement to the application of cost-reducing innovations or labour-saving devices. Apart from the lack of incentive from the supply side it must be remembered that new materials and methods of construction often created changes in the design of buildings which the general public were slow to accept. Even had prefabricated or industrialized systems of building been really commercially viable it is unlikely that they would have been used extensively in residential construction since the demand was largely for the traditional type of house. Finally, it can be argued that the fluctuating demand for buildings made it difficult for the industry to plan operations in such a way as to secure the greatest economies in costs of production.

III. *The Pattern of Aggregate Costs*

Given the limited technical progress and fairly modest improvement in the productive efficiency of the building industry in the inter-war years it would seem that the main cost-reducing element in building work came from the supply side. In this section we propose to draw together the cost items in building which have been discussed in the previous chapters. The main object here is to discover how far changes in the price of materials and labour were reflected in the actual cost of construction and whether changes in the costs of construction had any effect on the rate or level of building output, or conversely, whether changes in building output affected the level of costs.

To illustrate these points three statistical series will be used. The first of these is the index of building costs constructed by Maywald which includes the cost of materials (ten items) and labour weighted

[1] The ability of the small firm to carry out research into new materials and methods was also limited and this undoubtedly explains why knowledge about new techniques spread so slowly. The industry itself carried out little research, most of it being done by the Government sponsored Building Research Station.

equally. This index does not include, of course, changes in the cost of land and credit but since, as argued earlier, neither of these were very important in relation to total costs of construction we have assumed them to be constant. A satisfactory series for the actual costs of building construction presents greater difficulties. It would be easy to take the average cost of all dwellings built as a basis but this would not be very reliable since it does not allow for changes in the size and standard of accommodation. Hence we have used an index of the cost of building per square foot. The main objections to this series is that it relates only to the average contract price of three-bedroomed, non-parlour council houses. There is no reason to assume, however, that this index is not a reasonably reliable indication of trends in the cost of all building though there may be some discrepancy between tender and final prices and between council and non-council building costs. For the total output of building work we have used Feinstein's gross capital formation series relating to residential construction and other buildings. It was felt that in this context the Lomax index of building and contracting would not be entirely satisfactory since it includes certain public works and civil engineering projects the costs of which would not be reflected in the index of the cost of building per square foot.

The main statistical indices are reproduced in Table 16.[1] The first thing to notice is that the swings in actual costs of construction tended to be greater than the fluctuations in the price of materials and labour. This was true whether the market was a rising or a falling one. Between 1913 and 1920 the index of building costs rose by 197 per cent whereas the increase in the cost of building per square foot was 267 per cent. The same thing happened between 1923 and 1925 when the increases recorded in the indices were 3·9 and 13·6 per cent respectively. In the later 1930s (1934–8), however, the sequence was not repeated and both series rose by roughly 13·5 per cent. On the other hand, when prices fell, as they did between 1920 and 1922–3 and again 1925–34, final costs of building declined more rapidly than the price of materials and labour. Between 1925 and 1933, for example, the cost of building per square foot fell by 27·4 per cent whereas the index of building costs fell by no more than 19 per cent. In fact by the late 1920s and throughout the 1930s the final costs of building were lower than the price of materials and labour in relation to the pre-war levels. This suggests that for much of the period, and especially between 1925 and 1934, not only was the downward trend in the price of supply factors reflected in the

[1] The actual series are given in Appendix, Chapter 2, Tables 1, 4 and 7.

Table 16: INDICES OF COSTS OF CONSTRUCTION AND BUILDING OUTPUT

(1930=100)

	Index of building costs (labour and materials)	*Cost of building* per square foot*	*Total houses built*	*Local authority houses*	*GDCF in Building*	
					Non-residential building	*All building*
	(1)	(2)	(3)	(4)	(5)	(6)
1913	57·8	61·0				
1919	146·0	182·3				
1920	171·8	223·8	23·2	27·9	98·8	57·1
1921	140·5	178·7	58·2	142·6	75·3	66·5
1922	113·6	103·7	52·4	109·8	51·9	53·2
1923	106·9	107·9	45·2	32·8	60·5	53·6
1924	110·9	111·6	70·2	39·3	70·4	69·9
1925	111·1	122·6	88·9	82·0	74·1	82·3
1926	107·8	117·7	113·9	137·7	65·1	93·6
1927	105·9	118·3	124·0	196·7	66·6	99·0
1928	101·7	105·5	94·7	114·8	75·3	86·7
1929	102·2	101·2	109·6	119·7	88·9	99·5
1930	100·0	100·0	100·0	100·0	100·0	100·0
1931	96·2	96·9	105·3	126·2	69·1	90·1
1932	91·8	90·2	107·2	109·8	60·5	87·2
1933	90·0	89·0	146·2	114·8	65·4	108·9
1934	90·2	89·6	165·9	123·0	83·9	126·1
1935	92·0	87·2	167·3	114·8	95·1	126·1
1936	95·6	93·3	176·0	142·6	101·2	128·1
1937	100·4	103·7	175·0	150·8	129·6	134·0
1938	102·3	101·8	172·6	200·0	120·9	129·6

* Average cost of three-bedroom non-parlour council house reckoned per square foot within walls.

SOURCES: Based on Maywald, op. cit., R. L. Reiss, 'Municipal and Private Enterprise Housing', *Building and Society*, 1945; Feinstein, op. cit.

final costs of production but also that some improvement in the efficiency of building operations occurred the benefits of which were passed on to the consumer.

The relationship between costs and fluctuations in the level of building activity is by no means clear cut. One might expect a rough sort of positive correlation between costs and the level of output on the grounds that when the industry is working close to full capacity the pressure on supply factors increases and prices are likely to rise, whilst in times of slack demand and low output the opposite effect is likely to occur. In fact, however, this was not always the case in the inter-war years for the two variables were often inversely correlated. Between 1925 and 1934 when building costs were falling steadily there were considerable fluctuations in the level of output (all building) with peaks in 1927, 1930 and 1934. On the other hand, costs of building rose in the later 1930s by which time residential construction had already passed its peak and the curve of real investment in all building work was flattening out. This suggests, therefore, that for much of the time the costs of building were independently determined and were not particularly responsive to changes in the level of output. Furthermore, it means that expansion in building activity was never really checked by pressures from the cost side, though it is possible that the combined upswing in local authority building and non-residential construction from 1935 onwards was partly responsible for the shift upwards in the costs of construction and the decline in investment in private enterprise housing. Investment in non-residential dwellings was inversely correlated with that of residential accommodation.[1] Had this not been the case the index of building costs might well have fluctuated more closely with building activity between 1925 and 1934 instead of falling continuously as it did do.

The position in the early 1920s is more complicated because of the dislocating effects of war and the impact of the changes in subsidy policy. It has been argued that the subsidies were responsible for the fluctuations in the cost of housing in this period though the evidence is by no means conclusive on this point.[2] In 1920, when building costs were at their peak, the new housing programme had hardly got under way, and by the time it did, that is in 1921 and early 1922, costs had already fallen sharply. The pressure on costs was largely caused by the immediate post-war shortages of labour and materials, the low productivity in building at this time and the vigorous demand

[1] This aspect is dealt with fully in Chapter 10.

[2] J. Sykes, *A Study in English Local Authority Finance* (1939), pp. 8–9.

for new industrial and commercial building which seems to have reached a peak in 1919–20. Subsidies in fact had very little to do with the inflation in costs of this period though it is possible that the launching of the new housing programme in 1919 encouraged builders and producers of materials to revise their prices upwards before demand actually became effective.

The shift upwards in the final costs of building between 1922 and 1925 is less easy to explain since the index of building costs did not begin to rise until 1924 and even then the movement was very modest. Although the subsidy policy may have aggravated the situation in 1924–5 it cannot be held responsible for the initial increase in costs since the Chamberlain and Wheatley Acts did not become effective in terms of output until 1924. On the other hand, private unsubsidized housing and non-residential building moved up sharply from the low levels reached in 1922, which put pressure on the industry just at the time when the new subsidy terms were announced. Hence what seems to have happened is that builders took the opportunity of the favourable situation to inflate their earnings by raising contract prices unduly. Only this can explain the discrepancy between the movements in the index of building costs and the final costs of construction. After 1925 both series began a downward trend despite the fact that building activity in general continued to expand fairly rapidly until 1927. Changes in subsidy policy cannot explain the initial downturn since the first reduction did not take place until 1927, though the fairly sharp fall in costs in the following year was no doubt partly caused by the rapid contraction in subsidized building. However, by this time costs were obviously moving independently of building activity and the continuous fall which took place up to 1935 can be attributed to a secular fall in the price of factor inputs, together with improvements in the efficiency of building operations. It was in these years that the major cost-reducing improvements in the production of building materials took place, a fact which supports the conclusion that costs moved independently of building output.

Thus the fluctuations in the level of building activity had only a marginal effect on the costs of construction. For much of the period costs moved independently of output and there were few occasions when the pressure of demand on capacity brought about a sharp rise in production costs. Even between 1923–5, when output expanded sharply, it was the rise in builders' margins which was largely responsible for the inflation in selling costs. It is doubtful, too, whether building activity was ever seriously checked by high costs except in

1919–20.[1] On the other hand, did falling or low building costs stimulate building activity at all? Possibly the revival in private building after 1922 was a response to the dramatic fall in costs between 1920 and 1922, though by 1924 the position was distorted because of the Chamberlain subsidy. The impact of the much slower but protracted fall in building costs between 1925 and the early 1930s is more debatable, however. There are so many other factors involved, such as changes in subsidy policy, rising real incomes and cheap money policy, that it is difficult to isolate the effect of falling building costs.

Nevertheless, it is probable that the influence of this item on the housing market has been underestimated by many writers who have been more interested in the impact of cheap money. It is true that cheap money tends to coincide with a sharp upswing in residential construction in 1933 and 1934, but there is no doubt that it would not have been as effective had it not been preceded by a substantial fall in building costs. By 1933 when cheap money really began to be effective the final cost of construction was 26 per cent less than in 1925. It is difficult to believe that this did not have a significant effect in extending the market for housing. Moreover, there is evidence to suggest that falling costs were having an effect on the private sector long before the emergence of cheap money. Private unsubsidized building began to rise after 1927 and between 1928 and 1931 the number of houses produced doubled from 64,740 to 128,418, a rate of increase which was almost as great as that in the three years after the adoption of cheap money. Moreover, in 1935, when building costs turned upwards, activity in this sector began to decline. Although the evidence is by no means conclusive there is a case for arguing that not only was the fall in construction costs an important factor in sustaining the demand for housing after the cut in subsidies in 1927, but also that it played some part in determining the sharp upswing in building in the early 1930s.[2] These points will be analysed in greater detail in due course, but first we must examine how Government policy (including cheap money) affected the housing market in the inter-war years.

[1] Temporary saturation of the market was a more important factor in the decline in residential construction in the later 1930s than the rise in costs.

[2] It should, of course, be borne in mind that the prior fall in capital costs of construction tended to reduce the effectiveness of cheap money.

CHAPTER 8

GOVERNMENT POLICY: SUBSIDIES, SLUM CLEARANCE AND RENT CONTROL

I. *The Role of the State*

In the inter-war years Government policy had a considerable influence on the level of building output. Before 1914, however, the State, both at the central and local level, had played a relatively insignificant role in the provision of housing accommodation. In fact the central government took virtually no part at all and even the local authorities confined their activity largely to the task of ensuring that houses were provided with reasonably adequate sanitary arrangements. Only a very small proportion of the total houses built—less than 6 per cent in the years immediately prior to the war—were provided by local authorities and property development was left largely in the hands of the private builder or speculator. The war and its aftermath brought a radical change. The rapid rise in the rents of houses caused partly by the virtual cessation of building activity, forced the Government to take its first major step into this field. In 1915 rents of most houses were controlled or frozen at their pre-war level, and although this was only regarded as a temporary measure at the time the policy of rent restriction was continued throughout the inter-war years. The second legislative step took place soon after the war. The shortage of accommodation, coupled with the reluctance of private enterprise to build houses at a time when costs were high, forced the Government and local authorities to participate directly in the housing market. In 1919 two general Housing Acts were passed which provided Treasury subsidies to encourage housebuilding. These in fact were the first of a long series of Acts designed to stimulate the provision of accommodation especially for the working classes. Throughout the 1920s general subsidies were provided quite liberally by the Government, and when this source of funds was curtailed in the early 1930s the State did not withdraw from the field but shifted its attention to the problems of slum clearance and the abatement of overcrowding. During this period the municipal authorities built houses on a scale never before conceived possible. Their major contribution came in the first decade or so after the war, but even in the 1930s they continued to provide new accommodation and by 1939 they owned well over one million houses. The State's activity did not cease here. In various ways, especially in the 1920s, it attempted, albeit somewhat halfheartedly, to improve or facilitate the supply of building materials and labour. In addition a number of committees were set up to investigate the possibilities of using new materials and new methods of house construction.[1] Apart from its direct contribution Government policy also had an important—some would say crucial—indirect influence on the housing market in the 1930s. The shift to cheap money policy in 1932, together with measures which encouraged the development of domestic as opposed to export orientated industries, produced conditions which favoured investment in housing.

Quite clearly, therefore, the State's role in the housing market in the inter-war years was substantial and merits special attention. Over 40 per cent of the houses built in this period were subsidized either by central or local funds whilst nearly one-third of the new houses were provided by local authorities. The contrast with the pre-war policy, which was mainly of a permissive nature, is even more striking if we examine the early 1920s. In the three years 1919–22, local authorities built no less than 60 per cent of the new houses whereas in the late nineteenth and early twentieth centuries they had rarely provided more than 5 per cent in any one year. Undoubtedly this was a tremendous revolution and one which was largely brought about by the almost complete cessation of housebuilding during the war. The enormous backlog in supply which resulted forced the Government to take immediate action, and throughout the 1920s housing policy was designed to foster building in order to relieve the shortage of accommodation. Moreover, the growing problem of urban renewal, caused by the obsolescence of many houses built in the nineteenth century, ensured the continuance of State participation in the housing market during the 1930s. But at the same time one should also recognize the fact that social and political pressures in part determined the type of policy pursued. Throughout the inter-war years various attempts were made by the authorities to provide decent accommodation at a reasonable price for those sections of the community whose requirements were least likely to be satisfied if left to the forces of the free market. Thus, for example, the rent control and slum clearance legislation can be conceived in part as a response to the social needs of the community.

The State's activity in the housing market was therefore motivated by a variety of considerations, though its precise role was not always

[1] These aspects are discussed in Chapter 6.

made clearly explicit. Policy provisions, moreover, often varied, as in the 1920s, depending upon the prevailing financial and political circumstances of the time. In theory, of course, it is relatively easy to state explicitly what the chief aims of a housing policy should be. Ideally the State should take measures to ensure that the housing stock grows in relation to current requirements including the maintenance and repair of existing properties. Secondly, it should provide houses for those who cannot buy or rent them in a free market. At the same time in order to build houses as cheaply as possible it is desirable to maintain a fairly stable level of building output from one year to the next, since violent fluctuations in building activity tend to lead to low productivity in building. Not all these policies are mutually compatible, however. Rent control, for example, may provide houses at rents below the free market level for the poorer sections of the community but at the same time it could deter landlords from repairing their properties and discourage investors in housing and thus eventually reduce the supply of rented accommodation coming onto the market. Alternatively, if building is conceived as a stabilizing factor for offsetting fluctuations in other sectors of the economy, this may conflict with attempts to reduce the amplitude of fluctuations in the level of building activity in order to maintain a low level of building costs.

In practice, policy diverged considerably from these hypothetical criteria. Given the inexperience of the State in economic matters this is not surprising since some of the objectives, e.g. the role of stabilization policy, were only vaguely recognized at the time. Moreover, in the conditions obtaining at the end of the war the most essential task was to augment the supply of accommodation in order to relieve the general shortage. After this the second major problem to be tackled was the elimination of slum dwellings and the relief of overcrowding. Policy, therefore, tended to be of an *ad hoc*, short-term nature and it was designed primarily to relieve the more pressing housing problems rather than provide a lasting solution to them or fulfil the objectives of an ideal housing policy. In practice the policies adopted did in part meet these objectives, but it was more by chance than any express design on the part of the authorities that this was so.

In this chapter, therefore, we propose to discuss and assess the impact of the State's direct policy, namely the housing legislation and rent control. The following chapter will then be devoted to examining the influence of cheap money policy on the level of housebuilding in the 1930s.

II. *General Subsidy Policy, 1919–31*

a. The Housing Shortage

In the decade or so following the First World War the Government made its first major contribution towards housing the British people. Nearly two-thirds of the new houses built during the 1920s were either subsidized or constructed by municipal authorities. The scale on which the State participated in the housing market contrasts sharply with the pre-war period, but the reasons for its intervention are no secret. The most important single factor governing its actions was, of course, the acute housing shortage which existed at the end of the war. Housebuilding had virtually come to a halt during the period of hostilities and by the end of the war there was a considerable backlog of demand to be made good. Altogether in the UK the shortage amounted to roughly 865,000 houses. In addition, over 1·9 million new houses would be needed to satisfy the requirements arising from the growth in the number of families (1921–31) bringing the total to over 2·8 million in all (see Table 17).[1] This, in fact, represents the barest minimum number of houses required up to the end of 1931. It makes no allowance whatsoever for houses needed to replace slum dwellings and relieve overcrowding nor does it take account of the fact that a certain number of dwellings would come up for demolition.[2] Hence, even if the target were achieved, it would only mean that by 1931 the housing situation would be restored roughly to its pre-war position. Needless to say, the housing position in 1913 was far from satisfactory.[3]

If these requirements were to be fulfilled within a decade nearly 280,000 houses a year would need to be completed, that is a rate of

[1] The initial housing shortage is calculated by taking the excess of families over occupied houses from the 1921 Census for England and Wales, that is 979,000, subtracting all unoccupied houses (219,000) leaving a total of 760,000. To this must be added 95,000 for the estimated deficiency in Scotland and a rough estimate of 10,000 for Northern Ireland, giving a grand total of 865,000. This figure is an absolute minimum for it excludes single people wanting separate dwellings, assumes all unoccupied houses were occupied and makes no allowance for unhabitable houses. The basis of calculation of the growth in number of families is given in Chapter 2. These estimates differ somewhat from those of M. Bowley, *Housing and the State, 1919–1944* (1945).

[2] On the other hand, neither does it allow for the fact that new dwellings might be created by subdividing large buildings into flats, etc.

[3] This is particularly true of Scotland where at least 50 per cent of the population was living in overcrowded or slum dwellings. See *Report of the Royal Commission on the Housing of the Industrial Population of Scotland Urban and Rural*, Cmd. 8731 (1917).

building about double the annual rate of output in the peak pre-war boom decade 1897 to 1906. Moreover, nearly two-thirds of the additional new houses were required for the working classes. Clearly it was a gigantic task and one that private enterprise was unwilling to undertake alone in the uncertain conditions prevailing in the early post-war years. Supplies of materials and labour were short and the cost of building was prohibitively high. With competing claims for investors' funds the property market appeared a decidedly unattractive proposition. Under these circumstances, builders were extremely reluctant to produce houses either for sale or to let even for the wealthier classes. There was even less chance of the working classes

Table 17: HOUSING REQUIREMENTS IN THE UK, 1919–31 ('000)

Minimum shortage in June 1921	*Additional requirements for increase in families June 1921 to end of 1931*	*Total*	*Number required for working classes*
865	1,940	2,805	1,750–2,000

getting new houses at rents they could afford since, given the high costs, it would have been an unprofitable venture for either private enterprise or local authorities to undertake. The situation was obviously serious and one that would not resolve itself. There was an imminent danger, moreover, that unless immediate and drastic action was taken the shortage of houses would increase rather than diminish. The Committee on Working-Class Dwellings sitting in 1918 expressed grave alarm about the position and urged that immediate steps be taken: 'The shortage is so serious and the difficulty of meeting it so great that every assistance and inducement that can be offered to secure the building of suitable houses for the working classes ought to be carefully considered and none of them rejected that would help to remedy the present shortage.'[1]

b. Government Legislation

The Government's main solution to the problem was to stimulate both private enterprise and local authorities to build houses by subsidizing them. This policy was started immediately after the war, continued throughout most of the 1920s by a series of Acts and brought

[1] *Report of the Committee on the Provision of Dwellings for the Working Classes in England and Wales and Scotland*, Cmd. 9191 (1918), para. 18.

to an end in the early 1930s when official attention was diverted to the problems of slum clearance and overcrowding. Essentially the subsidy policy was a temporary expedient to tide over the period of high building costs. The fact that building costs failed to fall as far as anticipated whilst the shortage of houses continued explains why the subsidy policy was extended into the 1930s.

Basically the policy was a very simple one. The Treasury granted money (usually a fixed sum) towards the cost of construction of new houses whether built by local authorities or private enterprise. The terms and conditions on which the subsidies were made varied, of course, according to the legislative act under which they were granted. The first of these was passed in 1919 (the Addison Act) and was designed to encourage local authority housebuilding. The terms were extremely generous. All losses in excess of a penny rate incurred by local authorities were to be borne by the Treasury. The houses built were to be mainly working class dwellings the rents of which could be fixed independently of costs though these had to be approved by the Minister of Health since the lower the rents the greater the State's burden would be. Private enterprise was not included in this scheme but a further Act of the same year granted a small lump sum for houses built privately the size of which conformed to certain specifications. Both these subsidies were destined for a premature death. Because of the high building costs the first subsidy proved extraordinarily expensive and the Treasury was forced to retract. In July 1921 the number of houses eligible for assistance was limited to 170,000. Since this was only a little in excess of the number of houses for which contracts had already been agreed it virtually meant the end of subsidized housebuilding.

For nearly two years until the Housing Act of 1923 the Government remained aloof from the housing market apart from fulfilling the obligations it had already incurred under the Acts of 1919. The Chamberlain Act of 1923 was totally different from the first one passed in 1919. For one thing it safeguarded the position of the Treasury. The subsidy was limited to a maximum of £6 per house for twenty years and was made available for houses conforming to certain specifications built by private enterprise or local authorities. Secondly, houses subsidized under the Act were clearly not for the benefit of the working classes alone. The houses could be sold at any price or let at any rent and the local authorities were under no obligation to make any contributions from the rates. In fact the authorities were placed in a decidedly inferior position since they were only allowed to take advantage of the subsidy provided they could convince the Minister of Health that it would be better for them to build houses rather than private enterprise.[1] Clearly the aim of the Act was to prevent the local authorities from becoming permanent suppliers of working class housing as intended under the Addison Act. Moreover, the terms of the legislation were based on the erroneous assumption that the housing shortage would be over within two years, which explains why the subsidies were limited to houses built by October 1925.[2]

In view of the emphasis on private enterprise in the Chamberlain Act the Labour Government of 1924 introduced yet another subsidy scheme.[3] This made a number of changes. Local authorities were given back their powers to provide working class housing without first having to satisfy the Minister that they could not be provided by private enterprise. The houses they built were eligible for a subsidy of £9 per house per annum for forty years in urban areas and £12 10s in rural parishes, and the contribution from the rates was fixed at a maximum of £4 10s on each house built. These subsidies were also made available to private enterprise but only on condition that they built houses to let at rents which did not exceed those charged by local authorities for similar houses. In other words, all houses built with the subsidy whether by local authorities or private enterprise were to be for letting. On the matter of rents the Wheatley Act of 1924 was extremely vague. An attempt was made to return to the principles of the 1919 Act by fixing rents in relation to the controlled rents of pre-war houses. The controlled rents, however, were only to be a basis for the *average* rent charged by each authority and this average rent was not to exceed the rents of similar controlled houses unless annual costs incurred by local authorities exceeded their contribution of £4 10s per annum per house. Thus, as long as they satisfied these conditions, it was left to the discretion of the local authorities to fix the rents they would charge for individual houses. What this in effect meant was that the Wheatley subsidy might be as regressive as the Chamberlain one between families and areas. Apart

[1] Local authorities were empowered to advance money to people wanting to buy their own houses and also to make grants to landlords carrying out repairs to houses. These powers were only used to a limited extent. By 1935, for example, local authorities had only advanced £12·7 million for house purchase.

[2] A slum clearance grant was also available under this Act, but little use was made of it.

[3] The Chamberlain subsidy was not, however, abolished but in fact its provisions were extended practically unaltered for 15 years, that is the subsidy was available for houses completed before October 1, 1939. In 1929, however, the subsidy was withdrawn altogether. See below.

from the broad distinction between rural and urban areas little recognition was given to the fact that the needs of certain families and particular areas differed considerably. Although the Act did nothing to prevent the use of differential rents local authorities were unlikely to introduce them since it would entail shifting a greater financial burden onto some other section of the community. The one great asset of the Wheatley Act was that subsidies were only available for rented property which had to be let at reasonable rents.

The new provisions were accompanied by a long-term plan which envisaged the building of 2·5 million houses of the type required within fifteen years. This would involve constructing an ever-increasing number of houses each year, starting at the rate of 90,000 in 1925 and reaching a peak of 225,000 per annum in the years 1934–9. To achieve this target the Government made arrangements with representatives of the building industry and trade unions, the object of which was to devise means for ensuring that there would be sufficient labour and materials available.[1]

Such ambitious plans were never to be achieved—at least not by subsidies alone. The late 1920s saw the beginning of the end of the general subsidy policy. Various arguments were put forward to secure their reduction or abolition. It was claimed that they were proving excessively costly, and that when costs fell they ought to be reduced. Some argued in favour of their abolition altogether on the grounds that the housing shortage was almost over. The result was that in 1927 the Chamberlain and Wheatley subsidies were reduced; two years later the former was abolished altogether and the Wheatley subsidy was cut again.[2] The subsequent economic crisis accentuated the trend against general subsidies and as official attention turned towards problems of slum clearance in the early 1930s the demise of the Wheatley subsidy was only a matter of time. At the end of 1932 it was withdrawn thus bringing to a close the general subsidy policy which began in 1919.

c. Overall Effects of Policy

So much for the Government's housing legislation. Although official policy changed frequently in this period there was one underlying theme namely to encourage housebuilding by subsidies. How far did this policy succeed in fulfilling the main objectives of British housing policy in the decade or so after the war? The major task, as we have

[1] *Housing* (*Financial Provisions*), Cmd. 2151 (1924). See Chapter 5.

[2] In actual fact the second Wheatley cut was restored by the Labour Government in 1929.

already noted, was to build enough houses to eliminate the absolute shortage produced by the war and at the same time keep pace with additional requirements created by population growth. The majority of the new houses were needed for the working classes whose main requirements were that houses should be built to let at rents they could afford. Equally important were the problems of slum clearance and overcrowding which were already serious at this time, especially in Scotland. Until the early 1930s, however, virtually nothing was accomplished in this respect largely because official attention was occupied with the task of trying to solve the first two problems.

Although subsidized building continued after 1931 we have taken this year as the terminal date since most of the subsidized building under the general subsidy policy had in fact been completed by this time and the remaining building under the Wheatley Act was confined largely to the local authorities. The general results of the policy can be seen from Table 18. The most striking fact to emerge is the high proportion of houses that were subsidized. Nearly 60 per cent of the 2,051,000 houses built in the UK between 1919 and 1931 were subsidized and local authorities accounted for over one-third of the total output of houses. In Scotland the importance of subsidized building was much greater, accounting for about 85 per cent of the houses built. It would seem, therefore, that subsidies were relatively effective in getting houses built. On the other hand, even after a decade of subsidized building the housing shortage was greater than it had been at the beginning of the 1920s. When account is taken of the number of houses demolished, the outstanding deficit of houses in the UK in terms of immediate requirements amounted to over a million houses at the end of 1931.

Table 18: HOUSES BUILT IN THE UK, 1919–31
('000)

Houses built (1919–31)	2,051
Houses demolished	290
Net increase	1,761
Requirements	2,805
Deficit outstanding end 1931	1,044
Number of subsidised new houses	1,197
Number of houses built by local authorities	751

SOURCES: Table 17 above and Table 1, Appendix, Chapter 2.

The results are even more disappointing as regards the type of houses built. Roughly two-thirds of the estimated houses required up to 1931 were for working-class dwellings and the remainder for the upper and middle classes. In fact the proportions in which houses were built were almost the reverse. Just over 60 per cent of the new houses constructed in England and Wales between 1919 and 1931 were non-working class dwellings, that is with a rateable value of over £13. By the early 1930s enough houses had been built to cover all middle-class needs up to 1941.[1] In contrast working-class requirements were far from satisfied except in Scotland where local authority (low rateable value) building predominated. In Great Britain the number of working-class houses built was barely 700,000, that is, about 40 per cent of actual requirements.[2] The failure to meet working-class requirements is not difficult to explain. For one thing private enterprise contributed virtually nothing to this sector of the market. Only 14,000 houses of a rateable value up to £13 were built between 1919 and 1931. The reason for this is simply that private enterprise found it more profitable to build houses for those people who could afford to buy them or could pay economic rents. This is certainly true of unsubsidized building since it would have been economically impossible given the level of building costs to provide houses at a price the working man could afford. Even with a subsidy under the Chamberlain Act the lowest possible rent (excluding rates) worked out at over 10s a week, which was far too expensive for many working-class families. In any case there was no guarantee that houses would be let at the minimum rent. It is true, of course, that lower rents were possible with the more generous Wheatley subsidy but in

Table 19: HOUSES BUILT IN DIFFERENT RATEABLE CATEGORIES 1919–31

	Great Britain	*Metropolitan Police District*	*England and Wales*	*Scotland*
Class A	359	Over £45	Over £35	Over £45
Class B	747	£20–£45	£13–£35	£26 5s–£45
Class C	691	£20 or under	£13 or under	£26 5s or under

NOTE: The total of this column does not agree with the figure in Table 18 because of the exclusion of several months building in 1931 and the omission of Northern Ireland.
SOURCE: *Report of the Inter-Departmental Committee on the Rent Restriction Acts*, Cmd. 5621 (1937–8), pp. 13–15.

[1] M. Bowley, 'Fluctuations in Housebuilding and the Trade Cycle', *Review of Economic Studies*, 4 (1936–7), p. 174.

[2] Pressure on the working class housing market was relieved to some extent by a process of filtering-up. See below.

view of the attractive conditions on which private enterprise could build houses with the Chamberlain subsidy, little attempt was made to use the former subsidy to build working-class dwellings. In fact the terms of the Chamberlain subsidy were such (namely, freedom to sell or let houses at any price) as to encourage private builders to provide houses for the non-working-class market. It is not surprising, therefore, that nearly all the subsidized houses built by private enterprise in the 1920s were assisted by the Act of 1923.[1] Now even had all these houses been let at the lowest subsidized rent possible, they would still have been outside the means of many working-class families.[2] Thus in effect the subsidy policy allowed private enterprise to build houses for a class of people least in need of accommodation and who at the same time could generally afford to pay an economic rent for their accommodation.

d. Weaknesses in Local Authority Building

It was left, therefore, to the local authorities to provide the bulk of the working-class dwellings in this period. Had they maintained the 1921 (87,000 houses) rate of building up to 1931, some 225,000 additional houses could have been built. But, in fact, the output of local authorities fluctuated considerably and in some years it was extremely low.[3] The subsidy policy was partly to blame here. The sudden withdrawal of the Addison subsidy in 1921–2 checked local authority housebuilding. The Chamberlain Act of 1923 only served to discourage local authorities even further since it placed the main emphasis on private enterprise. Thus, by 1924, their output was not much more than one-quarter of 1921 and it was not until towards the end of 1925 that the Wheatley subsidy began to take effect. No sooner had local authorities begun to increase their output of houses appreciably than the Wheatley subsidy was cut. This again produced uncertainty and output of houses dropped sharply after 1927. But the subsidy cuts were not solely responsible for the relatively low level of local authority building in the years that followed. Despite the subsidy cut it was possible to let a Wheatley local authority house at 6s 6d in 1929 compared with 7s 5d in 1926 owing to the fall in construction costs. No doubt many authorities delayed expansion again

[1] It is not a coincidence that more houses were built with the Chamberlain subsidy in the 1920s than with any other subsidy. The totals built under the respective Acts in England and Wales up to March 1932 were as follows:
1919=174,635, 1919 (2)=39,186, 1923=438,047, 1924=411,135.

[2] See Bowley, op. cit., pp. 99 and 114.

[3] For details see Table 1, Appendix, Chapter 2.

until it was clear how far the fall in costs would compensate for the reduction in the subsidy, but perhaps an even more important factor was that local authorities in the less prosperous regions were reluctant to expand their building programmes again because of the danger of being unable to find tenants who could afford to pay the rents. Whatever the reason there is no doubt that had the subsidies been concentrated more heavily on those regions which needed them most, and had the Ministry exerted greater pressure on local authorities to maintain or expand their programmes, local authority building would have been considerably more buoyant after 1927.

Although most of the houses built by local authorities were of the working-class type it is doubtful whether they were occupied by those families who needed them most. Bowley has argued that it was a relatively small group of better-off working-class families who got the subsidized local authority houses. Yet it was precisely these families who were least in need of financial aid and could afford to pay economic rents.[1] Why did the poorest families with incomes below £3 a week not get these houses? There are a number of possible explanations for this. In the first place local authorities were inclined to let their houses to the more prosperous working-class families since they were less likely to default on their rent payments. Secondly, the rents charged for most local authority houses were beyond the means of most of the poorer working-class families. The lowest possible rent of houses built with the Wheatley subsidy was between 7s and 8s until the end of 1928, and even when building costs fell it was still around 6s 6d. This level of rents was about equal to or slightly above the national maximum of 6s to 7s a week, which it was considered could be afforded by this class of tenants.[2] But the local authorities were not obliged to charge the lowest rents possible and it is probable that the actual level of rents was higher than these figures suggest. Unfortunately, detailed statistics of local authority rents are not available for this period, but a survey carried out by the Ministry of Health in 1936 suggests that more than one-half of the local authority houses in county boroughs and other urban districts and roughly two-thirds in rural districts were let at rents above the appropriate maxima.[3] These proportions would probably be even

[1] M. Bowley, *Housing and the State, 1919–44* (1945), pp. 129–30.

[2] Ibid., pp. 96–9.

[3] *Rents of Houses and Flats owned by Local Authorities*, Cmd. 5527 (1936–7). The Ridley Committee in 1937 estimated that the average local authority rents were 16–25 per cent higher than those of controlled houses and only slightly below the uncontrolled rents.

greater for houses built before 1931 since the figures given in the survey included the houses built with the Greenwood subsidy when costs were lower. There were, of course, considerable variations in the level of rents between different areas but generally speaking the rents charged were too high for the lowest income families of the working-class community.

Furthermore local authorities did little to fix rents according to the capacity to pay of individual tenants. Few authorities introduced differential renting or rent rebate schemes before the 1930s.[1] This is perhaps not surprising since the subsidy policy provided no encouragement to do so. The only provision was that rents had to be reasonable and the importance of providing houses to let at various levels of rents was ignored. No attempt was made to grade subsidies according to variations in levels of rents and it was up to the local authorities themselves to choose whether or not they would provide houses to let at rents within reach of the lower income groups. In practice they chose to ignore the problem since it would probably have involved a greater financial burden on the rates.

e. Regional Variations

A further defect of the subsidy policy was that it did not differentiate between areas.[2] The same amount of subsidy was given regardless of where the houses were built. The result was that the financially weaker local authorities and those authorities in depressed regions were unable to take advantage of the subsidies to the same extent as the more fortunate authorities. Thus in Merthyr Tydfil and in West Hartlepool the Treasury contribution to the Chamberlain and Wheatley subsidies worked out at 6d and 2s respectively *per capita* in 1931 as against 6s 6d in Leeds and 3s 2½d in Birmingham.[3]

It is probable, too, that the flat rate type of subsidy which made no distinction between areas and income groups was partly responsible for differences in the rates of building in relation to requirements of different regions. Housing requirements differed considerably in various parts of the country yet there was no attempt to gear the subsidy accordingly. Where the demand was greatest, in the South and Midlands, the rate of building was higher than in the North and Scotland. On the other hand, in the latter areas the need for small subsidized houses was greater than elsewhere and it appears (see Table 20) that proportionately more local authority or subsidized

[1] See below.
[2] Except for the broad distinction between rural and urban areas.
[3] Bowley, op. cit., p. 131.

private enterprise houses were built in these regions than in the South. But a more detailed county breakdown gives the impression that there were wide discrepancies in rates of supply in relation to needs. Some counties, such as Cornwall, Sussex, Suffolk and Northumberland, did very well whilst others, e.g. Durham, London and Middlesex and Gloucestershire, fell far short of the requirements for additional houses over the period 1921–31.[1] It is true that the rate of increase in supply tended to be higher in counties where requirements were high but this was a result of private enterprise rather than local authority activity. Generally speaking, private enterprise proved

Table 20: HOUSES BUILT PER 1,000 OF 1931 POPULATION SINCE 1919

	South	*Midlands*	*North and Wales*	*Scotland*
Unsubsidized	21	10	8	4
All houses	41	42	33	28

SOURCE: M. Bowley: 'Some Regional Aspects of the Building Boom, 1924–36, *Review of Economic Studies*, 5 (1937–8).

to be much more responsive to local requirements than the local authorities; in thirty-seven counties the average rate of local authority supply was only half that of private enterprise. In fact, the proportionate contribution to requirements made by local authorities was inversely correlated with the rate of requirements, for in counties where requirements were high the local authority contribution tended to be relatively small.[2] In other words, as far as the local authorities were concerned, the subsidies did not produce rates of supply commensurate with requirements and their performance tended to be least satisfactory in areas with relatively large requirements of working-class houses. The conclusion to be drawn from this is obvious. To be really effective subsidies needed to be applied discriminately, that is in relation to the needs of particular areas and families, for local authorities with large working-class house requirements were unwilling, given the financial burden involved coupled with the inability of many tenants to pay their rents, to respond on the scale required without additional financial incentive. The net result was that in the absence of differential subsidies the local authorities

[1] See Bowley, op. cit., pp. 64 and 66.

[2] For a detailed analysis see Bowley, op. cit., pp. 61–9, and 'Local Authorities and Housing Subsidies since 1919', *The Manchester School*, 12 (1942).

confined their activities to providing houses for their more prosperous working-class citizens.

f. Appraisal of Government Policy

Taken all round the general subsidy policy was not an unqualified success. After more than a decade of subsidized building there was still a shortage of at least a million houses in the UK (1931). The position was even worse than on first sight. Virtually nothing had been done to tackle the problem of insanitary dwellings. Moreover, there were wide discrepancies in the performance rates of various counties; in 1931 over 30 per cent of requirements were still outstanding in several counties whilst in others the proportion was less than 10 per cent. By far the greater proportion of houses built in this period were designed for people whose needs were the least pressing. Private enterprise, though subsidized heavily, built practically no working-class houses. This job was left to the local authorities who built slightly less than 40 per cent of the houses required in this category. Even then, however, the poorest families appear to have had difficulty in acquiring council houses. Throughout the period there seems to have been a continuous built-in bias working in favour of the more affluent classes. Of course, indirectly the working classes stood to benefit in so far as it was possible for them to 'filter' into the old properties vacated by their more affluent neighbours. But old property was a poor substitute for new, especially after 1923 when the rents of vacated dwellings were determined in the free market.

The character of the Government's housing policy was largely responsible for the defects which occurred. The subsidy policy is especially open to attack. In the first place it was a mistake to subsidize private enterprise without ensuring that the houses built were sold or let at a price the working classes could afford. Secondly, little attempt was made to vary the scales of subsidy according to the differing needs of particular regions and families. The fixed or flat rate subsidy was given on the erroneous assumption that conditions were uniform throughout the country, and that all tenants could afford to pay the same rent. The absence of a clearly defined rent policy was a further major defect of the policy. Finally, the inadequate output of local authorities can be attributed to three factors: the absence of proper central control over their activities, the lack of a continuous national housing programme and the periodic interruption and alteration in the subsidy programme. Nevertheless, whatever its defects one thing can be said in its favour:

that without subsidies far fewer houses would have been built especially in the early 1920s when conditions were not propitious for unassisted private building. In contrast to the pre-war period the Government had made an important contribution to the housing market in the 1920s and though mistakes were made these can perhaps be partly accounted for by the fact that the State was still a novice in this field.

III. *Slum Clearance and Overcrowding*

a. Introductory

In the early 1930s the Government's housing policy changed dramatically. Regardless of the fact that there was still an overall shortage of houses, and an acute shortage of modern houses to let at reasonable rents for the working classes, the local authorities were told to restrict their building activities and it was announced that as from December 7, 1932, the general subsidies under the Wheatley Act would be discontinued. The economic crisis of 1931–2 was not wholly to blame for the rather sudden suspension of operations. The Ministry of Health was fully under the impression that the housing shortage had been solved by this time. Hence the obvious conclusion was drawn that subsidies and municipal building on a general scale were no longer necessary. Private enterprise would be able to provide all the working-class houses required in the future and local authorities would be able to confine their attention to special tasks such as slum clearance and the abatement of overcrowding.

Little had been done to tackle these twin evils before 1930. Although local authorities had possessed powers since 1875 to deal with slums, little attempt had been made to use them. Between 1875 and 1930 probably less than 200,000 people had been removed from slum areas and rehoused.[1] After the war local authorities had a legitimate excuse for their inactivity in this direction in that they were busy with the task of clearing away the shortage. Attempts at large-scale demolition of old houses at this stage would have only aggravated the situation. Moreover, apart from the Chamberlain Act of 1923, the housing legislation of the post-war period provided little financial incentive to deal with the problem. Yet by the end of the first post-war decade it was becoming clear that action would soon have to be taken. A large proportion of the houses which had been built in the nineteenth century were nearing the end of their

[1] *Particulars of Slum Clearance Programmes furnished by Local Authorities*, Cmd. 4535 (1934), p. 3.

life cycle and would require replacing in the near future. By the middle of the 1930s over 3 million houses, more than one-quarter of the total stock of houses in Great Britain (1935), were at least eighty years old.[1] Not all of these houses constituted slum dwellings in the strict sense of the term but it is fairly certain that the large majority of them failed to satisfy the minimum requirements of modern accommodation since many of them lacked even the most basic amenities. The position was most acute in the large towns such as Manchester, Glasgow, Liverpool, Birmingham and Leeds where by contemporary standards up to one-third to one-half of the existing dwellings could be classed as slum properties.

b. Slum Clearance

However narrow the definition of slum dwellings might be made, there is no doubt that the problem existed and that it was becoming steadily worse each year. This fact was recognized in 1930 when the Housing Act of that year introduced a new subsidy specifically for slum clearance. The subsidy was related not to the number of houses built but to the number of persons displaced and rehoused, which meant that it increased with the size of the family rehoused. In so far as the Treasury contribution varied according to differences in the ability of tenants to pay rents and differences in the costs of providing accommodation, it was more generous than the Wheatley subsidy, though on a flat rate basis there was little difference between the two scales.[2] The rents of houses built with the new subsidy were left to the discretion of the local authorities who could adopt rebate schemes and differential rent policies provided the rents were reasonably within the capacity of the tenants to pay.

Unfortunately the new scheme got off to a very bad start. It was introduced at a time when local authorities were running down their building programmes, and the subsequent economy campaign of 1931–2 made them unwilling to take effective action under the Greenwood Act. Apart from this the subsidy was inadequate to

[1] C. H. Feinstein, *Domestic Capital Formation in the United Kingdom, 1920–38* (1965), p. 218.

[2] Under the 1930 Act the Treasury contributed £2 10s for 40 years per person re-housed in rural parishes and £2 5s in urban parishes. The local authorities' contribution remained at £3 15s for 40 years per house. Under the Wheatley scheme the Treasury rate had initially been fixed at £9 per house per annum for 40 years in urban areas and £12 10s in rural parishes with a local authority contribution of at least £4 10s per house. Thus on the basis of four persons per new house the 1930 scale was less generous. After the reduction of the Wheatley scales in 1927 the Greenwood (1930) subsidy was slightly more advantageous.

enable local authorities to provide new houses at rents within the reach of displaced slum-dwellers until after 1933 when costs of building and rates of interest had fallen sufficiently to allow them to do so. Moreover, since there was little difference in the Wheatley and Greenwood rates of subsidy there was a strong temptation on the part of many authorities to continue building under the former until withdrawn at the end of 1932. Indeed, it was financially safer to do this since the type of tenants who occupied Wheatley houses were more likely to be able to pay a higher, that is economic, subsidized rent than slum dwellers rehoused under the 1930 Act.

It is not surprising, therefore, that by the spring of 1933, when economic conditions were becoming more favourable for subsidized building to take place under the 1930 Act, only 17,000 people had been rehoused from the slums under the new scheme. This inactivity prompted the Government to issue a circular to housing authorities in April 1933 informing them that progress with slum clearance schemes was far too slow, and that to ensure speedier action a combined effort between central and local authorities would be necessary. In future public money and effort were to be concentrated on clearing the slums whilst private enterprise would be left, unassisted, to provide accommodation for working-class requirements. In accordance with this new policy, every authority with a population over 20,000 was asked to submit programmes of action to be taken under the 1930 Act with a view to starting a five-year programme at once. The response was rapid. By the following year nearly all authorities had made surveys of their areas and presented estimates of the demolition and rehousing requirements. Altogether 266,851 houses were to be demolished in England and Wales and over 1 million persons rehoused which would require the construction of some 285,000 new houses. Similar, though less reliable, estimates are given for Scotland in Table 21. During the course of the programme, the estimates were revised, so that by 1939 the original demolition plans for England and Wales had been increased by 68 per cent.

The results of the slum clearance programme were satisfactory if the performance is judged by the original programmes of 1934. Over the period 1930 to the beginning of 1939 both England and Wales and Scotland exceeded their demolition targets of 1934 though the number of replacements fell slightly short of the original estimates. On the other hand, on the basis of the revised estimates progress was much less satisfactory. In Great Britain as a whole only 261,477 houses were demolished or closed out of a total of 604,517. It is doubtful, however, whether the housing authorities can be criticized too severely for failing to meet the revised targets since these were not drawn up until late on in the 1930s, by which time costs were rising and materials and labour for building were becoming more difficult to obtain. Moreover, one has to remember that in this period about five times as many people were rehoused from slum areas than in the fifty years prior to 1930. At the same time over 750,000 houses were rendered fit for human habitation by repair and renovation.[1]

Table 21: SLUM CLEARANCE PROGRAMME

At March 31, 1939	*England and Wales*	*Scotland*
New houses built (1930–9)	273,390	67,524*
Houses demolished or closed (1930–9)	272,836	70,104
Persons rehoused (1930–9)	1,092,526	315,578
Original programme (1934)—Demolition	266,851	66,417
Revised programme (1937–9)—Demolition	472,000	132,417
Deficit outstanding on revised programme	199,164	62,313

* Includes a small number of houses built before 1930 for slum clearance purposes.

SOURCES: *Twentieth Annual Report of the Ministry of Health, 1938–9*, Cmd. 6039 (1939) and *Tenth Annual Report of the Department of Health for Scotland, 1938*, Cmd. 5969 (1939).

The aggregate figures are somewhat misleading, however, for they conceal the geographical discrepancies in the achievements of various authorities. In some cases, e.g. Plymouth, Wigan and Dudley, where the scale of the slum problem was quite small, the original targets were far exceeded. In general it was in the large conurbations such as Liverpool, Manchester, Leeds and London, where the slum problem assumed gigantic proportions, that the programmes failed to be completed. To some extent this was the fault of the subsidy policy which did not make any distinction between rich and poor areas and those with large housing programmes and those with small ones. Thus authorities with heavy slum problems had to bear the greater absolute burden themselves. Although a discriminating subsidy policy would no doubt have facilitated progress in the worst areas the absence of this additional incentive was not the only reason for failure on the part of certain housing authorities. Sheffield, for example, with a programme approaching the dimensions of Liverpool, did far better than the latter and, in fact, built far more new replacement houses than Manchester whose target was con-

[1] M. Bowley, *Housing and the State, 1919–44* (1945), p. 152.

siderably greater (see Table 22). Moreover, although the absolute size of the slum problem was much less in the smaller towns than in the larger conurbations, in relation to the resources of the latter they may well have been as great. Thus the speed with which many of the smaller towns, even in the depressed areas, managed to fulfil or exceed their targets was evidence of the energy and willingness on their part to succeed rather than an indication of the relative insignificance of the problem within their boundaries. Much, therefore, depended on the initiative of individual authorities, particularly as

Table 22: SLUM CLEARANCE*

Area	*Houses to be demolished under 1934 plan*	*Number of houses built by Dec. 31, 1938*
London	33,000	22,656
Leeds	30,000	8,588
Liverpool	11,937	6,742
Manchester	15,000	7,888
Sheffield	9,000	10,012
Stoke-on-Trent	3,612	3,212
Birmingham	4,500	5,924
Bristol	2,900	3,400
Newcastle	2,253	3,999
Norwich	2,515	2,951
Nottingham	2,223	3,109
Plymouth	463	1,268
Wigan	470	1,116
Wolverhampton	2,378	3,004
Dudley	750	2,227

* We are indebted to Mr J. L. Marshall of Aberdeen University for these figures.

the Ministry of Health, once the initial directives had been issued and the programme was under way, did not take very much effective action to see that the programmes were carried out. Thus it was tempting when the initial surveys were being made for large city authorities in particular to under-estimate the extent of their slum properties. Towns such as Manchester, London and Liverpool contained at least twice as many slum dwellings as the targets originally set in the 1934 plan. Practically all housing authorities were guilty of this procedure and the fact that the original plans were revised considerably suggests that initial targets were far too small. For this the Ministry was as much to blame as its executive agents. Had the Ministry put pressure on the authorities to revise their targets at an earlier date instead of leaving it until the later 1930s when there was little chance of the revisions being completed in time, the results might have been better.

Probably the most satisfactory feature of the scheme was that the rents charged for the slum replacement houses were within the means of most of the former slum dwellers. On average the subsidized rents were 5s or less, which was below the national maximum rent fixed for the lowest class of workers. In 1934 average rents were as low as 3s 4d and even by 1938, after the rise in building costs, they had only risen to 4s 8d. But it was the fall in building costs and rates of interest in the early 1930s and not the subsidy which was responsible for the fall in rent levels. When the Greenwood Act was passed in 1930 local authorities could not afford to build houses to let at rents below about 6s a week, which was beyond the means of many inhabitants of the slum areas especially as removal to new areas often involved additional costs.[1] Even after the general level of rents had fallen it was found that some rehoused families could not pay their way. In order to alleviate the problem a number of authorities adopted rent rebate schemes or differential rents in order to assist those least able to afford the rents of the new houses. Although by 1938 only 112 authorities had introduced such schemes most of them were confined to assisting tenants rehoused under slum clearance and decrowding programmes. In all probably some 35,000–40,000 houses or families, or about 10 per cent of the rehoused total, were in receipt of rebates of one form or another.[2] Most of the authorities which granted rebates reported that without them it would have been impossible to carry out any comprehensive scheme of rehousing. The pity is that they were not applied more extensively particularly in areas where slum problems were serious. But the schemes tended to be least effective in areas with serious poverty and unemployment, that is where they were most needed. The obligation on the part of local authorities to balance their housing accounts meant that scales of rebate were generally less generous in those areas where large numbers of tenants were eligible for assistance of this kind. The problem could have been solved in one of three ways. The local authorities could have increased their own contribution from the rates for those dwellings occupied by the poorest members of the community, or they could have charged more realistic (economic)

[1] E.g. increased costs of travelling to and from work.

[2] See G. Wilson, *Rent Rebates* (1939, 3rd ed., Fabian Social Research Series, No. 28), pp. 10–14. Not all the rent rebates went to rehoused slum dwellers, of course.

rents for some of the houses built under earlier schemes (e.g. Wheatley) thus setting aside funds to subsidize less fortunate tenants. In 1936 the authorities had been given the power to amalgamate their housing accounts for houses built under the various Acts since 1919 so as to form one subsidy pool out of which rents of houses could be adjusted in accordance with tenants' capacity to pay. Little effort was made, however, to utilize this facility. The third alternative was to apply the Treasury subsidy more discriminately by concentrating it more on those areas which were most in need of it. But apart from variations in the subsidy according to the size of families, which seems to have been relatively ineffective, there was no attempt on a national basis to apply the subsidy more lavishly to those regions where the slum problem was most acute.

c. Overcrowding

The campaign for slum clearance was supplemented by a policy for the relief of overcrowding, initiated by the Housing Act of 1935. Local authorities were to survey the extent of overcrowding and provide sufficient accommodation to abolish it completely within five years following the slum clearance programme. Overcrowding was to be made a legal offence and local authorities were obliged to prevent its recurrence. Treasury subsidies were only available for specific cases and not, as for slum clearance, granted on all houses built to relieve overcrowding.[1] Exactly why subsidies for slum clearance and decrowding were differentiated in this way is unclear. Certainly it was not logical. The problems involved in clearing slums and abating overcrowding are very similar and in many cases they are caused by the same factors, namely because people cannot afford to live elsewhere or because insufficient accommodation is available. Recognition of these facts came belatedly in 1938 when the Housing Act of that year abolished the distinction between slum clearance and relief of overcrowding, and granted a uniform subsidy for both.

Before the authorities could set about their new task it was necessary to discover the extent of the problem. During the winter of 1935–6 the famous *Overcrowding Survey* was carried out; the investigation was mainly limited to working-class dwellings and in all

[1] Subsidies would only be available if (*a*) it was necessary to build flats, the subsidy being graduated according to the cost of site, (*b*) new houses were built to relieve overcrowding among agricultural workers, and (*c*) all things considered, the burden on the rates of providing new accommodation was unreasonable. The maximum grant was £5 per annum.

In all cases local authorities were to make contributions from the rates.

some 10 million or more were inspected throughout Great Britain. It revealed some 342,000 overcrowded dwellings in England and Wales equivalent to 3·8 per cent of the dwellings surveyed. In Scotland the position was much worse: nearly 259,000 dwellings or 22·6 per cent of the total were designated as overcrowded. The findings were not exactly startling. Indeed, the position was a good deal worse than these figures suggest. The standard set[1] was a very low one, the effect of which was to limit the schemes to the largest families living in the smallest houses. It failed to recognize that separate families require separate dwellings and in practice meant that living accommodation would have to be used as sleeping quarters. A family of eight allocated four small rooms would inevitably have to use one of its rooms for a dual purpose. Thus if a slightly higher standard had been adopted, requiring that the living accommodation should not be used for sleeping purposes, then the number of overcrowded families in England and Wales would have been 853,000, roughly 9·6 per cent of the total.

Unfortunately the operation of the scheme to abolish overcrowding was cut short by the war and the complete results of the progress made up to that time have never been published. Initially progress seems to have been quite rapid in England and Wales. By the end of 1937 sixty-five local authorities had completely abated overcrowding and the number of cases still outstanding was 258,792, a decrease of one-quarter on the original data. Only 6,547 houses had been built specifically for this purpose, which is not surprising in view of the unattractive nature of the subsidy. Progress had been achieved largely by rearranging tenancies and slum clearance projects, which in many cases helped to relieve overcrowding. After 1937 progress was probably slower; by March 1939, when nearly 24,000 houses had been built for decrowding, probably less than half the overcrowded families revealed in the 1936 Survey had been relieved. In Scotland little was achieved. By the end of 1938 it was reported that only 34,500 families, or just over 13 per cent of the total, had been removed from overcrowded houses. Even the Health Department acknow-

[1] The standard for measuring overcrowding was based on two factors: sex separation and capacity of the dwelling. As the number of rooms in a dwelling rose from one to five, the permitted number of persons was 2, 3, 5, 7½, and 10 respectively, and after that two persons for each additional room. Children under 1 were excluded and those from 1 to 10 counted as one-half. The sex separation test stipulated that two persons of opposite sex of 10 years or more should not sleep in the same room. Thus a couple with seven children under 10 years of age of which one was under 12 months might not be classed as overcrowded in a three-roomed dwelling!

ledged the fact that progress had been disappointing and excused itself on the grounds that local authorities found it more advantageous to pay greater attention to unfit houses than overcrowded ones.[1]

d. Conclusion

The achievements of the new policy of the 1930s were hardly spectacular, and by 1939 only the fringe of the problem had been attacked. Altogether barely 375,000[2] new houses had been built in Great Britain between 1930 and 1939 specifically for the purpose of abolishing the slums and overcrowded dwellings. To this must be added some 200,000 living units which provided relief to the problem but which did not involve new housebuilding.[3] This brings the total to 575,000, which may be compared with the total of roughly just over 1·2 million dwellings classified under the official decrowding and slum clearance schemes. Thus by 1939 the total arrears amounted to over 600,000 dwellings, though this does not make any allowance for the inevitable double counting between properties classified both as slums and overcrowded. Probably half a million or more would be a fairer estimate of the arrears on the official programmes.[4] But this represents the deficiency on targets embodying standards of the barest minimum. In other words, even if the housing authorities had managed to fulfil the targets set for slum clearance and decrowding they would only have made a beginning with the task of replacing the large amount of old nineteenth-century property which existed in Great Britain. Contemporary authorities on housing matters were not exaggerating when they suggested that 3 to 4 million or approaching one-third the total stock of houses were out of date and needed replacing. Official confirmation that their estimates were correct was given by the Minister of Health during the war. For England and Wales more than 1·5 million houses would be needed to provide each family with a separate dwelling and to relieve overcrowding, and a further 1·5 to 2·5 million would be required to replace slum dwellings and those grossly deficient in

[1] *Tenth Annual Report of the Department of Health for Scotland, 1938*, Cmd. 5969 (1939), pp. 21–2.

[2] This total includes a generous estimate of 10,000 new houses built by Scottish authorities to relieve decrowding.

[3] This again is a generous estimate. It does not include, however, the houses which local authorities renovated or repaired during the 1930s since most of these were not specifically classed as slum or overcrowded dwellings.

[4] A similar estimate was made by M. J. Elsas in *Housing Before the War and After* (1945), p. 68.

modern amenities.[1] Clearly the task was a gigantic one about which the pre-war housing authorities had only a hazy conception. The sanitary policy of the 1930s was no doubt novel and enlightened, but essentially it was designed to meet an emergency just as the general subsidy policy had been in the previous decade. The full implications of the policy were never pursued by the Government of that period and the resulting legacy was left for the planners of the post-war years.

IV *Rent Control*

a. Scope of Rent Control

It can be argued that a fair and equitable rent system is one of the chief prerequisites of a successful housing policy. Yet by 1939 no one had found a satisfactory method of ensuring that the most needy got houses at rents they could afford, or alternatively that houses with the highest rents were tenanted by families who could afford them most easily. Various schemes had been tried by local authorities to remedy the situation but little success was achieved. The rent system remained confused and haphazard with great variations in rents between areas and between types of houses. Different rents might be charged for old houses of the same type, size and age in the same area simply because some were controlled and some decontrolled, or because some were owned by local authorities and others by private enterprise. Rent control, whatever its advantages, only made things more complicated. So many statutes with overlapping clauses were passed that eventually few people knew exactly what the legal position was regarding rented property. One committee reviewing the position in 1945 was convinced that 'the difficulties and anomalies caused by the present system of control cause widespread and legitimate resentment and we are satisfied that the time has come for a determined effort to remove them'.[2]

When rent restrictions were first imposed in 1915 they were not designed exclusively for the benefit of the working classes. At that time most people lived in rented property and the purpose of control was to protect tenants from being evicted and prevent increases in rent. These restrictions applied to all houses except those with a very high rateable value and altogether 85 per cent of all dwellings were

[1] See 'The Assessment of Housing Needs' in *Planning*, No. 293, January 1949, p. 9.

[2] *Report of the Inter-Departmental Committee on Rent Control*, Cmd. 6621 (1945), p. 13.

subject to control. Contrary to original expectations rent control proved to be more than a temporary measure to meet war needs. The acute housing shortage coupled with the inflation in building costs after the war forced the Government to extend control in 1919–20 until it covered 98 per cent of all unfurnished tenancies.[1] Only new dwellings built after April 1919 escaped control. Rents could be raised by up to 40 per cent of the 1914 level. From then onwards rent control remained in force throughout the inter-war years though several attempts were made towards progressive decontrol of certain properties.

The first step in this direction was taken in 1923 following the Onslow report.[2] The Rent Act of that year continued to protect sitting tenants but provided for the decontrol of a house whenever a landlord regained possession of it. All houses then occupied by their owners were to be decontrolled immediately, and in certain cases rented properties could be freed from control where the landlord and tenant had reached agreement. When in 1931 the Marley Committee[3] reviewed the situation it found that decontrol had not progressed very far, except in the case of upper-class houses over one-third of which had been freed. On the whole the committee felt that decontrol had worked well in the case of upper- and middle-class housing and recommended that it should be continued. There was no longer an acute shortage of these houses and decontrolled rents had not risen steeply. On the other hand, the position was exactly the reverse as regards working-class houses. There was still a serious shortage and decontrol, in the few cases where it had taken place, had caused hardship to the tenants concerned. Hence it was suggested that no further decontrol should take place in this category.

Most of the committee's recommendations were embodied in the Rent Act of 1933. It divided all houses into three categories (A, B, C) according to rateable value. All class A houses were to be decontrolled at once. Those in the intermediate group were still subject to the Acts but became free when the landlord gained vacant possession. But for the lowest category of houses no further decontrol was allowed. As a result the proportion of controlled houses steadily diminished in the 1930s, the main changes taking place in Class B.

[1] Thus bringing houses of rateable value up to £105 in London, £90 in Scotland and £78 elsewhere within the orbit of control.

[2] *Final Report of the Departmental Committee on the Increase of Rent and Mortgage Interest (Restrictions) Act*, 1920, Cmd. 1803 (1923).

[3] *Report of the Inter-Departmental Committee on the Rent Restriction Acts*, Cmd. 3911 (1931).

By 1937 nearly 60 per cent of all houses were free of rent control (see Table 23). A further measure of decontrol was introduced in 1938 when the rateable values above which control could be removed were reduced. Thus by the beginning of the Second World War, when control was reimposed again, nearly 70 per cent of all dwellings were free, leaving about four million dwellings still subject to control.

This brief survey has shown that rent control was applied to a steadily diminishing proportion of houses throughout the inter-war years. Two questions are of immediate interest. How did control or decontrol affect the tenants and landlords and what impact did the rent restriction policy have on the housebuilding industry and on investors in property.

Table 23: THE EXTENT OF RENT CONTROL 1931–7
('000 houses)

	England and Wales		*Scotland*	
	1931	*1937*	*1931*	*1937*
Total number of Class C houses	5,600	6,300	792	819
Per cent controlled	78	57	77	60
Total number of Class B houses	2,250	2,950	260	293
Per cent controlled	60	32	74	50
Total number of Class A houses	1,200	—	71	—
Per cent controlled	49	—	63	—
Total number of houses in Classes ABC	9,050	10,500	1,123	1,185
Per cent controlled	69	43	76	54

SOURCE: *Report of the Inter-Departmental Committee on the Rent Restriction Acts*, Cmd. 5621 (1937–8), p. 16.

b. Tenants and Landlords

Briefly one can say that as far as middle- and upper-class tenants were concerned rent control was a welcome benefit in the immediate post-war years and that when decontrol was introduced in 1923 it caused no great hardship. By the early 1930s, when the general shortage of better-class property had disappeared and the middle classes were moving into house ownership, this was certainly true. The rapidity with which class B houses were vacated and decontrolled supports this conclusion. Rent control was, however, of considerable benefit to working-class tenants. At no time was there a real surplus of working-class dwellings and in view of the acute shortage in 1923 the decision to introduce decontrol on vacant possession for this class of property had an adverse effect since it tended to restrict the mobility of tenants. To move would have meant sacrificing the benefits of low rent since the only alternative was to purchase a house or take on an uncontrolled tenancy.[1] Both of these possibilities were out of the question as far as most working-class tenants were concerned. In many cases, especially areas most seriously affected by trade depression, tenants found it difficult to pay even the controlled rents. From Glasgow it was reported that arrears of rent amounted to one-fifth the annual rent in many cases.[2] Since the rents of uncontrolled dwellings were nearly double those of controlled ones in some cases, it is clear that they were beyond the reach of most people in a period of high unemployment and slowly rising real wages. The Marley Committee estimated in 1931 that decontrolled rents had risen by one-quarter since 1923 bringing the average level up to around 90 per cent above pre-war compared with 50 per cent for controlled tenancies.[3] It is not surprising, therefore, that tenants were unwilling to vacate pre-war houses. By 1931 less than one-eighth of the pre-war working-class houses had been decontrolled under the 1923 vacant possession clause.

Whether the decision to halt the process of decontrol for this category of houses in 1933 was a sound one or not is debatable. There was still a shortage of working-class accommodation as a result of which rents of uncontrolled dwellings rose steadily in the 1930s. Unfortunately the paucity of statistical data makes it difficult to say by how much exactly.[4] The Ridley Committee reckoned that in 1937 the rents of uncontrolled working-class houses were about 50 per cent higher than the controlled ones. On the basis of the 1931 data this would mean that non-controlled houses were about 100 to 125 per cent above the 1914 level as against 50 per cent for controlled dwellings—a significant difference. On the other hand, it is as well to remember that the rents of uncontrolled houses might well have been artificially inflated by virtue of the fact that there were so few free properties on the market. Many of them were new properties and it is only to be expected that they would command a higher price (rent) than the old pre-war houses. Nevertheless, this in no way alters the fact that many working-class people were unable to afford them. For those in regular employment, however, the position was not so bad as it might appear. Wage rates by the later 1930s were nearly double the level of 1914, which meant that they had not lagged

[1] Unless, of course, the tenant was fortunate to secure a council house.

[2] *Report of the Committee on the Rent Restriction Acts*, Cmd. 2423 (1925), p. 14.

[3] The average rent of a decontrolled tenancy was 11s 3d compared with 9s for a controlled one and around 6s for a local authority Wheatley house.

[4] There is no doubt about this. The Ministry of Labour's combined rent index (controlled and decontrolled working-class dwellings) rose from 152 in 1930 to 161 in 1939 (1914=100). The index for controlled dwellings only remained steady.

seriously behind the rise in the market rents.[1] The rise in real wages, moreover, allowed many working-class people to shift their expenditure patterns in favour of housing. Rent control, therefore, served a purpose if it protected those less fortunate members of the community whose employment was irregular and whose wages had lagged behind the general average. The snag was that rent controlled properties were not necessarily tenanted by those people most in need of assistance. Indeed, the most unsatisfactory feature about it was that it tended to protect all tenants irrespective of whether they could afford to pay for something better.

From the point of view of the landlord rent control was probably unfavourable, though again it is difficult to draw definite conclusions because of the inadequate data. Rents were frozen at the 1914 level and the only concession was a 40 per cent increase in 1920 of which 25 per cent was to cover the increased cost of repairs. When these adjustments were made the cost of repairs was 150 per cent above pre-war and the allowance of 25 per cent on the pre-war rent was made on the assumption that repairs constituted one-sixth of the net rent. This gave the landlord exactly the same net return as before the war, the only compensation being an addition of 5 per cent to the pre-war rent to allow for increased yield on owner's capital, which was hardly sufficient in view of the enormous increase in the price level between 1914 and 1920.[2] On the other hand, the repair costs now formed a much larger proportion of the total net rent. Around 1930–1, when repair costs were about 100 per cent above the 1914 level, the Marley committee estimated that repairs were then equivalent to about 50 per cent of the pre-war rent. Given these unfavourable conditions it is not surprising to find that landlords were unwilling to repair their property, and in the long term this led to an increase in the rate of obsolescence of old property. It was more profitable for them to sell their assets than to hang on to old properties, the upkeep of which tended to increase from year to year. Though the fall in building costs made things a little easier there is no question that pre-war houses were far from being the lucrative source of income they once were. Had it been possible many landlords would have sold out in the 1930s.

c. Rent Restriction and the Housing Market

A much more interesting point to consider is what effect rent restrictions had on the housing market as a whole. There are a number of

[1] The cost of living had, however, only risen by about 50 per cent.

[2] The remaining 10 per cent was to cover the increase in mortgage interest.

general theoretical considerations involved here. Broadly speaking, low rents will tend to discourage homebuilding. Rent control will have a similar effect, since with rents below the free market level investors will shy away from the property market. In time the amount of new rented accommodation will diminish and unless the Government intervenes the demand for housing will tend to exceed the supply. Families who cannot find rented accommodation will be forced to purchase houses, which should stimulate building in this sector. The rate of such building will be less, however, than it might have been had rents not been controlled, since families who are paying less rent than they can afford might well have decided to move into house purchase had they not managed to acquire controlled accommodation. This offsetting factor is accentuated by the fact that there will be a certain amount of doubling up of families in controlled dwellings because of the favourable rent terms. The removal of rent control may have a similar effect under certain conditions. As Grebler has pointed out, the producer of rented housing tends to consider the effects of an increase in controlled rents on decontrol.[1] If it is likely that rents will rise rapidly in the event of such action being taken it may well direct demand away from rented towards owner-occupied accommodation.

In practice things worked out somewhat differently since many assumptions have been made in the theoretical schema which are untenable in the real world. For one thing control was never complete even in the early 1920s since it did not apply to new properties. The existence of a small free market should have given a great incentive to build because of the high rents that could be charged. That so few unsubsidized private enterprise houses were built in the early years after the war cannot be attributed to the operation of the Rents Acts. Large-scale housebuilding was difficult for a time due to the shortages of labour and building materials, whilst the very high capital costs made investment in property an unattractive proposition. Investors, moreover, found more lucrative outlets for their money particularly in gilt-edged securities because of the high yields then prevailing. In any case private enterprise had to compete with the local authorities which could offer homes at rents much lower than those of private builders. It could be argued, of course, that the existence of such a large block of controlled houses limited the effective demand for new ones. This might well be true were it not for the fact that the housing shortage was so acute that demand was sufficient to keep the building industry fully occupied for some years.

[1] L. Grebler, *Production of New Housing* (1950, New York), pp. 136–7.

The only other deterrent effect, namely the prospect of control being extended to new houses, was discounted in 1923 when the first step towards general decontrol was taken.

It has been argued that indirectly rent control was an important factor in suppressing building activity in the 1920s.[1] The fact that rents were fixed at uneconomically low levels might indicate the probable level to which they would fall once the shortage had disappeared, and presumably this would discourage investors from building for letting until costs had fallen sufficiently. It is doubtful, however, if this reasoning is entirely sound. For one thing the housing shortage was so acute that it is highly unlikely that the level of rents would have fallen for some time to come. Secondly, it was in the provision of working-class housing that private enterprise was most noticeably deficient. Between 1919 and 1931 only 1 per cent of the houses built privately in England and Wales were in the class C category (i.e. rateable value of £13 and under). It is true that most pre-1914 houses in this category remained controlled, despite the introduction of decontrol in 1923, and conceivably this in itself deterred those who could afford from moving into better property. But from the builders' point of view, investment in this class of property was unattractive, not because it was expected that rents would fall, but because, given the high level of costs, it was not profitable to build and let at rents most working-class people could afford. Private builders, moreover, could not compete with the rents charged for subsidized accommodation, which accounted for 65 per cent of all houses built in the 1920s. The prospect of acquiring cheap subsidized dwellings would discourage tenants from seeking accommodation elsewhere. Now these factors would have continued to operate had all control been removed from class C properties, and though it is possible that some tenants might have chosen to move into new accommodation rather than pay a higher rent for decontrolled properties it seems unlikely that this would have led to a great increase in effective demand for new houses. Apart from this private enterprise obviously found it more profitable to concentrate its attention on the better end of the market, i.e. middle- and upper-class housing, where demand for new property was most effective. It was these classes that could afford to rent or buy new properties and it was for them the builders provided. Even in the middle-class range surprisingly few houses were decontrolled before 1931 and one can only assume that many people were encouraged to hang on to old

[1] D. J. Coppock, 'The Causes of Business Fluctuation', *Manchester Statistical Society*, December 1959, p. 34.

properties because of low rents. Here, then, the rent restriction had an adverse effect on demand. Had controls been removed sooner from this class of property the backlog of demand for new dwellings might have been worked off earlier.

The above argument is supported by the experience of the 1930s. Private building flourished in this period and an increasing number of houses were built to let at the lower end of the price scale. Rent control had little direct effect on housebuilding at this time, yet one might have expected that it would have operated indirectly as a deterrent in the same way as it is alleged to have done in the 1920s. The fact that it did not was due to a combination of favourable factors, in particular falling costs and rising real incomes, which made demand for new dwellings effective. Furthermore, cheap money, as we shall see, made property development relatively more attractive compared with other sources of investment and encouraged investors to divert their funds to this purpose. In other words, it was the absence of these favourable conditions in the previous decade rather than the adverse effects of rent restrictions on builders' plans which accounts for the lower volume of building in the 1920s.

Generally speaking, therefore, rent control only had a marginal effect on the volume of housebuilding. This was most noticeable in the 1920s, though even then its impact was relatively weak. The biggest drawback of the system was that it discouraged families with adequate means from moving into better accommodation since by so doing they would lose the benefits of controlled rents. It is unlikely that the indirect effects of rent control on builders' and investors' expectations of the future level of rents was sufficiently powerful to account for the relatively low level of private building after the war. The reason for this seems to lie chiefly on the demand side of the equation. Under the conditions obtaining in the 1920s the pent-up demand for new housing, especially at the lower end of the scale, could not be made effective. It was only when these conditions changed in the early 1930s that the demand was released and translated into new houses.

V. *Result of State Intervention*

Undoubtedly the Government's housing legislation was an important factor in stimulating the output of dwellings in the inter-war period. Of the 4,359,000 houses built between March 1920 and March 1939 nearly 1,805,000, or roughly 42 per cent, were constructed with the aid of subsidies. Moreover, local authorities were responsible for roughly one-third of the new houses coming onto the market. Clearly without treasury subsidies and the intervention of the local authorities in the housing market far fewer houses would have been built. On the other hand, had there been no Government participation, the supply of houses would not have been reduced by the number actually subsidized, since the level of private enterprise building would no doubt have been somewhat higher. The activity of the local authorities certainly tended to discourage both investors and private builders in the 1920s from expanding the supply of rented accommodation.

Though in numerical terms the State's contribution was fairly significant Government policy was hardly an unqualified success. As we have seen, not all the subsidized houses were built in the right places or for the right people. Many of the privately subsidized dwellings were built for non-working-class tenants whilst often local authorities failed to satisfy the needs of the poorest members of the community. Little in fact was done to ensure that subsidized building was concentrated in those regions where requirements were greatest. Furthermore, although an attempt was made to tackle the problems of slum clearance and overcrowding, Government policy only provided marginal relief to these problems before 1939. The operation of rent control did, however, provide some relief to working-class tenants, though at the same time it tended to restrict mobility. It seems unlikely, on the other hand, that rent control seriously affected the volume of housebuilding activity either in the 1920s or 1930s.

As far as solving the housing shortage is concerned Government action was undoubtedly a failure. Although directly the Government and local authorities were responsible for the building of over 1,800,000 houses between the wars, this was less than sufficient to meet even the additional requirements up to the end of 1931.[1] It did little therefore to reduce the original backlog outstanding in 1921. Thus the abandonment of the general subsidy policy in the early 1930s, under the mistaken impression that the housing shortage had been solved, was clearly premature. In fact even by the beginning of 1939, after a decade of unrestricted private building, the housing shortage was almost as bad as it had been in 1921. The increase in the UK housing stock between March 1921 and December 1938 (3,487,000) had barely kept pace with the estimated increase in the number of families (3,515,000) over the same period. Given an initial deficit of 787,000 houses at the beginning of 1921 the shortage

[1] This, of course, does not take account of the indirect effects of the Government's cheap money policy which will be considered in the following chapter.

at the end of the period amounted to over 800,000. In other words, the vast housing programme of the inter-war years was only sufficient to keep pace with current requirements and it did little or nothing to reduce the backlog which had accumulated in the war and the years immediately after.[1]

[1] This outcome is much less favourable than that given by Marian Bowley largely because of the different assumptions we have adopted in estimating family requirements. For the basis of calculation see Chapter 3.

CHAPTER 9

HOUSING AND MONETARY POLICY

I. *The Shift to Cheap Money*

Apart from houses built under the slum clearance and overcrowding schemes the local authorities contributed little to the housing market after the early 1930s, though their rate of building remained fairly steady throughout the remainder of the decade. Nor could they be said to have played a significant role in the housing boom of the period. Between 1930 and 1939 nearly 3 million houses were built in Great Britain, some 70 per cent of which were privately financed. Furthermore, practically all the private enterprise houses were built without any State assistance. In other words, the State did little directly to promote the housing boom of the 1930s. On the other hand, indirectly the conversion to a cheap monetary policy in 1932 probably did more to stimulate the housing market than much of the piecemeal legislation of the previous decade had done.

The building boom was not confined solely to the residential sector. Investment in other buildings, such as factories, shops, offices, schools, increased steadily in the 1930s. But in absolute terms housing continued to account for the major part of the fixed investment in building in this decade and initially it was responsible for most of the increase in investment. Between 1931 and 1934, for example, real gross investment in all buildings rose by £73 million, £61 million of which was in residential construction. The revival of non-residential building did not take place until 1934–5, and even by 1937 real investment in this sector was no greater than it had been in 1930.[1] It would appear, therefore, that lower interest rates had a much less dramatic effect upon this sector than they did on the housing market. The decision to build new factories and offices was probably influenced far more by the prospects of trade revival than by a fall in the interest rate of 1 or 2 per cent.[2] This being so, we shall confine our attention in this section to examining the way in which housebuilding, and more particularly house purchase, was affected by the cheap monetary policy of the 1930s.

[1] C. H. Feinstein, *Domestic Capital Formation in the United Kingdom, 1920–38* (1965), p. 38, Table 3.31.

[2] On this aspect see the general observations made in Chapters 4 and 10.

Throughout the 1920s interest rates had remained relatively high, and this had made the building and especially the purchase of houses a fairly expensive business. Mortgage rates on building society loans were stiff and the societies found it difficult to obtain funds at a time when returns elsewhere proved more attractive to investors. But the dampening effect of high interest rates on the housing market was alleviated to a large extent by the Government's general subsidy policy. But all other things being equal the shift to cheaper money in the early 1930s was bound to have some impact on building since it made it generally cheaper to build and purchase accommodation.[1] The question is more complex than it would appear to be at first sight, however. In the first place it had virtually no influence on local authority housing programmes. Secondly, cheap money was preceded by or ran parallel with falling building costs, rising real incomes, a reduction in Treasury subsidies and a shift in consumer tastes, all of which affected the demand for houses in one way or another. Most of these factors are discussed elsewhere,[2] and for our purposes here the main concern is with the cost element of housing. But it must be recognized that any attempt to examine the influence of cheap money must take into account factors which lie strictly outside the scope of this chapter. This is particularly true when discussing the timing of the upswing in housing construction since it is not altogether certain that the monetary factor was the major determinant. Thirdly, there is much more to a fall in interest rates than simply a reduction in the weekly payments of house purchasing. A prolonged period of low interest rates can be expected to have widespread repercussions on the supply of funds to, and investment policies of, various financial institutions. In other words, the extent to which housing is stimulated by a fall in interest rates depends very much on how the agents of house purchase, that is building societies, are placed *vis-à-vis* their competitors with regard to the supply of loanable funds and on what measures they take to encourage the use of their resources in times of easy money. Similarly investors in house property for letting with a view to a fixed return will no doubt reconsider their investment plans in the light of a permanent fall in interest rates. Clearly then the influence of a cheap money policy on the housing market can be expected to be widespread and intricate and a balanced account will necessitate a discussion of each of these factors in turn.

[1] This section is mainly confined to the house purchase side. The effect of lower interest rates on builders' credit facilities is considered in Chapter 6.

[2] See Chapter 3, Sections II and III, and Chapter 8, Section II.

II. *Cheap Money and the Building Boom*

At least one aspect of the problem, namely local authority housing, can be disposed of quite rapidly. As can be seen from Table 1 in the Appendix to Chapter 2, the number of houses built by municipalities showed no response at all to the fall in interest rates. This does not mean, of course, that local authorities were impervious to changes in interest rates. In a sense cheaper money allowed them to rehouse slum families, for it was not until the fall in rates of interest and other costs enabled them to build houses at rents within the reach of slum dwellers, without throwing an additional burden on the rates, that advantage was taken of the Greenwood Act. Conversely, of course, it could be argued that slum replacement depended on subsidies and had these been withdrawn replacement building would have been even lower than it actually was. Indeed, it is much more likely that the latter operation would have had a more disastrous effect, since, even if interest rates had not been reduced, the slum replacement programme would still have been left intact, and all that was necessary to see its execution was for the Ministry to exert greater pressure on the housing authorities.

After 1933 local authorities built few houses for general purposes, partly because they were occupied with their new sanitary programmes. But this is by no means the only reason for their failure to build general-purpose houses. In 1932 the Wheatley subsidy was terminated, and the effect of this was to more than offset the advantages which local authorities gained from a fall in interest rates. By 1935, when interest rates were at their lowest, the minimum economic rent at which new local authorities houses could be let was just under 8s, and by the later 1930s it had risen to 9s. Wheatley houses, on the other hand, were being built in the early 1930s at around 6s per week. Thus new houses could only be let at rents above those of the original subsidized houses, and these rents were nearly twice the level of those charged for slum replacement dwellings. Now, since many of the pre-1933 subsidized rents were outside the range of the poorest members of the community, it follows that the unsubsidized houses built after the termination of the subsidy were even more so. Consequently, if local authorities had continued to build general-purpose, unsubsidized houses they would have had to make a greater contribution from the rates in order to bring the rents down to reasonable levels. This they were not prepared to do. In any case, they had been given a specific mandate to clear the slums and were told that private enterprise would cater for the working classes.

In contrast to the local authorities private enterprise built an increasing number of houses in every year until 1935 and in the latter half of the 1930s the rate of output was more than twice that of the previous decade, and at least three times that of the local authorities (see Table 1, Appendix, Chapter 2). It is not difficult to explain this boom in private housebuilding, since there were a large number of favourable factors present at the time. The existence of so many variables, however, makes it all the more difficult to assess the importance of any one particular factor. Recently the monetary factor has been singled out as the chief element in both the initial upswing and continuance of the boom in house construction. Although we would not quibble with the second of these assumptions, the evidence relating to the first is so conflicting that it requires further investigation.

In a closely argued chapter Nevin maintains that cheap money was the key factor in the sharp acceleration in private housebuilding between 1931 and 1933.[1] This clear-cut conclusion is open to a number of objections. For one thing he fails to take account of the fact that 1931 was a low year for private enterprise building following the collapse of subsidized building after the withdrawal of the Chamberlain subsidy. This, of course, tends to accentuate the rise in the early 1930s. Rather more important is the fact that by lumping subsidized and unsubsidized private building together the movements in the latter sector, which are more likely to be effected by changes in costs, are obscured. A glance at Table 1 (Appendix, Chapter 2) will show that the upswing in unsubsidized building began in 1929 and, apart from a temporary interruption in 1931, which can be attributed to the financial crisis, continued unchecked until 1935. Thus between March 1929 and March 1932 unsubsidized building doubled, from 66,000 to 133,000, and by March 1933 had reached 149,000. During the same period (1929–33) the number of building society borrowers rose by over 300,000, most of which represented advances for new houses. Quite clearly, then, the house purchase market was turning upwards before the conversion to cheap money.

This conclusion is supported by evidence about the movements in interest rates. The first general fall in building society mortgage rates took place in the autumn of 1932, but it was not until the summer of 1933 that a reduction of 1 per cent became general. Yet in the year ending March 1933 private enterprise built 18,000 more

[1] E. Nevin, *The Mechanism of Cheap Money* (1955), pp. 273–6. Using figures for England and Wales he gives a rise of 68 per cent for all private enterprise housing.

houses than in the preceding twelve months. By the first half of 1933 the annual rate of completion of new houses had increased by 34,000 over that for the latter half of 1932.[1] Now it is inconceivable that the initial fall in interest rates could have been translated into effective demand for new houses so rapidly, since there is inevitably a time lag involved. In any case the houses which were completed in the year ending March 1933 would all have been started before the first fall of 0·5 per cent in the mortgage rate became effective.[2] Moreover, there is evidence to suggest that the demand for houses is not particularly responsive to small changes in interest rates *per se*. A fall of 0·5 per cent is hardly likely, initially at least, to attract a big response for at the most it would only involve a reduction in weekly purchase payments on a small house of up to 1s. Much more effective would be a liberalization of the terms on which building societies are prepared to make advances for house purchase. These include the lengthening of the period over which repayments are made and a reduction in the initial deposits required. The latter is particularly important for, as Nevin himself has pointed out, the difference between a cash deposit of £25–£40 and £100 would mean the difference between buying and not buying a house for many people. But such changes in the terms on which advances were offered did not really become generally available until after the middle of 1933.[3]

Additional evidence in support of the hypothesis that the upswing in house purchase preceded an effective fall in interest rates is available for Scotland, an area where one would expect such developments to be somewhat slower.[4] The number of houses purchased in Scotland with the aid of building society loans increased rapidly from 1927 onwards. Between 1928 and 1932 the number of new properties purchased with mortgages quadrupled from 288 to 1,165, and, taking the five years as a whole, new properties bought on mortgage accounted for 60 per cent of the total houses purchased with the aid of loans, as against 20 per cent or less in the years immediately preceding. The rate of increase, moreover, far exceeded that which took place after 1933. In fact, between 1934 and 1936, when the impact of reduced interest rates was most effective,

[1] These figures are for England and Wales only. See W. F. Stolper, 'British Monetary Policy and the Housing Boom', *Quarterly Journal of Economics*, 56 (1941–2), p. 6, Table IV. Cf. M. Bowley, 'Fluctuations in Housebuilding and the Trade Cycle', *Review of Economic Studies*, 4 (1936–7), p. 177.

[2] Cf. Stolper, loc. cit., p. 59.

[3] The widespread adoption of the Builders' pool system which reduced the initial deposit required did not occur until 1934.

[4] Unfortunately, detailed data are not available for Great Britain as a whole.

the number of new houses bought on mortgage increased very slowly indeed.[1] It would seem, therefore, that in so far as Scottish experience is concerned, demand was not particularly responsive to the fall in interest rates.

Monetary enthusiasts have, moreover, overlooked one point: that the weekly cost of buying houses was falling well before the conversion to cheap money. According to Bowley's calculations the carrying charges on house purchase began to decline in the late 1920s and between 1930 and 1932 there was a fall of 11·9 per cent. This is similar in magnitude to the reduction of 11 per cent between 1932 and 1933 which, according to Nevin, did so much to stimulate

Table 24: COST OF HOUSE PURCHASE

	Average capital cost of houses being built	*Weekly cost of buying*	
	£	*s*	*d*
1928	432	10	0½
1929	416	9	9
1930	411	9	9
1931	404	9	4
1932	375	8	7
1933	362	7	8
1934	361	7	10

SOURCE: M. Bowley, *Housing and the State, 1919–44* (1945), p. 278, Table 6. The calculations are based on a loan of 70 per cent repaid over 20 years at current mortgage rates.

the marginal purchaser.[2] If this is so why did the first reduction have so little effect on the marginal purchaser? To argue that it required a second reduction to bring the cost of house purchase down to around the level of renting similar accommodation in order to get a response is misleading. On the basis of Bowley's figures the cost of buying a house was by 1931 already equivalent to the economic rents paid for similar property. In practice, of course, the real weekly cost of house purchase was much greater than the data in Table 24, since it represents the minimum cost of purchase of the smallest type of house that could be realized and takes no account of the annual burden of rates. In practice the average weekly carrying charges on new mortgages over a twenty-year period in the early 1930s was around 16s to 18s, which was well above the level of rents of either controlled

[1] See *Provision of Houses for Owner Occupation in Scotland*, Cmd. 6741 (1945), p. 17, Table V.

[2] Nevin, op. cit., p. 289.

or decontrolled properties.[1] Thus the class of people moving into house purchase at this time were probably motivated more by the actual fall in weekly payments of purchase than by the prospect that these costs were equivalent to the cost of renting accommodation.

Nevertheless, it still remains true that as far as new mortgages are concerned the average weekly carrying charges fell considerably in 1931–2, before the new mortgage rates became effective, and that in the following year the reduction was quite small. This could only have been brought about by the fall in the capital costs of houses and at this point the level of building costs becomes important. These had been falling slowly in the late 1920s and between 1930 and 1933 the cost of materials fell by nearly 13 per cent and the overall index of building costs by roughly 10 per cent.[2] Now a fall in building costs of this magnitude is sufficient to reduce the weekly costs of house purchase by rather more than a 1 per cent fall in mortgage rates, assuming a twenty-year repayment period. Furthermore, by reducing capital costs a fall in building costs has the added advantage that it automatically lowers the initial deposit required. Since these changes took place before the first 1 per cent reduction in mortgage rates became operative, it suggests that the initial upswing in building was a reaction to a fall in building costs,[3] which was sufficiently sharp to produce a response. It is also possible to explain the even earlier upturn (1929) in private unassisted building in similar terms. Furthermore, when lower interest rates did become effective after the middle of 1933 their impact was undoubtedly strengthened by the fact that capital costs had already fallen appreciably.

III. *The Role of the Building Societies*

If the timing of the boom is open to debate there can be no doubt that the influence of cheap money was sufficient to maintain a fairly high rate of housebuilding for most of the 1930s. By August 1935 mortgage rates were down to 4·5 per cent, and they remained at this level until the end of the decade. This represented a reduction of 25 per cent on the rates in force prior to the autumn of 1932. At the same time the building societies now had ample funds and they endeavoured

[1] R. M. MacIntosh, 'A Note on Cheap Money and the British Housing Boom, 1932–7', *Economic Journal*, 61 (1951), p. 169.

[2] Most of the fall occurred before 1933. See K. Maywald, 'An Index of Building Costs in the United Kingdom, 1845–1938', *Economic History Review*, 7 (1954), p. 192.

[3] Assisted from the demand side no doubt by rising real incomes.

to attract customers by liberalizing the conditions on which advances were made. One method was to lengthen the period of repayment. Prior to 1932 the majority of advances were limited to sixteen to twenty years; in 1933 the twenty-year period became common and by 1934–5 advances were being made for twenty-five years and longer. Even more important, particularly to the person of small means, was the reduction in the initial deposit which mortgagees were required to provide on buying a house. In the early 1930s societies rarely advanced more than 80 per cent of the purchase price of properties and sometimes even less. But with the development of special insurance guarantees and other forms of security, loans of up to 90 and 95 per cent were becoming common in the later 1930s. One of the most effective schemes was that known as the 'builders' pool' whereby the housing contractor agreed to supply collateral security for extensions of advances beyond the conventional limit. In case of default on the part of the mortgagee the society had recourse to the builder. This system began to develop in 1934 and by 1938 it had become so widespread that something approaching one-half of the business of the larger societies was transacted on this basis.[1] At that time probably over one-half the new houses sold were being bought with advances which required low initial deposits from the purchasers.

From the point of view of the house purchaser, these measures were of considerable benefit. A buyer was certainly much better off than his counterpart of late 1920s and early 1930s. If he was fortunate he could expect to get a loan of 90 to 95 per cent. On a house costing £500 this would involve a deposit of £25 to £50 as against £100 with an 80 per cent advance. A reduction of 25 per cent (6 to 4·5 per cent) in the mortgage rate and a lengthening of the repayment period from fifteen to twenty-five years would save him anything up to one-third on his weekly payments. In actual fact, the longer repayment period increased the cost of the transaction, but what mattered to the small house purchaser was the absolute size of his weekly commitments, and even more important the initial outlay required. This, of course, is an extremely favourable example. Not all buyers would be fortunate enough to receive such good terms since the practice of each society varied depending to some extent on the status of borrowers involved. Nevertheless, the data relating to the pre-arranged monthly repayments for different classes of borrowers of one large metropolitan society shows that the monetary gains could be substantial. Between 1932 and 1936 average monthly

[1] Bowley, op. cit., p. 175.

payments dropped by about 20 per cent for most income groups. No doubt the decline meant more to small income receivers, though it is interesting to note that the poorest class, labourers, seem to have come off worst, with a reduction of less than 17 per cent.[1]

But for the facilities offered by the building societies it is doubtful whether there would have been a boom of such magnitude in this period. The investment expert Hargreaves Parkinson reckoned the movement was one of the major causal factors and indeed it was.[2] No less than 75 to 80 per cent of the new privately built properties coming onto the market in the 1930s were financed by it.[3] The vast scale on which funds were deployed can be seen from Table 6 (Appendix, Chapter 2). Altogether, between 1930 and 1939 building societies advanced on mortgage around £1,034 million as against £433 million in the previous decade.[4] We have already seen the way in which building societies sought to attract house purchasers in the 1930s, but the question remains how they acquired funds to finance operations on this scale.

Since the First World War the building societies had been an increasingly popular form of investment. People who before 1914 had invested in property to let now turned to the building societies as an alternative outlet for their funds. The gap left by the withdrawal of the former investors in rented property was only partially filled by the local authorities and so many people were forced to become owner-occupiers, which in turn assisted the growth and prosperity of the building society movement. The shares and deposits of building societies were made more attractive by the fact that though the yield on Consols (their closest competitors for investors' funds) was similar to that of building society shares, the gross yield of the latter was higher because of favourable tax arrangements.[5] After 1929 building societies became an even more attractive investment. The stock market crash disillusioned many investors and their funds took refuge in the safe security of the building societies. Thus between 1929 and 1931 their share capital alone increased by over £90

[1] H. Bellman, 'The Building Trades', in *Britain in Recovery* (1938), p. 430.

[2] H. Parkinson, 'The Building Society Outlook', *The Banker*, April 1935, p. 33.

[3] The remainder were either bought outright or financed by insurance companies, banks, co-operative societies, local authorities and employers.

[4] These figures are, of course, inflated somewhat since they include a certain number of conversion mortgages.

[5] Under special arrangements with the Inland Revenue, building societies paid the income tax. Thus recipients of interest on their shares got a tax-free return and hence a higher gross yield than from alternative investment income which was liable to tax. E. J. Cleary, *The Building Society Movement* (1965), p. 189.

million.[1] The fall in interest rates had a similar effect which lasted even longer. The yield on building society shares, which had been almost identical to that on Consols in the 1920s, fell much less rapidly than the latter after 1931 with the result that from 1932–7 there was an average yearly differential of 0·5 per cent in favour of the building societies. This proved a source of embarrassment to the building societies since they were literally flooded with funds seeking temporary accommodation at high rates of return. To check the influx of 'hot money' selective quantitative restrictions were placed on investments which were relaxed only when the rate of return on their shares was reduced and the differential narrowed in 1937.[2]

The reason for the stickiness of building society share rates is not difficult to explain. The building societies could easily have kept out unwanted funds in the 1930s by reducing their interest on shares and deposits more quickly. Given the nature of their investment business,[3] however, a too rapid reduction in rates of return might have proved disastrous in the event of a sudden withdrawal of funds to take advantage of a rise in the yield on gilt-edged securities. A temporary withdrawal of this nature might well have exceeded current receipts and left the societies in a very awkward position. Thus it was not until cheap money came to be regarded as normal and as a result the chance of this happening was lessened, that interest on shares and deposits was reduced substantially and the selective measures of restriction on investments relaxed.

Clearly then the building societies faced a problem of repelling funds in the 1930s rather than one of trying to attract them. At times they had more money than they could profitably employ and this led to keen competition in the mortgage market. Yet despite the influx of funds into the movement as a result of cheap money shares and deposits were not the major source from which the societies made advances. Repayment of mortgages became steadily more important in the 1930s, increasing from roughly 40 per cent of total receipts in 1930 to 64 per cent in 1938. Thus in this period the building societies financed an increasing share of their business from repayment receipts. Of just over £1,030 million advanced on mortgage between

[1] For full statistical details of their growth see Table 6, Appendix, Chapter 2.

[2] *Building Societies Year Book 1934*, p. 52.

[3] That is borrowing short and lending long. 80 to 90 per cent of the assets consisted of long-term mortgages. Their chief sources of funds were shares and deposits, which were subject to almost immediate withdrawal The former was by far the most important of the two and accounted for 79·3, 87·3 and 77·9 per cent of total liabilities in 1922, 1930 and 1938 respectively.

1930 and 1938 nearly £615 million was derived from repayment of mortgages and the remainder from share and deposit investments. In the 1920s, on the other hand, only just under half the total amount advanced on mortgage (£433 million) was financed by repayment receipts (£211 million). Thus despite the importance of cheap money in attracting investment funds, building societies relied more heavily on mortgage repayments to finance their transactions than they had done in the 1920s.[1]

IV. *Private Enterprise and the Supply of Rented Accommodation*

Not all the houses built by private enterprise in the 1930s were sold to owner-occupiers through the building societies. In fact, 28·3 per cent of the houses built by private enterprise between 1933 and 1939 were for letting.[2] Investment in rentable property became steadily more attractive in the 1930s compared with the previous decade. This was largely due to the effects of cheap money. Whilst the returns on gilt-edged fell steadily, at least until 1937, the returns on rented accommodation actually rose. The Ministry of Labour's rent index increased from 152 in January 1930 to 161 in January 1939. The buoyancy of the rent market was greater than these figures suggest, however, since the index combines both controlled and decontrolled properties, the former of which remained more or less stable throughout the period. Consequently the rents of uncontrolled houses, which included all new rented dwellings, must have risen quite sharply in the 1930s. Moreover, the real return on rented property was increased even further by the fact that the capital cost of dwellings was falling for part of the time. Thus it is not surprising that the investment demand for housing increased as alternative outlets for investors' funds (e.g. gilts) became less attractive. Soon after the War Loan Conversion when the returns on Consols dropped sharply the property market was booming and it was reported that investors were anxious to place their savings in property.[3] Judging from the figures relating to rented accommodation this boom in investment property steadily increased throughout the 1930s. The proportion of small houses (up to £13 rateable value) constructed for

[1] The figures for mortgages and repayment income include a certain element of double counting because of the impossibility of separating the conversion figures. The amount representing conversions would no doubt be greater in the 1930s thus tending to exaggerate the proportion of business financed by repayments.

[2] This figure relates to England only and includes houses up to a rateable value of £26.

[3] Bellman in *Britain in Recovery* (1938), p. 421, note 1.

letting by private enterprise rose from 29 to 45 per cent between 1934 and 1938 whilst over the same period the share of the intermediate class of houses (rateable value £14 to £26) increased from 15 to 25·5 per cent. A similar trend can be discerned from statistics relating to property companies.[1]

Initially, of course, private enterprise built houses for the relatively prosperous sections of the community. The result was that far more houses were built in the upper ranges (that is above £13 rateable value) than was required to satisfy essential needs. The excess houses did not, of course, remain empty. The middle and lower middle classes left their old nineteenth-century dwellings for the more modern houses, whilst by a process of filtering-up the working classes occupied those older tenements which were vacated but not pulled down. As the market for the better-class type of house became saturated private builders began to construct smaller houses. Here they did very much better than in the 1920s. Nearly 38 per cent of the houses built by private enterprise between 1931 and 1939 fell into this category (that is with a rateable value of under £14) compared with a mere 1 per cent in the preceding ten years.

Yet though in numerical terms the number of working-class houses built privately was large (nearly 700,000) it was not even sufficient to clear off the outstanding deficit in 1931 let alone provide for the increase in family formation of the 1930s. It seems extremely doubtful, moreover, whether those who needed houses most, that is the poorest section of the working classes, did in fact manage to get them. Most of these houses were let or sold at prices beyond the reach of this section of the community. In other words, those who benefited were the better-paid artisans, clerks and even the lower middle classes. Although as we have seen the proportion of privately built rented accommodation in the lowest category (under £14 rateable value) increased steadily in the later 1930s, the rents charged were beyond the means of many working people. Most of these houses were provided by commercial undertakings and it was impossible to let them at much under 16s a week even when interest rates and capital costs were at their lowest.[2] This was almost double the rents charged by local authorities and even their rents were beyond the means of some people.

As far as house purchase was concerned, the working classes probably fared a little better. In some cases it was cheaper to buy a

[1] J. L. Marshall, and E. Nevin, op. cit., pp. 278–80.

[2] See R. L. Reiss, 'Municipal and Private Enterprise Housing', *Building and Society* (1945), pp. 65–7.

house than rent privately built accommodation.[1] Certainly owner-occupation was increasing among the working classes in this period because of the favourable terms on which houses could be bought. The figures produced below showing the social status of borrowers of one large building society suggest that the lower classes (wage earners and labourers) were becoming increasingly important as house purchasers. On the assumption that these proportions applied to all building societies Nevin has calculated that over 90 per cent of

Table 25: SOCIAL STATUS OF BORROWERS OF ONE LARGE BUILDING SOCIETY

	Up to 1930 *per cent*	*1933* *per cent*	*1936* *per cent*
Wage earner	34·8	41·2	50·5
Salaried	16·7	14·2	10·7
Independent (excluding professional)	15·5	14·3	13·7
Clerk	7·3	7·6	6·9
Professional	4·4	3·3	3·0
Labourer	0·6	0·8	1·3
Miscellaneous	20·7	18·6	13·9

SOURCE: Bellman, loc. cit., p. 430.

the increase of £198 million in outstanding mortgages between 1932 and 1936 was advanced to working-class borrowers.[2] These figures clearly give an exaggerated impression of the progress of house ownership among the working classes. It was very difficult to get the weekly cost of loan charges down to below 11s and even this was exceptional. In practice 12s to 15s a week was the best that could be expected even on a small house, and when rates, repairs and insurance were added the total might be over £1. Clearly then this was quite outside the range of all but the better-paid workers (that is those earning over £4 a week). It seems very unlikely, therefore, that more than a very small proportion of private enterprise houses were occupied by families which were in any sense working class. It is impossible to give precise quantitive information, but a return by the Ministry of Health for 1938 suggests that of 4,652 houses surveyed with a rateable value below £20 only 19 per cent were owner-occupied, a ratio which was only a little above that of pre-war.[3] For

[1] In actual fact when overhead charges are taken into account, such as rates, insurance and repairs, there was little difference between the two.

[2] Nevin, op. cit., p. 295.

[3] The return was not complete. Only 8·25 million houses were surveyed altogether and of those 34·9 per cent were owner-occupied. See *Valuation of Rates 1939* (HMSO, 1945).

a large proportion of the working class house purchase was out of the question, and the building societies catered largely for the middle classes, clerical workers and the better-paid artisans whose employment was regular and whose income was steady.

In short, the people most in need of houses in the 1930s were those who were least likely to get them. The bulk of the privately built houses in the suburbs went to the wealthier members of the middle and lower middle classes, that is the sort of people who were not likely to fall in arrears with their payments. Private enterprise failed, therefore, to solve the real housing problem of rehousing or providing reasonable accommodation for the submerged sector of society. It failed because, as Bowley says, what it succeeded in doing was to provide houses for just the same sort of market as the local authorities had catered for earlier.[1] In practice the rents and terms of house purchase of private enterprise houses of the 1930s were far above those of the local authorities in the previous decade even though the houses were generally of similar size and quality.

V. *Summary*

Although there are grounds for suggesting that the influence of cheap money in the initial upswing has been over-emphasized, all the evidence lends support to the conclusion that it was by far the most important agent in helping to maintain a rapid rate of housebuilding once the boom was under way. By making house purchase much cheaper and easier and property investment more attractive relative to alternative competitors for investors' funds it stimulated both sectors of the market considerably. It is worth noting that of the 2·5 million unsubsidized houses built by private enterprise in Great Britain over the whole of the inter-war period, just over 1·8 million or 72 per cent were constructed in the years 1932–9.[2] Even in Scotland, where local authorities continued to be the main housebuilders, private enterprise made its major contribution in the 1930s. One can, of course, only hazard a guess as to the number of houses built as a result of the cheap money policy. If we make the not ungenerous assumption that one-quarter of the total number of houses built privately between March 1933 and March 1939 can be attributed to this factor it would mean that indirectly Government policy was responsible for an additional 390,000 houses, which together with the subsidized

[1] Bowley, op. cit., p. 177.

[2] The total number of houses built by private enterprise between 1920 and 1938 was slightly over three million.

houses brings the total to 2,195,000. In other words, State action was responsible, either directly or indirectly, for the contribution of just over 50 per cent of the new houses over the entire inter-war period. The extent to which this helped to relieve the shortage has been discussed in the previous chapter and requires no further comment.

CHAPTER 10

INTER-WAR BUILDING FLUCTUATIONS

1. *Introduction*

Although there have been several studies of the causes of the housing boom in the 1930s, the analysis of building fluctuations in the UK over the inter-war period as a whole has been more or less ignored. The mainstream of historical analysis of building with its concentration on the causes of long building cycles in (relatively) free market economies has passed the inter-war period by, probably because it is a special case not easily fitted into general explanations of building fluctuations geared to pre-1914 experience. The causes of long building cycles are not irrelevant to a study of the inter-war years, but their direct application is very limited. The pattern of recurrent cycles was halted by the First World War, and the war through its effects on the rate of building, income growth and population was the greatest external disturbance on the tempo of building activity known up to that time. Public intervention in the housing market materially influenced the fluctuations in building, and because of the lack of cohesion in, and spasmodic character of, policy the influence was irregular and unpredictable. General economic tendencies of the inter-war period—a fairly firm upward trend in real incomes but combined with heavy unemployment, a secular fall in prices and costs, a reversal of previous internal migration trends, transport and new industrial developments affecting the pattern of urbanization—also had an impact on building which made its fluctuations less explicable in pre-1914 terms. Finally, the inter-war years, with the two world wars as rigid boundaries, form too short a period for long cycles to be evident. In these circumstances building fluctuations in the inter-war period are not amenable to interpretation by *sole* aid of the general theories deduced from longer historical periods. A balance between the separate and often conflicting causal factors is not easily created, and this chapter claims merely to contribute a first approximation to an understanding of inter-war fluctuations in building.

The accepted generalization is that building (especially house-building) activity fluctuates in cycles of wider amplitude and longer than cycles in the economy at large. This probably holds in market economies, and one of the aims of this chapter is to show why this should be so and to relate the analysis to inter-war experience.

II. *General Considerations*

Before an empirical analysis of inter-war building fluctuations, it is necessary to discuss the reasons for the special character of building fluctuations. As is well known, cycles in housebuilding tend to be longer and more severe than cycles in the aggregate economy.[1] The causes of fluctuations in housebuilding[2] fall into two main groups, those not connected with the business cycle but which follow from the special character of the industry (durability of the product, 'reaction lags', the speculative nature of much of housebuilding, the diversity of regional housebuilding cycles) or from the fact that building is subject to long-lasting shocks, and the influences closely related to phases of the business cycle (national income, costs relative to rents and interest rates). The former group provides an explanation of why housebuilding fluctuations should follow a course very different from business cycles while the latter operates in a manner which tends to make the rate of building change through different phases of the business cycle, even to the extent that some observers have argued that housebuilding is anti-cyclical. The first group of forces is discussed in this chapter, while the influence of the second group is analysed in Chapter 11.

a. Durability of Product

One of the main reasons for the long periodicity of fluctuations in building is the exceptional durability of buildings. It is true of all consumer durables that what affects the price of services rendered by these goods is not the volume of production in a given time unit but the total stock available. Where the commodity is very durable like a house each year's production adds only a small percentage to the total stock. In the UK in the inter-war period the maximum annual addition to supply was 3·1 per cent in the mid-1930s. The low proportion of annual output to the total stock means that it takes a considerable period of time for an excess demand for houses to be met or for an excess supply to be eliminated.

[1] The average length of building cycles varies widely from place to place and time to time, but observed cycles have fallen within the minima of 12–14 years and the maxima of 25 years and over, in all cases longer than the business cycle with its range of 6–11 years.

[2] Non-residential fluctuations are considered separately; see Section V below.

The durability of houses affects the links between population changes and building output. For instance, assuming constant average real incomes, the output of a commodity with only a single use (e.g. a non-durable commodity such as bread) will vary with the size of the population as a whole; but housing output (since houses are very durable) will vary with *increases* in population and will fluctuate more severely.[1] The durability of a commodity is also connected with the length of its cycle in production via the needs for replacement; goods with a fixed life of twenty years will tend, if production was bunched in the past, to experience twenty-year cycles in its production. Now it is obvious that the durability of a house is too long to explain building cycles in terms of replacement demand, but the psychological life of a house may be far shorter than its physical life. It is possible that after twenty to thirty years demand may swing away from houses of a particular type and design in favour of new houses which are more modern; of course, it would be very surprising indeed to find a regular, recurrent shift in tastes, say, every two decades, but then the periodicity of building cycles is not exceptionally regular.

The durability of houses also means that replacement can easily be deferred, and in fact the timing of replacement of a particular vintage of houses can be varied significantly according to general economic considerations. The result is that fluctuations become much less predictable. Nevertheless, Burns argues that particular combinations of population changes and required replacements may give rise to long cycles in construction, even though population movements are not characterized by cycles.[2] In other words, differing increases in the size of the population account for annual variations in housebuilding output, while replacement demand makes these variations cyclical.

b. Production and Reaction Lags

Building cycles are also longer than business cycles as a result of the

[1] To give an example, if population remains stable at 1,000,000 in year 1 and 2, then rises to 1,005,000 in year 3 and to 1,011,000 in year 4, and each person consumes 100 loaves a year, bread output will be 100,000,000, 100,000,000, 100,500,000 and 101,100,000 through years 1–4, changing by 0·0, 0·5 and 0·6 per cent. But if a new house is required for every additional three people in the population, the annual output of houses will be zero, 1,667 and 2,000. The output of houses will consequently fluctuate to a far greater extent than the output of bread.

[2] A. F. Burns, 'Long Cycles in Residential Construction' in *The Frontiers of Economic Knowledge* (1954), especially pp. 314–18.

length of the lag between the development of housing deficiency and additions to the stock of houses to rectify it (and conversely the lag before the industry responds to the emergence of a housing surplus). The total lag could take anything up to four years.[1] The lag will, of course, not necessarily remain constant over time or in different institutional environments. The long lag is due to more than one cause. One factor is the time period of production which, varying between several months and more than two years (for certain types of non-residential buildings), is longer than for most products. The production period will lengthen when the supply of labour and materials is inelastic. Thus in the early 1920s and from the middle 1930s the lag between housebuilding plans and completions lengthened noticeably relative to the rest of the inter-war period. The main reasons for this were intermittent shortages of skilled labour in the 1920s and the competing demands of industrial and commercial building in certain years of the 1920s and after 1935. A related point is that the long period of production intensifies building's dependence on credit since it necessitates the builder having to pay his wage bill long before he gets paid. This dependence may assume critical significance in a building slump because of the reluctance of financial institutions to lend to builders at that time.

General 'reaction lags' have very similar effects. The structure of the industry with its conglomeration of small independent firms and heavy reliance on casual labour makes for poor and belated communication of, and responses to, changes in market conditions. The low dependence on capital equipment means that firms leave the industry in a slump, labour is not retained and the flow of apprentices dries up. When demand revives it takes time for the industry to expand capacity again to meet it. The poor communications within the building industry only partly explain the slow response to changing conditions. Another cause is the weakness of market indicators. How are builders to know that there is a housing shortage or surplus? Presumably, because of changes in the price of the services which housing gives, that is, in the movement of rents. But rents are notoriously 'sticky', and quite a severe excess of demand or supply may have to build up before rents rise or fall. In other sectors of the economy, manufacturing, for example, changes in the state of demand are communicated quite easily through changes in stocks. The sluggishness of responses in the building industry means, of

[1] J. B. Derksen ('Long Cycles in Residential Building: An Explanation', *Econometrica*, 8 (1940), p. 113) suggested that building activity was related to a shortage or excess supply of dwellings two years before.

course, that quite a severe housing shortage may develop before the building industry expands output. In the boom, on the other hand, over-building may occur because of the lag in building output behind changes in demand. This not only prolongs the upper turning point, but also makes the ensuing depression of longer duration. On the other hand, both the long time-period of production and the characteristic reaction lags mean that building activity is very often immune to temporary recessions in the economy.

c. Demographic Forces

The influence of population changes on construction has been analysed in some detail in Chapter 3, so its general impact can be given cursory treatment here. The main point is that population movements are not generally related to the business cycle but tend to change direction over rather longer periods, thus giving building fluctuations (assuming a degree of response to changes in the size of the population) a periodicity longer than economy-wide fluctuations. Long cycles in the total population do not of course generally exist, but some people have argued (notably A. Losch and W. H. Newman)[1] that there are long cycles in population increases and that these show a correlation with long building cycles. However, inter-war experience clearly demonstrates that a progressive slowing down in population growth does not eradicate the influence of population on building fluctuations if there are marked changes in the structure of the population—such as changes in marriage rates, age composition and family size due to a falling birth rate—and a high rate of inter-regional migration. Many of these structural changes in the population reflect changing customs and social habits rather than cyclical movements. A boom in marriages and births will tend to result in a potential echo effect from one generation to the next, though the repercussion may be very damped unless it coincides with a favourable movement in real incomes (which of course is not completely independent of the business cycle). But given that housebuilding responds to changes in the number of families, an initial disturbance in the size or structure of the population will tend to set up long building cycles.

However, the hypothesis that long cycles in population increases, or alternatively echo effects stemming from random disturbances in the population trend, are associated with long building cycles is not

[1] A. Losch, 'Population Cycles as a Cause of Business Cycles', *Quarterly Journal of Economics*, 51 (1936–7), and W. H. Newman, 'The Building Industry and Business Cycles', *Journal of Business of the University of Chicago*, 8 (1935).

clearly substantiated. The reason for this is that certain demographic forces tend to move in line with the business cycle. For instance, the correlation between changes in the number of marriages and real national income in the UK between the wars is very close; this is especially the case in the latter half of the period since from 1928 both indices moved in the same direction year after year. Similarly, net emigration tended to move in line with the international business cycle at least after 1929, with the result that the high net emigration in 1929 became negative in 1931 and remained negative for the rest of the decade. In the 1920s there was a relatively stable net emigration throughout the decade (apart from the exceptional level of 1923). This meant that isolating the effects of net emigration and immigration, we find that it should have depressed building activity in the 1920s and boosted it in the 1930s, and further that the stimulus of the 1930s was a counter-cyclical one, being at its peak in the period 1931–3.

Finally, internal migration movements show a tendency to move pro-cyclically. Although the migration of people and the associated shift in industry from Scotland, Wales and the North to the South-East and the Midlands was a trend factor, the tempo of migration changed with each phase of the business cycle, partly because changes in industrial location are stimulated by boom rather than slump conditions, partly because migrants have stronger financial resources with which to move in upswings rather than in depressions. The effect of internal migration, therefore, would be to pull building activity into line with the business cycle. However, the impetus of migration was probably small relative to, say, the growth of real incomes and changes in tastes, so that this effect may have been secondary to other factors. It should be noted, of course, that because migration was associated with changes in industrial location the pro-cyclical effects of these changes apply to industrial and commercial building as well as to housebuilding.

d. Expectations

Changing expectations and the growing importance of speculative building play a part in determining the special character of building fluctuations. This is particularly true of residential building. Some of the earliest investigations into building fluctuations found that building moved more closely in correspondence with share prices than with economic activity.[1] Another examination of US data for the period 1868–1940 showed a close association between building

[1] For example, J. B. Hubbard, 'An Analysis of Building Statistics for the United States', *Review of Economics and Statistics*, 6 (1924).

and stock-price cycles.[1] These findings suggested that expectations were an important element in the inducement to invest in building. If expectations influence housebuilding more than non-residential construction they could help to explain some of the cyclical divergences between the two types of building, for instance the tendency for residential to lead non-residential at the upper turning point (most non-residential buildings are tailor-made by order, rather than built by the speculative builder who hopes to sell his products to the house-buyer or the housing investor). Also, if speculative building is important over-building might occur early in the boom, which could explain the tendency for housebuilding to tail off in the later stages of the upswing while industrial and commercial building continues to rise (as in the late 1930s).

Expectations will also influence demand as well as supply. The decision to buy houses is based on expectations of ability to repay over twenty to thirty years (or from the point of view of the housing investor on expectations of favourable rent movements), but current trends will be given a high weighting in such expectations. If current conditions are interpreted pessimistically, people living in existing houses can easily postpone decisions to buy new houses; conversely, the demand for new houses may be anticipated with the result that sudden changes in income, prices or other conditions may induce quite large changes in market demand. There may therefore be some tendency for house-buyers to over-estimate their ability to make payments in the upswing, but also to be unduly put off house-buying in a building slump. These forces will be accentuated by the activities of speculative builders who, because they build houses not for their own use or for investment but to sell at a profit to owner-occupiers and investors, run a severe risk of over-supplying demand. If speculative building is extensive, activity will tend to be concentrated more and more in boom periods and less and less in depressions. Although, as argued above, expectations enter into housing consumption decisions, their role is not as great as on the supply side; thus Grebler argues that the spread of speculative building will intensify building fluctuations by increasing the weight of entrepreneurial decisions relative to the decisions of individual consumers.[2] Similarly, as the building industry becomes increasingly dependent on monetary and credit conditions speculative influences will be reinforced. On the

[1] C. D. Long, *Building Cycles and Theory of Investment* (1940), pp. 113–14.

[2] L. Grebler, 'Housing Policy and the Building Cycle', *Review of Economics and Statistics*, 24 (1942), pp. 67–8; see also ILO, *Housing and Employment* (1948), pp. 95–6.

other hand, Parry Lewis argues that building was becoming less sensitive to changes in credit between the wars, partly because of the emergence of *large* speculative builders who could obtain their working capital at low interest rates, partly because of the entry of building societies into the finance of flat developments.[1]

The effect of expectations and increased dependence on speculative building will be that a rising trend of demand for houses will be interpreted optimistically, while a falling trend will usually be interpreted pessimistically. Builders will tend to over-build in the boom and house-buyers and investors may over-estimate their ability to finance house purchase; in building slumps, on the other hand, both builders and purchasers will tend to hold back. What will this mean in terms of the amplitude and periodicity of building fluctuations? Firstly, fluctuations will be made more severe. The tendency for builders to build in anticipation of demand will mean a steep upswing, while the likelihood of over-building will result in very low levels of activity in the slump which follows. The impact of expectations and speculation on the periodicity of fluctuations is somewhat more complex to unravel. A housing shortage will be made up more quickly because of building running ahead of demand so that the upswing will be steep and shorter; once the over-building is recognized builders will drastically reduce their output and the downswing will also be sharp and short. On the other hand, at the upper turning point even when over-building is recognized current projects will have to be completed; this will tend to prolong the crisis at a stable level of activity. The lower turning point may be long drawn out because it may take quite marked shifts in demand conditions before builders interpret the market optimistically again. Consequently, though both the upswing and downswing will, as a result of expectations and speculation, be short and severe the upper turning-point and (especially) the lower turning-point will be prolonged. How these opposite effects will balance it is difficult to say. It is possible that they cancel out so that the factor of expectations considered in isolation may not alter the length of the cycle overall but will influence its character by changing the length of each phase (i.e. shortening the upswing and downswing but lengthening the peaks and troughs).

e. The Effects of Regional Cycles

How are national building fluctuations modified by the existence of different regional cycles? One suggestion is that regional building cycles may be closely associated with fluctuations in business activity

[1] J. Parry Lewis, *Building Cycles and Britain's Growth* (1965), p. 231.

or other factors (e.g. growth of population within the region) operating within the region rather than with building fluctuations in other regions. Bowen, for example, found that cyclical fluctuations in building craft employment by region moved closely with general fluctuations, and US investigations also show a tendency for building in various localities to conform more closely with general business than with each other.[1] In inter-war Britain it is clear that regional fluctuations in business activity varied quite widely: for instance, in the South and Midlands the depression of the early 1930s had virtually no effect on employment, while in other regions not only was the slump severe but the 1929 position was not retrieved until very late in the 1930s. If regional building cycles varied with local business then regional differences in building fluctuations could be great and would also vary markedly from building fluctuations in the aggregate economy. The turning-points in the building cycles of different regions would vary (as would the periodicity and amplitude of the cycles themselves), and the effect of different regional cycles and an increase in the number of cycles would be to lengthen national building cycles, and to moderate them.[2]

It is arguable that the consequence of varied regional building cycles, each of which moved in accord with local business activity (and were therefore similar to regional *business* cycles), would be a long building cycle (i.e. longer than the business cycle). The objection to this view is that just as regional differences in business activity are pulled into conformity and averaged out to give a recognizable business cycle then why should not regional differences in building activity (which are found to vary with business activity) average out into a national building fluctuation with a periodicity similar to the economy's business cycle? The answer is possibly to be found in the fact that building fluctuations are more intense than general fluctuations, and the response of building activity to a percentage point difference in business activity in region A may be far greater than the response in region B. This combination of the greater severity of building than general fluctuations and variations in the degree of association between building and business from one region to another may result in an overall building cycle that bears only a limited resemblance to the business cycle and is in fact considerably longer. This explanation could be a factor in why building fluctua-

[1] Bowen, 'Building Output and the Trade Cycle (UK 1924–38)', *Oxford Economic Papers*, No. 3 (1940), pp. 110–30.

[2] H. J. Habakkuk, 'Fluctuations in Housebuilding in Britain and the United States in the Nineteenth Century', *Journal of Economic History*, 22 (1962), p. 209.

tions are wider and more intense than economic fluctuations in general.

f. Institutional Changes and Random Shocks

Building activity may be influenced by changes in the institutional environment and by general economic trends. Between the wars such forces included the southward migration of industry and population, the expansion in the building society movement, the effects of transport innovations, the prohibition of capital exports in the 1930s and the associated drying up of emigration, and changes in tastes. The importance of factors of this kind is that they influence building over many years, usually over a period far longer than the business cycle. If their impact is strong, they may sustain building activity over time periods longer than the periodicity of economy-wide fluctuations.

The effects of random shocks may be of greater significance. These act as a sudden, sharp stimulus, and affect the pattern of fluctuations by distorting the phase to phase development of the endogenous cyclical mechanism. The building cycle models constructed by some theorists (Tinbergen and Derksen, for example)[1] exhibit marked dampening tendencies, and shocks may be crucial for keeping damped cycles oscillating.[2] During the inter-war period two outside shocks, the First World War and the timing of Government subsidy changes, had such a tremendous impact on the cyclical pattern that they require separate consideration.

III. *Two External Shocks*

Of random shocks acting on building fluctuations between the wars the First World War and public policy had the greatest impact. The effect of the war, by creating an exceptional housing shortage, and of State intervention, by making a sizeable fraction of total output dependent on public policy decisions rather than on strictly economic considerations, pulled the course of housebuilding out of conformity with the path which might be predicted from a market model.

a. The War

The war and its aftermath influenced building for the whole of the 1920s and possibly well into the 1930s as well. Although it may be

[1] Derksen, loc. cit., p. 115, and J. Tinbergen and J. J. Polak, *The Dynamics of Business Cycles* (1950), p. 245.

[2] R. Frisch, 'Propagation Problems and Impulse Problems in Dynamic Economics', in *Economic Essays in Honour of Gustav Cassel* (1933), pp. 171–205.

preferable to regard it as an outside shock acting upon the building cycle, some observers hold wars to be one of the causes of the cycle.[1] At first sight, wars would seem to be far too irregular to justify this role but the shortages of dwellings to which wars give rise may result in several large fluctuations (at least if one assumes the possibility of over-building in boom phases), though the fluctuations would obviously be damped and unless subject to another disturbance would sooner or later die out. Moreover, wars influence population movements, and the 'echo' effect of the demographic changes created by the war may last for many decades. Since our concern is only with the inter-war period it is unnecessary to speculate on these possibilities, for the impact of the First World War on building within this period is undeniable.

A broad distinction may be drawn between the war itself and its after-effects. The more immediate effects of the war were a virtual halt to residential building,[2] stagnation in the growth of real incomes, diversion of resources to war purposes and general economic uncertainty. Building restrictions discouraged residential building activity, but industrial building in armament and related industries proceeded faster than the average peacetime rate. Even in the absence of controls, few houses would have been built. Wartime uncertainty put off the housing investor, while rent control introduced in 1915 and sharply rising construction costs made housing investment unprofitable. At the same time, real incomes of the mass of the people fell, interfering with their ability to buy houses or pay market rents. The obvious consequence of the housebuilding stoppage was a severe deficit in the stock relative to households once the war was over.

This might be expected to have generated an immediate post-war building boom, but it failed to materialize. Firstly, there were marked reaction lags. The industry, composed primarily of small independent units, was slow to reorganize. Small building firms were lacking in capital (no profits accumulated in the war period), and were unable to obtain access to sources of capital in the general post-war boom since capital was scarce. The lack of stocks meant that

[1] This argument is usually the prerogative of American economists who have the United States institutional environment in mind when presenting the thesis. In particular they stress the echo effects on building activity of the consequences of the Civil War. It is, of course, far more difficult to relate an argument of this kind to a British context in view of the absence of major wars before 1914 and the relatively short time span between the First World War and the Second.

[2] In fact, 49,000 houses were built in 1915 and 1916, but almost none in the years 1917-19.

building materials were in very short supply up to 1922. Most serious of all, the labour situation was very difficult. In 1918 employment in building was only 50 per cent of the 1914 level.[1] Skilled labour was very scarce, partly because of the refusal of trade unions to relax conditions so that demobbed soldiers up to the age of 26 could be trained.

Apart from these supply problems, private builders thought the outlook unprofitable despite the severity of the shortage. Rents remained controlled (though not on new houses after 1919) while building costs rose sharply in the post war boom (by 46 per cent, 1918–20). Rising costs partly reflected the general rise in prices, partly the shortages of building materials, but there were other factors such as low efficiency and the effects of monopolies in the building material trades. Interest rates were also high, with the result that private builders held off, waiting for costs and wages to fall. It was this reluctance, above all, which accounted for the high proportion of houses built by local authorities in the early 1920s, more than 60 per cent of the houses built in the period 1919–22. Finally, there were the demographic effects of the war: a high marriage rate in 1919–21 which was the main factor in the increased rate of family formation; a high post-war birth rate which had few immediate consequences but was capable of affecting the future level of building through the 'echo' effect; a dampening effect on the birth rate over the 1920s and early 1930s resulting from the loss of potential fathers in the war. The first of these factors meant substantial additions to the number of families just at the time when housebuilding activity was low. As a result the severe shortage of houses already existing at the end of the war increased, and it was not until 1926 that a year's housebuilding exceeded the annual increase in families.

The war thus created such a serious housing shortage that this should have resulted in an intense post-war housing boom. The consequence of the war and immediate post-war conditions was a failure by the private sector to respond to housing needs. As a short-term solution (i.e. 1920–2) the State intervened and boosted housebuilding by its subsidy policy but from 1923, now that building costs had fallen, private housebuilding revived. There was still no immediate boom because the large-scale intervention of the public sector into housing interfered with the expansion of the private sector. But there *was* a boom later in the 1920s. Commentators have been deceived by the expansion in houses built in 1933 and afterwards into

[1] A. J. Brown, 'Resources Available for War', *Oxford Economic Papers*, No. 3 (1940), p. 6.

arguing that the building boom occurred in the 1930s not in the 1920s. Certainly, there was a housing boom in the 1930s based primarily on privately built houses for sale, but there was also a boom in the period 1925–9 (or even to 1932 since the depression had only slight adverse effects on the rate of building), based up to 1929 on local authority and private *subsidized* building.

In 1925 and the years that followed the number of houses built far exceeded the levels previously known in pre-1914 Britain[1] (including the booms of 1875–7 and 1897–1907 with the highest points in 1898–9 and 1902–3). The period 1925–9 was, therefore, characterized by a housing boom according to any reasonable standard. The inference is that attempts to explain the absence of a boom in the late 1920s due to high interest rates and other factors are grossly misplaced. What does require an explanation is the shift in the intensity of the boom from the conditions of 1925–32 to the super boom of 1933–8. The implication to be drawn from the occurrence of two housing booms, one superimposed upon the other, is that the theory of building cycles with its emphasis on the usual cyclical sequence (from trough to peak and back to trough again) can scarcely in itself satisfactorily explain inter-war building fluctuations.

b. Public Policy

Public housing policy may be used for stabilization purposes, either directly or by compensating for fluctuations originating elsewhere in the economy. Housing output can be controlled because the need for dwellings changes sluggishly (at least under normal conditions) and the extreme durability of a house means that annual additions to stock have only a slight impact on total supply, with the result that varying the rate of production from year to year counter-cyclically will only have slight adverse effects on welfare.[2] In the inter-war period, however, the counter-cyclical function of State intervention was not exercised so that public policy could as easily play a destabilizing as a stabilizing role. Instead the State intervened (as Chapter 8 shows) as a short-term remedy to the post-war housing shortage, to help provide working-class families with houses at rents lower than those offered by the private sector, and (later) to ac-

[1] See B. Weber, 'A New Index of Residential Construction, 1838–1950', *Scottish Journal of Political Economy*, 2 (1955), pp. 131–2.

[2] See, for instance, the examples suggested by L. Grebler, 'Housing Policy and the Building Cycle', *Review of Economics and Statistics*, 24 (1942), pp. 66–74. Although it is relatively easy in principle to control housebuilding for stabilization purposes, the technical difficulties involved are in practice considerable.

celerate slum clearance and to relieve overcrowding. If such action moderated fluctuations in building this was not the result of deliberate policy.

As far as building fluctuations were concerned, therefore, public policy would tend to act as an erratic shock, destabilizing or dampening according to the phase of the cycle reached when increases or cuts in subsidies were introduced. Fluctuations in building, therefore, followed a pattern different from that moulded by market forces. One line of analysis is to examine the changes in annual building due to State assistance separately from the forces at work on housebuilding by the private sector, and to regard the latter as the course of building activity according to a 'pure' market model. Unfortunately, an independent consideration of public housebuilding on the one hand and private housebuilding on the other is not practicable (certainly in the 1920s), because activity in the private sector was influenced by State intervention in a number of ways. Rent control, though not a direct obstacle to the building of rented houses by the private sector (new houses were not subject to restriction), nevertheless hindered private housebuilding. This was partly due to the (possibly unjustified) fear of investors that rent restriction on newer properties could be restored, partly to the fact that rent movements were less reliable as a market indicator of the profitability of housing investment, and partly because a large stock of rent controlled houses made people reluctant to move into uncontrolled houses at much higher rents. Secondly, private firms probably found it more profitable to build subsidized than unsubsidized houses, and also the extent of local authority building had an impact on the level of activity in the private sector because local authority houses were more often than not built by private contractors rather than by the local authorities themselves. Most important of all, as is shown in Chapter 8, the middle income groups and the better-off sections of the community benefited most from State-assisted building rather than the needy, and this obviously meant a reduced demand for output produced by the private unassisted sector. It follows that the extent of private housebuilding was not determined independently of the level of public housebuilding. The implications of this important point will be considered later.[1]

The varying role played by State-assisted building is an integral part of any sound explanation of inter-war building fluctuations. Firstly, the contribution of State-assisted to total UK housebuilding varied considerably over the inter-war period—the range spread

[1] See Section IV below.

from 70 per cent (local authority plus private subsidized houses) in 1927 down to 20 per cent (local authority houses, since private subsidized housebuilding had now become negligible) in 1934 and 1935. Secondly, the fluctuations in local authority housing expenditure in the 1920s were mainly due to changes in the type and amounts of subsidies.[1] This accounts for the peaks in local authority housebuilding in 1921–2 and again in 1925–7, while the sharp fall in local authority housebuilding in 1928 coincided with a reduction in the level of subsidy. Thirdly, apart from the spasmodic effect of changes in subsidies, housebuilding by the public sector tended to follow a path closely in line with the general business cycle. This reflected the tendency for public spending to be high in periods of prosperity and curtailed in depression. This pro-cyclical course of public housebuilding is particularly noticeable in the 1930s. Apart from a slight hump in 1931 (due possibly to a desire to obtain the final benefits before withdrawal of the Wheatley subsidy, or to initiate expenditure on slum clearance before the impact of the economy campaign was felt), local authority housing expenditures fell year by year from 1928 to 1933 (initially, of course, partly because of the subsidy cuts), then rose again up to 1938, very steeply indeed from 1935. These three rather different elements (the relative size of State-assisted and private housebuilding, the impact of changing subsidies, and the tendency for public expenditures on housing to move—with a lag at the lower turning-point—in the same direction as the business cycle) provide a substantial basis for analysing the role of public policy in residential building fluctuations.

IV. *Inverse Cycles in Public and Private Housebuilding*

a. The Housing Boom of the 1920s

Annual estimates of total capital formation in dwellings over the period 1920–38 at 1930 prices, and its allocation between the public and private sectors, are shown in Fig. 4 (p. 328). The total capital formation curve reveals a slow climb from very low levels indeed in 1920 up to 1927, with a moderate dip in 1922 and 1923. In 1928 there was a steep decline, followed by minor ups and downs over the next few years. In the period 1932–4 there was a sharp (and brief) upswing, but after 1934 there was a ratchet-like unsteady decline down to 1938 bringing real capital formation in dwellings back to slightly below the level of 1933.

Although the average level of residential capital formation in the

[1] These were outlined in Chapter 8.

1930s was considerably higher than in the previous decade, it is misleading to speak of a long housing boom in the 1930s and the absence of a boom in the 1920s. The fact was that the upswing of the 1930s was steep but its duration was short; a slight rise of about 5 per cent in the years 1930–2 was followed by an increase of 47 per cent between 1932 and 1934. From 1934 residential capital formation fell off, though the decline in terms of houses built was not as noticeable. However, there was a marked peak in the previous decade in 1926 and 1927. As was suggested above, this should undoubtedly be regarded as a housing boom. It is partially masked by the upward trend in housebuilding; if the trend were eliminated the 1920s boom would appear as intense as that in 1930s. Another reason why the 1920s boom is overlooked is that it was certainly not as obvious to contemporaries. The housebuilding of the 1930s probably made a stronger impression because of its heavy concentration on privately built houses, while in 1926 and 1927 both local authority building and private subsidized building were individually considerably more extensive than private unsubsidized building. Furthermore, the chronic housing shortage, the legacy of the war, made it more difficult for contemporaries to appreciate the existence of a boom. This housing shortage, in fact, intensified absolutely up to and including 1925. Did it make sense to believe there was a housing boom at a time when houses were in very short supply and the pressure on accommodation was very great? By the 1930s, on the other hand, the housing shortage was being alleviated. Many new houses were sprouting up in new privately developed suburbs, and the boom made a striking visual impression on contemporaries.

The housing boom of the 1920s can be demonstrated in other ways. The *absolute* rise in residential capital formation in the upswing of 1923–7 was considerably greater than the rise in the upswing of 1930–4—£87 million as against £66 million. The marginal housing coefficient, expressing the relationship between net *additions* to the housing stock and the number of families respectively, stood in the region of 1·3 in 1926 and 1927, a level that if lower than in the period 1933–7 (1·46 average) was considerably higher than in the years 1928–32 (0·98 average).[1] For the first time since the war a real bite was being taken into the housing shortage.

Furthermore, the term 'housing boom' is rather imprecise. If it relates to a sustained high level of housebuilding, this could easily be taken account of by a strong upward trend in housing expenditures and the cyclical implications of the word 'boom' may easily be lost.

[1] See Fig. 1, p. 325.

Alternatively, how can it be decided whether a cyclical peak is a boom or not? The peak of 1926 and 1927 was unsurpassed in the many vigorous pre-1914 housing booms but was nevertheless below the level of the 1930s. Consequently, should it qualify for the description 'boom'? As objective a criterion as any is to compare the house-building peak with the performance of the economy as a whole. In this test, the residential capital formation of 1926 and 1927 comes out very well. In these two years the share of residential in gross domestic capital formation averaged 35·7 per cent, a little higher than the average for 1932–8 (less than 35·6 per cent) and surpassed only in 1933–5. Finally, the share of residential in total construction (excluding civil engineering works) was higher in 1926 and 1927 (73·7 per cent) than in any year of the inter-war period except 1933 (76·0 per cent).[1]

It must be stressed that the case for a building boom in the 1920s, as well as in the 1930s, holds only in regard to residential building. When total building is considered[2] the argument in favour of a single boom, in the 1930s, becomes very strong as a result of the very steep rise in non-residential capital formation between 1932 and 1937. This was not because non-residential capital formation failed to rise in the second half of the 1920s, because it expanded quite steeply to a peak in 1930 which was not overtaken until 1936.[3] But at the time when housebuilding was rising rapidly between 1925 and 1927 industrial and commercial building was declining, and in 1929 and 1930 when non-residential building was booming housebuilding activity was markedly below the peak level of 1927. As a result, the residential building peak of 1926–7 and the non-residential peak of 1929–30 were flattened considerably, and in total construction the boom of the 1920s disappears. In the 1930s, on the other hand, between 1932 and 1934 housebuilding and non-residential building moved rapidly upwards together, and although the decline in residential capital formation set in from 1934, non-residential building continued to expand rapidly enough up to 1937 to keep the direction of total building slightly upwards. Paradoxically in view of the stress of the textbooks on the *housing* boom of the 1930s, a distinction between the 1920s and the 1930s is most clearly made if attention is riveted on total building rather than housebuilding alone. If one wishes to argue the case for a *single* building boom in the inter-war period, the foundations are stronger for a general building

[1] See Chapter 2, Appendix, Table 4, columns 2 and 3.

[2] See Fig. 3, p. 327.

[3] As shown by Fig. 8, p. 332.

boom in the 1930s rather than merely a housing boom. The inverse pattern of housebuilding and non-residential building in the second half of the 1920s erases the possibility of a boom, apparent in both branches of building when considered separately, from the pattern of overall building fluctuations.

b. The Inverse Relationship

The year-to-year movements in total residential capital formation show very different cyclical patterns for local authority and for private building.[1] The fluctuations in local authority building point to two full cycles, 1921–7 and 1927–38 with troughs in 1923 and 1934 respectively. The main factor behind these fluctuations was changes in the conditions and in the nature of Government subsidies. The sharp rise in local authority building in 1920–1 was due to the generous terms of the Addison Act of 1919, and the consequent steep decline in 1921–3 to the Treasury restrictions on the use of these subsidies under the Chamberlain Act of 1923 and the Wheatley Act of 1924. The year 1927 was the inter-war peak for local authority residential capital formation; in that year the scale of subsidies was reduced and despite a temporary restoration of the Wheatley reduction in 1929 further cuts were made in 1932. The steady fall in the level of subsidies and the eventual natural death of the general subsidy policy were associated with a decline in local authority building. Subsidies were then given for slum clearance under the Greenwood Act of 1930, but these merely had the effect of giving rise to a slight hump in local authority building in 1931. The general decline in local authority expenditures due mainly to adverse expectations brought on by the depression and the 1931–2 public economy campaign resulted in a continued fall in local authority building expenditures down to 1934. From 1934 local authority housing expenditures rose steadily up to 1938. The Housing Act of 1935 supplemented slum clearance by subsidies to relieve overcrowding.[2] Low interest rates favoured a revival of local authority spending, and there was a certain amount of pressure exerted by the Government on local authorities to step up their programme. By 1938 the real value of local authority housebuilding was almost back to the peak of 1927. Apart from the random effects of changes in subsidies, public housing expenditures followed a definite pro-cyclical course though lagging at the lower turning-point until 1934.

Private residential capital formation moved in a very different

[1] See Fig. 4, p. 328.

[2] These considerations were examined in some detail in Chapter 8 above.

fashion from local authority expenditures. In fact, private housebuilding displayed a strong upward trend from 1920–34, interrupted only in 1927–8 and more mildly in 1929–30. From 1934, however, private housebuilding expenditures declined steeply over the rest of the period. The contrast between fluctuations in local authority and private residential building expenditures is easily noticeable from a glance at Fig. 4 (p. 328). Only in 1920–1 and in 1923–8 did both move in the same direction. In the periods 1921–3, 1928–34 and 1934–8 their respective fluctuations followed an inverse pattern, local authority spending falling in 1921–3 and 1928–34 but rising in 1934–8 and private spending rising in the former periods but falling in the latter. In 1920–1 and in 1923–7 both sectors rose together and in 1927–8 both fell steeply. Moreover, the tendency for inverse cycles was far stronger than this contrast suggests at first sight, because the private residential capital formation aggregates of 1924–9 contain a substantial proportion of houses built by private enterprise but with the aid of subsidies. It is very doubtful that these should be given an unequivocal place in the private sector. Such building was very important since private subsidized houses built in 1926 and 1927 were considerably in excess of private unsubsidized houses.[1] If private subsidized building is excluded, the inverse pattern between private and local authority housebuilding fluctuations becomes almost exact. Virtually all the expansion in private housebuilding between 1923 and 1927 consisted of houses built with State assistance, and the numbers of unsubsidized houses built over this period actually fell slightly. On the other hand, in 1927–8, when both local authority and private subsidized housebuilding declined sharply, the number of houses built privately without State assistance actually rose slightly. Even in 1920–1 the expansion in private housing expenditures was accounted for, probably totally but at least primarily, by subsidized building. The statistics of private houses built in the early 1920s are very defective, but it is quite likely that private unsubsidized building was actually lower in 1921 than in 1920.

Thus, when the houses built by the private sector with State assistance are ignored, housebuilding by the private sector probably fell in 1920–1 and again in 1923–7 when local authority building was expanding and rose slightly in 1927–8 when local authority building was declining. This finding, in combination with the more strongly based opposite movements of 1921–3 and 1928–38, leads to the conclusion that private (unsubsidized) and local authority housing expenditures gave rise to inverse cycles throughout the inter-war

[1] As shown in Fig. 5, p. 329.

period. Spending on housing by the public sector operated as a stabilizer on the amplitude of residential building fluctuations. Consequently, the movement in total housing expenditure took far more the form of an upward trend and far less the form of severe ups and downs than if both sectors, public and private, had been moving in the same direction at the same time.

It is interesting to speculate why the inverse cycles developed. It could not have been due to conscious measures by the Government to stabilize residential building activity because the changes in subsidies and policy were dictated by *ad hoc* considerations, and the stabilization possibilities were very remote from the policy-makers' minds. This leaves two possibilities: either the inverse cycles were accidental, the result of pure chance, or there were adjustments on the side of private housebuilding to offset an upward or downward movement in public housing expenditures. The first explanation is, of course, the simplest but, unfortunately, the inverse pattern of the cycles is far too regular for pure accident to provide a plausible solution. We are inexorably driven to the second explanation where local authority expenditures have to be accepted as given and private housebuilding has to make the adjustments by changing in the opposite direction. There is a parallel between this situation and the old Treasury view about the futility of public works, that public spending will always be at the expense of private spending. As is well known, the weakness in this argument is that it holds only when there is a full employment and is irrelevant to conditions where resources are idle and can be brought into employment. Can the Treasury view be refashioned to explain the inverse cycle in public and private house expenditures in the inter-war period, that is, at a time characterized by high levels of unemployment and idle resources in general?

The renovation of this thesis is, in fact, feasible. Although heavy unemployment and excess capacity was widespread in the economy, and even though the average level of unemployment in building was high (10·5 per cent at its best in 1924 and 30·2 at its worst in 1932),[1] the supply of key building resources, particularly craftsmen and skilled labour generally, was often inelastic in periods of peak demand.[2] This meant that a boom in local authority housebuilding had to take place, to some extent, at the expense of private. Conversely, when public housebuilding declined this released resources, especially skilled craftsmen, for employment in the building of

[1] See Chapter 2, Appendix, Table 5.

[2] As argued in Chapter 5, pp. 123–7.

private houses. Admittedly, by the early 1930s the labour supply situation had eased compared with many years of the 1920s, but it is also true that the average level of total housebuilding activity had risen as well.

A supplementary explanation relates to the widespread tendency, stressed earlier, for local authorities to contract out their housebuilding to private builders. This led to a situation where private builders moved in and out of the public sector according to the direction of local authority housebuilding activity. Consequently, at a time when local authority building was expanding rapidly the increased number of contracts on offer to private builders inevitably meant a temporary decline in housebuilding by the private sector. When local authority building was falling off, on the other hand, it was natural for the contractors to return to building houses for sale to owner-occupiers or private investors. The extent to which this moving to and fro of private builders accounted for the inverse cycle is difficult to assess, but its influence may have been far from negligible.

A third explanation is connected with the argument advanced in Chapter 8, that the bulk of local authority and State-assisted houses built, at least before the slum clearance activities of the late 1930s, went not to the most needy in the community but to those best able to pay, probably to the better-off workers and even to the middle classes. The growth in total housebuilding was governed by the level of *effective* (not potential) demand. It is arguable that at times when local authority building was at a high level and rising, given the type of family to whom local authority houses were being allocated, this creamed off the effective demand for private housing with the result that the level of current demand for houses to buy or rent privately and consequently private housebuilding activity were low. When public housebuilding was low, on the other hand, the effective demand for housing was left almost untapped. On this view, the running down of the general subsidy policy and the growth in demand for houses to buy through building societies in the late 1920s and early 1930s were far from coincidental.

The pattern of fluctuations in residential building as measured in physical units, i.e. number of houses built, is shown in Fig. 5B.[1] The annual aggregate totals are given as well as the respective contributions of local authorities, private subsidized building and private unsubsidized building, but the aggregate figures have been estimated for calendar years while the sectoral totals refer to years ending

[1] This, in turn, is based on Chapter 2, Appendix Table 1.

March 31st (e.g. the figure for 1938 actually means the twelve months ending March 31, 1939). The broad cyclical pattern is, not surprisingly, similar to that shown in fluctuations in residential capital formation, but there are some significant differences. In the aggregate housing totals, the main difference is that from 1934 the expansion in houses built merely flattens out whereas the capital formation curve plunged downwards. The reconciliation between the two curves is achieved by the fact that average costs per dwelling continued to fall (by 6·3 per cent between 1934 and 1937),[1] despite the fact that the index of building costs rose sharply from 1934. However, the building cost index takes no account of changes in productivity and input efficiency in building itself, and falling average costs also reflected a switch to smaller houses.

The more interesting fluctuations are to be found in houses built in the different categories. The relatively high level of capital formation in the private sector in the middle 1920s was largely due to private building with the aid of subsidies. Private subsidized building was at a low though not negligible level in the period 1920–3, though rather extensive in 1921 before the lavish subsidies of the 1919 Act ran out. After 1923 private subsidized housebuilding soared to a peak in 1926 then dropped steadily down to 1929, but in both 1926 and 1927 was considerably more important than private unsubsidized building. Over the 1930s, and especially after 1934, private subsidized building virtually disappeared due to the change in emphasis in housing policy away from general subsidies in favour of slum clearance and overcrowding relief. The decline in subsidized building was not of course harmful to the private sector because private housebuilders found more than ample compensation in building houses without State assistance primarily for sale.

The annual estimates of private unsubsidized houses built are not available before 1923, but some 59,000 such houses were built between 1919 and March 1923. Between the years 1923 and 1928 private unassisted building remained remarkably stable within a range of 62,000 and 71,000 houses per annum. After 1928 expansion in houses built became very rapid, a fact obscured by the private sector capital formation series which includes subsidized houses which were now declining. The number of private unassisted houses built doubled between 1928 and 1930, then the upward movement flattened out over the next two years though houses built continued to increase. Between 1932 and 1934 the rate of expansion was as fast as in 1928–30, again almost a doubling of output in terms of

[1] Feinstein, op. cit., p. 216.

houses built. However, 1934 represented the inter-war peak. There was some fall in the level of houses built in 1935 and 1936 and a more marked decline through to 1938. The expansion in private unsubsidized housebuilding was therefore concentrated in a relatively brief period, the years 1928 to 1934.[1] This tends to give some support to those who argue that residential building in a free market will follow an anti-cyclical course.

The answer to why private unassisted building ceased to expand after 1934 is not easy to find. The sharpness of the upswing of 1932–4 could indicate the influence of speculative building with houses being built ahead of demand. An upswing of this kind could not go on very long and from 1934 output flattened out to permit demand to catch up despite further relaxation in the conditions of house purchase. It is clear that the boom of 1932–4 despite its strength failed to wipe out the housing shortage, so that any obstacle on the demand side was due to effective not potential demand. From 1934 average annual real earnings started to fall off and the expansion in aggregate real income slowed down. At the same time building costs started to move upwards again.[2] These facts are consistent with a stagnation in effective demand.

The movements in local authority housebuilding were not far different from the fluctuations revealed in the capital formation series.[3] The peaks of 1921 and 1927 and the trough of 1923 are well defined in both cases, as is the sharp fall in local authority housebuilding after 1927 and revival from 1935. The main dissimilarity is that the relatively smooth hollow over the period 1927–38 in capital formation takes on a more angular shape in the series of local authority houses built. Between 1928 and 1935 the annual output of local authority houses remained remarkably stable within a range 61,000 to 77,000, and averaged 70,400 houses per year. There was thus no real tendency for local authority housebuilding to be cut back in the depression once the effects of the subsidy cuts of 1927 had worked themselves out.

The inverse cycle pattern of housebuilding by the private and public sectors is also apparent in terms of houses built but not as strongly as shown by the investment curves. The hump of 1921 was based entirely on local authority assisted by private subsidized building and the boom of 1926–7 had the same foundations since there was no expansion whatsoever in private unassisted building.

[1] See Chapter 2, Appendix, Table 1 and Fig. 5, p. 329.

[2] Chapter 2, Appendix, Table 7, columns 4, 6 and 7.

[3] Shown in Fig. 4, p. 328.

The relative stability of housebuilding as a whole between 1929 and 1932 was explained by the fact that local authority building remained on more or less an even keel, while the sharp drop in private subsidized housebuilding was cancelled out by the expansion in unsubsidized building. The intense boom of 1932–4 was, of course, entirely due to the unsurpassed rate of growth in private building, while after 1934 the fall in private housebuilding was fully offset by the revival in local authority building.

c. Regional Housebuilding Fluctuations

Because of the immobility of the product housing markets are inevitably local. The national picture of building fluctuations is merely an average of a large number of local cycles, and the greater the degree of disaggregation the wider the differences between area fluctuations become. If building shows some response to changes in the rate of family formation, then heavy interregional migration such as took place between the wars will result in different patterns of building fluctuations between regions. It did not result in high levels of building activity in the regions into which the migrants were moving and stagnation in building in the areas from which the migrants were leaving, but merely different, but positive, rates of building. One reason for this was the higher average age of the existing stock in the North, Wales and Scotland which meant that replacement demands and slum clearance activity were higher in these areas. Another factor was the greater role played by local authority building in these areas aimed at the provision of subsidized homes for working families. This kept a relatively high floor on the extent to which building activity might fall. The differences between counties in the relative provision of local authority to private enterprise houses in the inter-war period varied tremendously: the range varied from 50–55 per cent local authority houses built between 1918 and 1939 in London and Cumberland, 40–45 per cent in the West Riding, Northumberland, Shropshire, Staffordshire and Norfolk, to 9–12 per cent only in Middlesex, Surrey and Essex. Rather surprisingly, the North and Midlands increased their share in total private sector housebuilding compared with the South in the 1930s despite the fact that the prosperity differential had probably widened in favour of the South. A possible explanation is that the demand for middle-class houses was satisfied earlier in the South and was only just being catered for in the other regions in the early 1930s.

There was a greater preponderance of local authority and subsidized building in the older industrial regions than in the prosperous areas of the South, and consequently the North was much more seriously affected by the decline in subsidized building after 1927. At the sub-regional level, however, there were considerable differences in the extent of local authority building. This reflected not only differences in political views between authorities, but also the fact that some methods of subsidy favoured the larger, richer authorities and discriminated against the poorer ones. Housing expenditures by the more prosperous authorities moved closer together, but were generally characterized by large fluctuations, whereas housing expenditures by the poorer authorities showed much greater stability. Bretherton and his collaborators noticed that as far as individual county boroughs were concerned there was a tendency for one year of expansion to be followed by a year of contraction. Their housing expenditures, therefore, proceeded by 'biennial jerks', though this did not show in overall figures because the timing was not uniform between boroughs.[1]

V. *Non-residential Building Fluctuations*

Fluctuations in industrial and commercial building move very closely in line with business activity. Investment is highly correlated with the level of business activity, and there is no *a priori* reason why investment in building should follow a different path from investment in plant and equipment, except perhaps the longer gestation period of buildings could give rise to some tendency to lag at the upper turning-point. There might be a case for arguing in favour of a lag at the lower turning-point as well on the grounds that businessmen may be less chary about investing in new machines in response to a recent rise in demand but may wish to be convinced that the expansion in demand is permanent before investing in new factories. Another view is that the timing of factory building will be dictated, except in very severe slumps, by the level of building costs and interest rates.[2] These may touch bottom either at or after the general turning points in the economy. But the level of interest rates is not going to be a crucial consideration in a situation where most firms rely on internal financing, and low building costs will normally be a minor factor compared, say, with profit expectations.[3] In any event, arguments about leads and lags are not particularly relevant to the

[1] R. F. Bretherton, F. A. Burchardt and R. G. S. Rutherford, *Public Investment and the Trade Cycle* (1941), p. 170.

[2] Robinson, op. cit., pp. 59–61 and 155.

[3] See Chapter 4, B.

inter-war period (at least to the latter half of the period), since major turning-points occurred in 1929, 1932 and 1937 in both industrial and commercial building and business activity.

As for non-residential building by the public sector, building work accounted for a higher proportion of public than for private investment. Most public construction was not subject to purely commercial influences—a possible exception was Post Office buildings but items of this type were quantitatively insignificant in the inter-war period.[1] In education and health the pressure for improved social services was the main stimulus within the constraints imposed by the budgets. In fact there was a long slow climb in social and public services building investment in the 1920s, a two-year lag at the upper turning-point with 1931 the peak year, a fairly sharp decline to 1933 and then a revival to unprecedented heights in 1938. The lags at the turning-points are a familiar occurrence in investment which depends upon fiscal decisions. The only influence of building in the public sector on the pattern of non-residential building fluctuations as a whole was to prolong the expected peak of 1929 into 1930. Otherwise the turning-points were the same as if only industrial and commercial building were under scrutiny.

An important question is how will non-residential building fluctuations affect the pattern of overall building fluctuations? There is no definite answer. If booms and troughs in non-residential building coincide with booms and troughs in housebuilding then the effect will be destabilizing. But if the peaks and troughs differ by substantial time periods, say, a few years, then overall building fluctuations will be milder. There are occasions when a trough in industrial and commercial building may occur simultaneously with a trough in housebuilding, and the result will be a severe building slump. This situation will be the exception, however, not the rule. As is argued in the next chapter, building is stimulated anti-cyclically by movements in building costs and interest rates, and though these are only two influences among many, they will normally be strong enough to pull housebuilding out of line with general fluctuations in economic activity. Housebuilding is, therefore, quite likely to be expanding when non-residential building is very low. Conversely, the counter-cyclical forces will tend to depress housebuilding just at the time when industrial building is attaining its peak. Consequently in the boom the flattening out or shrinkage in residential building need not necessarily involve a decline in total building activity because it will be generally replaced by other forms of building. Thus,

[1] Bretherton, *et al.*, op. cit., p. 100 et seq.

in the UK in the 1930s although capital formation in dwellings reached its peak in 1934, building as a whole continued to expand until 1937.

The overall pattern of gross capital formation in non-residential buildings can be discerned from Fig. 8A (p. 332).[1] Gross investment in buildings other than dwellings plunged downward in the years 1920–2 as an aftermath to the 1919–20 boom. From 1922 to 1925 there was a degree of recovery followed by a decline to 1927. From 1927 to 1930 non-residential building experienced a sharp intense boom restoring investment to a level not reached since 1920. This was the peak of the upswing, however, for the following year non-residential building declined rapidly, then more mildly in 1932. The trough of 1932 was lower than that of 1927 but not so deep as in 1922. After 1932 non-residential building recovered, at first slowly, but very steeply between 1933 and 1935. The expansion flattened out in 1935–6, but in 1936–7 the real value of non-residential building investment increased by 28 per cent.[2] In 1938 there was a mild relapse.

As suggested above, non-residential building responds to the same influences which operate on general investment decisions. For this reason, one would expect investment in non-residential building to follow a path similar to that pursued by the economy as a whole. That this generalization is broadly true is confirmed by Fig. 8A (p. 332) which compares fluctuations in non-residential building with fluctuations in business activity (as indicated by the *Economist* index). After 1930 the two series move closely in line. Before 1930 the similarity in the pattern of their fluctuations is not so clear. There are, in fact, two main differences. Firstly, non-residential building lagged behind business activity at both the lower and the upper turning-points by one year in 1927 and 1930 respectively. This phenomenon is not particularly unusual since the long gestation period in the production of non-residential buildings often makes for a lag at the peak. But the lag of 1930 behind 1929 in this case is not explicable in terms of long gestation building in industry and commerce; instead, the main factor was a further rise of building invest-

[1] No reliable estimates of net capital formation exist, for Feinstein's estimates of the difference between gross and net investment are based on a straight line depreciation method and the scrapping rate for other buildings and works averaged only about 32 per cent of assumed depreciation between the wars. The fluctuations in Feinstein's net capital formation estimates are consequently almost identical, apart from slight differences in amplitude, with those of gross capital formation. There is consequently little point in discussing fluctuations in gross and net investment separately.

[2] Chapter 2, Appendix, Table 3, column 1.

ment in social and public services, a rise which continued into 1931. In 1926–7 both industrial and commercial building declined, possibly because the repercussions of the General Strike meant a blow to business confidence.[1]

The second difference is that while non-residential building fell in 1927 and rose again in 1928, business activity improved in 1927 but fell off in 1928. The most plausible explanation of this is that the components weighted heavily in the *Economist* index expanded rapidly in 1927 to make up for the losses of the 1926 strike and the associated long coal strike and its effects, and that this resulted in a slight reaction in 1928. Had this not occurred business activity would have risen steadily from 1926 to 1929 bringing the direction of change into line with non-residential building investment which rose steadily between 1927 and 1930. Thus, there is little doubt about the close association between fluctuations in non-residential building investment and in the level of business activity. Probably both were subject to the same forces, so that the factors which made business boom and decline also stimulated and depressed industrial and commercial building.

Further observations may be made on these fluctuations in non-residential building if the aggregate total is split up into sectors.[2] The three most important sectors are manufacturing, retail distribution and the social and public services and their cyclical patterns are shown in Fig. 8B (p. 332).[3] Concentration on these three sectors alone covers a high proportion of total non-residential building (at least 75 per cent and in many years considerably more). A glance at the three series shows that the aggregate total masks quite considerable

[1] On the other hand, investment in plant and machinery revived quite strongly, and, moreover, the decline in non-residential building was very slight.

[2] A possible starting point is to take the Parry Lewis-Weber index of value of plans approved for new factories and workshops over the period 1923–38. However, because or its narrow scope and the fact that the plans were obtained only from the 146 local authorities submitting returns to the Ministry of Labour its usefulness is seriously reduced. For instance, the value of the plans in this series in 1936 was only about 12 per cent of total non-residential building investment. Suffice it to say that the fluctuations show turning points in 1926, 1929, 1931 and 1936 a year ahead of the aggregate series discussed above—this is explained by the lag between plans passed and their execution, so in effect the Parry Lewis-Weber index confirms the cyclical pattern of the aggregate capital formation curve. (B. Weber and J. Parry Lewis, 'New Industrial Building in Great Britain, 1923–38', *Scottish Journal of Political Economy*, 8 (1961).)

[3] See also Chapter 2, Appendix, Table 3, columns 2–4. In the manufacturing sector it is not possible to make a distinction between buildings and civil engineering works so the series is a composite one and is therefore an overestimate of building investment.

differences between the three sectors. There is some correspondence, not unnaturally, between the manufacturing and distribution series, but building in the social and public services followed a path of its own. Fluctuations in building investment in manufacturing were similar to those in total non-residential building after 1930, but not so clearly in the 1920s. There was a strong boom in 1920 (the level of activity was unsurpassed in the inter-war period), a drastic decline, then two minor cycles (with troughs in 1923 and 1928 and peaks in 1925 and 1929) fluctuating very much about the same level. The peak of 1925 was in fact higher than that of 1929, so the most noticeable aspect of the building cycle in manufacturing was the absence of a boom in the late 1920s. In the period 1932–7, on the other hand, the upswing was quite strong. This finding fits neatly the generalization of relative industrial stagnation in the 1920s and a marked revival in the recovery period of the 1930s.[1] There can be little doubt that the effect of the tremendous factory building boom of 1920 (though heavily concentrated on a limited range of industries—iron and steel, cotton, food, drink and tobacco, electrical engineering and chemicals) was to depress the level of factory building over the rest of the decade.

Building investment in retail distribution experienced fluctuations of rather similar periodicity to manufacturing, though this series led manufacturing in 1922, 1924 and 1927 and failed to decline in 1938. The contrast between the two series is really to be found in the amplitude of fluctuations. The amplitude of fluctuations in retail distribution building was certainly much narrower, especially after the mid-1920s; for instance, after 1924, in the peak year 1938 building investment in distribution stood at a level of 78 per cent above the trough (1932) compared with a peak (1937) in manufacturing 171 per cent above the trough. Apart from a severe slump in the early 1920s, especially in 1922, the average level of building investment in distribution in the 1930s was scarcely above the level prevailing in the previous decade. Even by 1936–8 investment in building in distribution had only just regained the level of 1924. On the other hand, the slump of the early 1930s was not marked in this sector, £9–12 million per annum still being invested in the

[1] This generalization may not be unanimously accepted, and here the authors found it difficult to ride two hobby horses at the same time. See H. W. Richardson, 'The Basis of Economic Recovery in the 1930s', *Economic History Review*, NS 13 (1962–3), and *Economic Recovery in Britain, 1932–9* (1967), and D. H. Aldcroft, 'Economic Progress in Britain in the 1920s', *Scottish Journal of Political Economy*, 13 (1966).

period 1930–3, though this is scarcely surprising considering how fast employment in distribution was expanding at this time.[1] These facts testify to the stabilizing influence of distribution on non-residential building fluctuations in the inter-war period.

The rough image of aggregate non-residential building fluctuations can still be discerned in the manufacturing and distribution series despite their individual differences. This suggests that both these series showed some response to variations in the level of economic activity—at least as represented by the index of business activity. When building investment in the social and public services is considered, however, it is apparent that this pursued an independent course. Building in this sector was not, of course, influenced by the business investment decisions which determined the direction of change in other branches of non-residential building. Instead, investment responded to social needs and pressures. The need for improved social and public services (more schools, libraries and hospitals, for example) was expanding, and it is therefore scarcely surprising to find an upward trend in expenditures on such items. Indeed, there is little evidence of a cycle at all in building in this sector. Apart from a minor dip in 1921–2, investment rose year by year (except for 1922–3 and 1927–8 when it remained stable) up to 1931. There was a decline in spending between 1931 and 1933, but from 1933 investment revived and gathered force up to 1938. The reductions of 1932 and 1933 were certainly the consequence of the economy campaign started in late 1931, and it is arguable that had it not been for these crisis restrictions on spending the course of building investment in this sector would have been continuously upward throughout the inter-war period. It is clear that this branch of investment had little impact on aggregate non-residential building fluctuations. The only way in which it influenced the aggregate pattern was that the steep rise in building in the social and public services in 1929–30 outweighed the decline in factory and shop-building and helped the upswing of the late 1920s to survive until 1930.

The causes of fluctuations in the shares of non-residential and residential building in total output can now be more clearly understood than when housebuilding fluctuations alone had been considered. The very high proportion of total building accounted for by non-residential building in 1920 was mainly due to the factory building boom of that year. The trough in non-residential building's

[1] Chapter 2, Appendix, Table 3.

share in 1926 was not purely the consequence of boom conditions in subsidized housebuilding but was also due to low levels of non-residential building in the year of the General Strike. The peak of 1930 was accounted for by a peak in non-residential building at a time when housebuilding had declined considerably below the levels of 1926–7, while the trough share of 1933 reflected not so much the slump in non-residential building, since the series had revived considerably above the level of 1932, as the tremendous surge forward in housebuilding. The subsequent revival in the share of non-residential building is similarly explained by a moderate falling off in housing expenditures as well as by the impact of recovery in industrial and commercial building.

VI. *Maintenance and Repairs*

Maintenance and repairs expenditures show characteristics different from new building expenditures which make for a different pattern of fluctuations. Maintenance jobs are less durable than original buildings and for this reason fluctuations in maintenance and repairs are shorter and less intense. They are also less liable to deferment than new construction which makes for greater stability. Maintenance and repairs are, of course, closely substitutable for new buildings because the obvious alternative to putting up a new building is to repair the old. To the extent that this substitutability operates, the result will be a tendency for repairs and maintenance to show an inverse cycle compared with new construction. Moreover, the need for repairs is related to the age distribution and quality of the existing stock of buildings; this will make for fluctuations in maintenance expenditures even if the total demand for buildings remains constant. Expenditures on alterations and conversions will give rise to no special cycle. Alterations to industrial and commercial buildings will probably move in harmony with business activity, that is, pro-cyclically. Alterations to houses will either take place at random or will vary according to long run changes in the average size of households; an increase in the average size will result in additions and alterations to existing houses while a fall in the average size will tend to give rise to conversions of existing large houses into flats. Alterations of this type, however, will only account for a small proportion of total maintenance and repairs expenditure.

Maintenance and repair expenditures on construction were characterized by relative stability with an upward trend in the inter-war period.[1] The trend was clearly associated with a similar upward trend in total building expenditures. Virtually stable between 1920 and 1925 (at £61·5 million, 1930 prices) spending on repairs rose steadily from that year until 1930 when they reached £77 million. The years 1930–2 saw a sudden jump in the scale of maintenance and repairs to £98 million in 1932, followed by a very gradual rise through to 1938 (£106 million), involving a rise of only 8 per cent over the period 1932–8.[2] These stability characteristics were very important for the overall amplitude of building fluctuations because of the high proportion of total investment in construction which went into repair work between the wars. Maintenance and repair expenditures averaged about 30 per cent of total building (including civil engineering) work over the period, being considerably lower than this in 1920–1 (averaging 25 per cent) but much higher in 1931–4 (an annual average of 39·2 per cent).

If the trend in maintenance and repair expenditures were eliminated, there would be some tendency for the inverse cycle to appear. This can most easily be observed by comparing fluctuations in the share of maintenance and repairs in total construction with fluctuations in total construction. Between 1920 and 1923 the share of maintenance expenditures rose at a time when construction was declining, whereas in the period 1923–7 an upswing in total construction was matched by a fall in the share of repairs. Similarly, the downswing in construction between 1927 and 1932 was associated with a rise in the share of repairs which was especially marked in the years 1930–2; from 1932 to 1937 construction expanded again while the share of maintenance and repairs fell steadily back to the 1928 level, and in 1938 construction declined but spending on repairs rose. The year by year inverse correlation was therefore exact. This would of course have been the case had expenditure on repairs remained constant throughout the period, but the tendency for an inverse cycle can be gleaned from the fact that the maintenance expenditures rose fastest between 1930 and 1932, that is, in years characterized by a rapid fall in total construction expenditures. The inverse cycle in maintenance and repair expenditures *per se* was not very marked, however, over the inter-war period as a whole. It would be more accurate to stress the stability of maintenance expenditures and their upward trend. They thus had a considerable moderating influence on the amplitude of overall building fluctuations, particularly by filling in the potential depressions.

[1] See Fig. 3, p. 327.

[2] Chapter 2, Appendix, Table 4.

VII. *The Overall Pattern*

The separate descriptions of fluctuations in each sector now make it possible to outline the pattern of fluctuations in building considered as a whole. This overall pattern can be discerned from the gross capital formation series for all building (Fig. 3A, p. 327).[1] The quite severe fluctuations in non-residential building disappear, partly because the weighting of this sector is smaller than that of housebuilding but mainly because the peaks and troughs are ironed out by offsetting movements in each sector. The peak housebuilding of 1927 cancels out the slump in industrial and commercial building, while in 1930 boom activity in non-residential building outweighs the fall in local authority and private subsidized housebuilding. The overall building levels of 1927 and 1930 were, therefore, about equal. Similarly, in the 1930s the severe industrial building slump of 1930–2 is moderated though by no means eliminated by a modest upswing in private housebuilding, while booming industrial and social service building after 1934 keeps the overall capital formation series on an upward path in spite of the relapse in housing expenditures.

As a result of the partially inverse pattern of housebuilding and non-residential building fluctuations, the cycle in building activity as a whole is evened out. The sharp depressions disappear and the upward trend in building becomes much more apparent. Fluctuations are not eliminated altogether: there remains the sharp upswing and downswing of 1920–2 and the depressions of 1928 and 1931–2. The upward trend is, however, only strongly marked in two periods, 1923–7 and 1932–4. It is perhaps significant that these were the years characterized by rapid expansion in housebuilding. Thus, the position may be summarized in this way: housing expenditures dictated the timing and the strength of the upswings in total building, but apart from in 1921–2 (when both sectors declined) sharply expanding industrial and commercial building offset falling housing investment in 1927–30 and 1934–8 thus avoiding serious slumps in building as a whole.

Nevertheless, the upward trend was apparent in both the residential and the non-residential sectors. In the latter, the main factor in the trend was the much greater buoyancy of industry and business activity in the 1930s. In the 1920s after the collapse of the post-war boom industrial investment in building failed to revive, and the upward movement of that decade was accounted for by building

[1] See Chapter 2, Appendix, Table 4, column 1. The series cover houses and non-residential buildings, but excludes civil engineering works.

in the social and public services. As for housebuilding, the trend showed itself only in the private sector—local authority housebuilding fluctuated about the same level over the period, though the troughs and peaks were more intense in the 1920s. The upward trend in private housebuilding was due to a host of favourable influences: the rise in real incomes, the expansion in building societies, a change of tastes in favour of new suburban houses which became more potent in the 1930s, the effects of the housing shortage. Expenditure on maintenance and repairs also exhibited the same upward trend.

A fact associated with the upward trend, almost a corollary, was the absence of severe contractions in building between the wars. The sharpest declines in building investment were 20 per cent in 1921–2, 12·4 per cent in 1927–8, and 12·8 per cent in 1930–2, all measured from peak to trough.[1] Although these falls could not be described as mild, the recessions were very short and less severe than experienced before 1914. The relative mildness of building slumps must be explained by factors on the housebuilding side, since non-residential building investment fell by 47·5 per cent and 38·8 per cent in the periods 1920–2 and 1930–2 respectively.[2] The absence of a major housebuilding slump is to be explained primarily as a consequence of the interruptions to building in the First World War and the severe housing shortage that developed. This housing shortage was never eliminated though it eased after the great upswing of 1932–4. The fall in investment in private housebuilding after 1934 might have had serious repercussions had it not been offset by increased local authority expenditures on new housing for slum clearance and to relieve overcrowding and by the steep recovery in non-residential building.

VIII. *Summary*

Fluctuations in building differ markedly in periodicity and in amplitude from fluctuations in economic activity as a whole. The reasons for these differences include the durability of buildings, the long production planning period and various reaction lags, demographic influences, the speculative character of the private housing sector and random shocks such as the effects of war and changes in Government subsidies. In addition, as shown in the next chapter, building is influenced by determinants which change cyclically such

[1] Chapter 2, Appendix, Table 4, column 1.

[2] Chapter 2, Appendix, Table 3, column 1.

as costs, rents, income and interest rates; the net effect of these variables on the level of building activity is usually to throw it out of line with economy-wide fluctuations. However, non-residential building follows a pattern similar to business activity generally.

In an analysis of inter-war building there are dangers in over-emphasizing the boom of 1932–4 and the role of private unsubsidized housebuilding. There was, in fact, a sharp but strong housing boom in 1926 and 1927, though based on local authority and subsidized private building. This boom is partially obscured in housebuilding since residential and non-residential building rose together (exceptionally) in the years after 1932 whereas they tended to offset each other in the latter half of the previous decade.

The main characteristic of cycles in non-residential building was their very wide amplitude with particularly sharp downswings in 1920–2 and 1930–2 and strong revivals in 1926–9 and 1933–7. These severe fluctuations failed, however, to impart an equivalent intensity to fluctuations in total building, partly because the weighting of non-residential building was smaller than housebuilding but mainly because housebuilding and industrial and commercial building tended to offset each other. Thus local authority building kept total building up in 1921 despite the slump in factory building, and private unsubsidized building expanded modestly between 1930 and 1932 moderating the decline in non-residential building. Conversely, the boom of the late 1920s in non-residential building helped to offset the effects of subsidy cuts on local authority housebuilding while the even sharper boom of the middle 1930s more than compensated for the post-1934 slump in private unsubsidized housebuilding.

Although all sectors of building were subject to the same causal forces in varying degrees they were each influenced by factors peculiar to their individual sector. The fluctuations in each sector were often sharp—in local authority housebuilding in the 1920s, in private housebuilding after 1932, in non-residential building over the whole period. The destabilizing tendencies in any single sector, however, were not allowed to determine the course of fluctuations in building as a whole because such tendencies were offset by counter movements in other sectors. There were strong inverse cycles in private and local authority housebuilding and, to a lesser extent, in housebuilding and non-residential building. These inverse patterns were not primarily accidental: the opportunities for private housebuilding were often dependent on the level of activity in the local authority cycle; non-residential building moved pro-cyclically for obvious reasons while housebuilding was stimulated by forces at work near the trough of the business cycle. Moreover, even maintenance and repairs expenditures played a stabilizing role: in no year did they experience a serious decline, and they expanded most rapidly of all between 1930 and 1932 thereby helping to offset the deep slump in non-residential building. The stabilizing consequences of these inverse cycles meant that total building fluctuations escaped the serious contractions experienced by individual sectors. The slumps were ironed out and the fluctuations became much milder, apart from the steep upswings of 1923–7 and 1932–4 which assist the impression of the course of building activity between the wars as an upward trend rather than a marked cycle.

CHAPTER 11

COSTS, INCOME AND BUILDING FLUCTUATIONS: THE WEBER THESIS

I. *Cyclical Variables*

a. Interrelationships

We have seen that secular forces, unrelated to the business cycle, may have powerful effects on building activity. It is equally clear, however, that the level of building is influenced markedly by variables that change in magnitude and in a regular, predictable way over the business cycle. The impact of these cyclical determinants vary, in some cases stimulating, in others depressing, building costs. On the one hand, building costs and interest rates fall in the depression and rise in the boom relative to rents, and in this way tend to make building fluctuations anti-cyclical. On the other hand, cyclical variations in real income have a pro-cyclical impact. The question is: how is building activity as a whole affected by the resultant of these opposing forces? Although they operate in opposite directions they do not necessarily cancel out. Some writers[1] have argued that the pattern of fluctuations in building is definitely inverse to the business cycle in general, even if perception of this fact is made more difficult by the complicating effect of long cycles.

In fact, there seems no *a priori* reason why one group of factors, whether the pro-cyclical or anti-cyclical forces, should always predominate under all conditions and at all times. Weber made an important explanatory suggestion in this respect by making the cyclical impact of each of these influences dependent upon the direction of the trend. He argued that if the trend of costs and prices is rising, then building will tend to be affected more by cost factors than by changes in income. Similarly, the income demand for houses over the business cycle will be of great influence if the trend of real incomes is rising and less important if the trend is falling. It follows that if the trend of real incomes is rising and is in reverse

[1] H. W. Robinson, *The Economics of Building* (1939), p. 156; K. Pribram, 'Residual, Differential and Absolute Urban Ground Rents and Their Cyclical Fluctuations', *Econometrica*, 8 (1940), pp. 62–78; and L. Grebler, 'House Building, the Business Cycle and State Intervention', *International Labour Review*, 33 (1936), Pt. 1, pp. 337–55, are three examples.

direction to the trend of costs and interest rates then building will tend to move in accord with cycles in the economy at large.[1] Since the trends of incomes, costs and interest rates were in broad agreement with this condition between the wars, Weber's hypothesis is very relevant to an appraisal of inter-war building fluctuations. Its theoretical justification and its value as a predictor of the pattern of building fluctuations in the inter-war period are considered in this chapter. The significance of the hypothesis is that it supports the view that the relative importance of individual determinants of the level of building activity may alter drastically over time and according to circumstances.

b. Building Costs and Interest Rates

The fall in building costs and in interest rates in the downswing would not *ceteris paribus*, act as an incentive to builders and housing investors if it were matched by an equivalent fall in house prices and rents. The investor would find the rent/cost ratio unchanged and the *expected* yield from house investment might well fall since his expectations could be adversely affected by general slump conditions. What overcomes the depressive effects of expectations is the tendency in slumps for the gap between rents (and to a lesser extent house prices) and costs to widen thereby increasing profitability. Rents tend to be inflexible, partly because of maintenance costs which have to be covered in the long run and which are not appreciably alleviated by short run falls in costs, partly because of the existence of leases. Even in the later stages of an upswing, when construction costs may rise rapidly, rents will adjust to this only very slowly. Thus in the inter-war period, after a peak in 1921 and 1922 and a slight decline thereafter, the Ministry of Labour rent index rose annually from 1924 up to the outbreak of the Second World War.[2] There were fairly marked variations in the annual rate of increase but in no year did rents actually decline. There is no concrete evidence of relative movement in construction costs and selling prices; US evidence suggests close conformity between the construction cost index and price index with certain short run divergences.[3] It is probable that in conditions of overall rising demand for houses falls in costs will not be fully reflected in price reductions (especially because of the lack

[1] Weber's argument is summarized in Parry Lewis, op. cit., Appendix 10, pp. 357–63.

[2] See Chapter 2, Appendix, Table 7.

[3] L. Grebler, D. M. Blank and L. Winnick, *Capital Formation in Residential Real Estate* (NBER, 1956), p. 358.

of homogeneity in houses not only in design and materials but particularly in sites, which gives considerable scope for price differentiation). However, if costs are rising rapidly the margin between cost and price may very well be narrowed if houses are ordered before completion and there are no adjustment clauses in the contracts.

Building costs are generally held to be less flexible than changes in interest rates (though more flexible than rents).[1] Although they rise early in the upswing and may increase very rapidly in the later stages when competition between house and non-residential building becomes intense, they are supposed to be resistant to depression. It is argued that building costs fall markedly only after depression has become intense, and often when demand has fallen to such low levels that reduced costs can have little effect. This view is not fully justified by inter-war experience. Demand remained buoyant throughout, and therefore a situation where demand was so low as to be impervious to changes in costs was irrelevant. Even more important, available cost indices indicate some cyclical flexibility in costs. The cyclical variations are rather difficult to perceive since the trend of costs was downward between the wars, but the Maywald index shows an 8·5 per cent fall between 1925 and 1928 and a 10 per cent fall between 1930 and 1933.[2] The estimates of average costs per dwelling based on the returns for 146 local authorities show a greater fall between 1930 and 1933 (15 per cent) compared with only a very slight downward trend in the late 1920s, and this index may be more reliable because it takes account of changing inputs.[3] Moreover, the rise in costs in the later 1930s was not as great as the *a priori* argument would lead one to expect. The downward adjustment in costs in the depression of the early 1930s shows a weaker cyclical response than prices in general, but does not indicate strong resistance to cost reduction.

The reasons for the supposed inflexibility of building costs are well known. Firstly, wage costs are higher in building than in most other industries and the price of labour is considerably less flexible than prices in general. Though unskilled labour in building was mainly casual, craft unions in the skilled categories were, partly in consequence of their shortage, able to resist substantial wage cuts.

[1] For example, see ILO, *Housing and Employment* (1948), pp. 96–98, and L. Grebler, 'House Building, the Business Cycle and State Intervention', loc. cit., pp. 339–40.

[2] Chapter 2, Appendix, Table 7.

[3] Feinstein, op. cit., p. 216.

Secondly, the building material industries are notorious for being riddled with restrictive agreements which make for very slow price reductions in slumps and accelerating price increases in booms. Thirdly, building costs tend to remain high and adjust much more easily in an upward than in a downward direction because of the consequences of irregularity in building activity, tardy infiltration of modern industrial methods and the resulting low productivity. Finally, as already suggested, the increased demands of commercial and industrial building tend to boost both wage and material costs at the peak of the boom.

One reason why building costs fell more than these considerations would suggest in the early 1930s is that the supply of labour was reasonably elastic. The pressure of policy in the 1920s had led to a substantial expansion in the labour force with the result that labour could easily be recruited in the early 1930s. The relatively consistent level of activity of the 1920s meant a stable labour force so that the fall in numbers employed between 1930 and 1932 (by 94,800) was easily recovered in the following two years.

However, there are limitations to the impact of building costs on the rate of building activity. For one thing, reduced construction costs are unlikely to cause families to move from existing into new houses, because older properties will be revalued sufficiently to erase any abnormal cost-price spread. The price elasticity of demand for houses is generally regarded as fairly low. As far as investors are concerned this would depend on how far rents and costs diverged, but for the potential house purchaser the fact that houses are bought on credit means that a 10 per cent fall in costs may have a far smaller effect on housebuilding than, say, a liberalization of building society lending terms and conditions. Probably, high building costs are more effective in choking off booms than low costs are in stimulating revivals, but standing in the late 1960s one is likely to be much more sceptical of this generalization than if one were in the late 1930s.

Changes in interest rates may have more influence on building than changes in costs. For instance, interest rates can change overnight, whilst movements in building costs may be spread over several years. But it should be noted that, given a twenty-year repayment period and assuming house purchase is financed entirely by borrowing, an 8 per cent fall in building costs will have as much effect as a reduction in interest rates from 5 per cent to 4 per cent.[1] On the other

[1] Moreover, falling building costs if passed on may have an important effect on the size of deposit required. The argument is elaborated in Chapter 9 above, pp. 203–4.

hand, repercussions of low interest rates and their corollary, easy credit conditions, are wider than those of lower building costs because they influence supply conditions as well as demand. Credit for builders will be more freely available when interest rates are low, an important point because of the predominance of small firms in the industry and the long period of production which results in heavy reliance on credit. The supply of finance will also be greater because funds will tend to move into building societies where returns remain higher than gilt-edged yields in periods of low interest rates and because investors will be wary of equities in depression. Monthly payments for house purchasers will fall, and the investment demand for houses will rise because lower interest rates will mean, *ceteris paribus*, a rise in the rent/cost ratio.

Some writers have regarded changes in the rate of interest as the critical variable in building fluctuations. Grebler, for example, found with pre-1914 data that housebuilding and the interest curves followed opposite courses, and that the opposition was almost exact, or else with a one-year lag.[1] The housing boom in the UK in the 1930s has also been mainly explained by the effects of cheap money. The stress on changes in building costs and interest rates is most relevant in conditions where the demand for housing is predominantly an investment demand, for in such circumstances a marked and growing divergence between rents and costs should act as a powerful stimulus. Where the demand is for owner occupation these changes become less important. On the other hand, even if they cannot explain a reversal in the direction of building activity they might help to account for the timing of the turning points.

c. Income Effects

Income effects on building activity tend to make building move pro-cyclically. Building activity is an obvious derivative of national income, and should show some response to changes in income. On the other hand, the observed fact that building cycles are of longer duration than business cycles means many fluctuations in national income have little or no effect on building. It is clear that building is far less sensitive than most other forms of investment to changes in income. In spite of this, it is often argued,[2] that housing demand responds more to income than to changes in costs and prices. How

[1] Grebler, loc. cit., p. 347.

[2] For example, Long, op. cit., *passim*, and L. Winnick, 'Housing: Has there been a downward shift in Consumers' Preferences?', *Quarterly Journal of Economics*, 69 (1955), pp. 85–98.

is this apparent contradiction reconciled? The answer is that there is a definite positive correlation between housing demand and long-run income changes, but that the cyclical effects of income changes are not great.[1] This is certainly the case when cyclical income changes are related to the *total* demand for housing, since, for instance, sharp temporary falls in income do not result in people moving into cheaper housing. It is not so clear when transitory income movements are examined in relation to the demand for new houses, since the durability of houses makes the rate of additions to the stock very sensitive to such changes. This is not because a fall in income reduces the incentive of people to want houses either to rent or to buy, but rather that these cyclical changes in income adversely affect the expectations of builders and investors.

Broadly speaking, housing demand will be associated with long-run expected income but cyclical changes in real income will not in themselves have a major direct impact on housing activity. This is not to deny that the rapidly rising real incomes of the majority of the population in the early 1930s was an important cause of the housing boom, since this was associated with other favourable factors such as a shift in the demand curve due to changing tastes, and other stimuli such as availability of housing finance. Moreover, this case was an unusual one in that the depression meant large increases in real incomes for many people (partly because of very favourable terms of trade) which to the extent that income demand was important tended to make building anti-cyclical, or more accurately helped to account for a rise in building while the general depression was still under way. Related to this, falling real wages in the late 1930s may have played a role in the flattening of the housebuilding curve at that time. Normally, however, national income movements will stimulate building in the upswing and depress it in the contraction. This is especially the case when construction as a whole is considered since non-residential building tends to follow national income very closely.

To sum up, cyclical movements in variables influential in building but which change considerably over the business cycle cannot in themselves account for fluctuations in building activity. This is partly because these variables tend to offset each other, and partly because they have to compete with strong trend forces (such as changes in the number of families) acting upon building. The cyclical movements are likely to be more influential when they are

[1] For a general statement of this view see M. G. Reid, *Housing and Income* (1962). See also Chapter 3, II.

combined with secular trends or sudden shifts operating in the same direction, but will not predominate sufficiently to make building follow a course which is directly or inversely in line with the business cycle.

II. *The Weber Thesis*

It has been observed that, due to the influence of housebuilding, fluctuations in building as a whole show two strong upswings in the years 1923–7 and 1932–4. Consideration of private unassisted housebuilding in itself, however, points to only one period of expansion over the years 1928–34. In the light of these facts what can be said about the pro- or anti-cyclical tendencies of housebuilding? In particular, what can be made of Weber's thesis that housebuilding will pursue a pro-cyclical course in periods when the trend of incomes is rising while the trend of costs falls, but an anti-cyclical course if costs are rising from a trend point of view while incomes are not? The hypothesis has its attractions. Its flexibility is shown by its prediction that housebuilding will show varied responses to changes in business cycles phases according to the changing set of economic conditions, a view superior to dogmatic assertions of a one-way causal relationship. Moreover, since any convincing interpretation of fluctuations requires a judicious blend of trend factors and cyclical impulses the explanation of the character of fluctuations in terms of trend influences is appealing. But the worth of the argument depends upon its theoretical plausibility and whether or not it predicts the facts.

The argument sounds reasonable in theory. If the trend in incomes is upwards then presumably the greatest increases in income will be concentrated in upswings. Provided the lag of housebuilding behind income is not too long then housebuilding should tend to pursue the course of the business cycle. Similarly, this tendency will be accentuated by a downward trend in costs and interest rates, since this trend will be stronger in depressions than booms. As the downswing proceeds circumstances will become more favourable to building, but costs and interest rates will not impart their greatest stimulus until the trough is reached, or possibly after the trough. Moreover, if the trend is downwards costs and interest rates will probably not rise sharply enough in the later stages of the upswing to choke off building and give it the anti-cyclical pattern which cost influences alone lead one to expect. One drawback to this thesis relates to the influence of income. When private houses are built for sale the demand for houses may respond more to changes in annual average earnings than to changes in aggregate income. These may not move in line; for instance, real earnings often increase fastest in downswings when overall income falls or at best remains stable. The rise in real average earnings was particularly noticeable in the depression of the early 1930s partly due to the effects of improving terms of trade. This point may call for qualifications to the Weber thesis.

Does the model fit the facts? In part, yes. The downward trend in interest rates (as measured by the yield on Consols) was most marked (apart from the rapid fall of 1920–2) between 1929 and 1935 (and especially after 1931), while building costs fell sharply between 1929 and 1933.[1] This bears a close association with the period of expansion in unsubsidized building, the years 1928 to 1934. The trend in real national income was clearly upwards over the inter-war period, but the two periods of decline were 1925–6 and 1930–2 and both these periods experienced expansion in housebuilding. Looking at the inter-war period as a whole, housebuilding did not show a definite pro-cyclical tendency since the two phases of rapid expansion were, as has been pointed out, the years 1923–7 and 1932–4 which fell within the early stages of an upswing. The later phases of upswings, 1927–9 and 1934–7, witnessed declining housebuilding activity. However, if the argument is amended to refer to the trend of average real earnings rather than to real national income then the concentration of tremendous expansion in housebuilding in the early stages of revivals can be explained. In a period when the trend of costs and interest rates is markedly downwards while the trend in real earnings is upwards both cost and income influences will be more favourable to housebuilding at the trough of depression. Real earnings expanded fastest in the year 1930–1, interest rates fell sharpest between 1931 and 1933 and building costs between 1930 and 1932. On the reasonable assumption of a one- or two-year lag these influences could account for the sharp housing boom of 1932–4. But the interaction of these influences cannot adequately explain the housebuilding boom of 1923–7. Average annual real earnings remained almost stable between 1923 and 1926, interest rates tended to move upwards, while building costs rose in the first two years, 1923–5, but fell thereafter. On the other hand, it has been shown that this earlier housing boom can scarcely be explained in terms of market forces at all, being primarily caused by the stimulus of subsidies.

Broadly speaking, therefore, interesting though the analysis may be, the Weber thesis is not an adequate predictor of the character of

[1] See Chapter 2, Appendix, Table 7, columns 4 and 5.

housebuilding fluctuations in the inter-war period. It is useful, on the other hand, to the extent that it shows how the interaction of cost and income trend factors may influence the character of the housebuilding cycle. When suitably modified it helps to account for the concentration of upswings in housebuilding in the early phases of business revival in the inter-war period.

Another criticism of the Weber thesis advanced by Parry Lewis is that it is too aggregative. Building markets are essentially local, and housebuilding at the regional or sub-regional level tends to follow the cyclical pattern of business activity in the area regardless of trends in incomes and costs.[1] But the Weber thesis is merely a generalization which intends to give a summary of tendencies rather than provide a detailed explanation. The pro-cyclical character of regional building fluctuations was discussed in the last chapter, and Parry Lewis's point may well be true. On the other hand, the differences in timing, periodicity and amplitude of regional building cycles may give rise to a far different national cycle. In addition, of course, local movements in business activity will vary from the aggregate business cycle. Thus, there is no reason why the aggregation of regional building fluctuations moving in line with regional business cycles could not result in an anti-cyclical pattern of building fluctuations in the national economy.

The limitations of the Weber thesis are obvious. It concentrates attention on income and cost factors alone which fluctuate cyclically. It says nothing about other influences on building which may bear little relation to the business cycle. For instance, the demographic shocks connected with the First World War, particularly the exceptionally high post-war marriage rate, had a marked impact on housebuilding in the years that followed.[2] Although it may be argued that its cyclical effects are neutral simply because it was an external shock this is not necessarily the case. It accentuated the housing shortage which induced large-scale Government intervention in the housing market in the 1920s, and was, therefore, in a sense partly responsible for the 1923–7 upswing. Another point is that certain demographic changes, such as migration and marriages, vary cyclically with business activity. However, if migration and the number of marriages change positively with national income, it might be answered that their influence is fully accounted for by the effects of national income on housebuilding. Moreover, population influences show themselves in changing housing needs which may not elicit much response in terms of changes in effective demand. Since effective demand deter-

[1] Parry Lewis, op. cit., pp. 362–3. [2] See Chapter 3, Section I.

mines housebuilding output it might be argued that Weber's argument concentrates on the crucial variables.

Weber's framework is too narrow, however, to deal with the causes of the private housebuilding boom of the early 1930s. Rising real incomes for those in work were a favourable factor but worked only because other circumstances were conducive to expansion in private housebuilding. Similarly, cheaper building costs helped the boom but the cost reductions were not extensive enough to explain the intensely sharp upswing of 1932–4. Finally, the reduced interest rates assisted the boom by providing easy credit for builders, by attracting investors into the relatively more profitable housing market and by leading to a fall in mortgage rates. But even these three factors considered together—all of which are taken into account in the Weber thesis—do not fully explain the boom. Rising real incomes led to increased effective demand only because of the inflow of funds into building societies and the very liberal relaxations in their credit terms and restrictions. The boom was accentuated by the size of the housing shortage bequeathed by the war and the failure to relieve this shortage in the intervening period, and by the effects of shifts to the South of population and industry. Cost reductions were only made effective because the supply inelasticities which had handicapped expansion in parts of the 1920s had been eliminated. The development of an investment demand for new houses was facilitated not only by low gilt-edged yields but by the absence of rent control on new houses making them more attractive (once fears of an extension of control had been allayed) to investors than existing houses. The sharp rise in output by the private sector did not result in much of a fall in public housebuilding because of growing public pressure for slum clearance, overcrowding relief and improvements in housing standards. A major cause of the boom was probably a change in tastes, a preference for new, smaller suburban houses made more attractive by design improvements and by new types of fittings and fixtures. Although this change in tastes was facilitated by rising incomes it was precipitated by all kinds of influences: transport improvements and increasing use of the motor-car, declining availability of domestic servants, a substantial decline in average family size.[1] It is not possible to give each factor its relative causal weight but it is clear that no single influence predominated; rather, a large number of favourable factors emerged simultaneously.

[1] On the other hand, the change in tastes thesis is not fully satisfactory as an explanation of the boom since by its nature such a change would tend to show itself in the long run rather than suddenly in the one phase of the cycle.

CHAPTER 12

BUILDING FLUCTUATIONS AND BUSINESS CYCLES

I. *The Problem*

The previous two chapters have concentrated attention on fluctuations in building itself and on the influences behind these fluctuations. Although some of these causal influences moved, either directly or inversely, in line with the business cycle, others bore no relation to cyclical changes but were long-term changes such as population movements or exogenous impulses such as the war. The interrelationship between fluctuations in building and fluctuations in general business now requires explicit discussion. One aspect, the way in which building is affected by cyclical forces which are the product of fluctuations in the aggregate economy, such as changes in costs and interest rates, was considered in the last chapter. But it is not necessarily the case that building merely responds to movements in the economy in general. It is also possible that in part building and general business are correlated not causally but rather because they are both strongly influenced by a common third factor. Even more likely, building may itself be the cause and general fluctuations the effect. One of the main objectives of this chapter is to explore the impact of building on fluctuations in the economy as a whole.

An important question is how movements in the aggregate economy should be measured. There is no strong case to be made for any single indicator, and consequently several will be used. These are: the most recent estimates of real national income as computed by Feinstein, the Lomax index of industrial production excluding building, the *Economist* index of business activity which is only available from 1924, and the level of employment as determined by Chapman and Knight's estimates. The level of total investment is not used as an indicator primarily because of the quantitative predominance of building investment in the total. As indicators of fluctuations in building the series of gross capital formation in dwellings and other buildings (excluding civil engineering works) employed earlier is adopted, supplemented by the Lomax index of building and contracting.[1] It will sometimes be necessary to separate

[1] As pointed out in the statistical appendix to Chapter 2, the Lomax index is

residential building from non-residential building fluctuations. The reason for this is that most branches of non-residential building do not change autonomously but respond to general investment decisions originating in, for example, the public and the industrial sectors. On the other hand, residential building does, as has been shown, follow an independent course and is therefore much more likely to be a causal stimulus to changes in general economic activity than other kinds of building.

The exact nature of the relationship between building and general fluctuations is not easy to unravel. It has already been noted that residential building while not moving in an exact anticyclical fashion shows some tendency to respond to forces operating in the depression, a tendency suggesting the possibility that building does in fact run counter to the business cycle. Other writers[1] have asserted in the light of US experience that building and general business go together, with building tending to lead business activity. An even stronger thesis is to assert that not only do they move together but that the turning-points and amplitude of general business cycles are causally determined by movements in building. In fact, those who favour the counter-cyclical fluctuations of building thesis often argue that building is causally influenced by overall fluctuations, while those who hold that both run together sometimes believe that building is the basic 'cause' of the business cycle. It is unnecessary, of course, to take the step beyond the pro- or counter-cyclical movement in building to subscribe to a causal relationship one way or the other. Furthermore, there is no inherent reason why building should move *either* pro-cyclically *or* anti-cyclically all the time. The Weber thesis discussed in the last chapter suggests that building may sometimes move with the cycle and sometimes against it depending on the direction of the trends in costs and incomes. The situation is consequently rather confused. Tinbergen summed it up in this way: 'Some hold that the building cycle runs counter to the cycle of the general economy, others that the building cycle leads, and still others again that it lags behind the general cycle. This in itself throws doubt on the existence of any clear-cut and simple relation.'[2]

---

less reliable partly because it underestimates the level of activity before 1923, partly because it includes public works contracting which is not specifically within the present scope.

[1] Long, op. cit., p. 102, J. R. Riggleman, 'Building Cycles in the United States', *Journal of American Statistical Association*, 28 (1933), and J. M. Clark, *Strategic Factors in Business Cycles* (1935) are merely three examples.

[2] J. Tinbergen and J. J. Polak, op. cit., p. 65.

II. *Building as a Cause of Fluctuations?*

In spite of the conflicts of opinion, the argument that building plays a causal role in economic fluctuations merits some attention. British experience in the 1930s provides the classic application of this thesis because of the widely held belief that the housing boom *caused* the general recovery after 1932. There is little doubt that building has a substantial impact on the rest of the economy and this impact takes many forms. For instance, building is of tremendous quantitative size in total investment. Taking residential building alone, dwellings accounted for over 30 per cent of total capital formation in normal years in the inter-war period (i.e. after 1925 when housebuilding had fully recovered from the effects of the war) and reached over 40 per cent in 1933 and 1934. When non-residential buildings are included, the proportion rises much higher reaching a maximum of almost 58 per cent in 1933.[1] Because of the tendency for investment in building to fluctuate in wider extremes than other kinds of investment, year to year changes in building investment will have a more than negligible effect on fluctuations in aggregate investment. Moreover, the influence of building on investment spreads far beyond its own boundaries. Building is only a part of total construction but it exercises a considerable impact on the remainder, particularly on contracting—roads, utilities, sewers and gas mains—and this impact is particularly strong when building is being extended into new suburbs. Building also gives rise to consequential investment in transport facilities and in electric power and consumer durables (e.g. for fittings and fixtures in houses). Building is, therefore, an important component of investment and income, but in itself it is relatively impervious to minor fluctuations in national income. Other kinds of investment, on the other hand, tend to be more sensitive to short-run income changes and for this reason are more likely to be pulled into conformity with building than the reverse.

But building's quantitative predominance in total investment and its influence on the rest is not sufficient proof that building is the major force behind investment fluctuations. One factor is that industrial and commercial building is not autonomously determined but is the result of investment decisions elsewhere.[2] Although building stimulates investment in its supplying industries the building materials sector is very much a closed group in the economy with less than average input-output connections with other sectors. The

[1] See Chapter 2, Appendix, Table 4.
[2] As was argued in Chapter 4, Part B.

impetus given to transport investment by building does not always, or even generally, show itself immediately, and is more relevant to a discussion of the connection between building and long-term growth.[1] Certainly, the lag between the investment in buildings and in transport is too long to account for synchronization in building and general fluctuations. In many cases, investment in transport developments may come first and stimulate building rather than the reverse.

Another common justification of building's supremacy in general fluctuations is its tendency to lead other sectors of the economy. This tendency has often been noticed, and is far stronger at the lower turning-point than at the upper turning-point.[2] Building probably led the way out of the depression in the 1930s. The trough in residential building actually is to be found in 1928 before the general depression materialized, and private unsubsidized building was expanding year by year after 1928. The fall in residential building due to subsidy reductions in 1928 pulled total building in that year down to trough level, but total building fell into another trough of similar depth in 1932 due to a slump in industrial and other kinds of non-residential building at a time before housing investment had surged forward (which it did in 1933). The upturn from this 1932 trough was apparent in building before most other sectors,[3] as is shown by the revival in building plans some months before signs of recovery elsewhere. However, it is a big step from the often empirically justified fact that building leads at the lower turning-point to the proposition that revival in building causes recovery. The lead of building at the lower turning-point is easily explained by the fact that it responds to depression influences (reduced interest rates and lower costs, for example) more easily and quickly than other branches of the economy. Whether or not building causes revival depends on how the upturn in building influences other sectors and requires a demonstration of the response of other sectors to the stimulus imparted by building. As it stands, without a detailed analysis of the nature of the causal relationship, the jump from building leading recovery to causing recovery is inadmissible.

Almost equally crude is to infer causal dependence from a close association between movements in building and general business.

[1] See the discussion in Chapter 14, pp. 305–11.

[2] For example, see C. D. Long, op. cit., pp. 155–7, J. B. Hubbard, loc. cit., and J. M. Clark, op. cit.

[3] Though building did not revive ahead of the Lomax index of industrial production. See IV below.

In the 1920s in the US a boom in building was coupled with a general boom, while in Britain in the 1930s there was a close association between the housing boom and the recovery. Moreover, in both cases the rate of expansion in building was higher in the early stages of the economy's upswing. From these facts it is easy to assume that the general boom was induced by the building boom which preceded and accompanied it. It is, however, a logical error to transform a correlation between two variables into a causal relation. Moreover, if the argument is that building always causes recovery this is a generalization from a very narrow range of experience—in fact, two examples. It is not difficult to find other examples which contradict the argument even from the same period. Thus, Japan experienced probably the strongest recovery in the world in the 1930s, but there were few signs of a building boom in the Japanese economy. Similarly, while a building boom developed in Sweden in the 1930s it lagged behind the general recovery of the economy by well over a year.[1] On the occasions when there is an association between a building and a general boom it is more often than not explained by both being the consequence of a common stimulus, such as economy-wide favourable expectations or a sustained rise in average real incomes, rather than by the general upswing being caused by expansion in building.

III. *Multiplier Effects*

A popular support of the argument that building is the major factor in business cycles is the view that building has a high employment multiplier. As a labour-intensive industry, it is argued, one unit of investment in building directly employs more labour than one investment unit in other parts of the economy. The direct increase in employment resulting from an expansion in building stimulates growth in other parts of the economy through the usual secondary consumption effects. Again taking the UK upswing of the 1930s as an example, building employment expanded considerably faster than employment in general. Between 1932 and 1937 employment in building and contracting expanded by 35·9 per cent whereas total UK employment increased by only 16·6 per cent.[2] This is not exactly a fair comparison since total employment as a weighted average of growing, stagnant and declining sectors is bound to grow more slowly than one rapidly expanding sector. Thus, there were several

[1] H. W. Richardson, op. cit., Chapter 12.

[2] Chapman and Knight, op. cit., p. 18.

sectors and industries such as metal manufacture, electrical engineering and vehicle production where employment increased much faster than in building.

Although this type of comparison supports the view that rapid expansion in building production will be accompanied by a rapid growth in building employment, it does not substantiate the argument that building has a high employment multiplier. To show this it would be necessary to compare the different employment effects of an identical injection of investment into separate sectors of the economy. Moreover, it is not enough to look at the direct effects, that is, the direct increase in employment within the sector benefiting from the injection. There may also be important indirect effects on employment, for instance, increased employment in industries supplying the sector where investment is rising with inputs. This, in turn, will set up repercussionary employment effects in other parts of the economy and these ought properly to be taken into account. Another indirect employment effect will, of course, be increased employment in consumer goods industries resulting from increased spending by newly hired workers in the sector where the injection is given (and in the industries indirectly affected as well). To be able to calculate whether or not building has a higher employment multiplier requires considerable empirical evidence and certain analytical assumptions. For instance, one really needs an input-output matrix to be able to assess the impact on supplying industries. It is also necessary to know whether the marginal propensity to consume differs, and if so by what extent, between building workers and workers in other sectors, and also whether or not there are any marked differences between their respective patterns of expenditure. Furthermore, assumptions have to be made about where to draw the line on the indirect effects: for instance, it may be reasonable to estimate increases in employment due to the first and second rounds of higher consumption spending of newly hired workers and due to expanding employment in the building materials industries, but is it also necessary to make estimates of increases in employment in transport developments which may follow from the expansion in building and in consumer durables industries the products of which may be in joint demand with houses?

The task is much more complicated than it appears at first sight, and it is virtually certain that those who argued that building had a high employment multiplier in Britain between the wars simply meant that building was quite a labour-intensive industry and productivity growth was very slow, so that an increase in output gave rise to an almost equivalent increase in employment, whereas other expanding sectors exhibited a close correspondence between output and productivity growth with relatively small increased employment effects. There is insufficient evidence available relating to the UK economy between the wars to examine whether building had a high employment multiplier or not. The only study known to the authors which tackles this question for this period is an inquiry by Leontief relating to 1939.[1] Its relevance is limited since it is based on US data, but it offers little comfort to those who argue for building having a high employment multiplier.

IV. *Correlation of Building and Business Fluctuations*

The argument so far suggests that there are no strong grounds for holding that building fluctuations will causally determine general fluctuations, but that building may be a powerful influence on economic fluctuations because of the sheer volume of building investment and the repercussionary effects of building on the rest of the economy. The extent to which they were interrelated in the inter-war period depends on how closely building fluctuations and business cycles moved together. The materials for this comparison are assembled in Fig. 10 (p. 334), which includes the four measures of general fluctuations, referred to at the beginning of this chapter (national income, business activity, employment and industrial production) and three indicators of building fluctuations, capital formation in all buildings and in residential dwellings alone (at 1930 prices), and an index of building and contracting. The first question is whether or not the general indicators provide a reasonable measure of business fluctuations. In fact, they move quite closely together. Employment and industrial production fluctuated in line with each other from 1920–37, with the year to year direction of change being the same throughout. The only divergence was in 1937–8 when employment continued to rise while industrial production fell. Business activity followed a similar course except that the sharp rise in 1927 from the trough of 1926 (accounted for by the General Strike) was followed by a slight decline in 1928, while in the slump after 1929 business activity con-

[1] W. W. Leontief, 'Output, Employment, Consumption and Investment', *Quarterly Journal of Economics*, 58 (1944), p. 290–314. Leontief's estimates for the construction industry were in fact calculated subsequently. His analysis showed that, taking into account both direct and indirect employment effects, one million dollars spent on construction gave rise to the employment of 448 men as against 489 in rail transport, 506 in metal fabrication, 518 in fuel and power, 566 in minerals, 770 in textiles and leather and 1,139 in agriculture.

tinued to fall until 1932 whereas both employment and industrial production revived after 1931. The path of national income was somewhat different from that followed by the other three but not exceptionally so. The most marked differences were that the troughs in national income were very shallow so that the upward trend is much smoother and the fact that national income went on rising in 1930 (rather than 1929) and in 1938 (rather than reaching a peak in 1937). The trough in the early 1930s came in 1932 synchronizing with business activity rather than with employment and industrial production.

As is not surprising, the fluctuations in the three building indicators were fairly similar. The overall building capital formation curve and the index of building and contracting moved in line together year after year with the exceptions that capital formation remained stable in 1922–3 and 1929–30 when building and contracting declined. The course pursued by residential building fluctuated in similar fashion to the building and contracting index up to 1930 but then diverged. Residential building expanded slightly in 1930–2 and rapidly in 1932–4 and declined thereafter, whereas the other two building indicators continued to move downwards after 1930 to 1932 then rose year by year up to 1937 (though the rate of expansion was at its highest in 1932–4) with a mild recession in 1937–8. Broadly speaking, any of the building indicators would show the same cyclical pattern up to 1930, but for the period 1930–8 total building and residential building must be considered separately.

Because the fluctuations in general business indicators were so similar while the building indices moved closely in line with each other, it does not matter very much which indicators are chosen. As representatives, gross capital formation in all buildings may be compared with the index of industrial production (excluding building, of course). Up to 1930 there is not much correspondence between the two cyclical movements. In 1920–1 building investment expanded while industrial production declined, in 1921–2 the reverse happened. Between 1922 and 1925 they moved upwards together, though the rate of expansion showed some tendency to decelerate in industrial production but to accelerate in building. In 1926 industrial production plunged downwards but building activity continued to expand, whereas in 1928 building activity slumped at a time when industrial production was slightly rising. Building revived and continued to rise a little in 1930, though now industrial production had started to fall off. In the 1930s the two series moved closer together, though building activity as a whole touched bottom in 1932 when industrial production had already begun to show a few signs of recovery. Both indicators moved up year by year to 1937 and were affected by the recession of 1937–8. However, the character of the upswing differed between the two, for industrial production climbed steadily while building activity showed a considerable upsurge in 1932–4 but a flattening out in the upswing between 1934 and 1937.

Thus, the cyclical fluctuations in building and business are not close enough to sustain the hypothesis that building activity was the decisive influence in economic fluctuations. The discrepancies are greater, however, in the 1920s. Building followed a different course from business in certain important respects: the expansion of 1920–1, the decline of 1921–2, the continued upswing between 1925 and 1927, and the marked decline of 1927–8. These divergences were not, except in one case, accountable in terms of any interrelationship between building and business but are to be explained by exogenous factors. The exception is the decline in building in 1921–2 which was more marked in non-residential building; non-residential building declined sharply in that year as a lagged reaction to the collapse of the post-war boom in 1920–1. Thus if there was a causal influence it was the wrong way round. The exogenous factors making for variations in the turning-points were undoubtedly connected with changing Government subsidies. The expansions of 1920–1 and in 1926 and 1927 were due to high subsidies favourable to building, while the declines of 1927–8 and to a lesser extent 1921–2 were due to subsidy reductions. In the 1930s, the discrepancies are not as marked but the variations in the rate of expansion at different phases of the upswing were significant enough to cast doubt on any clear causal relationship.

Looking over the inter-war period as a whole, there is a strong tendency in the annual series for troughs in building activity to lag behind the troughs in industrial production (apart from 1937–8 when both fell at the same time.) Thus, the troughs in industrial production of 1921, 1926 and 1931 were followed by troughs in building in 1922, 1928 and 1932. Whereas it would be stretching a point to invert the argument by arguing that business activity determined movements in building (because of the factors outlined above as well as the fallacy of mistaking a lead for a cause), it certainly puts an awkward fact in the way of the original thesis. How can changes in building causally determine economic fluctuations if the evidence indicates that building activity in this period lagged behind changes in business? Reference to the other indicators of general fluctuations fails to redeem the position for the 1920s, though the lag of 1931–2 is made less clear-cut since the troughs in national income and the business activity index both occurred in 1932.

Those who argue that building plays a decisive role in general economic fluctuations usually mean housebuilding rather than building as a whole. This follows from acceptance of the fact that non-residential building (especially industrial and commercial building) moves pro-cyclically, primarily due to the fact that both non-residential building and business activity respond to the same stimuli and depression impulses originating outside the building industry. Therefore, a brief examination needs to be given of the links between housebuilding and general business. There is no need to dwell upon the 1920s since housebuilding and total building fluctuations moved very closely together. In the 1930s, however, residential building fluctuations diverged from the total building cycle in very marked fashion. There was no correspondence between residential building fluctuations and the business cycle in this decade. Housebuilding expanded slightly between 1930 and 1932 whereas business activity declined; after 1934 housebuilding fell off as the economy approached boom. Residential building and business moved together only in 1932–4 (and to a slight extent in 1937–8). It is clear that the dominant role of housebuilding in the 1930s was to act as a stabilizer, moving counter-cyclically and offsetting fluctuations elsewhere in the economy. This is not inconsistent, on the other hand, with housebuilding behaving in a critical manner at the turning-points. The rapid upsurge in housebuilding in 1932–4 was of material importance in facilitating the general upswing in the economy after 1932, though its causal significance is difficult to estimate because of the presence of other circumstances favourable to revival in that year. Moreover, the temporary running down of the recovery in 1934–5 and the decline in housebuilding from that year were probably not entirely coincidental.

V. *Conclusions*

To sum up, there is no inherent reason why fluctuations in building should determine general fluctuations, and arguments used to support this thesis are far from convincing. This is not to deny that in a specific case building might induce a recovery provided that the mechanism of the stimulus can be demonstrated. Nor does it deny the quantitative importance of building, though the share of building in GNP in the US had been declining since the 1890s (apart from a temporary upsurge in the 1920s), while in Britain the weighting of building in overall industrial production had been decreasing probably up to 1914.[1] Building investment was of such quantitative importance that an exceptionally severe slump was probably impossible unless there was also a building slump, so that recessions would be mild if building activity remained brisk. This, of course, scarcely indicates that building plays a causal role in fluctuations. Rather it suggests that building may exercise an important stabilizing function, a finding which would tend to support the counter-cyclical tendency of building fluctuations rather than the pro-cyclical correspondence that is probably a necessary but not sufficient condition of causal dependence. There can be little doubt that residential building, by remaining on an even keel in the years before 1933, acted as such a stabiliser. In fact, the share of residential construction in total investment rose year by year from 28·0 per cent in 1930 to 43·7 per cent in 1933. On the other hand, it remains true that investment in residential construction only surged forward in 1932–3, the year in which business activity also made a great leap. But in itself this cannot imply a causal relationship.

Sometimes building and business moved together and sometimes their fluctuations were inverse. On occasion, a reversal in the direction of business brought about a change in the direction of building activity, for instance when a business slump pulled down non-residential building far enough to offset any tendency for house-building to continue undisturbed. Conversely, a surge in building was capable, as in 1932–4, of influencing the course of the general economy by injecting a massive boost of investment with repercussionary effects on employment and other sectors of the economy. Both building and business were from time to time the object of the same external impulse, for instance a sudden change in expectations or a transformation in credit conditions. Building could be destabilizing at one time, yet would offset general fluctuations at another. Both the empirical evidence of the inter-war period and *a priori* theorizing fail to substantiate the case for a one-way causal connection. This is not surprising since it is almost certain that no clear-cut causal relationship operative at all times and under all conditions exists. On the other hand, it would be impossible to understand fully the nature of business cycles without considering the quantitative and sometimes strategic role exerted by building. It would be equally ridiculous to attempt to explain building fluctuations without reference to fluctuations in general business.

[1] As suggested by W. G. Hoffmann, *British Industry, 1700–1950* (1955), p. 19.

CHAPTER 13

BUILDING AND ECONOMIC GROWTH

It is generally acknowledged that building forms an important sector of the economy, a fact which is true of both the past and the present. But the links between the industry and the rest of the economy are often inadequately appreciated even today. It is somewhat debatable, for example, whether a high rate of building activity has a beneficial effect on long-term growth or not. For one thing its relative importance varies considerably depending on the type of aggregates with which it is compared. At any one time building output accounts for but a small proportion of the total product or income generated in the economy. On the other hand, something like one-quarter to one-half of the total fixed capital formation is absorbed by building work. By contrast, as an employer of labour the building industry's demands are relatively modest for rarely has direct employment reached 10 per cent of the total labour force in Great Britain. The indirect multiplier effects of building activity may, however, be quite considerable. A large number of industries are either wholly or partly dependent on building, and employment in these trades may well be greater than the numbers engaged in the building industry itself. The indirect repercussions of the building industry on ancillary or associated industries is likely to be greater, moreover, in an economy which commands the production of a wide range of household consumer durables. In this respect the response produced by building activity might be expected to be greater in the twentieth than in the nineteenth century since at that time the number of consumer durable goods was very limited. On the other hand, in so far as building remained a traditional industry in the twentieth century, that is an industry largely unaffected by revolutionary techniques, the technological linkages or repercussions on other sectors of the economy would be relatively weak, though possibly the expansion in demand for factor inputs tended to stimulate improvements in the productive techniques of the building materials trades.

Apart from its impact on the deployment of economic resources and the economy as a whole building has some influence on the location of residential and industrial units and in turn on the course and nature of urban growth. In the inter-war years the most notable development was the rapid acceleration in suburban growth associated with a new form of transportation. The interrelationships of, together with the social problems arising from, these developments will form the basis of the concluding chapter of this study. In the present chapter, however, we propose to analyse the impact of the building industry on the economy as a whole.

I. *Building: An Expanding Sector*

It will already have become apparent that the building industry belonged to the expanding sector of the economy in the inter-war years. As Table 26 below shows its growth in percentage terms was substantially greater than the national average for all industrial groups combined, and in fact it was only surpassed by the performance of the electrical and electricity supply industries and vehicle manufacturing. Clearly in relation to the industrial sector of the

Table 26: INDICES OF INDUSTRIAL PRODUCTION (1924=100)

	1913	*1920*	*1929*	*1938*	*Rate of growth (per cent per annum)* *1913–38*	*1920–38*
Building and contracting	64·0	66·2	142·2	171·8	4·0	5·4
Total all industries*	90·5	90·3	115·8	146·4	2·0	2·7
Total all manufacturing	92·2	93·6	114·5	147·8	1·9	3·2

* Including mining, building, gas, water and electricity.

SOURCE: K. S. Lomax, 'Production and Productivity Movements in the United Kingdom since 1900', *Journal of Royal Statistical Society*, A122 (1959).

economy building was increasing its relative importance. But how did building compare with the economy as a whole? Was it an expanding or declining sector of the total economy? Recent research suggests that in the US residential construction, and possibly all building, has steadily declined in importance since the late nineteenth century. Apart from the later 1920s, when there was a temporary building boom in America, residential construction has accounted for a smaller and smaller proportion of the total national resources, that is of national product, capital formation and con-

Table 27: SHARE OF RESIDENTIAL CONSTRUCTION IN TOTAL OUTPUT, CAPITAL FORMATION AND CONSUMERS' EXPENDITURE
(*Average annual estimates at current prices*)

	(1) *Expenditure on dwellings* (£m.)	(2) *Total gross domestic capital formation* (£m.)	(3) *GNP* (£m.)	(4) *Consumers' expenditure* (£m.)	(5) *Col* 1 *as per cent of Col* 2	(6) *Col* 1 *as per cent of Col* 3	(7) *Col* 1 *as per cent of Col* 4
1870–9	21·3	101·8	1,223	1,082	20·9	1·7	2·0
1880–9	15·8	83·0	1,318	1,162	19·0	1·2	1·4
1890–9	21·8	112·0	1,549	1,362	19·4	1·4	1·6
1900–9	29·4	168·2	2,043	1,749	17·5	1·4	1·7
1920–9	106·8	413·8	4,620	4,106	25·8	2·3	2·6
1930–8	150·6	451·3	4,514	4,053	33·4	3·3	3·7
1950–9	565·0		16,450			3·4	

SOURCES: Based on C. H. Feinstein, 'Income and Investment in the United Kingdom, 1856–1914', *Economic Journal* 71 (1961); 'National Income and Expenditure, 1870–1963', *London and Cambridge Economic Bulletin*, No. 50, in *Times Review of Industry and Technology*, June 1964, and *Domestic Capital Formation in the United Kingdom, 1920–38* (1965). Dr. Feinstein also very kindly supplied the authors with some unpublished data on investment in buildings for the nineteenth century.

sumers' expenditure, throughout the period 1890 to 1950.[1] This trend is not repeated in the British case; if anything the reverse process occurs.

As Table 27 shows residential construction became much more important in the inter-war years compared with before 1914 when it had accounted for a fairly constant share of the nation's total resources. Thus in the forty years or so before 1914 investment in dwellings accounted for nearly one-fifth of the total domestic capital formation whereas by the 1930s it had increased to one-third. In terms of gross national product it had more than doubled its share from 1·4 to 3·3 per cent. Even in the 1950s, when for part of the period building restrictions were still in force, residential construction's share of GNP was about the same as in the 1930s, though as a proportion of total investment it had fallen quite considerably.

There are a number of possible explanations that can be put forward to account for the difference in the relative importance of residential construction between America and Great Britain. Before 1914 the proportion of total resources devoted to investment in dwellings in the US was much higher than in Britain. It averaged between 4 and 6 per cent of the GNP as against barely 1·5 per cent in this country. Even in the 1920s it was considerably higher than the British rate and it was only in the following decade, when American housing activity was cut back sharply in the depression, that it fell to somewhere near the proportion recorded in Britain before 1914. But the depression was not solely responsible for the lower level of American housing construction in the 1930s; it can be argued that without the economic crisis the rate of housebuilding would have declined in the inter-war years. Before the war and shortly afterwards America had increased her stock of houses considerably and given their durability there was obviously less scope for replacement in the near future. By 1929, and possibly even earlier, America was already overstocked with houses in relation to the level of prices and incomes and contraction was more or less bound to set in.[2] In actual fact housebuilding activity had already reached a plateau by the middle 1920s and between 1926 and 1929 there was a sharp fall in new construction. In other words, the depression merely served to accentuate the downward trend in house construction and the slow recovery in the later 1930s can be explained partly by long-term

[1] L. Grebler, D. M. Blank and L. Winnick, *Capital Formation in Residential Real Estate* (1956).

[2] See R. A. Gordon, 'Population Growth, Housing and the Capital Coefficient', *American Economic Review*, 46 (1956).

factors operating against housebuilding activity. The decline in the rate of growth of population and formation of households tended to reduce the demand for residential accommodation. But the most important single long-term factor affecting the demand for houses was the shift in the consumer preference curve. As real incomes rose consumer preferences shifted away from housing in favour of other commodities, especially consumer durables and service facilities. There was a distinct trend against large houses in the twentieth century, a point borne out by the fact that the average real input into newly constructed dwelling units fell by almost 10 per cent between 1900 and 1950.[1] In view of this factor it is not surprising that the residential sector in America declined in importance.

In Britain, on the other hand, many of these influences failed to operate. Prior to the First World War resources devoted to housing were low compared with American standards, and housing standards were generally poor. Because of under-investment in residential construction in the past many houses were old and ripe for renewal at the end of the war. Thus even had the war not created a serious shortage there would still have been a considerable replacement demand in the inter-war years. Hence any increase in real incomes was likely to be reflected in a rising effective demand for new houses as families sought to escape from the dingy quarters of the cities. This was particularly true of the poorer sections of the community whose housing conditions were especially bad. Given an improvement in their incomes their first preference was for better housing rather than anything else. Moreover, although the average size of new upper-class dwellings decreased after 1914 it is more than probable that the real inputs into lower middle-class and working-class dwellings increased due partly to the influence of Government policy which set higher standards for new accommodation than had previously been enjoyed.[2] In Britain, of course, the Government was more active in the housing market than in America during this period. One final factor might be noted, that there were less powerful alternative outlets in Britain for consumers' incomes in the form of cars and durable household equipment than there were in America in the inter-war years.

[1] L. Winnick, 'Housing: Has there been a Downward Shift in Consumers' Preferences?', *Quarterly Journal of Economics*, 69 (1955), p. 86.

[2] This is particularly true of Scotland where according to the census of 1921 almost 52 per cent of the total houses were one or two apartment dwellings. By way of contrast 61·7 per cent of the local authority houses built between 1919 and 1939 had three apartments or more, whilst only 12 per cent had two or less. The remainder (26·3 per cent) had four apartments or more.

It is too early to say as yet whether residential construction is likely to become a declining sector of the British economy. There was certainly no trend in this direction before 1939, for, as we have already seen, this sector became far more important than it had been before the war. Even so in relation to total income its importance was still fairly small and it is in terms of capital formation that it made its greatest impact. Throughout the entire period it accounted for about 30 per cent of gross domestic capital investment, as against less than 20 per cent pre-war. If non-residential building is included the total capital formation devoted to all building work rises to around 47 per cent for the inter-war years as a whole and to about 50 per cent in the 1930s, roughly equivalent to 5 per cent of the total national product. In this respect the period is unique since it is very unlikely that such a large proportion of domestic capital resources went into building at any other time either before or since. Prior to 1914 investment in buildings accounted for about one-third of the total and only in the 1870s did it approach 40 per cent (see Table 28). Although non-residential construction as a proportion of residential investment declined during these years it accounted for a slightly larger share of total domestic investment than before 1914.

II. *Building and the Allocation of Investment Resources*

It might be questioned whether the very high level of building activity in the inter-war years was necessarily the most beneficial form of investment as regards the long-term growth of national income or output. Certainly the expansion in building construction itself was important to the short-term growth process since the higher the level of building activity the higher the growth of total output was likely to be, assuming all other things being equal. On the other hand, recent empirical studies have drawn attention to the importance of breaking down the pattern of investment sectorally and it is often suggested that a high proportion of investment resources devoted to building work, particularly residential construction, can have deleterious effects on the long-term rate of growth of income. This argument is largely based on the assumption that investment in building is essentially unproductive in that a house (or any other building) cannot, like plant and machinery, produce new goods and therefore adds nothing to the flow of income. The proposition is misleading in at least two respects, however. In the first place buildings do contribute indirectly to the output of new goods since it would be difficult to conceive of a situation in which plant and

Table 28: INVESTMENT IN RESIDENTIAL AND NON-RESIDENTIAL BUILDING AS PERCENTAGE OF TOTAL FIXED INVESTMENT

(*Average annual estimates at constant prices*)

	(1) *Investment in dwellings* (*£m.*)	(2) *Non-residential investment* (*£m.*)	(3) *Total building investment* (1+2) (*£m.*)	(4) *Total fixed investment* (*£m.*)	(5) *Col* 1 *as per cent of Col* 4	(6) *Col* 2 *as per cent of Col* 4	(7) *Col* 3 *as per cent of Col* 4
1870–9	20·2	15·5	35·7	94·0	21·5	16·5	38·0
1880–9	17·2	11·3	28·5	92·4	18·6	12·2	30·8
1890–9	26·0	17·6	43·6	132·0	19·7	13·3	33·0
1900–9	35·2	24·5	59·7	186·7	18·9	13·1	32·0
1920–9	95·4	59·2	154·6	349·8	27·3	16·9	44·2
1930–8	158·0	74·3	232·3	467·2	33·8	15·9	49·7
1950–9	155·0			785·0	19·7		

NOTE: Base years—1870–1909 at 1900 prices
1920–1959 at 1930 prices

SOURCE: As for Table 27.

machinery could operate effectively without an adequate building infrastructure. Hence buildings can be regarded as much a part of the fixed productive equipment as plant and machinery which produces the new output. Moreover, the production and sale of commodities require in turn the provision of a varied range of ancillary services supplied by financial and commercial institutions, transport undertakings and business offices, all of which make use of buildings. But a second and more important criticism is that relating to income generation. It is wrong to assume that buildings do not contribute to the annual flow of income simply because they cannot produce new goods directly. A house, for example, is an investment good which provides a flow of services to the occupant the value of which can be calculated on the basis of an imputed rent. In other words, houses and buildings can be regarded as income generating assets because of the value of rent arising from the services they provide. Indeed, it is possible that the income-generating effect of a house may be greater in the long run than a machine on account of the more durable nature of the former asset.[1]

Thus, although it is inaccurate to regard buildings as having no income generating properties, this does not necessarily mean that a rising volume of investment in construction is always beneficial to the economy as a whole. A situation in which an increasing share of the nation's resources are earmarked for construction, as in the case of the inter-war years, may well lead to a misallocation of resources if other sectors of the economy, especially industry, are deprived of capital and labour because of the stronger competing claims of building. This in turn would ultimately have an adverse effect on the long-term rates of growth of these other sectors and possibly on the growth of the economy as a whole. This kind of situation is, of course, more relevant to full employment situations and is less applicable to the inter-war period when factors of production were often under-utilized. Nevertheless, it is well worth while to

[1] This possibility can be illustrated with a purely hypothetical example. Let us compare the expenditure of £500 on a house with £500 on a machine. Assume that the life of the house is 50 years and that of the machine is 10 years. Let us further assume that the gross annual income flow (i.e. rent) from the house is £60 and that the capital-output ratio is 4:1 so that the annual flow of goods from the machine is £125. For repairs let us make an allowance of £10 per annum in both cases. Although the net annual income flow from the machine is much larger than the net annual flow of services rendered by the house, the position is reversed when the aggregate flows over the life of the assets are compared. Assuming a discount rate of 5 per cent, the net present value of the house is £412·8, while that of the machine is £388·0.

explore briefly the implications of this thesis whether they be adverse or otherwise.

If these general assumptions are correct one would expect some sort of inverse correlation between building and non-building investment since as building activity rises it would presumably tend to draw resources away from other sectors of the economy. This does not seem to be borne out by pre-1914 experience, however. The building booms of the mid-1870s and the turn of the century were accompanied by an increase in most other forms of investment, though largely at the expense of foreign investment. On the other hand, the pattern seems to have changed in the inter-war years. Apart from 1921, when most forms of investment were at a peak, building and non-building investment did tend to move inversely. This is particularly true of the period 1925 to 1931 when peaks in building activity tended to be accompanied by low levels of investment in plant and machinery and transport equipment. For the early 1930s the position is somewhat less clear-cut since most of the investment series moved up together, but it is noticeable that the real peak in non-building investment was delayed until the latter half of the period when residential construction was declining.

This, of course, is by no means conclusive proof that the high level of building activity had an adverse effect on the provision of productive capital. The fact that non-building investment tended to be lower at times when building investment was high provides no justification for arguing that industry and commerce were starved of capital on account of the demands made by the construction industry. Pressure on the capital market was no doubt relieved by the fact that the capital requirements of the former basic industries were reduced in this period whilst exports of capital were substantially lower than they had been in pre-war years. In fact, in the 1930s foreign investment dried up altogether and by the Second World War the total overseas investment of the UK outstanding was lower than it had been in 1914. In other words, in this respect the pre-war pattern was being repeated: investment in building and elsewhere at home was taking place at the expense of capital exports.

If, however, it is assumed that because of the large volume of resources going into construction work other sectors of the economy were deprived or starved of capital one would expect that in time this would be reflected in the overall performance of the British economy. This was certainly not the case, however. The rates of growth of industrial production, productivity and total product were well above those of pre-war and compared favourably with those recorded in other industrial countries. In fact, in the inter-war years the British economy performed very well in the light of previous experience and the only black spots were the high level of unemployment and the failure of exports to recover. Moreover, what is particularly important from our point of view is that growth rates (especially in industry) were considerably higher in these years, when the proportion of resources devoted to building work was at an all-time record, than in the years prior to 1914 when building investment was considerably less. And, in fact, if anything, non-residential domestic investment accounted for a slightly higher proportion of the total national product in the inter-war years than before 1914.[1] It would be difficult to argue on the basis of this achievement that industrial growth was hampered by a shortage of capital. It is difficult therefore to resist the conclusion that a high level of building activity need not restrict an economy's capacity for growth except in cases where there is a fundamental scarcity of investment resources. There was, of course, no such scarcity at this time and possibly this is one reason why the building industry was able to expand so rapidly without apparently affecting adversely the rest of the economy.

III. *The Saving-Investment Relationships*

It was argued in the last section that the expansion in building did not appear to have had any serious repercussions on the rest of the economy. In fact one can go further than this and suggest that the characteristics of building made it a particularly suitable form of economic activity to expand at a time when resources were under-utilized. In the first place, building work requires large amounts of fixed investment which the building industry itself cannot generate through internal saving. This is, of course, true of most capital goods industries though it is probable that building absorbs a greater proportion of its investment resources from the rest of the economy than do most other industries. Unfortunately, there are no exact estimates of the savings generated by the industry for the inter-war years, but as a rough guide we have taken the total gross margins of the industry (that is total value added minus employee compensation) plus 10 per cent of the total wages and salaries bill. This in fact probably exaggerates the savings generated by the industry since the gross margin figures make no allowance for selling, transport and other incidental costs, whilst the assumption of a propensity to save of 0·1 is probably somewhat generous. Nevertheless, it does give an

[1] 6·2 per cent, 1890–1909, as against 6·8 per cent, 1920–38.

approximate idea of the savings derived from this sector. As Table 29 shows the total savings in building were generally less than one-third of the actual value of building work in any one year, which means that the building sector absorbed a substantial amount of capital from the rest of the economy. The second feature of the industry is that it is labour intensive, for the amount of capital

Table 29: INVESTMENT AND SAVINGS IN BUILDING

	Investment in all building work (£m.) (1)	*Savings generated by building industry* (10 *per cent of wage bill +gross margins*) (£m.) (2)	*Column* 2 *as percentage of Column* 1 (3)
1920	199	64·3	32·3
1921	188	48·9	26·0
1922	123	34·4	28·0
1923	116	31·8	27·4
1924	157	33·5	21·3
1925	186	57·3	30·8
1926	204	74·3	36·4
1927	213	83·2	39·1
1928	179	48·6	27·2
1929	207	62·1	30·0
1930	203	46·9	23·1
1931	176	39·8	22·6
1932	163	36·3	22·3
1933	199	47·6	23·9
1934	231	55·4	24·0
1935	236	55·0	23·3
1936	248	67·6	27·3
1937	273	63·5	23·3
1938	269	57·5	21·4

SOURCES: Based on C. H. Feinstein, *Domestic Capital Formation in the United Kingdom, 1920–38* (1965), p. 38, Table 3.30; A. L. Chapman and R. Knight, *Wages and Salaries in the United Kingdom, 1920–38* (1954), p. 22, Table 4; and P. E. Hart, *Studies in Profit, Business Saving and Investment in the United Kingdom, 1920–62*, Vol. 1 (1965), p. 96, Table 5.3.

employed per unit of labour is very small indeed. In 1924 and 1935 the capital per head amounted to only £71·7 and £63·2 respectively as against £235·8 and £201·5 for all manufacturing. In fact, the building industry was probably the most labour intensive of all industries.

These features of the building industry have important implications as regards the economy as a whole. Given a full employment situation a large expansion in building work might well be harmful to the rest of the economy since it would attract resources into building at a time when other sectors were in need of them. In turn this might well lead to a slowing down of plant replacement in industries on which the future growth of the economy depended, and at the same time encourage inflationary conditions. This is not to imply that erecting buildings serves no useful purpose but rather to emphasize the fact that at a time when resources are fully employed it is desirable to damp down the level of building since otherwise scarce resources will be absorbed into producing capital assets which have limited reproductive qualities. On the other hand, at times when the economy is slack raising the volume of building work can be expected to absorb unemployed resources fairly rapidly since the industry itself is labour intensive and its final product capital intensive. Thus in the conditions prevailing in the inter-war years the rapid expansion in building activity can be regarded as having a favourable influence on the economy since it absorbed a considerable volume of under-utilized resources, though the extent to which the level of building activity alternated to correspond with the cyclical variations in the rest of the economy was probably largely fortuitous.[1] Moreover, the fact that building tends to be a labour intensive industry will affect the pattern or level of consumption. The growth of a labour intensive industry, and particularly one in which the proportion of wage to salary earners is relatively high as in this case, will tend to redistribute income towards those groups with a high marginal propensity to consume. In other words, the expansion of building in the inter-war years probably resulted in a slightly higher level of aggregate consumption than would have been the case had it been a more capital intensive industry.

In effect, building provided a double-edged weapon for combating a deflationary situation, since it absorbed considerable amounts of both labour and capital. Furthermore, it produced fairly extensive indirect multiplier effects through its demands for products of other industries.[2] Thus given the conditions prevailing in these years an expansion in building provided one of the best ways of alleviating the under-utilization of resources. The main difficulty was the rather lengthy gestation period, and as a short-term counter-cyclical policy measure it was found to be too inflexible. Moreover, despite its particular attributes it is not altogether clear whether building was necessarily the most efficient or, alternatively, the least expensive way

[1] See Chapter 12.
[2] See below.

of absorbing unemployed resources. We shall consider this point shortly, but first let us examine in some detail the employment generation effects of building in the inter-war years.

IV. *Building and Employment*

a. Employment Generation

As the building industry was an expanding sector of the economy in the inter-war years one would naturally expect that it would have a favourable impact on employment opportunities both within and without the industry. Moreover, since it is a relatively labour intensive industry and its demand for products of other industries is fairly large, the total increase in employment generated directly and indirectly by a given increment in investment in building should be quite considerable. It has been estimated in the US, for example, that for every five workers actually employed on the construction site six workers may be engaged in activities serving their needs.[1] On the other hand, it has also been suggested that in comparison with other types of economic activity investment in building work may be a fairly expensive way of generating employment and creating a demand for the products of other industries.[2]

First of all let us consider what effects the expansion of building work had on the labour market. For this purpose we have taken the number of insured persons in employment (as published by the Ministry of Labour) in June 1923 when the series first became comprehensive, and compared it with the data for June 1938. By the latter date all building had in fact passed its peak but for our purposes this does not matter too much. The employment figures have been broken down into direct or primary employment and employment arising indirectly as a result of expansion in building activity. The former category is of course quite straightforward and consists solely of those people actively engaged in constructing dwellings or other buildings. Indirect employment is more tricky and obviously classification is at times somewhat arbitrary. Three categories are distinguished. The first of these includes industries which are more or less directly dependent on building work. Thus an expansion in numbers in paint, wallpaper, brick, cement trades, etc., is only likely to occur as a result of prior expansion in the volume of building activity. This is not, of course, completely true of iron and steel

[1] M. L. Colean and R. Newcomb, *Stabilizing Construction: The Record and Potential* (1952, New York), p. 10.

[2] International Labour Office, *Housing and Employment* (1945, Geneva), p. 46.

tubes, woodwork and ironfounding, but for purposes of simplicity it has been assumed that the bulk of the products produced by these industries are used in building work. The second category is quite small and consists of trades only partly dependent on building work. The distinction here is not perhaps at first sight very sharp but in fact most of these trades are by no means dependent upon the building industry as a customer. For example, glass was being used for car windows, wire and netting for a variety of odd jobs which have nothing to do with construction, whilst bolts, nuts, rivets, etc., were consumed in large quantities by civil engineering and the ship-building industry both of which lie outside the scope of this study. The third category presents the greatest difficulty since it is concerned with those industries which are only affected indirectly by the building industry. None the less it is an important category since it comprises a number of household goods, including consumer durables which are required by families moving into new houses. In this respect housing investment was likely to have a larger indirect impact than in the nineteenth century when the range of consumer goods was much smaller.

There are obvious objections to the system of classification adopted. It is fairly arbitrary as to the group in which an industry is placed, whilst some trades have been omitted, e.g. china and earthenware, and others are included whose products are by no means consumed solely by the building industry. In fact, the classification as a whole errs on the side of generosity since few of the industries or branches of industry included in Table 30 were producing exclusively for the building industry. Obviously, therefore, this will tend to over-inflate the number of workers dependent on the building industry, but it was found impossible in practice to make a more precise breakdown. Moreover, it has been impossible to estimate what proportions of the output of these industries were used in old or new dwellings or buildings. In some cases, e.g. paint and wallpaper, a fair proportion of the output may be used for repairing existing buildings. The same is true regarding the use of electrically operated consumer durables since in the 1930s more old houses were being wired for electricity than the number of new ones built.[1] Still, despite these reservations, it is felt that something useful can be said about the employment generated as a result of the expansion in building operations.

The first point to notice from Table 30 is that direct employment

[1] Political and Economic Planning, *The Market for Household Appliances* (1945), p. 372.

(that is in actual building work) increased by less than 300,000 or by 47 per cent between 1923 and 1938. This is not a very striking increase when set against the 141 per cent increase in real investment in building which occurred during the same period. Nevertheless, it was sufficient to raise building employment as a proportion of the total insured labour force from 6·2 in 1923 to 7·6 in 1938. Quite clearly it was an expanding industry in terms of employment; but although it was the largest single employer of labour, it was nowhere near as dominant in the labour market as it was in the capital market. The indirect employment effects of the expansion in building activity were, however, quite considerable. Apart from the few industries listed in category 2, most trades wholly or partially dependent upon the building industry increased their employment by more than the national average. Employment in those trades directly dependent on building (group 1) rose by about 160,000 between 1923 to 1938, that is an increase of 52·4 per cent compared with increases of 12·3 and 18·5 in manufacturing and the total labour force respectively. Even if group 2 industries are included in which the rate of increase was much smaller the percentage increase is still well above the national average. These two groups accounted for 5·7 per cent of total employment in 1938 as against 5·1 per cent in 1923. The largest absolute increase, however, was in the numbers employed in those industries indirectly affected by building activity. By 1938 the labour force in category 3 was over 220,000 greater than in 1928, despite a sharp fall in the numbers employed in steel smelting and iron puddling. This expansion was largely brought about by the rapid growth of electricity and electrical products and a good part of it was no doubt created as a result of the expansion in building during this period.

Taking the three categories together it is found that total employment rose by nearly 400,000 or by 33·5 per cent as against 18·5 per cent for the total labour force. This estimate is undoubtedly inflated, however, by the inclusion of workers not affected in any way by the building industry. It would be more correct to say therefore that this was the increase in numbers employed in industries connected in some way with building rather than the actual number of new jobs created in ancillary industries by virtue of the expansion in construction activity. The increase in numbers employed in trades serving on-site building workers was of course much smaller. It would consist mainly of those employed in classes 1 and 2 plus the addition of certain workers employed in the transport and distribution of materials and in electrical wiring and contracting and other fittings.

At the most, therefore, the increase in the number of service workers would amount to 250,000 as against under 300,000 on-site workers. These estimates are, however, very rough, but they do possibly indicate that the number of off-site workers required was perhaps somewhat lower than in the US. However, in view of the approximate nature of the data and the difficulties of precise inter-country comparisons, it would be extremely hazardous to draw more definite conclusions.

Table 30: NUMBERS IN INSURED EMPLOYMENT

	June 1923	*June 1938*	*Per cent increase*
Manufacturing employment	5,019,662	5,636,528	12·3
Total employment	10,188,101	12,075,268	18·5
(1)			
Stone quarrying and mining	30,574	45,181	
Slate quarrying and mining	7,781	9,110	
Artificial stone and concrete	9,039	26,934	
Cement, lime-kilns and whiting	14,946	16,985	
Brick, tile, pipe-making, etc.	56,240	94,490	
Iron and steel tubes	20,910	26,192	
Stove, grate, pipe, and general iron-founding, etc.	70,045	86,678	
Heating and ventilating apparatus	5,625	18,254	
Electrical wiring and contracting	9,924	38,169	
Sawmilling and machined woodwork	50,763	56,764	
Paint, varnish, red lead, etc.	12,978	22,979	
Wallpaper making	4,428	6,990	
Clay, sand, gravel, chalk pits	11,875	16,389	
Total	305,128	465,115	52·4
As per cent of manufacturing employment	6·1	8·3	
(2)			
Brass, copper, zinc, tin and lead	35,006	45,745	
Bolts, nuts, screws, rivets, nails, etc.	24,641	25,216	
Brass and allied metal wares	25,790	25,368	
Wire, wire netting, wire ropes	21,962	21,619	
Glass (excluding bottles)	23,070	27,379	
Other woodworking	23,652	21,391	
Total	218,446	227,765	4·3
As per cent of manufacturing employment	4·3	4·0	
(1)+(2)	523,574	692,880	32·3
As per cent of manufacturing employment	10·4	12·3	
As per cent of total employment	5·1	5·7	

Table 30: NUMBERS IN INSURED EMPLOYMENT (*contd.*)

	June 1923	*June 1938*	*Per cent increase*
(3)			
Electric cables, apparatus, lamps, etc.	64,989	163,698	
Electrical engineering	56,965	111,422	
Steel melting and iron puddling, iron and steel rolling	166,840	138,586	
Hand tools, cutlery, saws, files	25,132	26,496	
Furniture making, upholstery, etc.	87,349	132,422	
Rubber	50,887	56,280	
Oilcloth, linoleum, etc.	11,429	11,100	
Carpets	24,484	25,884	
Gas, water, electricity supply	160,027	205,177	
Total	648,102	871,065	34·4
(1)+(2)+(3)	1,171,676	1,563,945	33·5
As per cent of total employment	11·5	13·0	
(4)			
Employment in building work	626,440	919,338	46·8
As per cent of total employment	6·2	7·6	
(1)+(2)+(3)+(4)	1,798,116	2,483,283	38·1
As per cent of total employment	17·7	20·6	
Building+(1)+(2)	1,150,014	1,612,218	40·2
As per cent of total employment	11·3	13·4	

SOURCE: *Ministry of Labour Gazette.*

An overall picture of the total possible employment effects can be obtained by combining the building labour force with those employed in the three categories of related industries. In 1923 total employment amounted to 1,798,000 and by 1938 it had increased to 2,483,000, an increase of 685,000. In the latter year this was equivalent to 20·6 per cent of the total labour force as against 17·7 per cent in 1923. If we exclude trades listed in class 3 from the calculation the expansion in employment in building and service industries amounted to 462,000, whilst the proportion of the total labour force so employed increased from 11·3 to 13·4 per cent over the period 1923–38.

Despite the approximate nature of the estimates it is possible to summarize with some degree of precision the impact of the building industry on the employment market. Apart from one or two exceptions most of the industries connected with building, including of course the construction industry itself, were expanding industries in terms of employment, and they accounted for an increasing share of the national labour force throughout the period. At the most, however, the total increase in employment brought about either directly or indirectly by the expansion in building was less than 700,000, of which building workers alone accounted for less than one-half. If this estimate is correct it means that in June 1938 roughly one-fifth of the national labour force was employed in building or related industries as against 17·7 per cent in 1923. These estimates are, however, rather on the high side. If we exclude industries only indirectly affected by building (that is, class 3) then employment generated amounts to around 450,000 or 500,000 which might be regarded as a safe minimum estimate.[1] None the less, whichever estimate is used, the increase in employment in building and related trades accounted for more than one-quarter of the total increase in employment in Britain between the years 1923 and 1938. On the other hand, perhaps the most surprising thing is the relatively small increase in numbers employed in building work in relation to the enormous expansion in output during the period.[2] Furthermore, the impact of this increase was fairly small in relation to the total labour force. Altogether it accounted for no more than one or two percentage points' addition to the share of the total insured employment. This provides a sharp contrast with the capital position for real investment in all building work as a percentage of the total domestic investment rose from 37·7 to 47·3 per cent between 1923 and 1938. This suggests that building was a capital consuming, rather than an employment generating, industry. It is true that the industry can be regarded as labour intensive, but it would seem that from a given increase in investment in building the employment effects are relatively modest, whilst the cost in terms of capital resources is fairly high.

b. The Regional Employment Pattern

Unfortunately adequate statistics are not available which would allow a detailed regional analysis of both the direct and indirect employment effects arising from building. It is possible, however, to break down building employment regionally in order to find out whether areas like London and the South-East in particular had a higher concentration of building activity in relation to their resources and needs compared with regions further north. It is well known that the southern regions, especially the South-East, tended to have a higher proportion of their resources located in the newer expanding

[1] Thereby reducing the proportion of the natonal labour force so employed to 13·4 per cent in 1938 as compared with 11·3 per cent in 1923.

[2] This point has already been discussed in Chapter 5.

industries in this period, a factor which was inevitably associated with a marked difference in the degree of prosperity between the North and South. It is important, therefore, to see whether the building industry accentuated this regional imbalance in any way. Given the ubiquitous nature of the building industry, one would expect, of course, that a higher proportion of its resources would be located in the southern areas of Great Britain, since it was here that the volume of building was greatest in absolute terms during the inter-war years. But this in itself does not mean that it was over-concentrated in these regions.

A crude way of measuring the degree of regional concentration of an industry is to compare its percentage share of the labour force in relation to that of the population of the region in question. Table 31

Table 31: PERCENTAGE EMPLOYMENT IN BUILDING IN VARIOUS REGIONS IN 1931 AND LOCATION QUOTIENTS

Greater London	24·53	1·3
South-East (excluding Greater London)	16·62	1·5
Midlands	14·39	0·9
Eastern Counties	3·61	1·0
South-West	5·62	1·3
Northern Counties	22·52	0·77
Wales	3·64	0·8
Scotland	9·07	0·82
	100·0	

SOURCE: Political and Economic Planning, *Report on the Location of Industry* (1939).

shows the percentage shares of building employment for the main regions. As one would expect, the South (including London) and the Midlands accounted for a large share of the total employment in the building industry. Altogether over 50 per cent of the numbers engaged in the industry were concentrated in these regions. In relation to the distribution of population London and the South-East were very well represented indeed. Whilst they contained about 23 per cent of the total population of Great Britain they accounted for no less than 41 per cent of the employment in the building industry. By way of contrast areas further north were less favourably placed. Scotland, for example, contained nearly 11 per cent of the British population but only 9 per cent of the building labour force. Population itself, of course, is not an accurate guide to the rate of volume of building activity. The industry's resources will, all other things being equal, be more heavily concentrated in those regions where the demand for new buildings is made most effective irrespective of the distribution of population and the need for housing. Since the effective demand for new houses and factories was greater in the South than elsewhere one would naturally expect that a higher proportion of the industry's resources would be located there. Of the new houses built between 1919 and 1930 roughly 42 per cent were erected in the South of England, a proportion which is almost identical to the proportion of the building labour force employed in that region in 1931. In other words, in terms of the volume of building activity the South does not appear to have been unduly favoured. On the other hand, what is important is that as regards employment opportunities in building the South would appear to be more favoured simply by virtue of the fact that in relation to the distribution of population building employment tended to be higher than elsewhere. This conclusion would probably apply also to those industries closely related to building in so far as many of them were situated in close proximity to their major customer.

The above analysis does not of course tell us whether building was more highly concentrated in the South relative to other industries. Strictly speaking, an industry can only be said to be concentrated in a region when there is more of it there than would be expected in proportion to the total industrial population of that region. For this reason the location quotient provides a more accurate measure of the degree of industrial concentration. This is derived quite simply by dividing the percentage of employment of a given industry in a particular region by the employment percentage of all industry in that region.[1] Given the fact that building, like retailing and bread-baking, tends to be a ubiquitous industry which follows closely the pattern of demand one would expect that its locational quotient for any particular region would be close to unity.

Table 31 lists the location quotients for building in the major regions previously referred to. As was to be expected the building

[1] An example will make the point clear. In 1931 Greater London contained 19·56 per cent of the total insured labour force of Great Britain and 24·53 per cent of the persons engaged in the building industry. The location quotient would therefore work out as follows:

$$\frac{24\cdot 53}{19\cdot 56}=1\cdot 3$$

An industry with a location quotient approaching unity would indicate that it was fairly evenly distributed in relation to industrial employment as a whole in a particular region. Factors which exceed unity imply an over-concentration, whilst conversely those below unity suggest that an industry is under-represented.

industry was not highly concentrated since in many regions the location quotient is not far removed from unity. In comparison with a number of other industries, such as glass and coal, which in certain regions have a very high location factor, the building industry was fairly evenly spread throughout the country. Even in the Midlands the degree of concentration was not much higher than in the North. Yet the economic fortunes of these regions varied enormously, especially in the 1930s. Nevertheless, it is clear that Southern England is over-represented particularly in relation to all other areas. This is especially true of the South-East, where the location quotient is almost double that of Wales, Scotland and the Northern Counties. These three regions in fact were under-represented by the building industry with location quotients below unity.

The greater concentration of building employment in the South as compared with other regions is not difficult to explain. To a large extent it can be attributed to the predominance of London and its environs. The concentration of administration and commerce in London meant a much higher rate of office, hotel and other similar building there. The subsequent growth of these functions in the capital meant more and more office buildings, etc., in the centre of the city, a tendency which encouraged suburban housebuilding. Moreover, the very size of London also resulted in a much greater need for suburban housebuilding around London, whilst the relatively higher level of income per head in the South-East made this need effective. It is not surprising, therefore, that a disproportionate amount of private housebuilding and non-residential building occurred in the South of England in the inter-war period.

From what has already been said it would appear that the expansion in the building industry tended to accentuate the North-South differential growth pattern of this period.[1] Naturally given the greater volume of demand for new buildings in the South compared with elsewhere it was in some respects inevitable that this region should benefit more than others. Whether, of course, the degree of concentration in building increased in the South during this period or whether it had always been higher than in other regions is difficult to say. Probably since the later nineteenth century the building industry had been weighted slightly in favour of this region and that this tendency was accentuated in the inter-war years on account of

[1] Though it did not necessarily create the disparity between the two areas since the concentration of building in the South was apparent in the early 1920s, that is before the differences in prosperity between the South and the rest of the country had become clearly marked.

the large volume of residential and factory building which took place in the South. But for our purposes this point is not very relevant. What matters is that in the inter-war years the South had a higher proportion of building activity than elsewhere and that, since building was a growth industry, in terms of employment opportunities this area came off best. But this point should not be pushed too far since it does not necessarily follow that these regions with the highest degree of concentration in building employment were the ones in which the labour force expanded most rapidly. Table 32 shows the percentage increase in employment in building and in all industries for the main regions between the years 1923 and 1937. The most obvious point to emerge is that building employment increased by a larger percentage than all industry employment in every region

Table 32: PERCENTAGE RATES OF CHANGE BETWEEN 1923 AND 1937 IN THE NUMBER OF INSURED PERSONS IN BUILDING AND IN ALL INDUSTRIES

	Building	*Total all industries*
London and Home Counties	+41·6	+42·7
Midland Counties	+74·7	+28·2
West Riding, Notts and Derby	+57·5	+15·0
Mid-Scotland	+51·2	+ 9·5
Lancashire	+42·8	+ 7·5
Northumberland and Durham	+62·7	+ 4·7
Glamorgan and Monmouth	+19·8	− 4·3
Great Britain	+51·4	+22·3

SOURCE: *Royal Commission on the Distribution of Industrial Population*, Cmd. 6153 (1940), p. 271.

except London and the Home Counties. Some of the Northern Counties did not do too badly at all. In Northumberland and Durham, for example, employment in the building industry increased faster than in any other region barring the Midland Counties. Moreover, in most of the Northern areas including Scotland, the difference between the expansion in building employment and that in all industries was greater than that of either London and the Home Counties and the Midland Counties. Thus, although the greater degree of concentration of building in the South gave this region an initial advantage as regards employment opportunities, this was to some extent offset by the fact that employment in building tended to expand more rapidly in those counties situated further north. However, one must also bear in mind the fact that in the latter areas unemployment tended to be considerably higher than in the London area and the South.

V. *The Cost of Building Employment*

Whether in fact building work was a relatively expensive way of generating employment as American experience suggests is somewhat debatable. According to Leontief's calculations $1 million spent on the final output of the construction industry in the US in 1939 gave rise to the employment of 448 men (174 direct and 274 indirect) as against figures ranging from 1,139 for the same amount spent on agricultural products to 489 for a similar amount spent on railroad transportation. In fact, in terms of a given expenditure building had one of the lowest employment generation multipliers of all industries, which suggests it was a fairly costly way of creating new employment.[1] Yet the fact that building was a labour intensive industry with a relatively low output per man would seem to suggest that the employment generating effects would be fairly high in comparison with other industries.

Direct comparisons between Britain and America of the employment generation effects of a given expenditure on building are not possible, partly because of the lack of reliable data and partly because of the exchange rate problems involved in comparisons of this sort. There is no guarantee, for example, that the official exchange rate would reflect the real exchange rate, that is, the real comparative cost of investment in building, and we have no reliable conversion factor which would enable us to overcome this difficulty. This does not mean, however, that there is nothing more to be said on the matter. Data is available for the employment generation effects of a given expenditure on housing and certain public works in Great Britain and this is presented in Table 33. It will be seen at once that the proportions of direct and indirect employment created by a £1 million expenditure in this country were almost the reverse of the American. Nearly 60 per cent of the employment was directly generated in Britain as against 39 per cent in the United States, a difference which might be explained partly by the fact that American building firms tended to buy from outside more standardized fittings or components for assembly on the site. The second point to note is that the total employment effects of £1 million spent on

[1] International Labour Office, *Housing and Employment* (1948), p. 45.

building were greater than the same amount spent on other public works and services. There were, of course, variations in the direct and indirect employment repercussions between the various works in question. Water-drainage, for example, was far more productive in terms of direct employment than housing, whilst road works created considerably more indirect employment. Such differences might well be important in determining the types of work on which local authorities should concentrate. If unemployment is fairly evenly spread throughout the country expenditure on road works and housing would be the most obvious choices from a national point of view since the employment effects of such expenditures would be widely felt. Conversely, where unemployment is localized, drainage works are to be preferred because of the large proportion of direct employment created.

Table 33: PRIMARY EMPLOYMENT CREATED IN MAN-YEARS BY THE EXPENDITURE OF £1 MILLION BY LOCAL AUTHORITIES IN 1931

	Total	*Direct per cent*	*Indirect per cent*
Housing	3,990	59	41
Sewerage	3,710	87	13
Roads	3,110	40	60
Public Health other than sewerage	3,590	59	41

SOURCE: R. F. Bretherton, F. A. Burchardt and R. S. G. Rutherford, *Public Investment and the Trade Cycle in Great Britain* (1941), p. 303.

Whatever the advantages and disadvantages of housing expenditure compared with alternative expenditures from a local or national point of view, it is clear that housing was, in comparison with other public works, the least expensive way of generating employment. Similar estimates have not been made for manufacturing industry, but it is possible to obtain a rough idea of the relative cost of generating direct employment from a given expenditure by comparing the gross output (or final selling value) per man employed of the building industry with that of other trades. As one might expect, gross output per head in building fell below that of most other industries by a substantial margin. This would seem to suggest, therefore, that the labour content of a unit of output in building was fairly high and hence a given expenditure on building work would generate considerably more employment than a similar expenditure on the final output of most other industries. From the gross ouput per man figures given in the census of production the direct employment effects of a £1 million expenditure on the final output of building and other industries have been calculated and the results tabulated below (see Table 34). It can be seen clearly that the amount of employment created by a given expenditure on building was far greater than that from a similar amount spent on the final output of most other industries.[1]

Thus, in direct terms at least, building does not appear to have been a particularly costly way of generating new employment. On the basis of the evidence presented there are grounds for suggesting that British experience differed from that of the American.

A word of caution should be added, however, about the statistical basis of comparison. In the first place, the statistical data used here

Table 34: DIRECT EMPLOYMENT CREATED BY £1 MILLION EXPENDITURE ON FINAL OUTPUT

	Men employed	
	1924	*1935*
Building	3,448	3,155
Iron and steel	1,689	1,923
Engineering, shipbuilding and vehicles	2,451	2,247
Textiles	1,653	2,364
Clothing	2,584	2,994
Food, drink and tobacco	657	784
Chemicals	918	997
Clay and building materials	2,545	2,941
Total factory trades	1,605	1,818
Total all industries	1,949	2,049

SOURCES: Based on data in *Fifth Census of Production 1935*, and Feinstein, op. cit.

is not strictly comparable since the British figures refer only to housing and other buildings whilst the American analysis is based on all construction work, including public works, though there is no reason to suppose that the employment generation effects of non-building construction were widely different from those of building itself. But more important is the fact that our findings are based on

[1] The Feinstein and Chapman data have been used here for building output and employment, since the census data is incomplete and includes certain public works. If the census data is used the employment generation effects in building appear somewhat weaker though still considerably higher than those of other industries.

fairly crude data and there is no guarantee that it reflects precisely the true position. Despite these reservations about the data the employment differences are of sufficient magnitude as to justify the conclusion that building work was a relatively inexpensive way of creating employment.[1]

VI. *Inter-Industry Relationships*

It was pointed out earlier that our employment analysis tended to exaggerate the impact of building on the rest of the economy since it included employment figures for a number of trades which produced only a small part of their output for building. This is particularly true of those industries in category 3 of Table 30 which were only very indirectly affected by building work, whilst even those most closely associated with the industry did not sell all their output to the one customer. An input-output analysis of the 1935 Census of Production data provides some indication of the demand created by the building industry for the products of other industries in the economy.[2] Altogether the building industry bought products from twenty-four of the thirty-six main industrial groups classified by Barna. The total inter-industry transactions on behalf of the building industry amounted to nearly £213 million in 1935. This was a very small proportion indeed of the total industrial production of Great Britain, but what is important is that only two industries, food processing and the distributive services, had a greater volume of transactions with other industries than building. In other words, building had a greater impact on the rest of the industrial economy than almost any other industry. Nevertheless, apart from one or two exceptions, the proportion of total output of any one industry that was acquired by building was generally quite small. Table 35 lists ten of the most important industries with which building was associated together with the percentages of the gross output of those industries acquired by the building industry. As one might expect the bulk of the building materials were consumed by this industry but, apart from this, the proportion of output of the other industries

[1] Although there are a number of possible reasons which might be put forward to explain the contrast between American and British experience (e.g. differences in the structure and efficiency of the building industries in the two countries) it would be impossible to resolve this complex problem without a detailed comparative analysis of the American and British industries, a task which is clearly outside the scope of this study.

[2] T. Barna, 'The Interdependence of the British Economy', *Journal of Royal Statistical Society*, A 115 (1952).

which was sold directly to the building industry was fairly low, especially in the case of mechanical and electrical engineering. This analysis does tend to underestimate the impact of building on other industries, however, since it fails to take account of the more indirect repercussions on those industries not directly connected with construction work. Nevertheless, it does suggest that outside a fairly narrow range of trades which were directly linked with building work, the industry's demand for products of other industries formed a relatively small proportion of their total output. On the other hand, since the building industry expanded more rapidly than

Table 35: INTER-INDUSTRY DEMAND, 1935

	(1) (£m.)	(2) *Gross output* (£m.)	(3) *Column* 1 *as per cent of Column* 2
Building from:			
China and glass	6·9	31·4	21·9
Oils and paints	7·3	22·1	33·0
Iron and steel manufactures	22·6	175·7	12·8
Non-ferrous metals	4·8	54·5	8·9
Mechanical engineering	12·5	171·7	7·3
Electrical engineering	6·3	106·8	5·9
Metal goods	12·1	88·6	13·5
Manufactures of wood	14·0	71·7	19·5
Building materials	37·7	53·4	73·0
Mining other than coal	6·0	19·0	31·6

SOURCES: Based on *Census of Production 1935*, and T. Barna, 'The Interdependence of the British Economy', *Journal of Royal Statistical Society*, A 115 (1952).

most other industries in the inter-war years one can almost certainly say that, as in the case of employment, the building industry accounted for an increasing proportion of the total output of those industries with which it was associated during this period.

It is difficult to say exactly what effect the increase in building activity had on the market for household consumer goods. There is no doubt, of course, that the building of over 4 million houses in the inter-war years stimulated the demand for such products since families moving into new homes usually wanted the latest equipment to be installed. This is particularly true of the 1930s when the volume of housebuilding was at its highest. The output of electrical equipment including heating appliances, refrigerators, vacuum cleaners, etc., increased rapidly at this time and it seems probable that the new housing developments were an important factor in the situation. Even so, one must be careful not to exaggerate the position. The market for household appliances was still very limited before 1939. It was confined largely to the middle classes since the lower classes spent very little indeed on household durable goods. As Table 36 shows in most cases the penetration of the market had only just begun by the time war broke out. The number of vacuum cleaners, refrigerators and water heaters in use in 1939 was small even in relation to the new houses built since 1919. Nor can it be assumed that all the new equipment was bought by people moving into new houses since many pre-war houses were being wired for electricity during this period. By 1939 8·5 million homes were wired for electricity which means at least 4 million were old ones assuming the electricity was installed in all the new houses built since the First World War. Thus

Table 36: THE MARKET FOR HOUSEHOLD APPLIANCES

	Number in use in 1939	*Number per 1,000 wired houses*
Houses wired for electricity	8·5 m.	
Electric cookers	1·6 m.	190
Electric water heaters	480,000	56
Gas water heaters	1·1 m.	
Electric wash boilers	360,000	42
Electric washing machines	150,000	18
Vacuum cleaners	2·3 m.	270
Electric refrigerators	200,000	24
Electric irons	6·5 m.	800

SOURCE: Political and Economic Planning, *The Market for Household Appliances* (1945).

although housing developments in these years were likely to have a greater indirect effect on industry than in the nineteenth century when the new household appliances based on electricity were virtually non-existent, the impact before 1939 was relatively weak since use of the new appliances was confined largely to middle-class homes.

Finally in one respect the building industry had virtually no impact at all on the rest of the industrial economy and that was in the diffusion and transmission of new techniques. This is hardly surprising, of course, since technically the building industry remained largely traditional throughout the period. True, there were, as stated in Chapter 7, a number of new developments and improvements in production methods but the total effect of these was quite small and there was certainly no massive application of new technology in building which could possibly have resulted in the industry becoming a major centre for the transmission of new techniques and ideas to other sectors of the economy. The only development which could possibly have had any real effect in this respect was industrialized or prefabricated building techniques but since progress in the field had hardly got past the experimental stage even by 1939 the repercussions were negligible. If anything new developments occurred outside the building industry and percolated inwards as in the case of new building materials. Possibly the expansion in the demand for factor inputs stimulated improvements in the techniques used in producing building materials but even here the response was confined to a narrow range of industries. Nor is it certain that the introduction of new techniques in material-producing industries was always occasioned by the high level of demand generated by the building industry. The rotary kiln in cement making, for example, had been applied extensively long before the demand for cement from the building industry had reached its peak.

VII. *Summary*

Taken as a whole the building industry by no means exercised a dominant influence on the economy of Britain in the inter-war years despite the rapidity with which it expanded. It has already been shown in previous chapters that the housing boom of the 1930s was not the generally accepted key factor in the recovery from the slump and there is reason to believe that the role of building in long-term growth was less important than is often supposed. One should not, however, underestimate the impact of the building sector. It was, as we have seen, one of the fastest growing industries and it became a far more important sector of the economy than it had been in the years prior to 1914. On average it accounted for about 5 per cent of the national product in the 1930s,[1] whilst between 10 and 15 per cent of the total labour force was employed in building and related industries. Altogether the building and related trades accounted for roughly one quarter of the increase in employment in this period, whilst building work alone absorbed well over 40 per cent of the total domestic investment. Thus, in view of the industry's heavy requirements in terms of factor inputs, this sector was a particularly suitable form of economic activity to expand in the conditions

[1] This is almost twice the pre-war proportion. If maintenance and repairs are included the building sector's share of national product rises to over 6 per cent.

prevailing in the inter-war years, though it should be emphasized that the regional concentration of building activity did tend to accentuate the imbalanced growth pattern between the North and the South.

The assertion that building was a relatively expensive way of generating new employment has little foundation, and in this respect British experience differs from that of the American. Moreover, despite the fact that building work consumed a considerable amount of the nation's capital resources there is no evidence that this had a detrimental effect on other sectors of the economy. On the other hand, despite the large volume of investment in building the impact in terms of new technical developments was relatively slight. The structure and organization of the building industry remained largely traditional throughout the period, with the result that it did not become a centre for the transmission and diffusion of new techniques and processes to other sectors of the economy.

CHAPTER 14

BUILDING, TRANSPORT AND SUBURBAN DEVELOPMENT

In most of the previous chapters we have been primarily concerned with the economic aspects of building development during the inter-war period. Yet however important the expansion in building might have been from a purely economic point of view it should not allow us to lose sight of some of the social implications arising from that development. The vast expansion in the supply of new accommodation was associated with a significant improvement in the social living standards of many people. This was largely the result of the marked shift in the geographical location of building activity. In contrast to the nineteenth century by far the larger part of the buildings erected in this period were located on the periphery of the large urban complexes which had developed during the previous century. This is particularly true of residential accommodation and there is little doubt that the inter-war years saw the most intensive phase of suburban housing development. The outward shift in population which this development inevitably entailed was not determined solely by supply factors, that is, the availability of accommodation. It can be argued that building in the suburbs was a response in part to changes in demand associated with rising real incomes and changes in tastes. Furthermore, the process of suburban development was made possible by the availability of cheaper land on the outskirts of towns and the development of a new and flexible form of transport which enabled housing development to take place in areas previously inaccessible by rail and tram.

But although suburban growth brought many benefits it was far from being an unmixed blessing. Much of the suburban development of this period was unplanned. Houses were erected in a haphazard manner, often merely as an extension of the old town. Rarely were new suburbs conceived or developed as viable economic and social units. Residential accommodation was often provided without the necessary community and social services such as schools, libraries, chapels, etc., whilst few deliberate attempts were made by local authorities to co-ordinate housing and industrial development. Thus, far from relieving the overcrowded cities, suburban development tended to increase the congestion at the centre since many suburban dwellers continued to depend on the city as a place of work and amusement. Indeed it has been argued that in trying to overcome the difficulties of the overcrowded and over-extended city the suburb proved to be both a temporary and costly solution.[1]

Some of the social problems associated with suburban development will be considered in the latter part of this chapter. It is essential, however, first of all to examine the main features of that development and its causes.

I. *Population Movements and Suburban Growth*

The building expansion of the inter-war years was unique not only in terms of its volume, but also on account of its geographical location. Regional concentration in the South was not, however, its most significant feature. Even more important was the locational pattern of building within the major regions. The majority of the new houses were built in the industrial suburbs and the growth of the latter was associated with a significant outward migration of the population from the centre of the cities.

This movement of population from the city centres to the outskirts did not of course originate in the inter-war years. Indeed it had already begun well before the end of the last century for, with increasing congestion in the towns and improved local transport facilities, mainly railways and trams, the more affluent city dwellers were encouraged to move to residences in the suburbs. But apart from London and one or two other areas, the migration was largely confined to the wealthier sections of the middle classes. This drift from the centre to the fringes was greatly accelerated in the early twentieth century and in the inter-war years it became by far the most prominent feature in the distribution of population. Of the 131 districts in England and Wales which increased their population by 30 per cent or more between 1921 and 1931 no less than 116 were suburban areas, the remainder being seaside resorts.[2] All the major conurbations, accounting for about one-half of Britain's population, experienced this centrifugal movement. Numbers in the centre remained constant or even declined, whilst all the growth took place in the suburbs. Thus the inner centres of the seven largest urban areas of London, Manchester, Birmingham, West Yorkshire, Glasgow, Merseyside and Tyneside showed a decline in population of 2·5 per cent between 1921 and 1938, whilst the population of their suburbs

[1] L. Mumford, *The City in History* (1966, Pelican ed.), p. 559.

[2] Political and Economic Planning, *Location of Industry* (1939), pp. 294–8.

expanded by no less than 32 per cent. Altogether Britain's population increased by 3·44 million during this period, 75 per cent of which accrued to the suburbs of the twenty-seven major urban conurbations.

The increase in population was very unevenly distributed. In London and the Home Counties, for example, the increase was about 18 per cent (1921–37), whilst in the Midland Counties (Staffs, Warwicks, Worcestershire, Leicestershire and Northants) it was about 11 per cent. On the other hand, all other regions increased their population by less than the national average of 7·5 per cent. The West Riding, Notts and Derby group increased their population by 6 per cent, mid-Scotland by 4 per cent and Lancashire by 1 per cent only, whilst Glamorgan and Monmouth, Northumberland and

Table 37: POPULATION DISTRIBUTION AND INCREASE FOR LONDON, THE SOUTH-EAST AND ENGLAND AND WALES, 1921–39

	Percentage distribution of population in 1921	*Increase (in '000) between 1921–39*	*Percentage distribution of increase*
County of London	11·8	−472	−13·2
Greater London Conurbation	19·8	1,240	34·7
South-Eastern England	32·2	2,413	67·5
Rest of England and Wales	67·8	1,160	32·5
	100·0	3,573	100·0

SOURCE: D. L. Foley, *Controlling London's Growth* (1963), Tables 1 and 2, pp. 10 and 12.

Durham all experienced a decline in population. Of the actual increase in population by far the larger part accrued to the South-East of England. In 1921 this area accounted for roughly one-third of the total population of England and Wales. Yet it absorbed just over two-thirds of the increase in population between 1921 and 1939 (see Table 37). The Greater London area alone accounted for just over one-third of the national increase in population, which was a greater relative share than in any period since 1801.[1]

The process of suburban growth is brought out very clearly by the case of the Greater London region. Although in percentage

[1] For further details see *Royal Commission on the Distribution of Industrial Population*, Cmd. 6153 (1940).

terms the region as a whole was growing less rapidly than in the later nineteenth century, the important feature to note is that in the early twentieth century the outer zone was expanding at the expense of central London. After the turn of the century the population of the outer zone increased in absolute terms more rapidly than in any other period (see Table 38). Thus between 1921 and 1937 the population of outer London rose by nearly 1·4 million whilst that of the inner zone fell by almost 400,000. On the other hand, what is even more noteworthy is the fact that in the inter-war years outer London gained far more people than inner London lost. This suggests that there was a fairly strong inward movement of population from the

Table 38: INCREASE AND MIGRATION OF POPULATION IN IN INNER AND OUTER ZONES OF THE GREATER LONDON AREA ('000)

	Actual increases in population		*Gain or loss by migration*	
	Inner London	*Outer London*	*Inner London*	*Outer London*
1871–81	568·9	312·1	108	198
1881–91	397·7	469·5	–118	278
1891–1901	308·3	639·3	–182	397
1901–11	– 14·6	684·5	–553	321
1911–21	– 37·2	266·0	–323	20
1921–31	– 87·5	811·3	–360	604
1931–7	–311·0	728·0	–348	604

SOURCE: *Royal Commission on the Distribution of Industrial Population*, Cmd. 6153 (1940), pp. 163 and 317.

rest of the country towards London and the two movements met or merged in outer London. In this aspect the pattern of redistribution probably differed from that which occurred in most other large urban regions. In one other aspect too the London area was different. Large-scale suburban growth was not a relatively new phenomenon in London as it was in other regions during this period. Well before 1914 London had developed an extensive suburbia and in the inter-war years it was the case of either new urban centres being created on the edge of the old suburban ring or filling in the gaps between the communities created by the railways in the period prior to the First World War. Thus the boundaries were gradually pushed out to Becontree in the east, Ilford and Wanstead in the north-east, Hendon and Edgware in the north-west, South Harrow and Hayes to the west and Morden and Cheam in the south and south-east. At the same time a number of older, semi-rural communities, such as

Hounslow, Kingston, Croydon and Eltham, continued to expand and helped to complete the ring of satellite towns spread over a radius of ten to fifteen miles or more from the city centre.

Despite these differences the pattern of suburban development of the London area was not so markedly dissimilar from that of provincial urban areas to warrant separate regional analysis even if reliable data were available. Basically similar developments were taking place in most of the larger provincial towns or urban communities such as Manchester, Glasgow, Liverpool and Tyneside, though on a somewhat smaller scale than around the metropolis. The important thing is to discern what caused this massive suburban migration to take place in these years.

II. *The Determinants of Suburban Development*

a. The Interaction of Demand and Supply Factors

The growth of the suburbs was conditioned by a complex set of interdependent factors operating from both the demand and supply side of the equation. It would be easy, of course, to express the problem in simple terms, namely to argue that population moved to the suburbs because accommodation was made available there, but this would merely represent a statement of fact of what happened and would not explain why, for example, houses were built there in the first place. Nor would it tell us how far building was determined by changes in the demand schedule or alternatively whether both building and population migration were dependent upon some exogenous factor, for example, a change in the pattern of transport.

On the supply side at least the problem is fairly easy to resolve. There can be little doubt that extensive suburban housebuilding was largely conditioned by the fact that the main city centres were congested. Even before 1914 many of the central areas of the large urban conurbations, in which the majority of the population resided, were already congested and as time went on congestion became an increasingly serious impediment to the proper economic functioning of the city. Land in the central zone became scarce and expensive and the obvious solution to the problem was to move out to the suburbs where land was cheaper and more readily available. It was cheaper and easier therefore to build houses on the outer ring of the cities rather than bid for land in the centre or demolish and rebuild on the old sites. The process was facilitated, moreover, by the fact that many local authorities encouraged suburban housebuilding in an effort to relieve population congestion in the towns.

On the other hand, it can be argued that demand factors had an equally important part to play. Though circumstances forced builders to develop the suburban areas this development would not have been feasible had demand expectations not been favourable. Moreover, it was not simply a matter of rising real incomes, since effective demand for new houses often required both a change in income and a concomitant change in consumer tastes. Larger incomes could easily have been spent on other consumer durable goods, but the fact that in many uses these incomes were translated into a demand for new housing can be explained by the change in consumers' preferences. The desire to escape from the confines of the congested urban areas and reside in the cleaner and aesthetically more pleasant surroundings of the suburbs was an important factor in making the demand for housing effective. The period was characterized by a marked shift in the socially acceptable standard of living accommodation and it is probable that many buyers of private houses were motivated by changes in their tastes rather than by changes in their incomes. This was particularly true of many middle- and possible lower middle-class families for whom new houses in new surroundings became a symbol of status.

Changes in the nature of demand function have already been discussed in an earlier chapter and require no further elaboration here. But this brief resume clearly illustrates that the suburban residential development was occasioned by a variety of social and economic factors operating at the same time. Rising real incomes and changes in tastes on the demand side together with rising land costs and congestion on the supply side inevitably forced buildings and population to gravitate to the suburbs. But could this movement have occurred without simultaneous improvements in transportation? How far was the massive application of motorized transport a crucial factor in the spread of communities beyond the confines of the old city boundaries? In other words can demand and supply factors be regarded as autonomous variables or were they dependent upon some third factor?

b. Transport and Building

(i) *The Transport Building Cycle.* Some years ago Isard developed the theory of the transport-building cycle.[1] This stressed the crucial role

[1] W. Isard, 'Transport Development and Building Cycles', *Quarterly Journal of Economics*, 57 (1942) and 'A Neglected Cycle: The Transport-Building Cycle', *Review of Economics and Statistics*, 24 (1942).

played by the growth and innovational aspects of transport facilities in determining waves in building activity. By reacting upon industrial location and consumer behaviour transport developments set the basic pattern to which building adhered to in the past. For the US he found six major innovational transport developments between 1825 and 1933 each one of which was followed or accompanied by a major upswing in building activity, whilst once the transport development had spent itself sooner or later the building boom collapsed. The last cycle, which is the one most relevant here, occurred between 1918 and 1933 and was based of course on road transport. Isard admits that the temporary shortage of houses and the wave of marriages shortly after the war were important factors in the housing cycle but argues that ultimately the basic stimulus to building was received from the dispersion of population brought about and encouraged by the motor-car.

It is difficult, of course, to isolate the impact of one particular factor. But the correlation between long waves in building and transport in America is sufficiently consistent to suggest that it was more than a chance association.

To see whether American experience was repeated in Britain the real investment in building and the annual increase in all motorized road vehicles were plotted on a graph. A glance at Fig. 11 (p. 335) will show that the two are by no means unrelated. There were two major upswings in building activity both of which were preceded by a similar cycle in the additions to the stock of road vehicles. In the early 1920s, for example, there was a sharp increase in the number of vehicles which reached a peak in 1924–5, three years before that of the peak in all building. The dramatic fall in the additions to road vehicles through to the slump of 1930 was not accompanied by a definite trend in building activity, though two minor troughs occurred in 1928 and 1931–2. But the second wave in building activity in the 1930s was again accompanied by a rapid growth of road vehicles the peak of which occurred two years before that of all building activity, though a year after the peak in residential building.

There would seem, therefore, to be some support for Isard's transport-building cycle thesis in the British data for the inter-war years. In case this was simply a chance association the relevant data was collected back to 1860 and plotted as before.[1] The period before 1914 saw two major upswings in building, one in the late 1860s and

[1] Real investment figures were used for building together with annual increments in rail and tram mileage. It was not thought necessary to reproduce the graph here.

early 1870s and the other around the turn of the century, both of which were accompanied by a surge forward in transportation, though in each case the latter tended to lag slightly behind the building cycle rather than precede it. A minor boom in building in the early 1880s, however, was preceded by a sharp increase in net additions to the tramway mileage. Conversely, the trough in building in the later 1880s occurred at a time when additions to the transportation network were at a minimum.

British experience suggests, therefore, that the tendency has been for building and transport cycles to be positively correlated. On the other hand, before 1914 there is no clear evidence that building booms were triggered off by prior innovations in transport, whereas in the inter-war years the data tends to point rather to the opposite conclusion. Such evidence is by no means conclusive proof that suburban housing development was solely a creation of the innovations in road transport. But it does suggest that transport was not an unimportant factor and it might be worth while to examine the position more closely at the regional or local level to see in what sort of context transport was the determining factor. Here we can distinguish between industrial and residential building units since the two were rarely planned in conjunction with each other.

(ii) *Motor Transport and Suburban Building Development.* One would expect motor transport to have been a decisive factor in shifting the pattern of industrial location. Not only did it offer a new freedom to the manufacturer in selecting a site but it also accentuated the disadvantage of locating factories or commercial buildings in the old urban centres. The location of factories was no longer tied to areas where railway facilities were available since the motor vehicle allowed a much greater freedom of choice in this matter. Thus it was possible for the new or light industries, such as chemicals, electrical goods and vehicle manufacturing, to be located in the suburbs of the urban conurbations away from the coal, iron and rail groupings which had been such a distinct feature of nineteenth-century development. There were distinct advantages in moving to the outskirts. Land was cheaper and more readily available than in the older developed centres, whilst reliance on road transport magnified the drawbacks of the obsolescent street layout of the cities which aggravated the problems of traffic congestion. To some extent location based on the new form of transport tended to reduce the possibilities of congestion since it differed from that of the old industrial centres. Whereas railway transport had tended to encourage the development of factories grouped around nuclear points with radial distribution of goods from the centre, motor transport, with its greater flexibility and ease of movement, made possible the building of factories along arterial roads with no specific focal point. In the long run this brought about a greater diffusion of industry and population which, though it had advantages, eventually produced ribbon development against which the Government was forced to take action in 1935.

Evidence suggests that there was a trend towards industrial decentralization and that rail connections became increasingly less important in determining the location of new factories. In a recent study of the New York Metropolitan region it was found that the percentage of new plant sites having railroad sidings fell from 63 per cent prior to 1920 to 50 per cent in the period 1920 to 1945.[1] The obvious conclusion to be drawn from this is that motor transport was becoming a more powerful factor in determining the location of new industrial developments. Little work has been done on the suburban industrial development of British towns, but what scanty data there is points to the same conclusion. The construction of a series of new arterial roads serving the Metropolis after 1918 provided transport facilities essential to the attraction of modern industry. It became possible, therefore, for factory estates to be established adjacent to arterial roads and this practice became increasingly common in the 1930s. Of the 470 factories opened or extended in the outer London region between 1933 and 1936 no less than two-fifths were established on such estates, most of them being independent of railway connections. The most outstanding example of extensive industrial development along an arterial highway was the Great West Road. Within a two-mile stretch more than fifty factories were established employing 11,000 people, and the road became one of the principal industrial centres of the outer London region.[2]

Much of the new factory development, especially in the 1930s, occurred in the London region,[3] and it was almost inevitable that

[1] E. M. Hoover and R. Vernon, *Anatomy of a Metropolis: The Changing Distribution of People and Jobs within the New York Metropolitan Region* (1959), p. 37.

[2] For details see S. V. Pearson, *London's Overgrowth and the Causes of Swollen Towns* (1939), p. 58.

[3] Of the net increase of 644 in the number of factories in Great Britain in the six years 1932 to 1937 no less than 532 or five-sixths were located in the Greater London area. These figures exclude new establishments employing less than 25 persons. *Royal Commission on the Distribution of Industrial Population*, Cmd. 6153 1940), p. 166.

some of it should take place on the outskirts of this congested area. Even so the central zone still held its attractions and on balance the process was one of increasing centralization of business and commercial premises. Between 1924 and 1934 the area devoted to industry alone (excluding docks) in the County of London rose from 3,000 to 3,660 acres, together with an unspecified increase in the area occupied by the business premises. In other large urban regions the attraction of the outer suburbs seems to have been even less marked than in the London area, and on balance the trend was towards increasing centralization of business and commercial premises. True, there are examples of industrial decentralization in some of the larger towns such as Manchester, Glasgow and Liverpool, but nowhere did it take place on a massive scale. Of course one must remember that new factory development was much less extensive than in the South-East region and it was this which was most likely to bring about decentralized location patterns of development. Establishments already located in the central zones of cities were unlikely to uproot and move outwards unless the existing sites were uneconomic or obsolete, or unless further expansion was restricted by a shortage of space. Admittedly site congestion was a problem but to some extent it was being relieved by the migration of population from the central zone, and in turn the vacated residential sites were then acquired by business and commercial interests. Thus, far from there being a diffusion or decentralization of business and commercial premises to correspond with the movement of population, there was in actual fact an increasing concentration of such activity in the inner zones of the provincial urban centres. The net effect of this process has been to increase the congestion in the centre of the city. Apart from the London region then—and even here the effect was limited—motor transport does not appear to have had a dramatic impact on the pattern of industrial location, at least not before 1939. It certainly made decentralization easier, but in practice its effects were very weak indeed.

As far as residential accommodation is concerned the pattern of location was quite different. Here, as we have already noted, the bulk of the new dwelling units were located on the fringes of the cities and it would be difficult, if not impossible, to deny that motor transport did not play some part in this suburban development. Yet it would be too easy and also misleading to state simply that it was caused by the development of a new medium of transport. Certainly it facilitated the whole process, but there is no reason to assume that it was always the key factor or that suburban development would not have taken place without it. The part played by motor transport varied enormously between areas or districts depending on the type of development and the adequacy of existing lines of communication.

It is possible to distinguish three of four main types of residential suburban development and examine the role of motor transport in each of these in turn. First there were those areas where the new form of transport had little influence on the siting of new residential estates. Glasgow is perhaps a typical example. Here the Corporation was responsible for most of the housebuilding in the inter-war years and by 1939 it had completed just over 50,000 new dwellings. Nearly all of them were located within easy access of the city centre. It was possible to do this since land was still available on the outer edge of the inner zone. Large housing estates were, therefore, erected at Mosspark, Bellahouston, Knightswood and Riddrie, and nearly all of these places were situated within easy reach of the existing transportation network, namely the tramways which had all but been completed before 1914. In time, of course, the tramway services were gradually replaced by buses, but by and large it was possible for suburban housing development to take place within the existing transportation framework and independently of the motor bus or private car.

At the other extreme there was the type of suburban development which depended heavily on the concomitant provision of road transport facilities. Residential growth along some of the main arterial highways leading out of London, for example, was largely occasioned by the private car or express coach service. Similarly, suburban housing development beyond the local city boundaries, where lines of communication were often weak, was made possible by the provision of bus services. This was the case, for example, of the Wythenshawe estate in Manchester, which was inaccessible by either rail or tram, and it only became possible to develop it extensively providing proper bus services to Manchester were laid on for the inhabitants. In fact, as suburban development began to take place further and further away from city centre, and hence from the old urban transportation network, the greater became the dependence on road transport.

In the majority of cases, however, suburban growth was made possible by utilizing both the old and the new forms of transport. Much of the new housing development did in fact follow the existing lines of communication. Where road transport became important was that it allowed the centres of development to spread away from the railhead and tramway networks or it made possible the development of empty areas which lay between railway stations on radial routes. Thus the development of extensive residential accommodation in places like Becontree, Dagenham, Romford and Thames Ditton would not have been feasible without the existence of rapid rail communication to the centre of London since a large proportion of the inhabitants of these districts continued to work in the Metropolis. Without suburban rail services this would not have been possible since it was too time-consuming and inconvenient to commute by road each day over such long distances. Nevertheless, motor transport still had a part to play in this daily migration since dispersion of population within the suburban satellite towns was only practicable providing the inhabitants had easy access by road to the local railway station.

There is no doubt whatsoever that motor transport facilitated inter-war suburban growth but we would question any assumption to the effect that it was the chief causal factor in the process. In some regions, especially Greater London, extensive suburban development had taken place long before the new form of transport had made its mark and this trend could have continued irrespective of whether the transport function had changed or not. Great Britain was already fairly well provided with a suburban transportation network when the 1914–18 war began, and it is quite realistic to assume that fairly extensive suburban growth could have taken place on the basis of the old system with a few extensions. True the pattern of that development might well have been different and its pace considerably slower but it would have taken place all the same. In so far as motor transport was a cheaper and more flexible form of transport than either the railway or tram, it made possible a more varied and haphazard pattern of development than the old transport system would have permitted. On the other hand, suburban development in turn increased the popularity of the new form of transport. The establishment of new estates away from the city centre created a heavy local demand for transport facilities for shopping, amusement and inter-urban travel, and the obvious choice was road transport because of its inherent advantages for short-distance work.

III. *Some Problems of Suburban Growth*

However debatable the causes of inter-war suburban growth might be few would deny that the housing accommodation provided, whether for the middle or lower classes, was markedly superior to that built before 1914. Not only was the quality of housing generally better and densities lower, but also most new houses had gardens attached and were situated in much more congenial surroundings. Yet despite these attractions suburban growth left much to be desired. In fact there were several undesirable features associated with the development of suburbia most of which sprang basically from one factor: the lack of proper constructive town planning. Most of the housing development of this period was haphazard and unregulated. Some of the results are of course obvious even today. New estates sprang up where land was cheap and access to transport facilities convenient. Inevitably this produced sprawling suburban growth either in the form of uncontrolled ribbon development along main arterial roads or nuclear groupings along radial access routes to the city. From an aesthetic point of view this type of development was highly unpleasant and it is perhaps this aspect of the question which has received most attention and comment in the past. But in comparison with the long-term social and economic consequences of suburban growth this point is rather a minor one.

a. Land Utilization

One question which received all too little consideration at the time was that regarding land utilization. At first perhaps this may have seemed a factor of little consequence since on the periphery of the urban complexes land was relatively cheap and plentiful. But this situation soon changed with the rapid spread of suburban housing since little consideration was given to economy in the employment of land.[1] The result was that the amount of land consumed was far greater than could be justified by the improvement in standards of residential housing conditions compared with pre-war. In the Manchester conurbation, for example, it has been estimated that the post-1918 development was spread over five times the area covered by earlier development though it only contained 25 per cent more people.[2] Admittedly post-war development was of a more spacious type but it is almost certain that the land available could have been used less extravagantly had effective planning control been operative. Furthermore, the movement of housing and industry into hitherto under-developed areas was often carried out without due regard to the value of land for alternative uses. In some counties housing often used up the very best agricultural land. The Special Areas Commissioners were informed in the 1930s that in Southern Essex alone building development had involved the loss of thousands of acres of

[1] See *Town Planning Review*, June 1936, p. 39, for a critical attack on this aspect.
[2] P. Self, *Cities in Flood* (1961), p. 23.

the most fertile land in Britain where market gardening in its highest form had been carried on for generations.[1] It is impossible of course to estimate quantitatively the effect of this development in terms of land utilization but the long-term economic implications of such extensive land use are noticeably apparent today and require little further comment in an age of high land values.

b. The Haphazard Growth of Suburban Communities

But perhaps the most unsatisfactory feature of the inter-war housing estates was that only rarely were attempts made to shape a town in accordance with some view as to the varied needs of the community. Suburban towns were not planned as viable economic and social entities. Generally speaking, they were simply places of residence whose inhabitants were forced to find their livelihood and amusement elsewhere. This is particularly true of private estate development, but even local authorities paid lip-service to effective economic and social planning of the communities they created. The co-ordinated development of industry, housing and public services, such as schools, churches, shops and transport facilities was conspicuous by its absence in most towns. It was sometimes a matter of years after the inception of a new estate before proper industrial and community facilities were provided. The London County Council's efforts to develop suburban estates in Essex was typical of many. In the 1920s the Council carried out a large working-class housing scheme at Becontree to relieve population congestion in London. By 1932 the Council was accommodating 103,000 on the new estate nearly all of whom had to commute daily to London since there was little new industrial work provided nearby. For some time, moreover, the area was deficient in social and public amenities. There was a severe shortage of school accommodation, especially for infants, and to begin with there were no shops, churches, public houses or other amenities within easy reach of some of the residential quarters.[2]

On the other hand, at Slough, to the west of London, almost the reverse process took place. Here a large modern industrial estate with magnificent social amenities was established which by 1938 was employing some 28,000 workers. But unfortunately the expansion in employment opportunities was not accompanied by a corres-

[1] *Royal Commission on the Distribution of the Industrial Population*, Cmd. 6153 (1940), p. 96.

[2] See W. Ashworth, 'Types of Social and Economic Development in Suburban Essex', in *London: Aspects of Change* edited by the Centre for Urban Studies (1964), p. 69.

ponding increase in residential accommodation so that many of the workers had to live outside the area and travel in each day. Such lack of balance between industrial and residential building was not uncommon in the Greater London region despite the fact that the trend towards industrial decentralization had made greater progress here than elsewhere. The greater part of the new industrial development occurred in the west and north-west of London, whereas the majority of the industrial workers tended to reside in the east and south-east, a situation which resulted in a heavy cross-city traffic in the morning and early evening.

Most inter-war satellite or suburban towns grew in a piecemeal fashion and it was usually many years before any of them reached a well-balanced, integrated stage whereby they could function as independent units. Few were conceived from the beginning as integrated communities with an economic life of their own. There were of course notable exceptions. The second garden city at Welwyn[1] was probably the outstanding example, for it had been designed specifically to avoid some of the typical drawbacks of suburban development by catering for both industry and residence. By 1939 it housed a population of 15,000, over one-quarter of whom were employed in nearby manufacturing firms. The example was followed by Manchester Corporation in the 1930s when it developed the Wythenshawe estate on the south side of the city. It was much less successful, however, than either Welwyn or Letchworth. Although it grew into a massive residential estate there was hardly any industrial development before 1939. Altogether the estate employed less than 1,000 workers and half of these lived outside its boundaries. In addition, there were a few notable private estates developed by industrial firms. Perhaps one of the most famous was the Bournville Estate. Although this had been started in 1895 the main expansion came after 1918. Between that date and 1938 the number of houses increased from 975 to 2,400 and the population of the estate nearly doubled. The Estate was a model of its kind. The average density of the houses was six to the gross acre and they were built against a background of parks, recreation grounds and open spaces and provided with all the necessary social amenities.

c. Suburban Growth and Urban Congestion

One important result of the suburban movement was that it increased congestion in the centre of cities and partly elsewhere. Although one would have expected some relief in the central zone on account of

[1] The first had been built at Letchworth before the war.

the outward movement of population, the fact that residential and industrial units were rarely planned in conjunction with one another meant that many suburban dwellers continued to depend on the city for employment.[1] The problem was accentuated, moreover, on account of the fact that new commercial and business premises were often built in the old urban areas rather than in the suburbs. In most towns therefore the proportion of people working in the centre but living elsewhere increased during the inter-war years and hence the flow of traffic into and out of the cities rose accordingly. In the late 1930s the London Passenger Transport Board estimated that the centripetal movement of population amounted to roughly 1,700,000 persons for every working day compared with only 850 to 900,000 in 1921.[2] Much of the traffic occurred at peak-hours which created additional problems for public transport undertakings, whilst an increasing number of journeys were being made by car or bus. The net result was that in relation to the volume of traffic road conditions definitely deteriorated in this period despite a considerable amount of road improvement, whilst in turn the cost to the community rose year by year.

The problem of traffic congestion was worst in and around the large urban conurbations; according to a survey of Sheffield it had already 'become extraordinarily acute in every big city by the early 1930s'.[3] The situation was probably very similar in most of the large cities and urban areas of Britain. In Central London the average speed of movement of motor vehicles was actually less in 1938 than it had been by horse vehicles thirty years earlier, and one large concern handling goods estimated that deliveries cost less than half as much on Sunday when traffic was freer. The total cost of traffic delays in that city alone was said to be in the region of £70 million per annum. Of course not all the traffic congestion can be attributed solely to the commuting habits of suburban dwellers. The volume of road traffic would have increased whether suburban housing development had taken place or not. Moreover, congestion occurred on some main highways which were not directly affected by daily commuters. Sir Charles Bressey in his *Report on London Traffic* in May 1938 pointed out that there was a bottleneck on average every mile all the way from London to Birmingham. Nevertheless, despite

[1] And usually, of course, for recreational facilities too.

[2] Furthermore the length of the average journey increased. The average distance travelled per passenger journey on the railways of Greater London rose from 3·90 miles in 1924 to 4·44 in 1932.

[3] A. G. Pool, *A Survey of Transport in Sheffield* (1933), p. 38.

these reservations there can be no doubt that traffic congestion in the cities increased as a result of suburban development.

d. The Failure of Town Planning

There is no question that the failure to relieve the problems created or aggravated by suburban development was largely due to inadequate town planning. Inter-war suburban development, apart from one or two significant exceptions, was as disorderly and haphazard as urban growth had been in the nineteenth century. In 1940 the Barlow Report summed up the position as follows: 'Except to a comparatively insignificant extent, industrial development and the building of the twelve million houses which today exist in this country have been carried out without the guidance of approved town plans. This is undoubtedly one of the main reasons for the maldistribution of new housing development in relation to new industrial development which is unfortunately often to be found in large towns.'[1] This is a sad commentary on the period, particularly in view of the fact that it was recognized in official circles at an early stage that without effective town and regional planning the bad conditions of the past were likely to recur.[2] Moreover, local authorities had been given town planning powers as early as 1909 and these were supplemented by further legislation in 1919 and 1932. Why then was so little done to implement town planning schemes?

The failure can be attributed to two factors—defective legislation and the apathy of the planning authorities. Although the Act of 1919 made it compulsory for every borough and urban district with a population of over 20,000 to prepare town planning schemes there was in fact little response from the municipal authorities. By April 1932 the total area fully planned, that is in the sense of being included in approved planning schemes, was a mere 75,020 acres, though some 7·5 million acres were already covered by approved resolutions to prepare such schemes. Within the next seven years progress was somewhat more rapid; even so by April 1939 only just over one million acres were fully planned, whilst more than half the area of the country, 26·5 million acres, was by that time subject to interim development control. This is far from being an impressive performance, however, for the amount of planning actually carried out was almost negligible. The reluctance of the local authorities to fulfil

[1] *Royal Commission on the Distribution of Industrial Population,* Cmd. 6153 (1940), p. 74.

[2] See *First Annual Report of the Ministry of Health, 1919–20,* Pt. II, Cmd. 917 (1920), pp. 45–6.

their functions is beyond dispute, though part of the blame can be attributed to the lack of pressure from the Ministry of Health which was responsible for seeing that schemes were, in fact, prepared and implemented. It is interesting, however, to note that when compulsion was dropped from the town planning law in 1932 the rate of progress increased indicating that local authorities were at last realising the virtues of town planning.

But even had the law as it then stood been applied more extensively it is doubtful whether it would have altered radically the pattern of development. For one thing, as Professor Ashworth has observed, there was rarely much recognizable difference between the outcome of development under town planning schemes and development outside them.[1] Few local authorities knew much about the subject and there was a lack of qualified personnel to advise them. Secondly, the legislation in itself was defective in several aspects and was hardly conducive to the implementation of proper planning schemes for large areas. Until 1932 the redevelopment of already built up areas fell outside the scope of the planning legislation. Hence it was virtually impossible to deal with the town as a whole unit and the problems of urban decay had to be treated under the Housing Acts. An even greater drawback of statutory planning was that it provided little scope for planning on anything other than a local basis. It was designed largely to achieve a more pleasant, healthier and more congenial local environment in newly developed areas rather than to check the spread of great towns and agglomerations or to correct the tendency towards increasing density and traffic congestion within large urban areas. In other words the planning legislation gave little incentive to plan on a regional basis.

Yet regional planning, made permanent and effective by national planning, was the key to the solution of many of the problems created by intensive urban and suburban development.[2] Many of these problems transcended local boundaries and could not be dealt with effectively unless co-operation on a regional scale was adopted. There were far too many local authorities with planning powers acting individually as if the economic problems with which they were faced were geographically exclusive to their own boundaries. In the area covered by the London Passenger Transport Board, for example, there were no less than 133 authorities exercising planning powers and it was obvious to anyone that effective planning required a

[1] W. Ashworth, *The Genesis of Modern British Town Planning* (1954), p. 212.

[2] See P. Abercrombie, *Town and Country Planning* (2nd ed. 1943), for an exposition of this view.

wider approach than this. The legislation was not completely silent on the matter of regional grouping of planning authorities. The Act of 1919 had made provision for the formation of joint town planning committees between neighbouring authorities, and by 1930 eighty joint committees had been set up representing over 1,000 local authorities covering a population of over 30 million.[1] But apart from the preparation of a series of regional plans these joint bodies accomplished very little in practice. They had no executive powers to carry out their plans and regional planning received little official support at the national level. In fact before 1939 effective regional planning was even less in evidence than town planning at the local level. Nevertheless, despite the disappointing performance it was clearly evident that a greater interest was being taken in town and regional planning, an interest which no doubt stemmed from the obvious shortcomings of the rapid but largely unregulated suburban growth of the early twentieth century.

e. The City and the Suburb

Apart from the more immediate and obvious problems connected with suburban development which have been discussed in the foregoing paragraphs there are other important economic and social aspects of city and suburban growth which were scarcely mentioned by contemporaries. Here we can but mention briefly only a few of the most relevant points since lack of space and empirical data preclude an extensive discussion. These comments are intended merely as a recognition that these problems exist.

The first point we have already touched upon briefly, namely, the viable economic size of the city or town. This is obviously a difficult question, the answer to which will vary according to differing conditions. Much will depend on the type and scale of the functions a city is expected to fulfil. Obviously the size of the metropolitan or parent town or city will be larger than its neighbouring satellite towns, since its range of services will be greater, some of which will be executed partly for the benefit of the inhabitants of the satellites. But the important point is when does a parent city become too big, that is, at what point does it begin to suffer diseconomies of scale? If at a certain size diminishing returns set in the obvious course of action is to create independent townships on the periphery of the original city. But how big should these be and how many? Would one or two economically self-contained towns be better than a large number of small villages or towns which are likely to be dependent

[1] Ashworth, op. cit., p. 203.

on the parent for many services. If it is possible to create one or two large and economically viable towns it might be better than a series of small but dependent townships since the latter course might result in a heavy drain on the resources of the parent town. Moreover, such townships might, because of their small size, prove an economically extravagant way of checking metropolitan growth. The point is an important one and has a direct bearing not only on past but also on future urban and suburban growth. It is a question of whether we could all move to small cities, as Lewis Mumford suggests, with economic impunity.[1]

Whatever the nature of the suburban growth, it is bound in some way to affect the economic balance of the metropolitan city. Whether the city gains or loses on balance is something of a moot point. If the city has already passed its optimum size then presumably decentralization will be a benefit. But even here this may not always be the case. Rapid spatial diffusion of population may impoverish the central zone and accentuate the problems of urban decay. Usually the first to move out are the younger and more prosperous elements and hence the central city tends to house the older and poorest section of the population. This raises the question of redevelopment of those quarters which have been vacated. Not only will new residential accommodation be expensive to build but it is unlikely to prove very attractive to any but the poorest kind of tenants. Thus it would seem that as income and wealth tend to migrate the city would be a net loser. In fact, however, the residential movement might be more than counter-balanced by an influx of business and commercial interests wanting to take advantage of convenient sites in the centre as and when they are freed. Inter-war experience suggests that the movement was by no means all one way. As population moved outward to suburban residences land values in the city tended to rise because of the demand on the part of business and industry for convenient central locations. Thus unless Government policy is directed towards wholesale decentralization of both industry and residential units there is every indication that the city might experience a net gain in terms of income by suburban residential development.

Extensive suburban development might, however, accentuate the socio-political problems of both the city and its environs. As the more

[1] This point has been raised recently by W. R. Thompson in his interesting article entitled 'Urban Economic Growth and Development in a National System of Cities', Chapter 12 in *The Study of Urbanization*, edited by P. M. Hauser and L. F. Schnore (1965, New York), p. 489.

prosperous sections of the community move further away from the city their proximity to the slum area diminishes and this in turn may lead to a decreasing awareness of the problem on the part of responsible members of society. As the city area and suburbs grow the slums become increasingly isolated and forgotten and a stage may be reached where the slum child may never transcend its immediate surroundings. As Michael Harrington has recently shown in parts of urban America this stage has certainly been reached.[1] In the suburbs too social and political segregation may have equally adverse results. The middle and upper class elements tend to cluster together and in time such groups become hardened by political boundaries. The same thing occurs with the lower classes. In so far as this political fragmentation leads to a divorce of the tax base from public service needs it will restrict the redistribution of income through public welfare services. How serious this will be in practice will depend of course on how rigid the political boundaries are and how extensive local as opposed to central welfare income redistribution services prove to be.

Such problems are largely inevitable in a rapidly growing urban society. Most of them were present, though only vaguely recognized, before 1939, but today they are of vital significance. No one supposes that their solution will be easy but action is imperative if our cities are to continue functioning effectively. All we have done here is to raise the questions; we do not pretend to know the answers.

IV. *Conclusions*

The social aspects of building development are less subject to precise quantitative analysis than those relating to aggregate growth which were explored in the previous chapter. Nevertheless, certain conclusions emerge from the last part of our study.

The most notable feature of inter-war building activity was its concentration in the suburbs, though the decentralization of industrial and commercial building was far less significant than that of residential accommodation. The location of new housing and the concomitant outward shift in population from the city centres was conditioned by a complex set of economic and social factors. The scarcity and expense of land in the central areas coupled with increasing congestion forced builders out towards the suburbs, whilst rising real incomes and shifts in consumer preferences created favourable conditions for the growth of suburban housing estates. Transport changes, too, were an important additional factor in-

[1] M. Harrington, *The Other America: Poverty in the United States* (1962).

fluencing the pattern of building activity. The two major upswings in building activity of the 1920s and 1930s were accompanied by similar movements in the growth of motor transport. This association between transport and building activity is probably more than accidental since a similar association is evident in the nineteenth century both in America and Great Britain. Whether at the regional or local level transport was a chief causal or determining factor in suburban building development is somewhat debatable. Certainly the two factors were inter-dependent and without innovations in transport suburban housing development would have been less pronounced. Indeed it is possible to argue that the volume of residential building would have been lower had new transport developments not allowed easier access to cheaper land and less congested sites. On the other hand, suburban development could, and did, take place without much extension to the transportation network, whilst in some areas development depended as much on the further exploitation of existing transport facilities (e.g. electrification of suburban railways around London) as it did on motor transport.

Though an economic and social necessity, given the conditions prevailing at the time, suburban development was accompanied by many social problems. These included questions such as land utilization, urban congestion, the development of viable communities and the relations between the city and the suburbs. The failure to alleviate these problems in any way was largely due to the inadequate and ineffective town planning machinery.

CONCLUSION

Building activity between the wars was much higher than before 1914, and compares well with experience since the Second World War. This was especially true of housebuilding. The number of houses built in the UK during the period 1920–38 inclusive totalled 4·359 million, equivalent to almost 81 per cent of the 5·418 million houses built between 1947 and 1965. The inter-war peak was not surpassed until 1964, and the houses built in the quinquennium 1934–8 amounted to more than in any post-war five-year period, even including 1961–5.[1] Although inter-war non-residential building did not show up as favourably, even here the inter-war peak was not overtaken until the middle 1950s. In view of the much higher post-war levels of industrial production and real income, inter-war building activity was remarkably brisk. Moreover, the upward trend in building was achieved with a low rate of growth in employment and with very little major reorganization in the industry's structure. The relative rates of growth in output and employment reflected a marked increase in productivity, if from a very low level in the early 1920s.

The industry's supply problems in the inter-war period were not serious. There were periodic shortages of skilled workers immediately after the war, in the middle 1920s and in the late 1930s, and these had a cost-raising effect. But, with substantial reserves of unskilled labour in a depressed labour market and considerable flexibility in the proportion of skilled craftsmen, it could scarcely be argued that labour shortages noticeably restricted building activity. Builders were able to obtain the credit they required from the banks or builders' merchants with relative ease. The building materials industries expanded vigorously, and materials were in plentiful supply. Material prices did not fall as rapidly as cost reductions justified, however, partly to be explained by the successful operations of oligopolies in the building materials trades in conditions of high demand for their products. Although there were no revolutionary advances in construction techniques and no striking developments in new materials, resources were more efficiently utilized, especially in non-residential building.

[1] Post-war figures obtained from *Annual Abstract of Statistics* and Ministry of Housing and Local Government *Housing Statistics*, No. 2 (1966), p. 3. 1,782,000 houses were built in the period 1934–8 compared with 1,699,000 in the years 1961–5.

Although supply conditions, especially of materials, were for most of the period reasonably elastic and aggregate costs fell substantially, probably demand forces had the strongest influence. Broadly speaking, demographic and sociological variables determined housing needs while the growth in incomes determined the rate at which demand could be made effective. State intervention in the housing market and its effects must be excepted from this general statement. A substantial proportion of houses built between the wars could be accounted for, directly or indirectly, by Government policy. The entry of the State was undoubtedly responsible for a higher level of housebuilding than would otherwise have been realized. Yet in many respects inter-war housing policy can be criticized, especially in the 1920s when subsidized houses were not built for the sections of the community or in localities most in need. Moreover, the housing shortage at the end of the inter-war period was as serious as at the beginning, reflecting the Government's too early acceptance of the judgment that the housing problem had been solved. With the expansion of local authority building and the increased supply of houses for owner occupation, the provision of private rented accommodation had declined greatly compared with before 1914. Investment demand for houses was important only in certain years of the inter-war period, especially the mid-1930s, while the level of replacement demand remained abnormally low throughout. In non-residential building too, demand forces, as shown in profit expectations, had a far greater impact than supply factors such as changing costs and interest rates.

The inter-war period is too short for us to be able to discern long building cycles, but nevertheless fluctuations in building, especially residential building, varied considerably in periodicity and in amplitude from fluctuations in the economy as a whole. Private housebuilding, local authority building and non-residential building all followed different, in some cases inverse, cyclical patterns. The net effect was stabilizing so that the path of building activity between the wars took much more the form of an upward trend than a cycle. The cyclical impact of building on the economy generally was far wider and more extensive than the 'housing boom of the 1930s caused recovery' thesis implies. For instance, there was the earlier housing boom in 1926–7 and in the 1930s housing investment began to fall off after 1934. Though monetary policy remained a crucial determinant of building activity, the influence of cheap money on the boom of the 1930s should not be exaggerated. Other factors such as the prolonged fall in building costs, rising incomes and changing tastes deserve serious consideration. The interrelationships between building and general business fluctuations were very complex and in a continuous state of transformation, but inter-war experience provides little evidence of a one-way causal sequence.

The net effect of expanding building activity on the growth of the economy may have been neutral rather than positive. In conditions of unemployed resources the high share of building in total investment did not harm growth in other sectors, but because of its high residential content neither did it stimulate future growth to any extent. On the other hand, in contrast with American experience, building was an expanding sector of the economy between the wars, and its relative weight in total output was increasing. Similarly, the tentative evidence available suggests that the employment generating effects of expenditure on building were higher relative to other industries in Britain than in the US. Building and allied industries accounted for a substantial share of total employment and their importance in the economy, reinforced by the associated phenomena of new transport and suburban developments, was far greater than before 1914.

A major feature between the wars was the extension of building, particularly residential building, into the suburbs. Though not a new phenomenon—there had been suburban development even in the nineteenth century—the pace of suburban activity quickened markedly. The causes of the extension of suburban building, such as rising land values and changing consumer tastes, are many and complex. The interdependence between building and transport developments was often close, but the evidence does not always point to an explicit causal relationship. The growth of suburbia raised many social and economic problems—the efficient utilization of land, the independence or dependence of satellite towns, the financing and provision of local public services, traffic flows and urban congestion, physical effects on the countryside—but few of these were solved. It is a repeated complaint of many that there has been too much intervention in the last twenty years, an excess of town and city planning regulations and restrictions. Would these critics deny that between the wars the trouble was the lack of urban planning and ordered development?

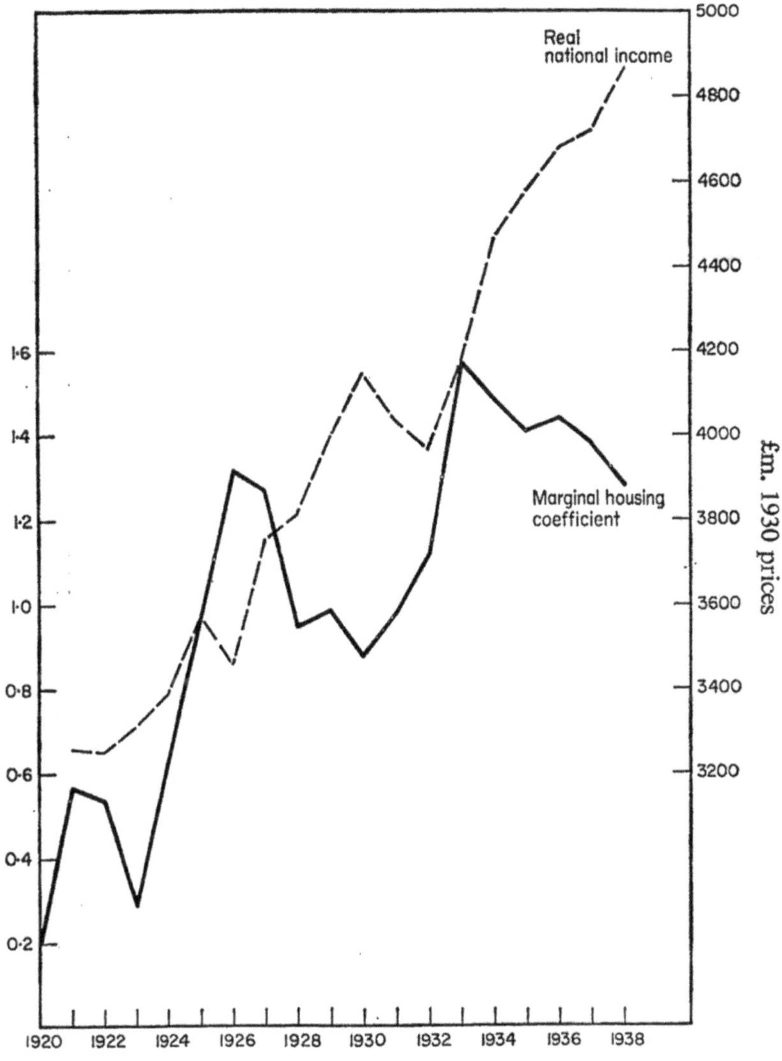

Fig. 1

The Marginal Housing Coefficient and National Income.

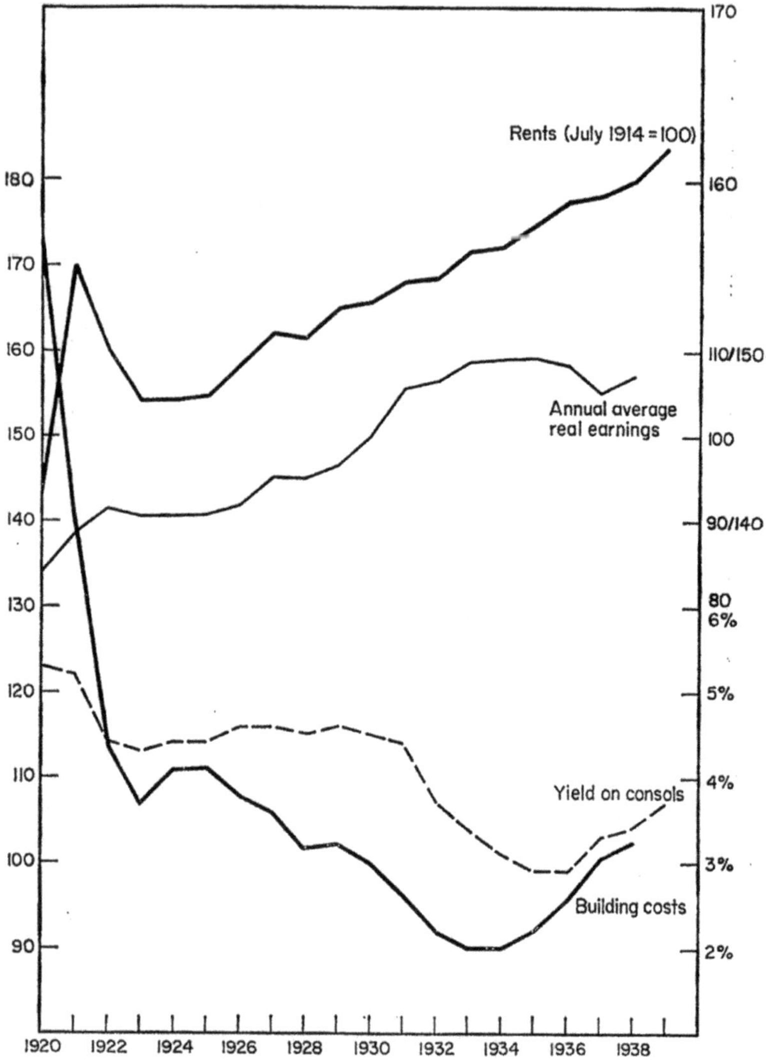

Fig. 2

Rents, Costs and Earnings.

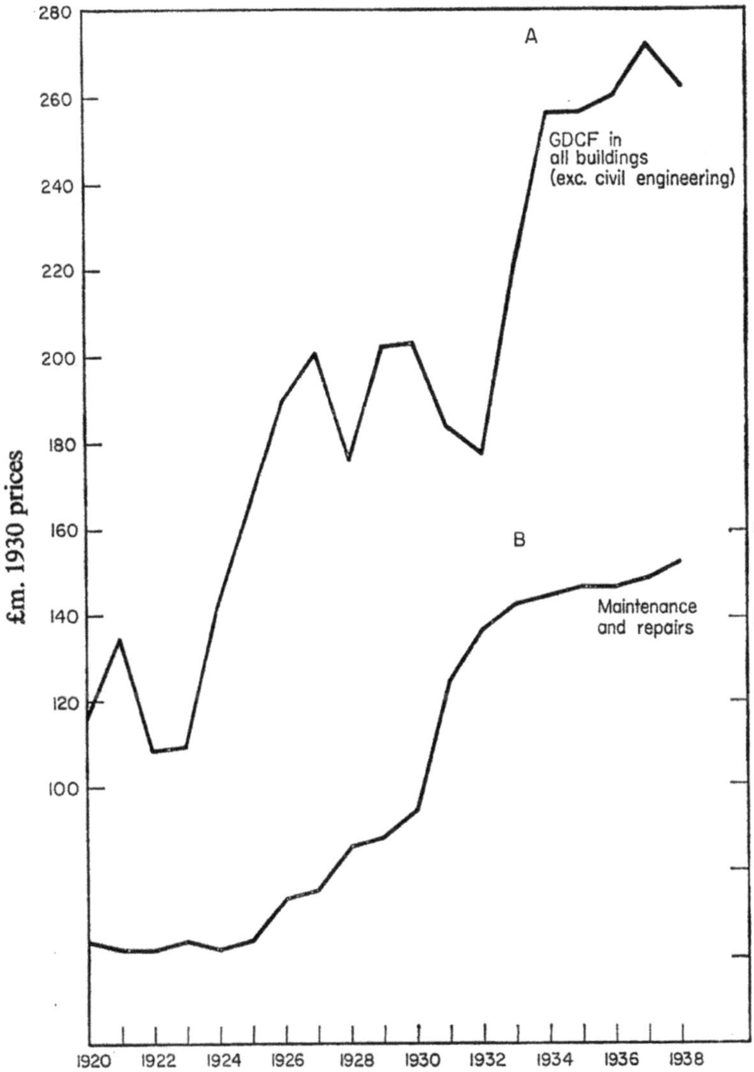

Fig. 3

A. Building Investment. B. Repairs.

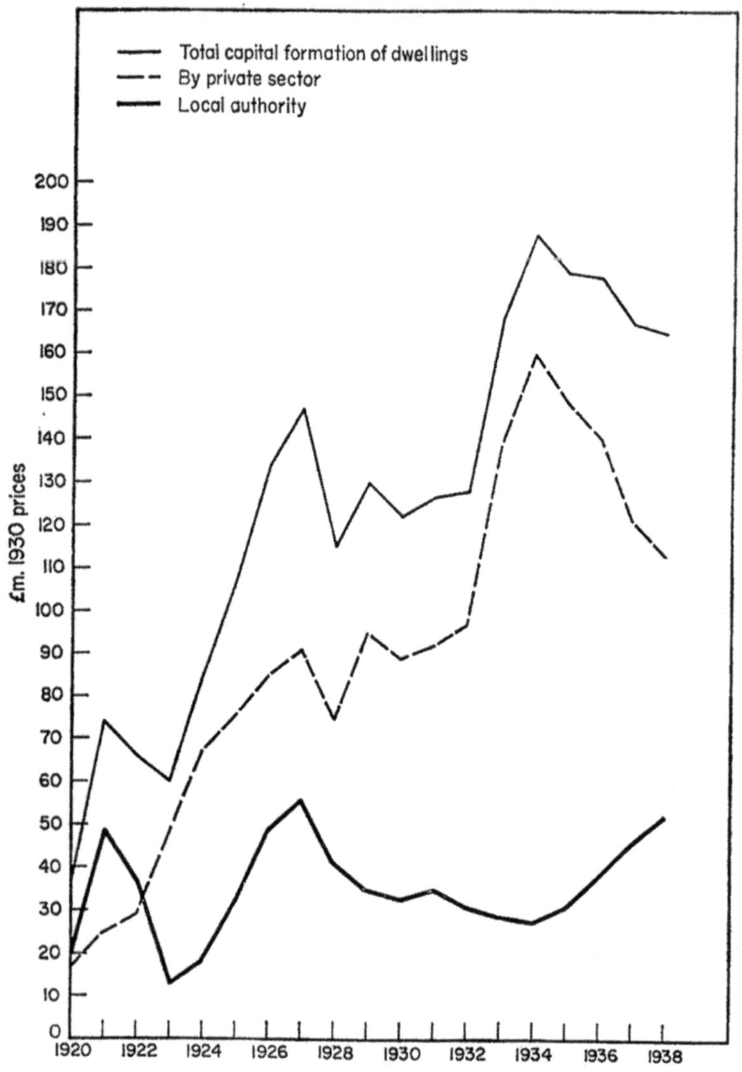

Fig. 4

Residential Building Investment.

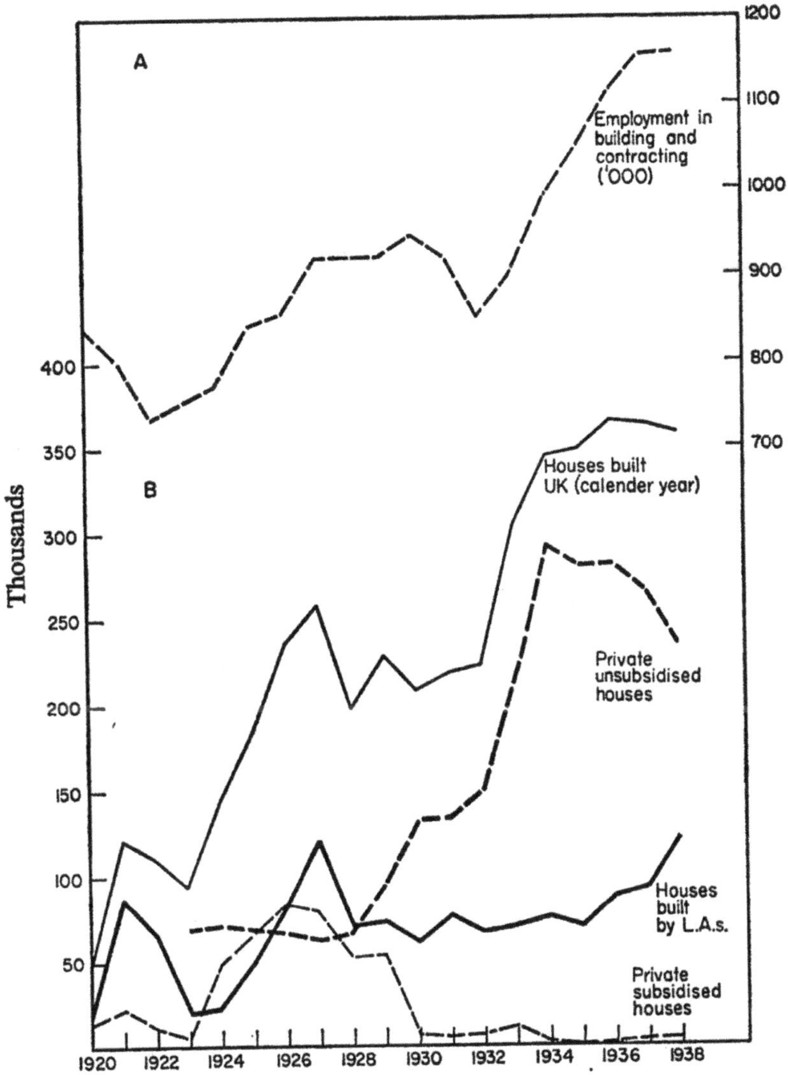

Fig. 5

A. Building Employment. B. Distribution of Housebuilding.

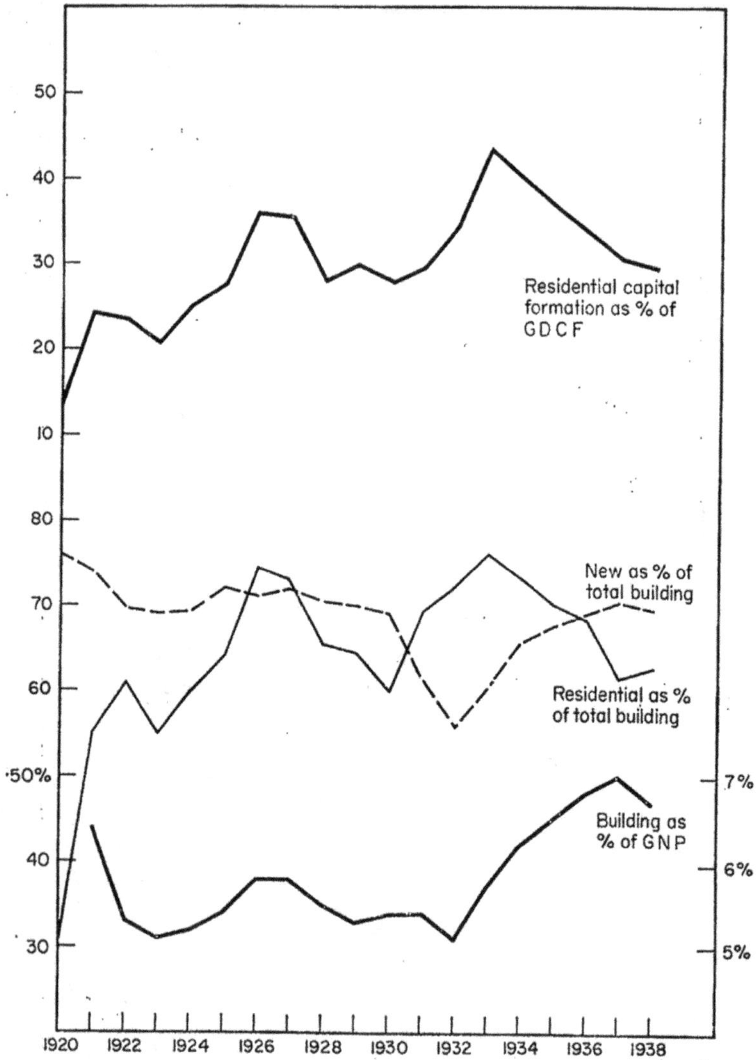

Fig. 6

Building, Output and Investment.

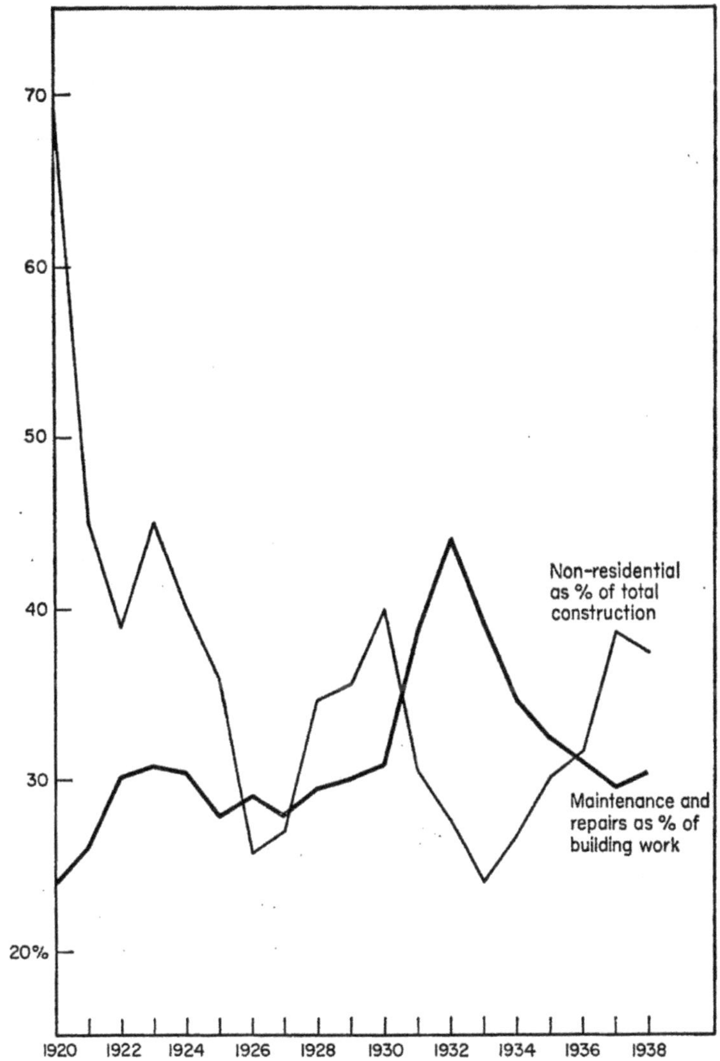

Fig. 7

The Shares of Non-residential Construction and Repairs.

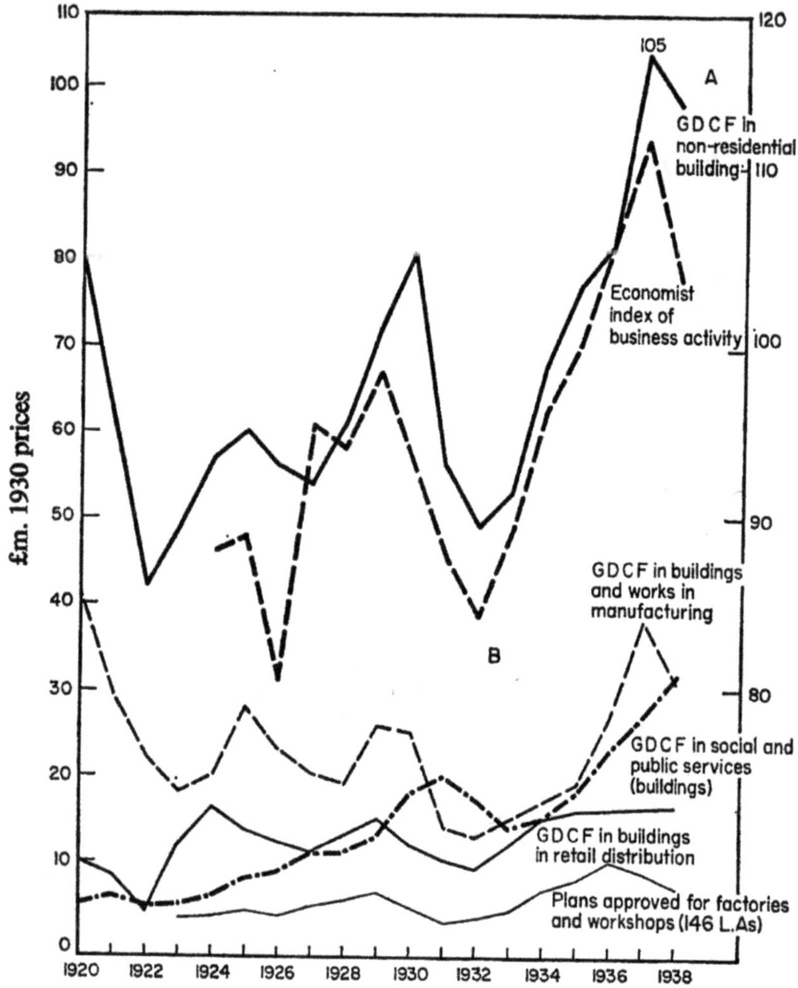

Fig. 8

A. Non-residential Building and Business Activity.
B. The Distribution of Non-residential Building.

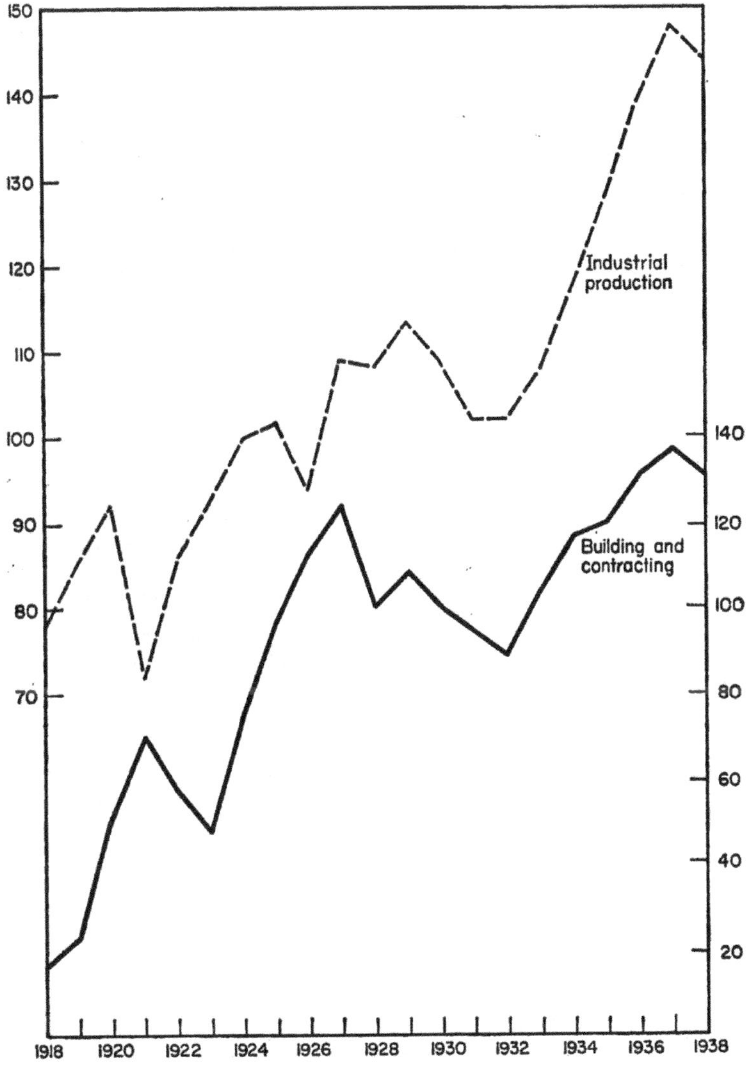

Fig. 9

Building and Industrial Production.

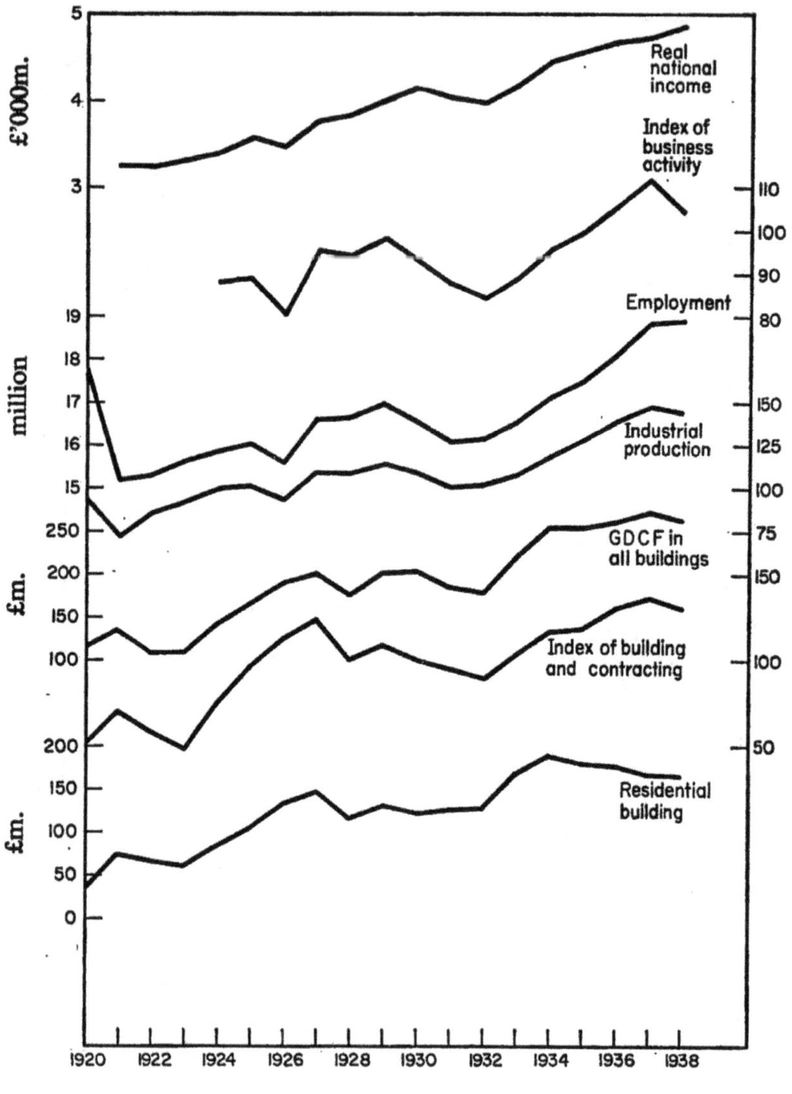

Fig. 10

Fluctuations in Building and Business Between the Wars.

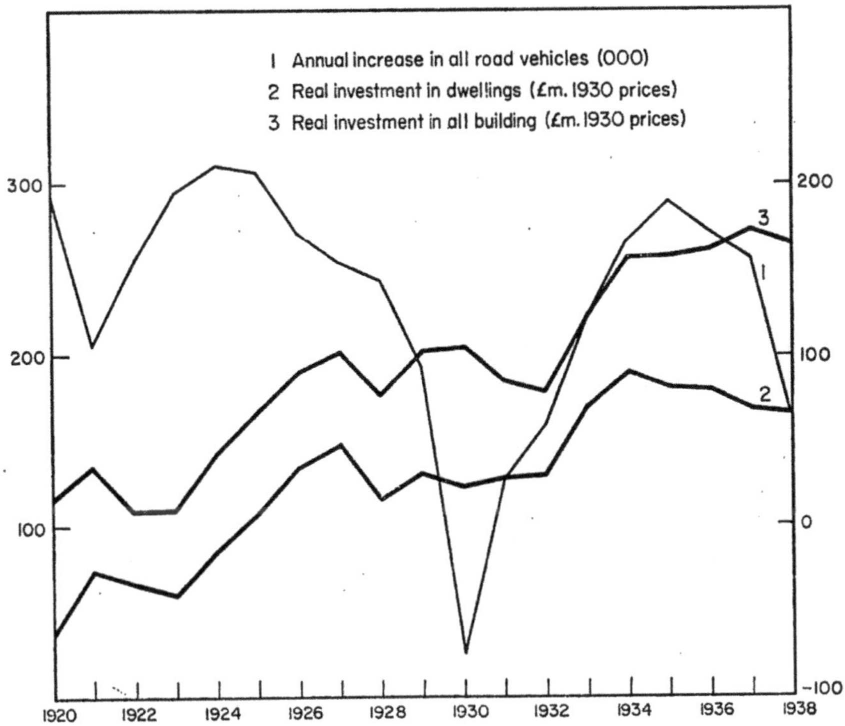

Fig. 11

Building and Transport.

SELECT BIBLIOGRAPHY

1. BOOKS AND PAMPHLETS

ABBEY, N. C.: *The Rent Acts, 1920–1957* (1957)

ABERCROMBIE, L. P.: *Town and Country Planning* (1943)

ABRAMS, M.: *The Condition of the British People, 1914–1945* (1945)

Anglo-American Council on Productivity: *Productivity Team Report on Building: Report of Visit to USA in 1949* (1950)

ASHWORTH, H.: *Housing Demand and Supply* (1946)

ASHWORTH, H.: *Housing in Great Britain* (1957)

ASHWORTH, W.: *The Genesis of Modern Town Planning* (1954)

BARHAM, H.: *The Building Industry* (1947)

BARNES, H.: *The Slum: Its Story and Solution* (1934)

BELLMAN, H.: *The Silent Revolution: the influence of building societies on the modern housing problem* (1928)

BELLMAN, H.: *Bricks and Mortals* (1949)

BLOCK, A.: *Estimating Housing Needs* (1946)

BOWLEY, M.: *Britain's Housing Shortage* (Oxford Pamphlets on Home Affairs, H.9, 1944)

BOWLEY, M.: *Housing and the State, 1919–1944* (1945)

BOWLEY, M.: *Innovations in Building Materials* (1960)

BOWLEY, M.: *The British Building Industry: Four Studies in Response and Resistance to Change* (1966)

BRETHERTON, R. F., BURCHARDT, F. A., and RUTHERFORD, R. S. G.: *Public Investment and the Trade Cycle in Great Britain* (1941)

British Association: *Britain in Recovery* (1938) ('The Building Trades' by H. Bellman).

British Building Commission: *Report of the British Building Commission on the Methods of Building in the United States* (1944)

British Productivity Council: *A Review of Productivity in the Building Industry* (1954)

BURN, D. (ed.): *The Structure of British Industry*, Vol. I (1958). ('The Building Materials Industry' by B. R. Williams.)

BURNS, A. F.: 'Long Cycles in Residential Construction' in *The Frontiers of Economic Knowledge* (1954)

CARR-SAUNDERS, A. M., and JONES, D. C.: *A Survey of the Social Structure of England and Wales* (1937)

CHAPMAN, A. L., and KNIGHT, R.: *Wages and Salaries in the United Kingdom, 1920–1938* (1953)

CHAWNER, L. T.: *Residential Building* (National Resources Committee Housing monograph, Vol. I, Washington 1939)

CLARK, J. M.: *Strategic Factors in Business Cycles* (NBER, 1935)

CLEARY, E. J.: *The Building Society Movement* (1965)

COHEN, J. L.: *Building Society Finance* (1933)

COLEAN, M. L., and NEWCOMB, R.: *Stabilizing Construction: the record and potential* (1952, New York)

DENBY, E.: *Europe Rehoused* (1938)

ELSAS, M. J.: *Housing Before the War and After* (2nd ed., 1945)

FAIRCHILD, E. C. (ed.): *Building and Society* (1945)

FEINSTEIN, C. H.: *Domestic Capital Formation in the United Kingdom, 1920–1938* (1965)

FLORENCE, P. S.: *The Logic of British and American Industry* (1953)

FOLEY, D. L.: *Controlling London's Growth* (1963)

GLOAG J. E. (ed.): *The Place of Glass in Building* (1943)

GREBLER, L.: *Production of New Housing* (1950, New York)

GREBLER, L., BLANK, D. M., and WINNICK, L.: *Capital Formation in Residential Real Estate* (1956, Princeton)

HARRISON, D. D.: *An Introduction to Standards in Building* (1947)

HART, P. E.: *Studies in Profit, Business Saving and Investment in the United Kingdom, 1920–1962*, Vol. I (1965)

HAUSER, P. M., and SCHNORE, L. F. (eds.): *The Study of Urbanisation* (1965, New York)

HEAKS, H. C., and KIRBY, C. H.: *Housing Finance in Great Britain* (1938)

HELGER, B.: *Urban and Rural Housing* (1939, League of Nations, Economic Intelligence Service)

HILL, H. A.: *The Complete Law of Housing* (1938)

HOFFMANN, W. G.: *British Industry 1700–1950* (1955)

HOOVER, E. M., and VERNON, R.: *Anatomy of a Metropolis: The Changing Distribution of People and Jobs within the New York Metropolitan Region* (1959, Harvard)

HOWKINS, F.: *The Development of Private Building Estates* (1938)

International Labour Office: *Housing Policy in Europe* (1930)

International Labour Office: *Housing Policy, housing standards, the organisation and financing of low-cost housing and the relations of housebuilding to the general level of employment* (1945, Geneva)

International Labour Office, *Housing and Employment* (1948)

JARMAIN, J. R.: *Housing Subsidies and Rents: a study of local authorities' problems* (1948)

KINGSBURY, L. M.: *The Economics of Housing (1957)*

LEWIS, J. P.: *Building Cycles and Britain's Growth* (1965)

LONG, C. D.: *Building Cycles and the Theory of Investment* (1940)

MADGE, J. (ed.): *Tomorrow's Houses, new building methods, structures and materials* (1946)

MANSBRIDGE, A.: *Brick upon Brick: Co-operative Permanent Building Society, 1884–1934* (1934)

MATTHEWS, R. C. O.: *The Trade Cycle* (1959)

MERRETT, A. J., and SYKES, A.: *Housing Finance and Development* (1965)

MITCHELL, B. R.: *Abstract of Historical Statistics* (1962)

MUMFORD, L.: *The City in History* (1966 ed.)

National Bureau of Economic Research (University Conference): *Demographic and Economic Change in Developed Countries* (1960)

National Housing Committee: *A National Housing Plan* (1934)

NEEDLEMAN, L.: *The Economics of Housing* (1965)

NEVIN, E.: *The Mechanism of Cheap Money* (1955)

OSBORN, F. S.: *Green-belt Cities: The British Contribution* (1946)

PEACOCK, A. T., and WISEMAN, J.: *The Growth of Public Expenditure in the United Kingdom* (1961)

PEARSON, S. V.: *London's Overgrowth and the Causes of Swollen Towns* (1939)

Political and Economic Planning: *Housing England, a guide to housing problems and the building industry* (1934)

Political and Economic Planning: *Report on the Location of Industry* (1939)

Political and Economic Planning: *The Market for Household Appliances* (1945)

POOL, A. G.: *A Survey of Transport in Sheffield* (1933)

PRICE, S. J.: *Building Societies: Their Origin and History* (1958)

PURDOM, C. B.: *The Building of Satellite Towns* (1949)

REID, M. G.: *Housing and Income* (1962)

RILEY, G. S.: *Building Society Practice* (1935)

ROBINSON, E., and KEEBLE, L. B.: *The Development of Building Estates* (1952)

ROBINSON, H. W.: *The Economics of Building* (1939)

ROSTAS, L.: *Comparative Productivity in British and American Industry* (1948)

ROSTAS, L.: *Productivity, Prices and Distribution in Selected British Industries* (1948)

Royal Institute of British Architects.: *Housing: A Report* (1944)

SALTER, W. E. G.: *Productivity and Technical Change* (1960)

SAUNDERS, S. E., and RABUCK, A. J.: *New City Patterns* (1946)

Scottish Council on Industry: *First Report of the Committee on Building Materials for Housing in Scotland* (1946)

SEGAL, W.: *Planning and Transport. Their Effects on Industry and Residence* (1945)

SELF, P.: *The Planning of Industrial Location* (1953)

SELF, P.: *Cities in Flood* (1961)

SHEPPARD, R.: *Prefabrication in Building* (1946)

SIMON, E. D.: *How to Abolish the Slums* (1929)

SIMON, E. D.: *The Anti-Slum Campaign* (1933)

SIMON, E. D.: *The Rebuilding of Britain* (1942)

SMITH, E. P.: *Structural Steelwork for Buildings* (1946)

STONE, J. R., and ROWE, D. A.: *The Measurement of Consumers' Expenditure and Behaviour in the United Kingdom, 1920–1938*. Vol. I (1954)

SVENNILSON, I.: *Growth and Stagnation in the European Economy* (1954)

SYKES, J.: *A Study in English Local Authority Finance* (1939)

TINBERGEN, J., and POLAK, J. J.: *The Dynamics of Business Cycles* (1950)

TITMUSS, R. M.: *Poverty and Population* (1938)

WARREN, G. F., and PEARSON, F. A.: *World Prices and the Building Industry* (1937)

WHITE, R. P.: *Prefabrication: A History of its Development in Great Britain* (1965)

WHYTE, W. E.: *Housing: a survey of the position in Scotland* (1932)

WILSON, G.: *Rent Rebates* (3rd ed. 1939, Fabian Social Research Series No. 28)

WILSON, R. M.: *Financial Freedom for Housing* (1945)

ZAIMAN, A., and MCINTYRE, W. A.: *Economic and Manufacturing Aspects of the Building Brick Industries* (1933)

2. ARTICLES

AINSWORTH, R. B.: 'Earnings and Hours of Manual Wage-Earners in the United Kingdom in October 1938', *Journal of Royal Statistical Society*, A 112 (1949)

ALLEN, R. G. D., and THOMAS, B.: 'The London Building Industry and its Labour Recruitment through Employment Exchanges', *Economic Journal*, 47 (1937)

ASHWORTH, W.: 'Types of Social and Economic Development in Suburban Essex', in *London: Aspects of Change*, edited by the Centre for Urban Studies (1964)

BARNA, T.: 'The Interdependence of the British Economy', *Journal of the Royal* Statistical Society, A 115 (1952)

BECKER, A. P.: 'Housing in England and Wales during the Business Depression of the 1930s', *Economic History Review*, 3 (1950–1).

BOWEN, I.: 'Investment in the Building Industry, 1930–1935', *Review of Economic Studies* 6 (1938–9).

BOWEN, I.: 'The Building Industry in War-Time', *Economic Journal*, 49 (1939)

BOWEN, I.: 'Building, Output and the Trade Cycle (U.K. 1924–38)', *Oxford Economic Papers*, 3 (1940)

BOWEN, I.: 'The Future Output of the Constructional Industries in the United States', *Economic Journal*, 56 (1946)

BOWEN, I., and ELLIS, A. W. T.: 'The Building and Contracting Industry', *Oxford Economic Papers*, 7 (1945)

BOWLEY, M.: 'Fluctuations in Housebuilding and the Trade Cycle, *Review of Economic Studies* 4, (1936–7).

BOWLEY, M.: 'Some Regional Aspects of the Building Boom 1924–36', *Review of Economic Studies*, 5 (1937–8)

BOWLEY, M.: 'Local Authorities and Housing Subsidies since 1919', *The Manchester School*, 12 (1942)

BRAAE, G. B.: 'Investment in Housing in the United Kingdom, 1924–38', *The Manchester School*, 32 (1964)

BROWN, A. J.: 'Resources Available for War', *Oxford Economic Papers*, 3 (1940)

CLARK, W. C.: 'Some Considerations affecting the Long-term Trend of the Building Industry', *Review of Economic Statistics*, 8 (1926)

COLEAN, M. L.: 'Housing—An Industrial Opportunity', *International Labour Review*, 41 (1944)

CONNOR, L. R.: 'Urban Housing in England and Wales', *Journal of Royal Statistical Society*, 99 (1936)

COPPOCK, D. J.: 'The Causes of Business Fluctuation', *Manchester Statistical Society* (1959)

DERKSEN, J. B.: 'Long Cycles in Residential Building: An Explanation', *Econometrica*, 8 (1940)

FAIRCHILD, E. C.: 'Building Societies: Their Reform and their Future', *Building and Society* (1945)

FEINSTEIN, C. H.: 'Income and Investment in the United Kingdom 1856–1914', *Economic Journal*, 71 (1961)

FEINSTEIN, C. H.: 'National Income and Expenditure, 1870–

1963', *London and Cambridge Economic Bulletin*, No. 50, in *Times Review of Industry and Technology*, June 1964.

FLEMING, M. C.: 'The Long-Term Measurement of Construction Costs in the United Kingdom', *Journal of Royal Statistical Society*, A 129 (1966)

GORDON, R. A.: 'Population Growth, Housing and the Capital Coefficient', *American Economic Review*, 46 (1956)

GOTTLIEB, M.: 'Building and Business Cycles', paper read before the *American Statistical Association* (1959)

GREBLER, L.: 'Home Building, the Business Cycle and State Intervention: I and II', *International Labour Review*, 33 (1936)

GREBLER, L.: 'Housing Policy and the Business Cycle', *Review of Economics and Statistics*, 24 (1942)

HABAKKUK, H. J.: 'Fluctuations in Housebuilding in Britain and the United States in the Nineteenth Century', *Journal of Economic History*, 22 (1962)

HILL, W.: 'What Housing Costs', *Building and Society* (1945)

HUBBARD, J. B.: 'An Analysis of Building Statistics for the US', *Review of Economics and Statistics*, 6 (1924)

ISARD, W.: 'A Neglected Cycle: The Transport Building Cycle', *Review of Economics and Statistics*, 24 (1942)

ISARD, W.: 'Transport Development and Building Cycles', *Quarterly Journal of Economics*, 57 (1942)

LESER, C. E. V.: 'Building Activity and Housing Demand', *Yorkshire Bulletin of Economic and Social Research*, 3 (1951)

LOMAX, K. S.: 'Production and Productivity Movements in the United Kingdom since 1900', *Journal of the Royal Statistical Society*, A 122 (1959)

LOSCH, A.: 'Population Cycles as a source of Business Cycles', *Quarterly Journal of Economics*, 51 (1936–7)

MACINTOSH, R. M.: 'A Note on Cheap Money and the British Housing Boom, 1932–37', *Economic Journal*, 61 (1951)

MAYWALD, K.: 'An Index of Building Costs in the United Kingdom, 1845–1938', *Economic History Review*, 7 (1954–5)

MAYWALD, K.: 'Fire Insurance and the Capital Coefficient in Great Britain, 1866–1952', *Economic History Review*, 9 (1956)

MURPHEY, G. W.: 'Some Aspects of Building Society Finance', *The Manchester School*, 24 (1956)

NEWMAN, W. H.: 'The Building Industry and Business Cycles', *Journal of Business of University of Chicago*, 8 (1935)

PARKINSON, H.: 'The Building Society Outlook', *The Banker* (1935)

PARKINSON, H.: 'Building Societies in 1935', *The Banker* (1936)

Political and Economic Planning: 'Building and Housing Progress', *Planning*, 5 (1937)

Political and Economic Planning: 'Trading Estates and Industry', *Planning*, 6 (1938)

Political and Economic Planning: 'Labour in the Building Industry', *Planning*, 10 (1943)

Political and Economic Planning, 'Old Houses', *Planning*, 10 (1944)

Political and Economic Planning: 'The Assessment of Housing Needs', *Planning*, 15 (1949)

Political and Economic Planning: 'Rent Control Policy', *Planning*, 16 (1949)

Political and Economic Planning: 'A New Policy for Housing Subsidies', *Planning*, 16 (1950)

Political and Economic Planning, 'Housing Policy and the Building Industry', *Planning*, 17 (1950)

PRIBRAM, K.: 'The Financing of House Building in Countries with Rent Restriction Legislation: I', *International Labour Review*, 33 (1936)

PRIBRAM, K.: 'Residual, Differential and Absolute Urban Ground Rent and their Cyclical Fluctuations', *Econometrica*, 8 (1940)

REISS, R. L.: 'Municipal and Private Enterprise Housing', *Building and Society* (1945)

RHODES, E. C.: 'U.K. Timber Trade Statistics', *London and Cambridge Economic Service* (Special Memorandum No. 30, 1929)

RIGGLEMAN, J. R.: 'Building Cycles in the United States', *Journal of American Statistical Association*, 28 (1933)

ROBINSON, H. W.: 'A Note on Unoccupied House', *Review of Economic Studies*, 6 (1938–9)

SAVILLE, J.: 'The Measurement of Real Cost in the London Building Industry, 1923–1939', *Yorkshire Bulletin of Economic and Social Research*, 2 (1949)

SCHIFF, E.: 'Family Size and Residential Construction', *American Economic Review*, 36 (1946)

SCHWARTZ, G. L., and RHODES, E. C.: 'Output, Employment and Wages in the United Kingdom, 1924, 1930 and 1935', *London and Cambridge Economic Service* (Special Memorandum No. 47, 1938)

SINGER, H. W.: 'Income and Rent', *Review of Economic Studies*, 4 (1936–7)

STOLPER, W. F.: 'British Monetary Policy and the Housing Boom', *Quarterly Journal of Economics*, 56 (1941–2)

STONE, P. A.: 'The Economics of Housing and Urban Development', *Journal of Royal Statistical Society*, A 122 (1959)

WALLIS, L.: 'The Building Industry: its Work and Organization', *Building and Society* (1945)

WEBER, B.: 'A New Index of Residential Construction, 1838–1950', *Scottish Journal of Political Economy*, 2 (1955)

WEBER, B., and LEWIS, J. P.: 'New Industrial Building in Great Britain 1923–38: A Problem of Measurement', *Scottish Journal of Political Economy*, 8 (1961)

WINNICK, L.: 'Housing: Has there been a Downward Shift in Consumers' Preferences?' *Quarterly Journal of Economics*, 69 (1955)

3. OFFICIAL PUBLICATIONS

(a) *Parliamentary Papers*

Cd. 8731, 1917–18: *Report of the Royal Commission on the Housing of the Industrial Population of Scotland, Rural and Urban.*

Cd. 9087, 1918: *Memorandum by the Advisory Housing Panel of the Ministry of Reconstruction on the Emergency Problem.*

Cd. 9179, 1918: *Report of the Committee on the Building Industry after the War.*

Cd. 9191, 1918: *Report of the Committee to consider Questions of Building Construction in Connection with the Provision of Dwellings for the Working Classes in England and Wales, and Scotland.*

Cd. 9235, 1919: *Report of the Committee of the Ministry of Reconstruction on the Increase of Rent and Mortgage Interest (War Restrictions) Act.*

Cd. 9238, 1919: *First Report of the Treasury Committee on Housing Finance.*

Cmd. 127, 1919: *Financial Assistance to Local Authorities.*

Cmd. 426, 1919: *Statement of Proposals for new methods of Constructing Houses.*

Cmd. 444, 1919: *Interim Report of the Treasury Committee on Housing Finance.*

Cmd. 658, 1920: *Reports of the Departmental Committee on the Increase of Rent and Mortgage Interest (War Restrictions) Act.*

Cmd. 959, 1920: *Standing Committee on Prices: Report on Bricks.*

Cmd. 985, 1920: *Standing Committee on Prices: Report on Timber.*

Cmd. 1091, 1920: *Standing Committee on Prices: Report on Cement and Mortar.*

Cmd. 1209, 1921: *Standing Committee on Prices: Report on Stone, Brick and Clayware Trades.*

Cmd. 1217, 1921: *Standing Committee on Prices: Report on Pipes and Castings.*

Cmd. 1268, 1921: *Standing Committee on Prices: Report on Iron and Steel Products.*

Cmd. 1338, 1921: *Standing Committee on Prices: Report on Slates.*

Cmd. 1411, 1921: *Report of the Committee of Enquiry into High Cost of Building Working-class Dwellings in Scotland.*

Cmd. 1447, 1921: *Report of the Departmental Committee on the High Cost of Building Working-class Dwellings.*

Cmd. 1803, 1923: *Final Report of the Departmental Committee on the Increase of Rent and Mortgage Interest (War Restrictions) Act, 1920.*

Cmd. 1908, 1923: *Report of the Committee appointed to survey the Prices of Building Materials* (and annual command reports to 1934)

Cmd. 2104, 1924: *Report on the Present Position of the Building Industry with regard to the carrying out of a full housing programme with reference to the supply of labour and materials.*

Cmds. 2310, 2334, 1924–25: *Interim Reports of the Committee on new methods of House Construction.*

Cmd. 2392, 1924–25: *Report by a Court of Inquiry concerning Steel Houses.*

Cmd. 2423, 1924–25: *Report of the Committee on the Rent Restriction Acts (Scotland).*

Cmd. 3482, 1930: *Report of the Standing Committee on Bricks, Tiles, etc.*

Cmd. 3897, 1931: *Report of the Committee on Finance and Industry* (Macmillan Committee).

Cmd. 3911, 1930–31: *Report of the Inter-Departmental Committee on the Rent Restriction Acts.*

Cmd. 4208, 1932–33: *Memorandum of Statistics on Houses.*

Cmd. 4397, 1932–33: *Report of the Departmental Committee on Housing.*

Cmd. 4469, 1933–34: *Report of the Departmental Committee on Scottish Housing.*

Cmd. 4535, 1933–34: *Housing Act, 1930: Particulars of Slum Clearance Programmes furnished by Local Authorities.*

Cmd. 5171, 1935–36: *Summaries of Reports and Building Proposals by Local Authorities in Scotland.*

Cmd. 5527, 1936–37: *Rents of Houses and Flats owned by Local Authorities (England and Wales).*

Cmd. 5621, 1937–38: *Report of the Inter-Departmental Committee on the Rent Restriction Acts.*

Cmd. 5667, 1937–38: *Government Policy on Rent Restriction.*

Cmd. 5913, 1938–39: *Rents of Houses and Flats owned by Local Authorities (England and Wales).*

Cmd. 5977, 1938–39: *Report of the Committee on Scottish Building Costs.*

Cmd. 6153, 1939–40: *Report of the Royal Commission on the Distribution of Industrial Population.*

Cmd. 6282, 1941: *Report of the Committee on Cement Production.*

Cmd. 6428, 1942–43, *Training for the Building Industry.*

Cmd. 6552, 1944: *Report by the Scottish Housing Advisory Committee on the Distribution of New Houses in Scotland.*

Cmd. 6609, 1945: *Housing.*

Cmd. 6621, 1945: *Report of the Inter-Departmental Committee on Rent Control.*

Cmd. 6741, 1945–46: *Report by the Scottish Housing Advisory Committee on the Provision of Houses for Owner-Occupation in Scotland.*

Cmd. 6901, 1945–46: *Report by the Scottish Housing Advisory Committee on Housing Management in Scotland.*

Cmd. 7507, 1948: *Total Provision of Housing Accommodation in Great Britain as at 31st July 1948.*

Cmd. 7695, 1948–49: *Report of the Royal Commission on Population.*

(b) *Other Official Publications (HMSO)*

Board of Health for Scotland: *Circular to Local Authorities on the Augmentation of skilled Labour in the Building Trades* (1925)

Building Research Board (DSIR): *Report of the Reinforced Concrete Structures Committee* (1933)

Building Research Board (DSIR): *The Application of Reinforced Concrete to Wartime Building* (1940)

Building Research Board (DSIR): *Steel and House Construction* (1940)

Building Research Board (DSIR): *Economy of Timber in Building* (1942)

Building Research Board (DSIR): *Reports on Bricks* (1948)

Building Research Station (DSIR): *Productivity in Housebuilding* (Special Report No. 21, 1953)

Council for Research on Housing Construction: *Slum Clearance and Rehousing: First Report* (1934)

Department of Health for Scotland: *State Assisted Housing Schemes* (1933)

Department of Health for Scotland: *Report of the Committee on Scottish Building Costs* (1948)

House of Commons Library: *Housing and Housing Subsidies since the End of the First World War* (Statistical memorandum, No. 29, 1955).

Ministry of Health: *Report of the Committee on Standardization and New Methods of Construction* (1920)

Ministry of Health: *Statement on the Future Housing Policy of the Government*, Circular 221 (1921)

Ministry of Health: *The Prevention and Abatement of Overcrowding*, Memorandum B (1935)

Ministry of Health: *The Redevelopment of Overcrowded Areas*, Memorandum C (1935)

Ministry of Health: *Consolidation of Housing Contributions and Accounts*, Memorandum E (1935)

Ministry of Health: *Departmental Committee on the Construction of Flats for the Working Classes: Interim Report* (1935), *Final Report* (1937)

Ministry of Health: *Report on the Overcrowding Survey in England and Wales* (1936)

Ministry of Health: *Report to the Ministry of Health by the Departmental Committee on the Valuation for Rates 1939* (1944)

Ministry of Health: *The Placing and Management of Building Contracts* (1944)

Ministry of Health: *Report on Private Enterprise Housing by the Sub-Committee of the Central Housing Advisory Committee* (1944)

Ministry of Health: *First Report of the Committee of Inquiry into the Cost of Housebuilding* (1948)

Ministry of Town and Country Planning: *Advisory Handbook on the Redevelopment of Central Areas* (1947)

Ministry of Works: *Reports of the Committee on the Brick Industry* (1942–43)

Ministry of Works: *The Standard of War-time Building* (1943)

Ministry of Works: *Report of the British Building Mission on Methods of Building in the USA* (1944)

Ministry of Works: *Reports of the Committee on the Use of Standards in Building* (1944, 1946)

Ministry of Works: *Reports of the Inter-Departmental Committee on Housing Construction* (1944, 1946, 1948)

Ministry of Works: *Production in Building and Civil Engineering: an analysis of man-hours and machine-hours expended in the execution of building and civil engineering works* (1945)

Ministry of Works: *The Architectural Use of Building Materials* (1946)

Ministry of Works: *Price Control of Building Materials and Components* (1946)

Ministry of Works: *Report of the Committee on Cement Costs* (1947)

Ministry of Works: *Report on Payment by Results in Building and Civil Engineering during the War* (1947)

Ministry of Works: *Report of the Committee on the Distribution of Building Materials and Components* (1948)

Ministry of Works: *Reports of the Committee on New Methods of House Construction* (1948–49)

Ministry of Works: *First Report of the Advisory Council on Building Research and Development* (1949)

Ministry of Works: *Working Party Report on Building* (1950)

National Housing Committee: *A National Housing Policy* (1934)

4. PERIODICALS, ANNUALS AND MISCELLANEOUS PUBLICATIONS

Annual Abstract of Labour Statistics, 1920–1938 (command papers)

Board of Trade Journal

Board of Trade Surveys of Industrial Development, 1932–1938

The Builder

Building Societies Gazette

Building Societies Year Book

Census Reports on Population

Census Reports on Production

Department of Health for Scotland, Annual Reports, 1930–1938 (command papers)

Economist

Ministry of Health Annual Reports, 1920–1938 (command papers)

Ministry of Labour Gazette

Scottish Board of Health Annual Reports, 1920–1929 (command papers)

Statist

Statistical Abstract of the United Kingdom, 1920–1938 (command papers)

INDEX